STUDENT SOLUTIONS MANUAL

TENTH EDITION

COST ACCOUNTING

A MANAGERIAL EMPHASIS

HORNGREN   FOSTER   DATAR

Prentice Hall
Upper Saddle River, New Jersey 07458

Acquisitions editor: *Annie Todd*
Assistant editor: *Kathryn Sheehan*
Project editor: *Joseph F. Tomasso*
Manufacturer: *Banta Book Group*

Printed in the United States of America

10 9 8 7 6 5 4 3 2 1

ISBN 0-13-040090-4

Prentice-Hall International (UK) Limited, *London*
Prentice-Hall of Australia Pty. Limited, *Sydney*
Prentice-Hall Canada Inc., *Toronto*
Prentice-Hall Hispanoamericana, S.A., *Mexico*
Prentice-Hall of India Private Limited, *New Delhi*
Prentice-Hall of Japan, Inc., *Tokyo*
Prentice-Hall (Singapore) Pte Ltd
Editora Prentice-Hall do Brasil, Ltda., *Rio de Janeiro*

TABLE OF CONTENTS

CHAPTER 1
THE ACCOUNTANT'S ROLE IN THE ORGANIZATION

1-2   *Management accounting* measures and reports financial and nonfinancial information that helps managers make decisions to fulfill the goals of an organization. It focuses on internal reporting.

   Financial accounting focuses on reporting to external parties. It measures and records business transactions and provides financial statements that are based on generally accepted accounting principles (GAAP).

1-4   The three important roles are:
1. Problem solving—comparative analysis for decision making.
2. Scorekeeping—accumulating data and reporting reliable results to all levels of management.
- Attention directing—helping managers to properly focus their attention.

1-6   The business functions in the value chain are:
- **Research and development** – the generation of, and experimentation with, ideas related to new products, services, or processes.
- **Design of products, services, and processes** – the detailed planning and engineering of products, services, or processes.
- **Production** – the acquisition, coordination, and assembly of resources to produce a product or deliver a service.
- **Marketing** – the manner by which companies promote and sell their products or services to customers or prospective customers.
- **Distribution** – the delivery of products or services to the customer.
- **Customer service** – the after-sale support activities provided to customers.

1-8   The four key themes are:
1. Customer focus.
2. Key success factors (such as cost, quality, time, and innovation).
3. Continuous improvement.
4. Value-chain and supply-chain analysis.

1-10   The three guidelines for management accountants are:
1. Employ a cost-benefit approach.
2. Recognize behavioral and technical considerations.
3. Adopt the "different costs for different purposes" notion.

1-12   The new controller could reply in one or more of the following ways:

(a)   Demonstrate to the plant manager how he or she could make better decisions if the plant controller was viewed as a resource rather than a deadweight. In a related way, the plant controller could show how the plant manager's time and resources could be saved by viewing the new plant controller as a team member.

(b)   Demonstrate to the plant manager a good knowledge of the technical aspects of the plant. This approach may involve doing background reading. It certainly will involve spending much time on the plant floor speaking to plant personnel.

(c)   Show the plant manager examples of the new plant controller's past successes in working with line managers in other plants. Examples could include:
- assistance in preparing the budget,
- assistance in analyzing problem situations, and
- assistance in submitting capital budget requests.

(d)   Seek assistance from the corporate controller to highlight to the plant manager the importance of many tasks undertaken by the new plant controller. This approach is a last resort but may be necessary in some cases.

1-14   The Institute of Management Accountants (IMA) sets standards of ethical conduct for management accountants in the following areas:
- Competence
- Confidentiality
- Integrity
- Objectivity

1-16   (10 min.) **Management accountants and customer focus.**

1.   Line managers are the primary customers of the management accounting function. Line managers in each of the six business function areas (R&D, design, production, marketing, distribution, and customer service) use management accounting information in their decisions.

2.   Line managers rely on the continued support of management accountants to justify their budgets and headcount approvals. If these line managers do not find the information provided both relevant and timely, management accountants will not receive the resources necessary to continue fulfilling their potential contributions. This is similar to Ford not being able to retain its customers if it does not continue to satisfy (and even exceed) their expectations as to the reliability and performance of Ford motor vehicles.

1-18 (15 min.)   **Problem solving, scorekeeping, and attention directing.**

Because the accountant's duties are often not sharply defined, some of these answers might be challenged:
1. Scorekeeping
2. Attention directing
3. Scorekeeping
4. Problem solving
5. Attention directing
6. Attention directing
7. Problem solving
8. Scorekeeping (depending on the extent of the report) or attention getting
9. This question is intentionally vague. The give-and-take of the budgetary process usually encompasses all three functions, but it emphasizes scorekeeping the least. The main function is attention directing, but problem solving is also involved.
10. Problem solving

1-20 (15 min.)   **Value chain and classification of costs, computer company.**

Cost Item	Value Chain Business Function
a.	Production
b.	Distribution
c.	Design
d.	Research and Development
e.	Customer Service
f.	Design (or Research and Development)
g.	Marketing
h.	Production

1-22 (15 min.)   **Management themes and changes in management accounting.**

Change in Management Accounting	Key Theme
a.	Value-chain and supply-chain analysis
b.	Key success factors (quality)
c.	Key success factors (cost)
d.	Continuous improvement
e.	Customer focus

1-24 (10-15 min.) **Professional ethics and reporting divisional performance.**

1.   Miller's ethical responsibilities are well summarized in the IMA's "Standards of Ethical Conduct for Management Accountants" (Exhibit 1-7 of text). Areas of ethical responsibility include:
- competence
- confidentiality
- integrity
- objectivity

The key area related to Miller's current dilemma is integrity. Miller should refuse to book the $200,000 of sales until the goods are shipped. Both financial accounting and management accounting principles maintain that sales are not complete until the title is transferred to the buyer.

2.   Miller should refuse to follow Maloney's orders. If Maloney persists, the incident should be reported to the corporate controller. Support for line management should be wholehearted, but it should not require unethical conduct.

1-26 (15 min.)   **Planning and control decisions; Internet company.**

1.   Planning decisions at WebNews.com focus on organizational goals, predicting results under various alternative ways of achieving those goals, and then deciding how to attain the desired goals. For example, WebNews.com could have the objective of revenue growth to gain critical mass or it could have the objective of increasing operating income. Many Internet companies in their formative years make revenue growth (and subscriber growth) their primary goal.

Control focuses on (a) deciding on, and taking actions that implement the planning decisions, and (b) deciding on performance evaluation and the related feedback that will help future decision making.

2.   **Planning decisions**
   a. Decision to raise monthly subscription fee
   c. Decision to upgrade content of online services
   e. Decision to decrease monthly subscription fee

Control decisions
   b. Decision to inform existing subscribers about the rate of increase—an implementation part of control decisions
   d. Demotion of VP of Marketing—performance evaluation and feedback aspect of control decisions

1-28 (30 min.) Software procurement decisions, ethics.

1.   Companies with "codes of conduct" frequently have a "supplier clause" that prohibits their employees from accepting "material" (in some cases, any) gifts from suppliers. The motivations include:

(a)   Integrity/conflict of interest. Suppose Michaels recommends that a Horizon 1-2-3 product subsequently be purchased by Fiesta. This recommendation could be because he felt obligated to them as his trip to the Cancun conference was fully paid by Horizon.

(b)   The appearance of a conflict of interest. Even if the Horizon 1-2-3 product is the superior one at that time, other suppliers likely will have a different opinion. They may believe that the way to sell products to Fiesta is via "fully-paid junkets to resorts." Those not wanting to do business this way may downplay future business activities with Fiesta even though Fiesta may gain much from such activities.

Some executives view the meeting as "suspect" from the start given the Caribbean location and its "rest and recreation" tone.

2.   **Pros of attending user meeting**
(a)   Opportunity to learn more about Horizon's software products.
(b)   Opportunity to interact with other possible purchasers and get their opinions.
(c)   Opportunity to influence the future product development plans of Horizon in a way that will benefit Fiesta. An example is Horizon subsequently developing software modules tailored to food product companies.
(d)   Saves Fiesta money. Visiting suppliers and their customers typically cost money, whereas Horizon is paying for the Cancún conference.

Cons of Attending
(a)   The ethical issues raised in requirement 1.
(b)   Negative morale effects on other Fiesta employees who do not get to attend the Cancún conference. These employees may reduce their trust and respect for Michaels' judgment, arguing he has been on a "supplier-paid vacation."

Conditions on Attending that Fiesta Might Impose
(a)   Sizable part of that time in Cancun has to be devoted to business rather than recreation.
(b)   Decision on which Fiesta executive attends is <u>not</u> made by the person who attends (this reduces the appearance of a conflict of interest).
(c)   Person attending (Michaels) does not have final say on purchase decision (this reduces the appearance of a conflict of interest).
(d)   Fiesta executives go only when a new major purchase is being contemplated (to avoid the conference becoming a regular "vacation").

A Conference Board publication on *Corporate Ethics* asked executives about a comparable situation:
- 76% said Fiesta and Michaels face an ethical consideration in deciding whether to attend.
- 71% said Michaels should not attend, as the payment of expenses is a "gift" within the meaning of a credible corporate ethics policy.

3. **Pros of having a written code**

The Conference Board outlines the following reasons why companies adopt codes of ethics:

(a) Signals commitment of senior management to ethics.

(b) Promotes public trust in the credibility of the company and its employees.

(c) Signals the managerial professionalism of its employees.

(d) Provides guidance to employees as to how difficult problems are to be handled. If adhered to, employees will avoid many actions that are unethical or appear to be unethical.

(e) Drafting of the policy (and its redrafting in the light of ambiguities) can assist management in anticipating and preparing for ethical issues not yet encountered.

Cons of having a written code

(a) Can give appearance that all issues have been covered. Issues not covered may appear to be "acceptable" even when they are not.

(b) Can constrain the entrepreneurial activities of employees. Forces people to always "behave by the book."

(c) Cost of developing code can be "high" if it consumes a lot of employee time.

1-30 (40 min.) **Global company, ethical challenges with bribery.**

1. The following decision tree is a useful way to structure the class discussion:

The comment by Shell's Chairman addresses the AI branch, which assumes that bribes are illegal. One difficult issue here is when certain kinds of payments are illegal in one country but not illegal in other countries.

Even if "bribes" are not illegal, students should debate two questions:

(a) Should Shell engage in activities many regard as unethical even if they are not illegal? Similar questions arise with tobacco companies.

(b) Do the "bribes" increase the market value of Shell?

Both (a) and (b) raise issues that are not black or white. Some students will argue on (a) that as long as the government does not prohibit an activity, it is commercially acceptable to undertake it. They will assert that as long as shareholders are aware of that activity (such as a company selling tobacco), those opposed to it can always not invest in the company. This is not as strong an argument for supporting bribes as it is unlikely that companies will admit to bribes being paid.

Even if bribes are not illegal, they do not always increase shareholder wealth. Bribery can become a very large cost in some areas. They may not generate revenues sufficient to offset the cost of bribes.

1-30 (Cont'd.)

2. The investigation could be made at several levels:
   (a) Ask Shell employees at the subsidiary to explain why payments are being made to the local law firm. What is the deliverable the law firm is providing to Shell?
   (b) Question the local law firm on what they are billing Shell for and whether they are making related payments to a third party.
   (c) Question those who it is alleged are being paid by the local law firm.

The billing rates and the services provided by the law firm could be examined to see how much other firms are charging for comparable work.

The Shell Chairman has outlined an outright prohibition policy on bribes. If this is company policy, then requesting a resignation may be the only viable course. The difficult issues here include:
   (a) What is and is not a bribe is sometimes not black or white, and
   (b) Even in the "gray" or "black" area, a company may be reluctant to request a resignation, especially for a highly valued employee. This person could feel he or she was doing what "many other competitors were doing" and had no option if the business was to be secured for Shell.

3. The Board presentation needs to promote a full and thorough debate on investment in the dictator's country. Even if the discovery was of lower financial value, the political and economic risks of investing in a country under questionable terms can be very high. Issues to consider are:
   (a) Are the requests "official" ones? The dictator's key advisor may not represent the government or indeed the dictator's son. It may be a "trial balloon" to see what was possible for one individual to obtain. Other companies may have agreed to make payments due to their not calling the advisor's bluff.
   (b) How will the proposed transaction be recorded? Some countries require a 10% (or more) equity in successful ventures. However, the request implies the 10% goes to a private individual. A good working requirement is that each board member should be able to publicly explain the payments made as being both economically justified and in accordance with Shell's ethical position.
   (c) What is the "world opinion" on the dictator's government? Does the dictator have a reputation for suppressing human rights, private wealth diversion, cronyism, and so on? Shell has to avoid being portrayed as a financial backer of a repressive regime. In some cases, there can be a backlash against companies that supported a prior regime when a dictator is replaced by another regime. Putting the son of a dictator on a board can be a visible signal (and symbol) of an association that over time Shell may wish to avoid.
   (d) What can be learned from the experience of other companies who have conducted business in the country? Are there allegations of them making facilitating payments? Are questions being raised in the press about those companies acting illegally or unethically?

CHAPTER 2
AN INTRODUCTION TO COST TERMS AND PURPOSES

2-2   Cost assignment is a general term that encompasses the assignment of both direct costs and indirect costs to a cost object. Direct costs are *traced* to a cost object while indirect costs are *allocated* to a cost object.

- Direct costs of a cost object are related to the particular cost object and can be traced to it in an economically feasible (cost-effective) way.
- Indirect costs of a cost object are related to the particular cost object but cannot be traced to it in an economically feasible (cost-effective) way.

2-4   Factors affecting the classification of a cost as direct or indirect include:
- the materiality of the cost in question,
- available information-gathering technology,
- design of operations, and
- contractual arrangements.

2-6   A *cost driver* is a factor, such as the level of activity or volume, that causally affects costs (over a given time span).A change in the cost driver results in a change in the cost of the cost object. For example, number of vehicles assembled is a driver of the costs of steering wheels on a motor-vehicle assembly line.

2-8   The *relevant range* is the band of activity or volume in which a specific relationship between the level of activity or volume and the cost in question is valid. This concept enables the use of linear cost functions when examining cost-volume-profit (CVP) relationships as long as the volume levels are within that relevant range.

2-10 Manufacturing companies typically have one or more of the following three types of inventory.
1. *Direct materials inventory.* Direct materials in stock and awaiting use in the manufacturing process.
2. *Work-in-process inventory.* Goods partially worked on but not yet fully completed. Also called *work in progress*.
3. *Finished goods inventory.* Goods fully completed but not yet sold.

2-12 No. Service sector companies have no inventories and, hence, no inventoriable costs.

2-14 *Overtime premium* consists of the wage rate paid to all workers (for both direct labor and indirect labor) in excess of their straight-time wage rates.

Idle time is a subclassification of indirect labor that typically represents wages paid for unproductive time caused by lack of orders, machine breakdowns, material shortages, poor scheduling, and the like.

2-16 (10 min.) **Total costs and unit costs.**

1. Total cost, $4,000. Unit cost per person, $4,000 ÷ 500 = $8.00
2. Total cost, $4,000. Unit cost per person, $4,000 ÷ 2,000 = $2.00
3. The main lesson of this exercise is to alert the student early in the course to the desirability of thinking in terms of total costs rather than unit costs wherever feasible. Changes in the denominator (the level of total activity or volume in this case attendance) will affect *total variable costs* but not *total fixed costs*. In our example, it would be perilous to use either the $8.00 or the $2.00 unit cost to predict the total cost because the total costs are not affected by the attendance. Instead, the student association should use the $4,000 total cost. Obviously, if the musical group agreed to work for, say, $4.00 per person, such a unit variable cost could be used to predict the total cost.

2-18 (15 min.) **Computing and interpreting unit manufacturing costs.**

1.

	Supreme	Deluxe	Regular
Direct materials costs	$ 84.00	$ 54.00	$ 62.00
Direct manuf. labor costs	14.00	28.00	8.00
Indirect manuf. costs	42.00	84.00	24.00
Total manuf. costs	$140.00	$ 166.00	$ 94.00
Pounds produced	80	120	100
Cost per pound	$ 1.7500	$ 1.3833	$0.9400

2. The unit costs in requirement 1 includes $20 million of indirect manufacturing costs that are fixed irrespective of changes in the volume of output per month, while the remaining variable indirect manufacturing costs change with the production volume. Given the unit volume changes for August 2001, the use of unit costs from the past month at a different unit volume level (both in aggregate and at the individual product level) will yield incorrect estimates of total costs in August 2001.

2-20 (15 min). **Cost drivers and the value chain.**

1.

Business Function	Representative Cost Driver
Production	• Hours the Tylenol packaging line is in operation
Research and Development	• Number of patents filed with U.S. Patent office.
Marketing	• Minutes of TV advertising time on "60 Minutes"
Distribution	• Number of packages shipped
Design of Products/Processes	• Hours spent designing tamper-proof bottles
Customer Service	• Number of calls to toll-free customer phone line

2.

Business Function	Representative Cost Driver
Research and Development	• Hours of laboratory work • Number of new drugs in development
Design of Products/Processes	• Number of focus groups on alternative package designs • Hours of process engineering work
Production	• Number of units packaged • Number of tablets manufactured
Marketing	• Number of promotion packages mailed • Number of sales personnel
Distribution	• Weight of packages shipped • Number of supermarkets on delivery route
Customer Service	• Number of units of a product recalled • Number of personnel on toll-free customer phone lines

2-22 (15-20 min.) **Variable costs and fixed costs.**

1. Variable cost per ton of beach sand mined:

Subcontractor	$ 80 per ton
Government tax	50 per ton
Total	$130 per ton

Fixed costs per month:

0 to 100 tons of capacity per day	=	$150,000
101 to 200 tons of capacity per day	=	$300,000
201 to 300 tons of capacity per day	=	$450,000

2.

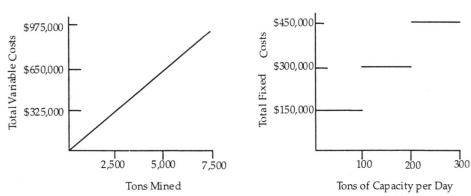

The concept of relevant range is potentially relevant for both graphs. However, the question does not place restrictions on the unit variable costs. The relevant range for the total fixed costs is from 0 to 100 tons; 101 to 200 tons; 201 to 300 tons, and so on. Within these ranges, the total fixed costs do not change in total.

3.

Tons Mined per Day	Tons Mined per Month	Fixed Unit Cost per Ton	Variable Unit Cost per Ton	Total Unit Cost per Ton
(1)	**(2) = (1) × 25**	**(3) = FC ÷ (2)**	**(4)**	**(5) = (3) + (4)**
(a) 180	4,500	$300,000 ÷ 4,500 = $66.67	$130	$196.67
(b) 220	5,500	$450,000 ÷ 5,500 =$81.82	$130	$211.82

The unit cost for 220 tons mined per day is $211.82, while for 180 tons it is only $196.67. This difference is caused by the fixed cost increment from 101 to 200 tons being spread over an increment of 80 tons, while the fixed cost increment from 201 to 300 tons is spread over an increment of only 20 tons.

2-24 (15-20 min.) Classification of costs, merchandising sector.

Cost object: Video section of store

Cost variability: With respect to changes in the number of videos sold

There may be some debate over classifications of individual items. Debate is more likely as regards cost variability.

Cost Item	D or I	V or F
A	I	F
B	I	F
C	D	V
D	D	F
E	I	F
F	I	V
G	I	F
H	D	V

2-26 (20-30 min.) Inventoriable costs vs. period costs.

1.   *Manufacturing-sector companies* purchase materials and components and convert them into different finished goods.

Merchandising-sector companies purchase and then sell tangible products without changing their basic form.

Service-sector companies provide services or intangible products to their customers—for example, legal advice or audits.

Only manufacturing and merchandising companies have inventories of goods for sale.

2.   *Inventoriable costs* are all costs of a product that are regarded as an asset when they are incurred and then become cost of goods sold when the product is sold. These costs for a manufacturing company are included in work-in-process and finished goods inventory (they are "inventoried") to build up the costs of creating these assets.

Period costs are all costs in the income statement other than cost of goods sold. These costs are treated as expenses of the period in which they are incurred because they are presumed not to benefit future periods (or because there is not sufficient evidence to conclude that such benefit exists). Expensing these costs immediately best matches expenses to revenues.

3.   (a) Mineral water purchased for resale by Safeway—inventoriable cost of a merchandising company. It becomes part of cost of goods sold when the mineral water is sold.

(b) Electricity used at GE assembly plant—inventoriable cost of a manufacturing company. It is part of the manufacturing overhead that is included in the manufacturing cost of a refrigerator finished good.

(c) Depreciation on Excite's computer equipment—period cost of a service company. Excite has no inventory of goods for sale and, hence, no inventoriable cost.

(d) Electricity for Safeway's store aisles—period cost of a merchandising company. It is a cost that benefits the current period and is not traceable to goods purchased for resale.

(e) Depreciation on GE's assembly testing equipment—inventoriable cost of a manufacturing company. It is part of the manufacturing overhead that is included in the manufacturing cost of a refrigerator finished good.

(f) Salaries of Safeway's marketing personnel—period cost of a merchandising company. It is a cost that is not traceable to goods purchased for resale. It is presumed not to benefit future periods (or at least not to have sufficiently reliable evidence to estimate such future benefits).

(g) Water consumed by Excite's engineers—period cost of a service company. Excite has no inventory of goods for sale and ,hence, no inventoriable cost.

(h) Salaries of Excite's marketing personnel—period cost of a service company. Excite has no inventory of goods for sale and, hence, no inventoriable cost.

2-28 (30-40 min.) Cost of goods manufactured.

Canesco Company
Schedule of Cost of Goods Manufactured for the Year Ended December 31, 2001
(in thousands)

1.

Direct materials costs:		
Beginning inventory, Jan. 1, 2001	$22,000	
Purchases of direct materials	75,000	
Cost of direct materials available for use	97,000	
Ending inventory, Dec. 31, 2001	26,000	
Direct materials used		$ 71,000
Direct manufacturing labor costs		25,000
Indirect manufacturing costs:		
Indirect manufacturing labor costs	15,000	
Plant insurance 9,000		
Depreciation—plant building and equipment	11,000	
Repairs and maintenance—plant	4,000	39,000
Manufacturing costs incurred during 2001		135,000
Add beginning work-in-process inventory, Jan. 1, 2001		21,000
Total manufacturing costs to account for		156,000
Deduct ending work-in-process inventory, Dec. 31, 2001		20,000
Cost of goods manufactured		$136,000

2.

Canesco Company
Income Statement for the Year Ended December 31, 2001
(in thousands)

Revenues		$300,000
Cost of goods sold:		
Beginning finished goods, Jan. 1, 2001	$ 18,000	
Cost of goods manufactured (requirement 1)	136,000	
Cost of goods available for sale	154,000	
Ending finished goods, Dec. 31, 2001	23,000	131,000
Gross margin		169,000
Operating costs:		
Marketing, distribution, and customer service	93,000	
General and administrative	29,000	122,000
Operating income		$ 47,000

2-30 (15-20 min.) **Interpretation of statements.**

1.   The schedule in 2-29 can become a Schedule of Cost of Goods Manufactured and Sold simply by including the beginning and ending finished goods inventory figures in the supporting schedule, rather than directly in the body of the income statement. Note that the term *cost of goods manufactured* refers to the cost of goods brought to completion (finished) during the accounting period, whether they were started before or during the current accounting period. Some of the manufacturing costs incurred are held back as costs of the ending work-in-process; similarly, the costs of the beginning work-in-process inventory become a part of the cost of goods manufactured for 2001.

2.   The sales manager's salary would be charged as a marketing cost as incurred by both manufacturing and merchandising companies. It is basically an operating cost that appears below the gross margin line on an income statement. In contrast, an assembler's wages would be assigned to the products worked on. Thus, the wages cost would be charged to Work-in-process and would not be expensed until the product is transferred through Finished Goods Inventory to Cost of Goods Sold as the product is sold.

3.   The direct-indirect distinction can be resolved only with respect to a particular cost object. For example, in defense contracting, the cost object may be defined as a contract. Then, a plant supervisor's salary may be charged directly and wholly to that single contract.

4.   Direct materials used   = \$320,000,000 ÷ 1,000,000 units = \$320 per unit
     Depreciation   = \$ 80,000,000 ÷ 1,000,000 units = \$ 80 per unit

5.   Direct materials unit cost would be unchanged at \$320. Depreciation unit cost would be \$80,000,000 ÷ 1,200,000 = \$66.67 per unit. Total direct materials costs would rise by 20% to \$384,000,000, whereas total depreciation would be unaffected at \$80,000,000.

6.   Unit costs are averages, and they must be interpreted with caution. The \$320 direct materials unit cost is valid for predicting total costs because direct materials is a variable cost; total direct materials costs indeed change as output levels change. However, fixed costs like depreciation must be interpreted quite differently from variable costs. A common error in cost analysis is to regard all unit costs as one-as if all the total costs to which they are related are variable costs. Changes in output levels (the denominator) will affect *total variable costs*, but not *total fixed costs*. Graphs of the two costs may clarify this point; it is safer to think in terms of total costs rather than in terms of unit costs.

2-32   (15-20 min.) **Interpretation of statements.**

1.   The schedule in 2-31 can become a Schedule of Cost of Goods Manufactured and Sold simply by including the beginning and ending finished goods inventory figures in the supporting schedule, rather than directly in the body of the income statement. Note that the term *cost of goods manufactured* refers to the cost of goods brought to completion (finished) during the accounting period, whether they were started before or during the current accounting period. Some of the manufacturing costs incurred are held back as costs of the ending work-in-process; similarly, the costs of the beginning work-in-process inventory become a part of the cost of goods manufactured for 2001.

2.   The sales manager's salary would be charged as a marketing cost as incurred by both manufacturing and merchandising companies. It is basically an operating cost that appears below the gross margin line on an income statement. In contrast, an assembler's wages would be assigned to the products worked on. Thus, the wages cost would be charged to Work-in-process and would not be expensed until the product is transferred through Finished Goods Inventory to Cost of Goods Sold as the product is sold.

3.   The direct-indirect distinction can be resolved only with respect to a particular cost object. For example, in defense contracting, the cost object may be defined as a contract. Then, a plant supervisor's salary may be charged directly and wholly to that single contract.

4.   Direct materials used $= \$105,000,000 \div 1,000,000$ units $= \$105$ per unit
      Depreciation $= \$\ \ \ 9,000,000 \div 1,000,000$ units $= \$\ \ \ 9$ per unit

5.   Direct materials unit cost would be unchanged at $105. Depreciation unit cost would be $\$9,000,000 \div 1,500,000 = \$6$ per unit. Total direct materials costs would rise by 50% to $157,500,000 ($105 × 1,500,000). Total depreciation cost of $9,000,000 would remain unchanged.

6.   Unit costs are averages, and they must be interpreted with caution. The $105 direct materials unit cost is valid for predicting total costs because direct materials is a variable cost; total direct materials costs indeed change as output levels change. However, fixed costs like depreciation must be interpreted quite differently from variable costs. A common error in cost analysis is to regard all unit costs as one-as if all the total costs to which they are related are variable costs. Changes in output levels (the denominator) will affect *total variable costs*, but not *total fixed costs*. Graphs of the two costs may clarify this point; it is safer to think in terms of total costs rather than in terms of unit costs.

2-34 (20-25 min.) **Finding unknown balances.**

Let G = given, I = inferred

Step 1: Use gross margin formula	Case 1	Case 2
Revenues	$ 32,000 G	$ 31,800 G
Cost of goods sold	A 20,700 I	20,000 G
Gross margin	11,300 G	C $11,800 I

Step 2: Use schedule of cost of goods manufactured formula		
Direct materials used	$ 8,000 G	$ 12,000 G
Direct manufacturing labor costs	3,000 G	5,000 G
Indirect manufacturing costs	7,000 G	D 6,500 I
Manufacturing costs incurred	18,000 I	23,500 I
Add beginning work-in-process, 1/1	0 G	800 G
Total manufacturing costs to account for	18,000 I	24,300 I
Deduct ending work-in-process, 12/31	0 G	3,000 G
Cost of goods manufactured	$ 18,000 I	$ 21,300 I

Step 3: Use cost of goods sold formula		
Beginning finished goods inventory, 1/1	$ 4,000 G	4,000 G
Cost of goods manufactured	18,000 I	21,300 I
Cost of goods available for sale	22,000 I	25,300 I
Ending finished goods inventory, 12/31	B 1,300 I	5,300 G
Cost of goods sold	$ 20,700 I	$ 20,000 G

For case 1, do steps 1, 2, and 3 in order.
For case 2, do steps 1, 3, and then 2.

2-36 (30 min.) **Comprehensive problem on unit costs, product costs.**

1.   If 2 pounds of direct materials are used to make each unit of finished product, 100,000 units × 2 lbs., or 200,000 lbs. were used at $0.70 per pound of direct materials ($140,000 ÷ 200,000 lbs.). Therefore, the ending inventory of direct materials is 2,000 lbs. × $0.70 = $1,400.

2.

	Manufacturing Costs for 100,000 units		
	Variable	**Fixed**	**Total**
Direct materials costs	$140,000	$ –	$140,000
Direct manufacturing labor costs	30,000	–	30,000
Plant energy costs	5,000	–	5,000
Indirect manufacturing labor costs	10,000	16,000	26,000
Other indirect manufacturing costs	8,000	24,000	32,000
Cost of goods manufactured	$193,000	$40,000	$233,000

Average unit manufacturing cost: $233,000 ÷ 100,000 units
= $2.33 per unit

Finished goods inventory in units: $= \dfrac{\$20,970 \text{ (given)}}{\$2.33 \text{ per unit}}$

= 9,000 units

2-36 (Cont'd.)

3. Units sold in 2001 = Beginning inventory + Production − Ending inventory
    = 0 + 100,000 − 9,000 = 91,000 units
    Selling price per unit in 2001 = $436,800 ÷ 91,000
    = $4.80 per unit

4.

Revenues (91,000 units sold × $4.80)		$436,800
Cost of units sold:		
Beginning finished goods, Jan. 1, 2001	$ 0	
Cost of goods manufactured	233,000	
Cost of goods available for sale	233,000	
Ending finished goods, Dec. 31, 2001	20,970	212,030
Gross margin		224,770
Operating costs:		
Marketing, distribution, and customer−service costs	162,850	
Administrative costs	50,000	212,850
Operating income		$ 11,920

Note: Although not required, the full set of unit variable costs is:

Direct materials costs	$1.40	
Direct manufacturing labor costs	0.30	
Plant energy costs	0.05	per unit manufactured
Indirect manufacturing labor costs	0.10	
Other indirect manufacturing costs	0.08	
Marketing, distribution, and customer−service costs	$1.35	per unit sold

2 − 11

2-38 (30 min.) Cost analysis, litigation risks, ethics.

1. Reasons for Savage not wanting Nash to record the potential litigation costs include:
(a) Genuine belief that the product has no risk of future litigation. Note that she asserts "she has total confidence in her medical research team."
(b) Concern that the uncertainties about litigation are sufficiently high to make any numerical estimate ""eaningless."
(c) Concern that inclusion of future litigation costs would cause the board of directors to vote against the project. Savage may be "overly committed" to the project and wants to avoid showing information that prompts questions she prefers not to be raised.
(d) Avoid "smoking gun" memos being included in the project evaluation file. Savage may believe that if subsequent litigation occurs, the plaintiffs will "inappropriately" use a litigation cost line item as "proof" FY "knew the product had health problems" that were known to management at the outset.

2. Information on which to estimate potential litigation costs include:
(a) The nature of potential damage done by the Enhance product and the possibility and cost of repairing that damage.
(b) The magnitude of verdicts given for related "product defect" situation. The Enhance product is bought primarily for "cosmetic" purpose. Information on litigation (including settlements) costs for a broad range of cosmetic-related products would be of interest.
(c) Past costs of hiring lawyers and expert witnesses in large complex litigation cases.
(d) Expected changes in litigation costs over the next 5 to 10 years. It is likely that the Enhance product would not result in litigation settlements for some time. A time trend of past increase in litigation settlements/verticts could assist in projecting the trend.

3. Nash has already registered his concern to Savage. The difficultly is that Savage asked that the presentation be "off-the-record." If there is no record of this presentation, then Nash may have several concerns.
(a) He may be accused at a later stage of not anticipating the costs of litigation. If litigation does occur, some people will try to distance themselves from the problems. It may be to Nash's advantage to have a record of his early concerns. (Although plaintiffs may make Nash's life very difficult if they get access to Nash's files). Nash may want to keep some record of his presentation to Savage.
(b) He may be portrayed as not being a "team player" if he continues his objections. Savage may have to silence his concerns if he decides to stay at FY.
(c) He may have difficult ethical objections with Savage's behavior. If he thinks she is acting unethically, his main options are to speak to her first (at least one time), speak to her supervisior, or as a final result resign –see Exhibit 1-8 of the text.

CHAPTER 3
COST-VOLUME-PROFIT ANALYSIS

3-2   The assumptions underlying the CVP analysis outlined in Chapter 3 are:

1.   Changes in the level of revenues and costs arise only because of changes in the number of product (or service) units produced and sold.
2.   Total costs can be divided into a fixed component and a component that is variable with respect to the level of output.
3.   When graphed, the behavior of total revenues and total costs is linear (straight-line) in relation to output units within the relevant range.
4.   The unit selling price, unit variable costs, and fixed costs are known and constant.
5.   The analysis either covers a single product or assumes that the sales mix, when multiple products are sold, will remain constant as the level of total units sold changes.
6.   All revenues and costs can be added and compared without taking into account the time value of money.

3-4   Contribution margin is computed as the difference between total revenues and total variable costs. Contribution margin per unit is the difference between selling price and variable cost per unit. Contribution-margin percentage is the contribution margin per unit divided by selling price.

3-6   Breakeven analysis denotes the study of the breakeven point, which is often only an incidental part of the relationship between cost, volume, and profit. Cost-volume-profit relationship is a more comprehensive term than breakeven analysis.

3-8   An increase in the income tax rate does not affect the breakeven point. Operating income at the breakeven point is zero, and thus no income taxes will be paid at this point.

3-10 Examples include:
Manufacturing—substituting a robotic machine for hourly wage workers.
Marketing—changing a sales force compensation plan from a percent of sales dollars to a fixed salary.
Customer service—hiring a subcontractor to do customer repair visits on an annual retainer basis rather than a per-visit basis.

3-12 Operating leverage describes the effects that fixed costs have on changes in operating income as changes occur in units sold and hence in contribution margin. Knowing the degree of operating leverage at a given level of sales helps managers calculate the effect of fluctuations in sales on operating incomes.

3-14 A company with multiple products can compute a breakeven point by assuming there is a constant mix of products at different levels of total revenue.

3-16 (10 min.) **CVP computations.**

	Revenues	Variable Costs	Fixed Costs	Total Costs	Operating Income	Contribution Margin	Contribution Margin %
a.	**$2,000**	$ 500	$300	$ 800	$1,200	$1,500	**75.0%**
b.	2,000	**1,500**	300	**1,800**	200	500	**25.0%**
c.	1,000	700	**300**	1,000	**0**	**300**	**30.0%**
d.	1,500	**900**	300	**1,200**	300	600	40.0%

3-18 (15–20 min.) **CVP analysis, changing revenues and costs.**

1. USP $=$ 8% × $1,000 = $80
    UVC $=$ $35 ($17 + $18)
    UCM $=$ $45
    FC $=$ $22,000 a month

a. $Q = \dfrac{FC}{UCM} = \dfrac{\$22,000}{\$45}$

    $=$ 489 tickets (rounded up)

b. $Q = \dfrac{FC + TOI}{UCM} = \dfrac{\$22,000 + \$10,000}{\$45}$

    $= \dfrac{\$32,000}{\$45}$

    $=$ 712 tickets (rounded up)

2. USP $=$ $80
    UVC $=$ $29 ($17 + $12)
    UCM $=$ $51
    FC $=$ $22,000 a month

a. $Q = \dfrac{FC}{UCM} = \dfrac{\$22,000}{\$51}$

    $=$ 432 tickets (rounded up)

b. $Q = \dfrac{FC + TOI}{UCM} = \dfrac{\$22,000 + \$10,000}{\$51}$

    $= \dfrac{\$32,000}{\$51}$

    $=$ 628 tickets (rounded up)

3-20 (20 min.) **CVP exercises.**

	Revenues	Variable Costs	Contribution Margin	Fixed Costs	Budgeted Operating Income
Orig.	$10,000,000^G	$8,200,000^G	$1,800,000	$1,700,000^G	$100,000
1.	10,000,000	8,020,000	1,980,000	1,700,000	280,000
2.	10,000,000	8,380,000	1,620,000	1,700,000	(80,000)
3.	10,000,000	8,200,000	1,800,000	1,785,000	15,000
4.	10,000,000	8,200,000	1,800,000	1,615,000	185,000
5.	10,800,000	8,856,000	1,944,000	1,700,000	244,000
6.	9,200,000	7,544,000	1,656,000	1,700,000	(44,000)
7.	11,000,000	9,020,000	1,980,000	1,870,000	110,000
8.	10,000,000	7,790,000	2,210,000	1,785,000	425,000

^{G}stands for given.

3-22 (10–15 min.) **CVP analysis, income taxes.**

1. Operating income $\quad$ = Net income $\div$ (1 – tax rate)
$= \$84,000 \times (1 - 0.40) \quad = \$140,000$

2. Contribution margin – Fixed costs $\quad$ = Operating income
Contribution margin – $300,000 $\quad$ = \$140,000
Contribution margin $\quad$ = \$440,000

3. Revenues – 0.80 Revenues $\quad$ = Contribution margin
$\quad$ 0.20 Revenues $\quad$ = \$440,000
$\quad$ Revenues $\quad$ = \$2,200,000

4. Breakeven point = Fixed costs $\div$ Contribution margin percentage
Breakeven point = $300,000 \div 0.20 = \$1,500,000$

3-24 (10 min.) **CVP analysis, margin of safety.**

1. $\text{Breakeven point revenues} = \dfrac{\text{Fixed costs}}{\text{Contribution margin percentage}}$

$\text{Contribution margin percentage} = \dfrac{\$400,000}{\$1,000,000} = 0.40$

2. $\text{Contribution margin percentage} = \dfrac{\text{Selling price} - \text{Variable cost per unit}}{\text{Selling price}}$

$0.40 = \dfrac{USP - \$12}{USP}$

$0.40\,USP = USP - \$12$
$0.60\,USP = \$12$
$USP = \$20$

3. Revenues, 80,000 units × $20 $\qquad$ $1,600,000
Breakeven revenues $\qquad\qquad\quad$ 1,000,000
Margin of safety $\qquad\qquad\qquad$ $\underline{\$\ \ 600,000}$

3-26 (30 min.) **CVP analysis, sensitivity analysis.**

1. USP   = $30.00 × (1 – 0.30 margin to bookstore)
            = $30.00 × 0.70 = $21.00

    UVC   = $ 4.00   variable production and marketing cost
                 3.15   variable author royalty cost (0.15 × $30.00 × 0.70)
              $ 7.15

    UCM   = $21.00 – $7.15 = $13.85

    FC   = $ 500,000   fixed production and marketing cost
                 3,000,000   up-front payment to Washington
              $3,500,000

Exhibit 3-26A shows the PV graph.

EXHIBIT 3-26A
PV Graph for Media Publishers

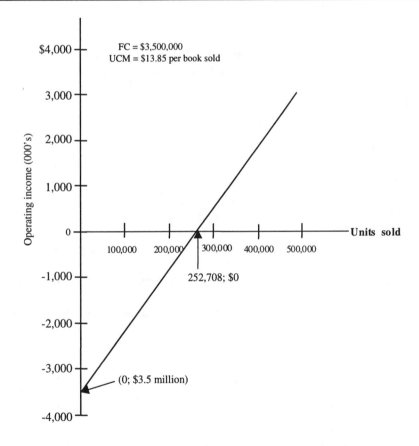

3-26 (Cont'd.)

2. a. Breakeven number of units $= \dfrac{FC}{UCM}$

        $= \dfrac{\$3,500,000}{\$13.85}$

        $=$ 252,708 copies sold (rounded up)

    b. Target OI $= \dfrac{FC + OI}{UCM}$

        $= \dfrac{\$3,500,000 + \$2,000,000}{\$13.85}$

        $= \dfrac{\$5,500,000}{\$13.85}$

        $=$ 397,112 copies sold (rounded up)

3. a. Decreasing the normal bookstore margin to 20% of the listed bookstore price of $30 has the following effects:

USP	$=$	$\$30.00 \times (1 - 0.20)$
	$=$	$\$30.00 \times 0.80 = \$24.00$

UVC	$=$	$ 4.00	variable production and marketing cost
		+ 3.60	variable author royalty cost $(0.15 \times \$30.00 \times 0.80)$
		$ 7.60	

UCM $=$ $\$24.00 - \$7.60 = \$16.40$

Breakeven number of units $= \dfrac{FC}{UCM}$

        $= \dfrac{\$3,500,000}{\$16.40}$

        $=$ 213,415 copies sold (rounded)

The breakeven point decreases from 252,708 copies in requirement 2 to 213,415 copies.

    b. Increasing the listed bookstore price to $40 while keeping the bookstore margin at 30% has the following effects:

USP	$=$	$\$40.00 \times (1 - 0.30)$
	$=$	$\$40.00 \times 0.70 = \$28.00$

UVC	$=$	$ 4.00	variable production and marketing cost
		+ 4.20	variable author royalty cost $(0.15 \times \$40.00 \times 0.70)$
		$ 8.20	

3-26 (Cont'd.)

$$\text{UCM} = \$28.00 - \$8.20 = \$19.80$$

$$\frac{\text{Breakeven}}{\text{number of units}} = \frac{\$3,500,000}{\$19.80}$$

$$= 176,768 \text{ copies sold (rounded)}$$

The breakeven point decreases from 252,708 copies in requirement 2 to 176,768 copies.

c. The answer to requirements 3a and 3b decreases the breakeven point relative to requirement 2 because in each case fixed costs remain the same at $3,500,000 while contribution margin per unit increases.

3-28 (30 min.) **Sales mix, new and upgrade customers.**

1.

	New Customers	Upgrade Customers
USP	$210	$120
UVC	90	40
UCM	120	80

Let S = Number of upgrade customers
$1.5S$ = Number of new customers
Revenues – Variable costs – Fixed costs = Operating income
$[\$210\,(1.5S) + \$120S] - [\$90\,(1.5S) + \$40S] - \$14,000,000 = \text{OI}$
$\$435S - \$175S - \$14,000,000 = \text{OI}$
Breakeven point is 134,616 units when OI = 0
$\$260S = \$14,000,000$
$\quad S = \underline{53,846}$
$1.5S = \underline{80,770}$
$\quad\quad\quad \underline{134,616}$

Check

Revenues ($210 × 80,770; $120 × 53,846)	$23,423,220
Variable costs ($90 × 80,770; $40 × 53,846)	9,423,140
Contribution margin	14,000,080
Fixed costs	14,000,000
Operating income (subject to rounding)	$ 0

3-28 (Cont'd.)

2. When 200,000 units are sold, mix is:

New customers (60% × 200,000)	120,000
Upgrade customers (40% × 200,000)	80,000

Revenues ($210 × 120,000; $120 × 80,000)	$34,800,000
Variable costs ($90 × 120,000; $40 × 80,000)	14,000,000
Contribution margin	20,800,000
Fixed costs	14,000,000
Operating income	$ 6,800,000

3a. Let S = Number of upgrade customers
then S = Number of new customers

$$[\$210S + \$120S] - [\$90S + \$40S] - \$14,000,000 = OI$$

$330S - 130S$	=	$14,000,000
$200S$	=	$14,000,000
S	=	70,000
S	=	70,000
		140,000 units

Check

Revenues ($210 × 70,000; $120 × 70,000)	$23,100,000
Variable costs ($90 × 70,000; $40 × 70,000)	9,100,000
Contribution margin	14,000,000
Fixed costs	14,000,000
Operating income	$ 0

3b. Let S = Number of upgrade customers
then $9S$ = Number of new customers
$$[\$210 (9S) + \$120S] - [\$90 (9S) + \$40S] - \$14,000,000 = OI$$

$2,010S - 850S$	=	$14,000,000
$1,160S$	=	$14,000,000
S	=	12,069
$9S$	=	108,621
		120,690 units

Check

Revenues ($210 × 108,621; $120 × 12,069)	$24,258,690
Variable costs ($90 × 108,621; $40 × 12,069)	10,258,650
Contribution margin	14,000,040
Fixed costs	4,000,000
Operating income (subject to rounding)	$ 0

3-28 (Cont'd.)

3c.   As Zapo increases its percentage of new customers, which have a higher contribution margin per unit than upgrade customers, the number of units required to break even decreases:

	New Customers	Upgrade Customers	Breakeven Point
Requirement 3(a)	50%	50%	140,000
Requirement 1	60	40	134,616
Requirement 3(b)	90	10	120,690

3-30 (20 min.) Gross margin and contribution margin.

1a.
Cost of Goods Sold	$1,600,000
Fixed Manufacturing Costs	500,000
Variable Manufacturing Costs	$1,100,000

Variable manufacturing costs per unit = $1,100,000 ÷ 200,000 = $5.50 per unit

1b.
Total marketing and distribution costs	$1,150,000
Variable marketing and distribution (200,000 × $4)	800,000
Fixed marketing and distribution costs	$ 350,000

2.   Selling price   = $2,600,000 ÷ 200,000 units = $13 per unit

$$\frac{\text{Contribution margin}}{\text{per unit}} = \frac{\text{Selling}}{\text{price}} - \frac{\text{Variable}}{\text{manufacturing}} - \frac{\text{Variable marketing}}{\text{and distribution}}$$
$$\text{costs per unit} \quad \text{costs per unit}$$

   = $13 – $5.50 – $4.00 = $3.50

$$\text{Operating income} = \left(\frac{\text{Contribution margin}}{\text{per unit}} \times \frac{\text{Sales}}{\text{quantity}}\right) - \frac{\text{Fixed manufacturing}}{\text{costs}} - \frac{\text{Fixed marketing}}{\text{and distribution}}$$
$$\text{costs}$$

   =   ($3.50 × 230,000) – $500,000 – $350,000
   =   –$45,000

Foreman has confused gross margin with contribution margin. He has interpreted gross margin as if it was all variable, and interpreted marketing and distribution costs as all fixed. In fact, the manufacturing costs, subtracted from sales to calculate gross margin, and marketing and distribution costs contain both fixed and variable components.

3.   Breakeven point in units $= \dfrac{\text{Fixed manufacturing, marketing and distribution costs}}{\text{Contribution margin per unit}}$

   $= \dfrac{\$850,000}{\$3.50} = 242,858$ units (rounded up)

Breakeven point in revenues   =   242,858 × $13 = $3,157,154.

3-32 (15–20 min.) Uncertainty, CVP analysis.

1. King pays Foreman $2 million plus $4 (25% of $16) for every home purchasing the pay-per-view. The expected value of the variable component is:

Demand (1)	Payment (2) = (1) × $4	Probability (3)	Expected payment (4)
100,000	$ 400,000	0.05	$ 20,000
200,000	800,000	0.10	80,000
300,000	1,200,000	0.30	360,000
400,000	1,600,000	0.35	560,000
500,000	2,000,000	0.15	300,000
1,000,000	4,000,000	0.05	200,000
			$1,520,000

The expected value of King's payment is $3,520,000 ($2,000,000 fixed fee + $1,520,000).

2.   USP = $16
     UVC = $ 6 ($4 payment to Foreman + $2 variable cost)
     UCM = $10
     FC   = $2,000,000 + $1,000,000 = $3,000,000

$$Q = \frac{FC}{UCM}$$

$$= \frac{\$3,000,000}{\$10}$$

$$= 300,000$$

If 300,000 homes purchase the pay-per-view, King will break even.

3-34 (20 min.) CVP analysis, cost structure differences, movie production.
(Continuation of 3-33)

1.   *Contract A*
     Fixed costs for Contract A:

Production costs	$21,000,000
Fixed salary	15,000,000
Total fixed costs	$36,000,000

Unit variable cost = $0.25 per $1 revenue marketing fee
Unit contribution margin = $0.75 per $1 revenue

$$\text{Breakeven point in revenues} = \frac{\text{Fixed costs}}{\text{Unit contribution margin per \$1 revenue}}$$

$$= \frac{\$36,000,000}{\$0.75} = \$48,000,000$$

3-34 (Cont'd.)

Box-office receipts of $76,800,000 ($48,000,000 ÷ 62.5%) translate to $48,000,000 in revenues to Royal Rumble.

Contract B

Fixed costs for Contract B:	
Production costs	$21,000,000
Fixed salary	3,000,000
Total fixed costs	$24,000,000

Unit variable cost =	$0.25	per $1 revenue fee to Media Productions
	0.15	per $1 revenue residual to directors/actors
	$0.40	per $1 revenue

Unit contribution margin = $0.60 per $1 revenue

$$\text{Breakeven point in revenues } = \frac{\$24,000,000}{0.60} = \$40,000,000$$

Box-office receipts of $64,000,000 ($40,000,000 ÷ 62.5%) translate to $40,000,000 in revenues to Royal Rumble.

Difference in Breakeven Points

Contract A has a higher fixed cost and a lower variable cost per sales dollar. In contrast, Contract B has a lower fixed cost and a higher variable cost per sales dollar. In Contract B, there is risk-sharing between Royal Rumble and Savage, Michaels, and Martel that lowers the breakeven point, but results in Royal Rumble receiving less operating income if *Feature Creatures 2* is a mega-success.

2.	Revenues, 0.625 × $300,000,000	$187,500,000
	Variable costs, 0.40 × $187,500,000	75,000,000
	Contribution margin	112,500,000
	Fixed costs	24,000,000
	Operating income	$ 88,500,000

Feature Creatures 2 has a higher breakeven point and lower operating income at $300 million in box-office receipts than *Feature Creatures* because of a higher level of fixed costs and a lower unit contribution margin.

3-36 (20–25 min.) **CVP analysis, shoe stores.** (Continuation of 3-35)

1.   Because the unit sales level at the point of indifference would be the same for each plan, the revenue would be equal. Therefore, the unit sales level sought would be that which produces the same total costs for each plan.

$$\text{Let } Q = \text{unit sales level}$$
$$\$19.50Q + \$360,000 + \$81,000 = \$21.00Q + \$360,000$$
$$\$81,000 = \$1.50Q$$
$$Q = 54,000 \text{ units}$$

2.

	Commission Plan		Salary Plan	
Sales in units	50,000	60,000	50,000	60,000
Revenues @ $30.00	$1,500,000	$1,800,000	$1,500,000	$1,800,000
Variable costs				
@ $21.00 and @ $19.50	1,050,000	1,260,000	975,000	1,170,000
Contribution margin	450,000	540,000	525,000	630,000
Fixed costs	360,000	360,000	441,000	441,000
Operating income	$ 90,000	$ 180,000	$ 84,000	$ 189,000

The decision regarding the plans will depend heavily on the unit sales level that is generated by the fixed salary plan. For example, as part (1) shows, at identical unit sales levels in excess of 54,000 units, the fixed salary plan will always provide a more profitable final result than the commission plan.

3.   Let TQ = Target number of units

a. $\$30.00TQ - \$19.50TQ - \$441,000 = \$168,000$
$$\$10.50TQ = \$609,000$$
$$TQ = \$609,000 \div \$10.50$$
$$TQ = 58,000 \text{ units}$$

b. $\$30.00TQ - \$21.00TQ - \$360,000 = \$168,000$
$$\$9.00TQ = \$528,000$$
$$TQ = \$528,000 \div \$9.00$$
$$TQ = 58,667 \text{ units (rounded)}$$

The decision regarding the salary plan depends heavily on predictions of demand. For instance, the salary plan offers the same operating income at 58,000 units as the commission plan offers at 58,667 units.

3-38 (30 min.) **CVP analysis, income taxes, sensitivity.**

1a. In order to break even, Almo Company must sell 500 units. This amount represents the point where revenues equal total costs.

Let Q denote the quantity of canopies sold.

$$
\begin{aligned}
\text{Revenue} &= \text{Variable costs} + \text{Fixed costs} \\
\$400Q &= \$200Q + \$100,000 \\
\$200Q &= \$100,000 \\
Q &= \underline{500} \text{ units}
\end{aligned}
$$

The calculation can also be expressed as

$$
\begin{aligned}
\text{Breakeven} &= \text{Fixed Costs} \div \text{Contribution margin per unit} \\
&= \$100,000 \div \$200 \\
&= \underline{500} \text{ units}
\end{aligned}
$$

1b. In order to achieve its net income objective, Almo Company must sell 2,500 units. This amount represents the point where revenues equal total costs plus the corresponding operating income objective to achieve net income of $240,000.

$$
\begin{aligned}
\text{Revenue} &= \text{Variable costs} + \text{Fixed costs} + \text{Operating income} \\
\$400Q &= \$200Q + \$100,000 + [\$240,000 \div (1 - 0.4)] \\
\$400\,Q &= \$200Q + \$100,000 + \$400,000 \\
Q &= \underline{2,500} \text{ units}
\end{aligned}
$$

2. To achieve its net income objective, Almo Company should select the first alternative where the sales price is reduced by $40, and 2,700 units are sold during the remainder of the year. This alternative results in the highest net income and is the only alternative that equals or exceeds the company's net income objective. Calculations for the three alternatives are shown below.

Alternative 1

$$
\begin{aligned}
\text{Revenues} &= (\$400 \times 350) + (\$360 \times 2,700) = \$1,112,000 \\
\text{Variable costs} &= \$200 \times 3,050 = \$610,000 \\
\text{Operating income} &= \$1,112,000 - \$610,000 - \$100,000 = \$402,000 \\
\text{Net income} &= \$402,000 \times (1 - 0.4) = \underline{\$241,200}
\end{aligned}
$$

Alternative 2

$$
\begin{aligned}
\text{Revenues} &= (\$400 \times 350) + (\$370 \times 2,200) = \$954,000 \\
\text{Variable costs} &= (\$200 \times 350) + (\$190 \times 2,200) = \$488,000 \\
\text{Operating income} &= \$954,000 - \$488,000 - \$100,000 = \$366,000 \\
\text{Net income} &= \$366,000 \times (1 - 0.4) = \underline{\$219,600}
\end{aligned}
$$

Alternative 3

$$
\begin{aligned}
\text{Revenues} &= (\$400 \times 350) + (\$380 \times 2,000) = \$900,000 \\
\text{Variable costs} &= \$200 \times 2,350 = \$470,000 \\
\text{Operating income} &= \$900,000 - \$470,000 - \$90,000 = \$340,000 \\
\text{Net income} &= \$340,000 \times (1 - 0.4) = \underline{\$204,000}
\end{aligned}
$$

3-40 (15–25 min.)   **Sales mix, three products.**

1.   Let A = Number of units of A to break even
        5A = Number of units of B to break even
        4A = Number of units of C to break even

Contribution margin – Fixed costs = Zero operating income

$$\$3A + \$2(5A) + \$1(4A) - \$255,000 = 0$$

$17A	=	$255,000
A	=	15,000 units of A
5A	=	75,000 units of B
4A	=	60,000 units of C
Total	=	150,000 units

2.   Contribution margin:

A: 20,000 × $3	$ 60,000	
B: 100,000 × $2	200,000	
C: 80,000 × $1	80,000	
Contribution margin		$340,000
Fixed costs		255,000
Operating income		$ 85,000

3.   Contribution margin

A: 20,000 × $3	$ 60,000	
B: 80,000 × $2	160,000	
C: 100,000 × $1	100,000	
Contribution margin		$320,000
Fixed costs		255,000
Operating income		$ 65,000

Let A = Number of units of A to break even
     4A = Number of units of B to break even
     5A = Number of units of C to break even

Contribution margin – Fixed costs = Breakeven point

$$\$3A + \$2(4A) + \$1(5A) - \$255,000 = 0$$

$16A	=	$255,000
A	=	15,938 units of A (rounded)
4A	=	63,752 units of B
5A	=	79,690 units of C
Total	=	159,380 units

Breakeven point increases because the new mix contains less of the higher contribution margin per unit, product B, and more of the lower contribution margin per unit, product C.

3-42 (20–25 min.)   **Sales mix, two products.**

1. Let Q   = Number of units of Deluxe carrier to break even
    3Q   = Number of units of Standard carrier to break even

    Revenues – Variable costs – Fixed costs = Zero operating income

$$
\begin{aligned}
\$20(3Q) + \$30Q - \$14(3Q) - \$18Q - \$1{,}200{,}000 &= 0 \\
\$60Q + \$30Q - \$42Q - \$18Q &= \$1{,}200{,}000 \\
\$30Q &= \$1{,}200{,}000 \\
Q &= 40{,}000 \text{ units of Deluxe} \\
3Q &= 120{,}000 \text{ units of Standard}
\end{aligned}
$$

The breakeven point is 120,000 Standard units plus 40,000 Deluxe units, a total of 160,000 units.

2. Unit contribution margins are: Standard: $20 – $14 = $6; Deluxe: $30 – $18 = $12
    a.   If only Standard carriers were sold, the breakeven point would be:
        $1,200,000 ÷ $6 = 200,000 units
    b.   If only Deluxe carriers were sold, the breakeven point would be:
        $1,200,000 ÷ $12 = 100,000 units

3. Operating income   =   180,000($6) + 20,000($12) – $1,200,000
                       = $1,080,000 + $240,000 – $1,200,000
                       = $120,000

    Let Q   =   Number of units of Deluxe product to break even
     9Q   =   Number of units of Standard product to break even

$$
\begin{aligned}
\$20(9Q) + \$30Q - \$14(9Q) - \$18Q - \$1{,}200{,}000 &= 0 \\
\$180Q + \$30Q - \$126Q - \$18Q &= \$1{,}200{,}000 \\
\$66Q &= \$1{,}200{,}000 \\
Q &= 18{,}182 \text{ units of Deluxe (rounded)} \\
9Q &= 163{,}638 \text{ units of Standard}
\end{aligned}
$$

The breakeven point is 163,638 Standard + 18,182 Deluxe, a total of 181,820 units.

The major lesson of this problem is that changes in the sales mix change breakeven points and operating incomes. In this example, the budgeted and actual total sales in number of units were identical, but the proportion of the product having the higher contribution margin declined. Operating income suffered, falling from $300,000 to $120,000. Moreover, the breakeven point rose from 160,000 to 181,820 units.

3-44 (30-40 min.) **CVP analysis, income taxes.**

1. Revenues – Variable costs – Fixed costs $= \dfrac{\text{Target net income}}{1 - \text{Tax rate}}$

    Let X = Net income for 2000

$$20{,}000(\$25.00) - 20{,}000(\$13.75) - \$135{,}000 = \dfrac{X}{1 - 0.40}$$

$$\$500{,}000 - \$275{,}000 - \$135{,}000 = \dfrac{X}{0.60}$$

$$\$300{,}000 - \$165{,}000 - \$81{,}000 = X$$

$$X = \$54{,}000$$

2. Let Q = Number of units to break even

    $\$25.00Q - \$13.75Q - \$135{,}000 = 0$

    $Q = \$135{,}000 \div \$11.25 = 12{,}000$ units

3. Let X = Net income for 2001

$$22{,}000(\$25.00) - 22{,}000(\$13.75) - (\$135{,}000 + \$11{,}250) = \dfrac{X}{1 - 0.40}$$

$$\$550{,}000 - \$302{,}500 - \$146{,}250 = \dfrac{X}{0.60}$$

$$\$101{,}250 = \dfrac{X}{0.60}$$

$$X = \$60{,}750$$

4. Let Q = Number of units to break even with new fixed costs of $146,250

$$\$25.00Q - \$13.75Q - \$146{,}250 = 0$$

$$Q = \$146{,}250 \div \$11.25 = 13{,}000 \text{ units}$$

$$\text{Revenues} = 13{,}000 \times \$25.00 = \$325{,}000$$

Alternatively, the computation could be $146,250 divided by the contribution margin percentage of 45% to obtain $325,000.

5. Let S = Required sales units to equal 2000 net income

$$\$25.00S - \$13.75S - \$146{,}250 = \dfrac{\$54{,}000}{0.6}$$

$$\$11.25S = \$236{,}250$$

$$S = 21{,}000 \text{ units}$$

$$\text{Revenues} = 21{,}000 \text{ units} \times \$25.00 = \$525{,}000$$

6. Let A = Amount spent for advertising in 2001

$$\$550{,}000 - \$302{,}500 - (\$135{,}000 + A) = \dfrac{\$60{,}000}{0.6}$$

$$\$550{,}000 - \$302{,}500 - \$135{,}000 - A = \$100{,}000$$

$$\$550{,}000 - \$537{,}500 = A$$

$$A = \$12{,}500$$

3-46 (20–30 min.) **CVP analysis under uncertainty.**

1. a. At a selling price of $100, the unit contribution margin is ($100 – $50) = $50, and it will require the sale of ($200,000 ÷ $50) = 4,000 units to break even. The sales in dollars is $400,000, and there is a 2/3 probability of equaling or exceeding this sales level.

   b. At a selling price of $70, the unit contribution margin is ($70 – $50) = $20, and it will require the sale of ($200,000 ÷ $20) = 10,000 units to break even. At the lower price, this sales in dollars is $700,000, and there is a 2/3 probability of equaling or exceeding this sales volume.

   Therefore, if you seek to maximize the probability of showing an operating income, you are indifferent between the two strategies.

2.

$$\begin{pmatrix} \text{Expected} \\ \text{operating income} \end{pmatrix} = \begin{pmatrix} \text{Selling} \\ \text{price per unit} \end{pmatrix} - \begin{pmatrix} \text{Variable} \\ \text{costs per unit} \end{pmatrix} \times \begin{pmatrix} \text{Expected} \\ \text{sales level} \end{pmatrix} - \text{Fixed costs}$$

At a selling price of $100:

Expected revenues	= $450,000 ($100 × 4,500)
Expected operating income	= [($100 – $50) × 4,500] – $200,000
	= $25,000

At a selling price of $70:

Expected revenues	= $750,050 ($70 × 10,715)
Expected operating income	= [($70 – $50) × 10,715] – $200,000
	= $14,300

A selling price of $100 will maximize the expected operating income.

3-48 (30 min.) Ethics, CVP analysis.

1. Contribution margin percentage $= \dfrac{\text{Revenues} - \text{Variable costs}}{\text{Revenues}}$

    $= \dfrac{\$5,000,000 - \$3,000,000}{\$5,000,000}$

    $= \dfrac{\$2,000,000}{\$5,000,000} = 40\%$

    Breakeven revenues $= \dfrac{\text{Fixed costs}}{\text{Contribution margin percentage}}$

    $= \dfrac{\$2,160,000}{0.40} = \$5,400,000$

2. If variable costs are 52% of revenues, contribution margin percentage equals 48% (100% − 52%)

    Breakeven revenues $= \dfrac{\text{Fixed costs}}{\text{Contribution margin percentage}}$

    $= \dfrac{\$2,160,000}{0.48} = \$4,500,000$

3.

Revenues	$5,000,000
Variable costs (0.52 × $5,000,000)	2,600,000
Fixed costs	2,160,000
Operating income	$ 240,000

4. Incorrect reporting of environmental costs with the goal of continuing operations is unethical. In assessing the situation, the specific "Standards of Ethical Conduct for Management Accountants" (described in Exhibit 1-7) that the management accountant should consider are listed below.

Competence
Clear reports using relevant and reliable information should be prepared. Preparing reports on the basis of incorrect environmental costs in order to make the company's performance look better than it is violates competence standards. It is unethical for Bush to not report environmental costs in order to make the plant's performance look good.

Integrity
The management accountant has a responsibility to avoid actual or apparent conflicts of interest and advise all appropriate parties of any potential conflict. Bush may be tempted to report lower environmental costs to please Lemond and Woodall and save the jobs of his colleagues. This action, however, violates the responsibility for integrity. The Standards of Ethical Conduct require the management accountant to communicate favorable as well as unfavorable information.

3-48 (Cont'd.)

Objectivity

The management accountant's Standards of Ethical Conduct require that information should be fairly and objectively communicated and that all relevant information should be disclosed. From a management accountant's standpoint, underreporting environmental costs to make performance look good would violate the standard of objectivity.

Bush should indicate to Lemond that estimates of environmental costs and liabilities should be included in the analysis. If Lemond still insists on modifying the numbers and reporting lower environmental costs, Bush should raise the matter with one of Lemond's superiors. If after taking all these steps, there is continued pressure to understate environmental costs, Bush should consider resigning from the company and not engage in unethical behavior.

CHAPTER 4
JOB COSTING

4-2   In a *job-costing system,* costs are assigned to a distinct unit, batch, or lot of a product or service. In a *process-costing system,* the cost of a product or service is obtained by using broad averages to assign costs to masses of similar units.

4-4   The seven steps in job costing are (1) identify the chosen cost object or job, (2) identify the direct costs of the job, (3) select the cost-allocation base(s) to use for allocating indirect costs to the job, (4) identify the indirect costs associated with each cost-allocation base, (5) compute the rate per unit of each cost-allocation base used to allocate indirect costs to the job, (6) compute the indirect costs allocated to the job, and (7) compute the total cost of the job by adding all direct and indirect costs assigned to it.

4-6   Three major source documents used in job-costing systems are (1) job cost record or job cost sheet, a document that records and accumulates all costs assigned to a specific job, (2) materials requisition record, a document used to charge job cost records and departments for the cost of direct materials used on a specific job, and (3) labor-time record, a document used to charge job cost records and departments for labor time used on a specific job.

4-8   Two reasons for using six-month or annual budget periods are:
a.   The numerator reason—the longer the time period, the less the influence of seasonal patterns, and
b.   The denominator reason—the longer the time period, the less the effect of variations in output levels on the allocation of fixed costs.

4-10   A house construction firm can use job cost information (a) to determine the profitability of individual jobs, (b) to assist in bidding on future jobs, and (c) to evaluate professionals who are in charge of managing individual jobs.

4-12   Debit entries to Work-in-Process Control represent increases in work in process. Examples of debit entries are: (a) direct materials used (credit to Materials Control), (b) direct manufacturing labor billed to job (credit to Wages Payable Control), and (c) manufacturing overhead allocated to job (credit to Manufacturing Overhead Allocated).

4-14   A company might use budgeted costs rather than actual costs to compute direct labor rates because it may be difficult to trace some costs to jobs as they are completed.

4-16 (20 min.) **Actual costing, normal costing, accounting for manufacturing overhead.**

1.
$$\text{Budgeted manufacturing overhead rate} = \frac{\text{Budgeted manufacturing overhead costs}}{\text{Budgeted direct manufacturing labor costs}}$$

$$= \frac{\$1,750,000}{\$1,000,000} = 1.75 \text{ or } 175\%$$

$$\text{Actual manufacturing overhead rate} = \frac{\text{Actual manufacturing overhead costs}}{\text{Actual direct manufacturing labor costs}}$$

$$= \frac{\$1,862,000}{\$980,000} = 1.9 \text{ or } 190\%$$

2. Costs of Job 626 under actual and normal costing follow:

	Normal Costing	Actual Costing
Direct materials	$ 40,000	$ 40,000
Direct manufacturing labor costs	30,000	30,000
Manufacturing overhead costs		
$30,000 × 1.75; $30,000 × 1.90	52,500	57,000
Total manufacturing costs of Job 626	$122,500	$127,000

3.
$$\text{Total manufacturing overhead allocated under normal costing} = \text{Actual manufacturing labor costs} \times \text{Budgeted overhead rate}$$

$$= \$980,000 \times 1.75$$
$$= \$1,715,000$$

$$\text{Underallocated manufacturing overhead} = \text{Actual manufacturing overhead costs} - \text{Manufacturing overhead allocated}$$

$$= \$1,862,000 - \$1,715,000 = \$147,000$$

There is no under- or overallocated overhead under actual costing because overhead is allocated under actual costing by multiplying actual manufacturing labor costs and the actual manufacturing overhead rate. This, of course equals the actual manufacturing overhead costs. All actual overhead costs are allocated to products. Hence, there is no under- or overallocatead overhead.

4-18 (20-30 min.) **Job costing, accounting for manufacturing overhead, budgeted rates.**

1. An overview of the product costing system is:

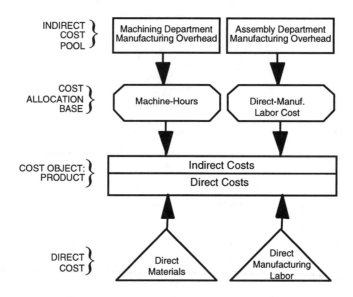

Budgeted manufacturing overhead divided by allocation base:

Machining overhead: $\dfrac{\$1,800,000}{50,000}$ = $36 per machine-hour

Assembly overhead: $\dfrac{\$3,600,000}{\$2,000,000}$ = 180% of direct manuf. labor costs

2.
Machining overhead, 2,000 hours × $36	$72,000
Assembly overhead, 180% of $15,000	27,000
Total manufacturing overhead allocated to Job 494	$99,000

3.
	Machining	**Assembly**
Actual manufacturing overhead	$2,100,000	$ 3,700,000
Manufacturing overhead allocated,		
55,000 × $36	1,980,000	
180% of $2,200,000		3,960,000
Underallocated (Overallocated)	$ 120,000	$ (260,000)

4-20 (20–30 min.) **Computing indirect-cost rates, job costing.**

1a.

	Budgeted Fixed Indirect Costs	Budgeted Hours	Budgeted Fixed Indirect Cost Rate per Hour	Budgeted Variable Indirect Cost Rate per Hour	Budgeted Total Indirect Cost Rate per Hour
Jan.–March	$ 50,000	20,000	$ 2.50	$10	$12.50
April–June	50,000	10,000	5.00	10	15.00
July–Sept.	50,000	4,000	12.50	10	22.50
Oct.–Dec.	50,000	6,000	8.33	10	18.33
b.	$200,000	40,000	$ 5.00	$10	$15.00

2a. All four jobs use 10 hours of professional labor time. The only difference in job costing is the indirect cost rate. The quarterly-based indirect job costs are:

Hansen:	$(10 \times \$12.50)$	=	$125.00
Kai:	$(6 \times \$12.50) + (4 \times \$15.00)$	=	$135.00
Patera:	$(4 \times \$15.00) + (6 \times \$22.50)$	=	$195.00
Stevens:	$(5 \times \$12.50) + (2 \times \$22.50) + (3 \times \$18.33)$	=	$162.50

	Hansen	Kai	Patera	Stevens
Revenues, $65 × 10	$650	$650	$650	$650.00
Direct costs, $30 × 10	300	300	300	300.00
Indirect costs	125	135	195	162.50
Total costs	425	435	495	462.50
Operating income	$225	$215	$155	$187.50

b. Using annual-based indirect job-cost rates, all four customers will have the same operating income:

Revenues, $65 × 10	$650
Direct costs, $30 × 10	300
Indirect costs, $15 × 10	150
Total costs	450
Operating income	$200

3. All four jobs use 10 hours of professional labor time. Using the quarterly-based indirect-cost rates, there are four different operating incomes as the work done on them is completed in different quarters. In contrast, using the annual indirect-cost rate, all four customers have the same operating income. All these different operating income figures for jobs with the same number of professional labor-hours are due to the allocation of fixed indirect costs.

4-20 (Cont'd.)

An overview of the Tax Assist job-costing system is:

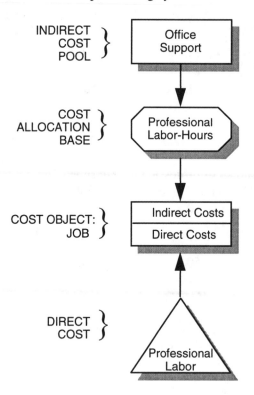

4-22 (20 min.) Job costing, journal entries, and source documents.
(Continuation of 4-21)

The analysis of source documents and subsidiary ledgers follows:

1. a. Approved invoice
  b. dr. Materials record, "received" column

2. a. Materials requisition record
  b. dr. Job cost records
   cr. Materials record, "issued" column

3. a. Materials requisition record
  b. dr. Department overhead cost records, appropriate column
   cr. Materials record, "issued" column

4. a. Summary of time records or daily time analysis. This summary is sometimes called a *labor cost distribution summary*.
  b. dr. Job cost records
   dr. Department overhead cost records, appropriate columns for various classes of indirect labor

5. a. Special authorization from the responsible accounting officer
  b. dr. Department overhead cost records, appropriate columns

6. a. Various approved invoices and special authorizations
  b. dr. Department overhead cost records, appropriate columns

7. a. Use of an authorized budgeted manufacturing overhead rate
  b. dr. Job cost record

8. a. Completed job cost records
  b. dr. Finished goods records
   cr. Job cost record

9. a. Approved sales invoice
  b. dr. Customers' accounts (or Cash)
   cr. Sales ledger, if any

10. a. Costed sales invoice
  b. cr. Finished goods records

11. a. Special authorization from the responsible accounting officer
  b. Subsidiary records are generally not used for these entries

4-24 (10–15 min.) **Accounting for manufacturing overhead.**

1. Budgeted manufacturing overhead rate $= \dfrac{\$7,000,000}{200,000}$

    $= \$35$ per machine-hour

2. Work-in-Process Control   6,825,000
       Manufacturing Overhead Allocated   6,825,000
    (195,000 machine-hours × $35 = $6,825,000)

3. $6,825,000 – $6,800,000 = $25,000 overallocated, an insignificant amount.

    Manufacturing Overhead Allocated   6,825,000
       Manufacturing Department Overhead Control   6,800,000
       Cost of Goods Sold   25,000

4-26 (20–30 min.) **Job costing; actual, normal, and variation of normal costing.**

1. Actual direct cost rate for professional labor $= \$58$ per professional labor-hour

    Actual indirect cost rate $= \dfrac{\$744,000}{15,500 \text{ hours}}$ $= \$48$ per professional labor-hour

    Budgeted direct cost rate
    for professional labor $= \dfrac{\$960,000}{16,000 \text{ hours}}$ $= \$60$ per professional labor-hour

    Budgeted indirect cost rate $= \dfrac{\$720,000}{16,000 \text{ hours}}$ $= \$45$ per professional labor-hour

	(a) Actual Costing	(b) Normal Costing	(c) Variation of Normal Costing
Direct-Cost Rate	$58 (Actual rate)	$58 (Actual rate)	$60 (Budgeted rate)
Indirect-Cost Rate	$48 (Actual rate)	$45 (Budgeted rate)	$45 (Budgeted rate)

2.

	(a) Actual Costing	(b) Normal Costing	(c) Variation of Normal Costing
Direct Costs	$58 × 120 = $ 6,960	$58 × 120 = $ 6,960	$60 × 120 = $ 7,200
Indirect Costs	48 × 120 = 5,760	45 × 120 = 5,400	45 × 120 = 5,400
Total Job Costs	$12,720	$12,360	$12,600

4-26 (Cont'd.)

All three costing systems use the actual professional labor time of 120 hours. The budgeted 110 hours for the Montreal Expos audit job is not used in job costing. However, Chirac may have used the 110 hour number in bidding for the audit.

The actual costing figure of $12,720 exceeds the normal costing figure of $12,360, because the actual indirect-cost rate ($48) exceeds the budgeted indirect-cost rate ($45). The normal costing figure of $12,360 is less than the variation of normal costing (based on budgeted rates for direct costs) figure of $12,600, because the actual direct-cost rate ($58) is less than the budgeted direct-cost rate ($60).

Although not required, the following overview diagram summarizes Chirac's job-costing system.

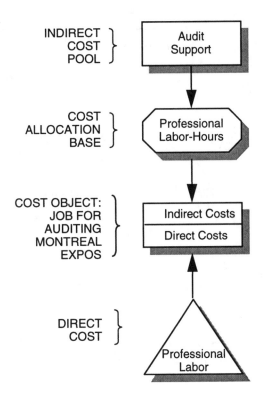

4-28 (20–30 min) **Job costing; accounting for manufacturing overhead, budgeted rates.**

1. An overview of the job-costing system is:

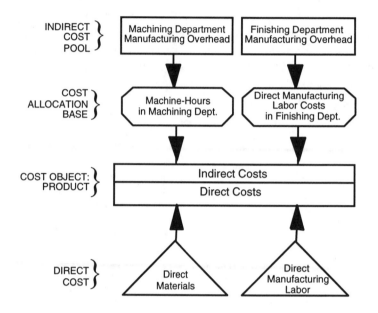

2. Budgeted manufacturing overhead divided by allocation base:
    a. Machining Department:
        $$\frac{\$10,000,000}{200,000} = \quad \$50 \text{ per machine-hour}$$
    b. Finishing Department:
        $$\frac{\$8,000,000}{\$4,000,000} = \quad 200\% \text{ of direct manufacturing labor costs}$$

3.
Machining overhead, $50 × 130 hours	$6,500
Finishing overhead, 200% of $1,250	2,500
Total manufacturing overhead allocated	$9,000

4-28 (Cont'd.)

4. Total costs of Job 431:
   Direct costs:

Direct materials—Machining Department	$14,000	
—Finishing Department	3,000	
Direct manufacturing labor —Machining Department	600	
—Finishing Department	1,250	$18,850

   Indirect costs:

Machining overhead, $50 × 130	$6,500	
Finishing overhead, 200% of $1,250	2,500	9,000
Total costs		$27,850

   The per-unit product cost of Job 431 is $27,850 ÷ 200 units = $139.25 per unit

5. The point of this part is (a) to get the definitions straight and (b) to underscore that overhead is allocated by multiplying the actual amount of the allocation base by the budgeted rate.

	Machining	Finishing
Manufacturing overhead incurred (actual)	$11,200,000	$7,900,000
Manufacturing overhead allocated		
220,000 hrs. × $50	11,000,000	
200% of $4,100,000		8,200,000
Underallocated manufacturing overhead	$ 200,000	
Overallocated manufacturing overhead		$ 300,000
Total overallocated overhead = $300,000 – $200,000 = $100,000		

6. A homogeneous cost pool is one where all costs have the same or a similar cause-and-effect or benefits-received relationship with the cost-allocation base. Solomon likely assumes that all its manufacturing overhead cost items are not homogeneous. Specifically, those in the Machining Department have a cause-and-effect relationship with machine-hours, while those in the Finishing Department have a cause-and-effect relationship with direct manufacturing labor costs. Solomon believes that the benefits of using two cost pools (more accurate product costs and better ability to manage costs) exceeds the costs of implementing a more complex system.

4-30 (25-30 min.)   **Service industry, job costing two direct- and two indirect-cost categories, law firm.** (Continuation of 4-29)

Although not required, the following overview diagram is helpful to understand Keating's job-costing system.

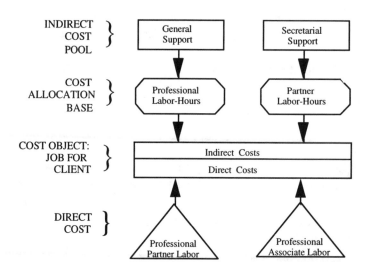

1.

	Professional Partner Labor	Professional Associate Labor
Budgeted compensation per professional	$200,000	$80,000
Budgeted hours of billable time per professional	1,600	1,600
Budgeted direct-cost rate	$125 per hour*	$50 per hour†

*Can also be calculated as $\dfrac{\text{Total budgeted partner labor costs}}{\text{Total budgeted partner labor - hours}} = \dfrac{\$200,000 \times 5}{1,600 \times 5} = \dfrac{\$1,000,000}{8,000} = \$125$

†Can also be calculated as $\dfrac{\text{Total budgeted associate labor costs}}{\text{Total budgeted associate labor - hours}} = \dfrac{\$80,000 \times 20}{1,600 \times 20} = \dfrac{\$1,600,000}{32,000} = \$50$

4-30 (Cont'd.)

	General Support	Secretarial Support
2.		
Budgeted total costs	$1,800,000	$400,000
Budgeted quantity of allocation base	40,000 hours	8,000 hours
Budgeted indirect cost rate	$45 per hour	$50 per hour

3.

	Richardson		Punch	
Direct costs:				
Professional partners, $125 × 60; 30	$7,500		$3,750	
Professional associates, $50 × 40; 120	2,000		6,000	
Direct costs		$ 9,500		$ 9,750
Indirect costs:				
General support, $45 × 100; 150	4,500		6,750	
Secretarial support, $50 × 60; 30	3,000		1,500	
Indirect costs		7,500		8,250
Total costs		$17,000		$18,000

4.

	Richardson	Punch
Single direct - Single indirect (from Prob. 4-29)	$12,000	$18,000
Multiple direct - Multiple indirect (from requirement 4 of Prob. 4-30)	17,000	18,000
Difference	$5,000 undercosted	no change

The Richardson and Punch jobs differ in their use of resources. The Richardson job has a mix of 60% partners and 40% associates, while Punch has a mix of 20% partners and 80% associates. Thus, the Richardson job is a relatively high user of the more costly partner-related resources (both direct partner costs and indirect partner secretarial support). The refined-costing system in Problem 4-30 increases the reported cost in Problem 4-29 for the Richardson job by 41.7% (from $12,000 to $17,000).

4-32 (40–55 min.) Overview of general ledger relationships.

1. & 3.   An effective approach to this problem is to draw T-accounts and insert all the known figures. Then, working with T-account relationships, solve for the unknown figures (here coded by the letter X for beginning inventory figures and Y for ending inventory figures).

Materials Control			
X	15,000	(1)	70,000
Purchases	85,000		
	100,000		70,000
Y	30,000		

Work-in-Process Control				
X		10,000	(4)	305,000
(1) DM	70,000			
(2) DL	150,000			
(3) Overhead	90,000	310,000		
		320,000		305,000
(a)		5,000		
(c)		3,000		
Y		23,000		

Finished Goods Control			
X	20,000	(5)	300,000
(4)	305,000		
	325,000		300,000
Y	25,000		

Cost of Goods Sold			
(5)	300,000	(d)	6,000

Manufacturing Department Overhead Control			
	85,000	(d)	87,000
(a)	1,000		
(b)	1,000		

Manufacturing Overhead Allocated			
(d)	93,000	(3)	90,000
		(c)	3,000

4-13

4-32 (Cont'd.)

Manufacturing overhead cost rate = $90,000 \div $150,000 = 60\%$

	Wages Payable Control	
	(a)	6,000

	Various Accounts	
	(b)	1,000

2. Adjusting and closing entries:

    (a)   Work-in-Process Control   5,000
           Manufacturing Department Overhead Control   1,000
                Wages Payable Control   6,000
           To recognize payroll costs

    (b)   Manufacturing Department Overhead Control   1,000
                Various accounts   1,000
           To recognize miscellaneous manufacturing overhead

    (c)   Work-in-Process Control   3,000
                Manufacturing Overhead Allocated   3,000
           To allocate manufacturing overhead

Note: Students tend to forget entry (c) entirely. Stress that a budgeted overhead allocation rate is used consistently throughout the year. This point is a major feature of this problem.

    (d)   Manufacturing Overhead Allocated   93,000
                Manufacturing Department Overhead Control   87,000
                Cost of Goods Sold   6,000
           To close manufacturing overhead accounts and over-
           allocated overhead to cost of goods sold

4-32 (Cont'd.)

An overview of the product-costing system is:

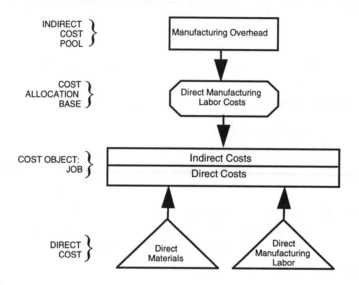

3. See the answer to 1.

4-34 (30 min.) **General ledger relationships, under- and overallocation, service industry.**

1. Summary T-accounts for year 2001 transactions follow.

Jobs-in-Process Control			
1-1-2000	200,000	Jobs completed	
Actual direct		and billed (6)	2,500,000
costs (1)	150,000		
Prof. labor			
allocated (4)	1,450,000*		
Supp.overhead			
allocated (5)	1,200,000†		
12-31-2001	500,000		

Cost of Jobs Billed			
Transferred from		Engineering	
Jobs in Process		support costs	
and billed (6)	2,500,000	overalloc. (8)	20,000
Professional			
labor			
underalloc. (7)	50,000		

Direct Professional Labor Control		
Actual prof.		Transfer to Cost of
labor costs (2) 1,500,000		Jobs Billed (7) 1,500,000

Direct Professional Labor Allocated		
Transfer to Cost		Allocated to WIP
of Jobs Billed (7) 1,450,000		Control (4) 1,450,000*

Engineering Support Overhead Control		
Actual support		Transfer to Cost of
overhead		Jobs Billed (8) 1,180,000
costs (3) 1,180,000		

Engineering Support Overhead Allocated		
Transfer to Cost		Allocated to WIP
of Jobs Billed (8) 1,200,000		Control (5) 1,200,000†

Cash Control	
Direct cash costs (1)	150,000
Prof. labor costs (2)	1,500,000
Support overhead	
costs (3)	1,180,000

*$50 per hour $\times$ 29,000 hours = $1,450,000
†80% $\times$ professional labor costs = 80% $\times$ $1,500,000 = $1,200,000

2. Operating income for 2001 is as follows:

Revenues	$2,800,000
Cost of jobs billed	
($2,500,000 + $50,000 – $20,000)	2,530,000
Operating income	$ 270,000

4-36 (30 min.) **Allocation and proration of manufacturing overhead.**

1. Although not required, an overview of the product costing system follows:

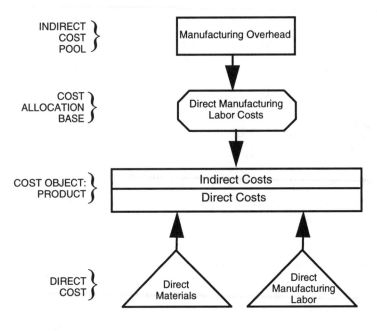

$$\frac{\$252,000}{\$420,000} = \$0.60 \text{ per direct manufacturing labor dollar}$$

The Work-in-Process inventory breakdown at the end of 2001 for Jobs 1768B and 1819C is:

	Job 1768B	**Job 1819C**	**Total**
Direct materials (given)	$22,000	$ 42,000	$ 64,000
Direct manufacturing labor (given)	11,000	39,000	50,000
Manufacturing overhead allocated,			
60% × DML$	6,600	23,400	30,000
Total manufacturing costs	$39,600	$104,400	$144,000

The finished goods inventory at the end of 2001 is $156,000 (given). A direct manufacturing labor cost of $40,000 implies a budgeted manufacturing overhead costs component of $24,000.

The COGS is $1,600,000 (given). The total direct manufacturing labor of $400,000 implies direct manufacturing labor in COGS of $310,000 ($400,000 – $11,000 – $39,000 – $40,000). Hence, manufacturing overhead allocated in COGS is 60% × $310,000 = $186,000. Direct materials in COGS is $1,104,000 ($1,600,000 – $310,000 – $186,000).

4-36 (Cont'd.)

The summary account information is:

	Direct Materials	Direct Manufacturing Labor	Manufacturing Overhead Allocated	Total
Work in process	$ 64,000	$ 50,000	$ 30,000	$ 144,000
Finished goods	92,000	40,000	24,000	156,000
Cost of goods sold	1,104,000	310,000	186,000	1,600,000
Total	$1,260,000	$400,000	$240,000	$1,900,000

2.

$$\begin{matrix} \text{Overallocated} \\ \text{manufacturing} \\ \text{overhead} \end{matrix} = \begin{matrix} \text{Manufacturing overhead} \\ \text{allocated} \end{matrix} - \begin{matrix} \text{Manufacturing overhead} \\ \text{incurred} \end{matrix}$$

= $240,000 – $186,840
= $53,160

3a.

Account	End-of-Year Balance (before Proration) (1)			Proration of $53,160 Overallocated Manuf. Overhead (2)	End-of-Year Balance (after Proration) (3)=(1)+(2)
Work in process	$ 144,000	(144/1,900	= 7.58%)	$(4,030)	$ 139,970
Finished goods	156,000	(156/1,900	= 8.21%)	(4,364)	151,636
Cost of goods sold	1,600,000	(1,600/1,900	= 84.21%)	(44,766)	1,555,234
Total	$1,900,000		100.00%	$(53,160)	$1,846,840

b.

Account	End-of-Year Balance (before Proration)	Allocated Overhead in End-of-Year Balance (before Proration)		Proration of $53,160 Overallocated Manufacturing Overhead	End-of-Year Balance (after Proration)
Work in process	$ 144,000	$ 30,000	(12.5%)	$(6,645)	$ 137,355
Finished goods	156,000	24,000	(10.0%)	(5,316)	150,684
Cost of goods sold	1,600,000	186,000	(77.5%)	(41,199)	1,558,801
Total	$1,900,000	$240,000	100.0%	$(53,160)	$1,846,840

4-36 (Cont'd.)

4.   The COGS amount when the overallocated overhead is immediately written off to COGS is $1,546,840 (see below) compared to $1,555,234 in 3(a) and $1,558,801 in 3(b) Thus, with a lower COGS, there is a higher operating income.

Account	End-of-Year Balance (before Proration)	Proration of $53,160 Overallocated	End-of-Year Balance (after Proration)
Work in process	$ 144,000	$ 0	$ 144,000
Finished goods	156,000	0	156,000
Cost of goods sold	1,600,000	(53,160)	1,546,840
Total	$1,900,000	$(53,160)	$1,846,840

5.   The adjusted allocation rate approach would adjust the cost of job 1819C for the amount of manufacturing overhead overallocated to it. For 2001, manufacturing overhead is overallocated to each job by 22.15% ($53,160 ÷ $240,000). Hence, the cost of job 1819C would be decreased by 22.15% × Manufacturing overhead allocated to 1819C = 22.15% × $23,400 = $5,183.10).

Cost of Job 1819C would then appear as follows:

Direct materials	$42,000.00
Direct manufacturing labor	39,000.00
Manufacturing overhead allocated	23,400.00
Adjustment for manufacturing overhead overallocated	(5,183.10)
Cost of job after adjustment for overallocation	$99,216.90

4-38 (25 min.) **Service industry, job costing, accounting for overhead costs, budgeted rates.**

1. Budgeted overhead rate $= \dfrac{\text{Budgeted overhead costs}}{\text{Budgeted direct labor costs}} = \dfrac{\$1,200,000}{\$1,500,000} = 80\%$

Jefferson allocates overhead costs at 80% of direct labor costs or \$0.80 per direct labor dollar.

2. Overhead allocated to Job A21 as of 1/31/2001 $= 0.80 \times$ Actual direct labor costs of Job A21 $= 0.80 \times \$50,000 = \$40,000$

Overhead allocated to Job A24 as of 2/28/2001 $= 0.80 \times$ Actual direct labor costs of Job A24 $= 0.80 \times \$40,000 = \$32,000$

3. Overhead allocated to jobs in February $= 0.80 \times$ Actual direct labor costs in February

$= 0.80 \times \$120,000 = \$96,000$

Actual overhead costs incurred in February = \$102,000
Underallocated overhead costs = \$102,000 − \$96,000 = \$6,000

4. To calculate Cost of Jobs Billed for February 2001 of \$400,000 we make entries to the Jobs-in-Process Control, Cost of Jobs Billed, Overhead Costs Control, and Overhead Costs Allocated T-accounts.

Jobs-in-Process Control

1-31-2001	\$120,000*	Costs of jobs completed and billed (2)	394,000
Direct materials	150,000		
Direct labor	120,000		
Overhead costs allocated (1)	96,000		
2-28-2001	92,000†		

Cost of Jobs Billed

Cost of jobs completed and billed	(2)	394,000	
Underallocated overhead costs	(3)	6,000	

Overhead Costs Control

Overhead costs for February	102,000	Transfer to Cost of Jobs Billed	(3)	102,000

Overhead Costs Allocated

Transfer to Cost of Jobs Billed	(3)	96,000	Overhead costs allocated in February	(1)	96,000

*Cost of Job A21 = Direct materials + Direct labor + Overhead allocated
= \$30,000 + \$50,000 + \$40,000 = \$120,000

†Cost of Job A24 = Direct materials + Direct labor + Overhead allocated
= \$20,000 + \$40,000 + \$32,000 = \$92,000

4-38 (Cont'd.)

Cost of jobs completed and billed from Jobs-in-Process Control account can be calculated by plugging for the missing number in Jobs-in-Process Control account, $120,000 + $150,000 + $120,000 + $96,000 − $92,000 = $394,000

Cost of Jobs Billed is also increased by the underallocated overhead costs of $6,000.

Hence, Cost of Jobs Billed for February 2001 = $394,000 + $6,000 = $400,000.

CHAPTER 5
ACTIVITY-BASED COSTING AND ACTIVITY-BASED MANAGEMENT

5-2   Overcosting may result in competitors entering a market and taking market share for products that a company erroneously believes are low-margin or even unprofitable.

Undercosting may result in companies selling products on which they are in fact losing money, when they erroneously believe them to be profitable.

5-4   An activity-based approach focuses on activities as the fundamental cost objects. It uses the cost of these activities as the basis for assigning costs to other cost objects such as products, services, or customers.

5-6   The purpose for computing a product cost will determine whether unit costs should be based on total manufacturing costs in all or only some levels of the cost hierarchy. Inventory valuation for financial reporting requires *total* or only some manufacturing costs (all levels of the hierarchy) to be expressed on a per output-unit basis. In contrast, for cost management purposes, the cost hierarchy need not be unitized, as the units of output is not the cost driver at each level in the hierarchy.

5-8   Four decisions for which ABC information is useful are:
(1)   pricing and product mix decisions,
(2)   cost reduction and process improvement decisions,
(3)   design decisions, and
(4)   planning and managing activities

5-10   "Tell-tale" signs that indicate when ABC systems are likely to provide the most benefits are:
1.   Significant amounts of indirect costs are allocated using only one or two cost pools.
2.   All or most indirect costs are identified as output-unit-level costs (i.e., few indirect costs are described as batch-level, product-sustaining, or facility-sustaining costs).
3.   Products make diverse demands on resources because of differences in volume, process steps, batch size, or complexity.
4.   Products that a company is well suited to make and sell show small profits, whereas products that a company is less suited to produce and sell show large profits.
5.   Complex products appear to be very profitable, and simple products appear to be losing money.
6.   Operations staff have significant disagreements with the accounting staff about the costs of manufacturing and marketing products and services.

5-12   No, ABC systems apply equally well to service companies such as banks, railroads, hospitals, and accounting firms, as well merchandising companies such as retailers and distributors.

5-14   Increasing the number of indirect-cost pools does NOT guarantee increased accuracy of product, service, or customer costs. If the existing cost pool is already homogeneous, increasing the number of cost pools will not increase accuracy. If the existing cost pool is not homogeneous, accuracy will increase only if the increased cost pools themselves increase in homogeneity vis-a-vis the single cost pool.

5-16 (30 min.) **Cost smoothing or peanut-butter costing, cross-subsidization.**

1.   Cost smoothing or peanut-butter costing is a costing approach that uniformly assigns the cost of resources to customers when the individual customers use those resources in a nonuniform way The reunion dinner averages the costs across all five people. These five people differ sizably in what they consume.

2.

Diner	Entree	Dessert	Drinks	Total
Armstrong	$27	$8	$24	$59
Gonzales	24	3	0	27
King	21	6	13	40
Poffo	31	6	12	49
Young	15	4	6	25
Average	$23.60	$5.40	$11.00	$40.00

The average-cost pricing will result in each person paying $40.

	Amount Over- or Undercosted
Accurately costed person	
• King, $40 – $40	$ 0
Undercosted people	
• Armstrong, $40 – $59	$(19)
• Poffo, $40 – $49	$(9)
Overcosted people	
• Gonzales, $40 – $27	$ 13
• Young, $40 – $25	$ 15

Yes, Young's complaint is justified. He is "overcharged" $15. He could point out likely negative behaviors with this approach to costing. These include:
   a.   It can lead some people to order the most expensive items because others will "subsidize" their extravagance.
   b.   It can lead to friction when those who dine economically are forced to subsidize those who dine extravagantly. At the limit, some people may decide not to attend the reunion dinners.

Likely benefits of this approach are:
a.   it is simple, and
b.   it (purportedly) promotes a group atmosphere at the dinner.

5-16 (Cont'd.)

3.   Each one of the costs in the data is directly traceable to an individual diner. This makes it straightforward to compute the individual cost per diner. Examples where this is not possible include:
- A plate of hors d'oeuvres is shared by two or more diners
- A loaf of garlic bread is shared by two or more diners
- A bottle of mineral water or wine is shared by two or more diners

Each of these items cannot be directly traced to only one diner.

Some possible behaviors if each person pays for his or her own bill are:

a.   Some people may reduce their ordering of more expensive items because they will not be subsidized by other diners.
b.   May encourage some potential diners to attend who otherwise would have stayed away.
c.   May encourage a person "trying to impress others with his or her success" to order the most expensive items.

5-18 (25 min.) Cost hierarchy, ABC, distribution.

1.   Total distribution costs (given), $2,130,000

$$\text{Distribution cost per case under existing system} = \frac{\text{Total distribution costs}}{\text{Total cases of specialty and regular wine shipped}} = \frac{\$2,130,000}{200,000} = \$10.65 \text{ per case}$$

| | Regular | | Specialty | |
	Total (1)	Per Case (2) = (1) ÷ 120,000	Total (3)	Per Case (4) = (3) ÷ 80,000
Distribution costs				
$10.65 × 120,000; $10.65 × 80,000	$1,278,000	$10.65	$852,000	$10.65

2a.   Promotional activity—distributor-level costs because these costs do not depend on the number of cases shipped or the number of batches in which the cases are shipped. An amount of $8,000 is incurred for each of Sonoma's distributors.

Order-handling costs—batch-level costs because these costs are incurred each time a customer places an order regardless of the number of cases ordered. These costs total $300 per order.

Freight distribution costs—Unit-level costs because a cost of $8 is incurred on freight for each case shipped.

2b.

	Regular		Specialty	
	Total **(1)**	**Per Case** **(2) =** **(1) ÷ 120,000**	**Total** **(3)**	**Per Case** **(4) =** **(3) ÷ 80,000**
Distribution costs of freight				
$8 × 120,000 cases	$ 960,000	$8.00		
$8 × 80,000 cases			$ 640,000	$8.00
Ordering costs				
$300 × 10 orders/year × 10 distr.	30,000	0.25		
$300 × 20 orders/year × 30 distr.			180,000	2.25
Promotion costs				
$8,000 × 10 distributors	80,000	0.67		
$8,000 × 30 distributors			240,000	3.00
Total costs	$1,070,000	$8.92	$1,060,000	$13.25

3. The existing costing system uses cases shipped, a unit-level cost driver, as the only cost allocation base for distribution costs. As a result, the distribution cost per case is the same for specialty and regular wines ($10.65). In fact, specialty wines use distribution resources more intensively than regular wines: (a) Sonoma spends $8,000 on promotional activity at each distributor independent of cases sold. Specialty wine distributors sell fewer cases a year than regular wine distributors. As a result the promotional cost per case of wine sold is higher for specialty wines than for regular wines. (b) Sonoma's cost per order is $300 regardless of the number of cases sold in each order. Because specialty wine distributors order fewer cases per order, the ordering costs per case are higher for specialty wines than for regular wines.

The existing costing system undercosts distribution costs per case for specialty wines and overcosts distribution costs per case for regular wines.

Sonoma's management can use the information from the ABC system to make better pricing and product mix decisions, to reduce costs by eliminating processes and activities that do not add value, to identify and evaluate new designs that reduce the activities demanded by various products, to reduce the costs of doing various activities, and to plan and manage activities.

5-20 (15 min.) **Alternative allocation bases for a professional services firm.**

1.

Client (1)	Direct Professional Time			Support Services		Amount Billed to Client
	Rate per Hour (2)	Number of Hours (3)	Total (4) = (2) × (3)	Rate (5)	Total (6) = (4) × (5)	(7) = (4) + (6)
SEATTLE DOMINION						
Wolfson	$500	15	$7,500	30%	$2,250	$ 9,750
Brown	120	3	360	30	108	468
Anderson	80	22	1,760	30	528	2,288
						$12,506
TOKYO ENTERPRISES						
Wolfson	$500	2	$1,000	30%	$300	$1,300
Brown	120	8	960	30	288	1,248
Anderson	80	30	2,400	30	720	3,120
						$5,668

2.

Client (1)	Direct Professional Time			Support Services		Amount Billed to Client
	Rate per Hour (2)	Number of Hours (3)	Total (4) = (2) × (3)	Rate per Hour (5)	Total (6) = (3) × (5)	(7) = (4)+(6)
SEATTLE DOMINION						
Wolfson	$500	15	$7,500	$50	$ 750	$ 8,250
Brown	120	3	360	50	150	510
Anderson	80	22	1,760	50	1,100	2,860
						$11,620
TOKYO ENTERPRISES						
Wolfson	$500	2	$1,000	$50	$ 100	$1,100
Brown	120	8	960	50	400	1,360
Anderson	80	30	2,400	50	1,500	3,900
						$6,360

5-20 (Cont'd.)

	Requirement 1	Requirement 2
Seattle Dominion	$12,506	$11,620
Tokyo Enterprises	5,668	6,360
	$18,174	$17,980

Both clients use 40 hours of professional labor time. However, Seattle Dominion uses a higher proportion of Wolfson's time (15 hours), which is more costly. This attracts the highest support-services charge when allocated on the basis of direct professional labor costs.

3. Assume that the Wolfson Group uses a cause-and-effect criterion when choosing the allocation base for support services. You could use several pieces of evidence to determine whether professional labor costs or hours is the driver of support-service costs:

a. *Interviews with personnel.* For example, staff in the major cost categories in support services could be interviewed to determine whether Wolfson requires more support per hour than, say, Anderson. The professional labor costs allocation base implies that an hour of Wolfson's time requires 6.25 ($500 ÷ $80) times more support-service dollars than does an hour of Anderson's time.

b. *Analysis of tasks undertaken for selected clients.* For example, if computer-related costs are a sizable part of support costs, you could determine if there was a systematic relationship between the percentage involvement of professionals with high billing rates on cases and the computer resources consumed for those cases.

5-22 (30 min.) Department indirect-cost rates as activity rates.
(Continuation of 5-21)

1.

	2001 Variable MOH Costs	Total Driver Units	Rate
Design-CAD	$ 39,000	390	$100 per design-hour
Engineering	29,600	370	$ 80 per engineer-hour
Production	240,000	4,000	$ 60 per machine

2.

	United Motors	Holden Motors	Leland Vehicle
Design			
$100 × 110; 200; 80	$11,000	$ 20,000	$ 8,000
Engineering			
$80 × 70; 60; 240	5,600	4,800	19,200
Production			
$60 × 120; 2,800; 1,080	7,200	168,000	64,800
Total	$23,800	$192,800	$92,000

5-22 (Cont'd.)

3.		United Motors	Holden Motors	Leland Vehicle
a.	Department rate (Exercise 5-22)	$23,800	$192,800	$92,000
b.	Plantwide rate (Exercise 5-21)	9,258	216,020	83,322
	Ratio of (a) ÷ (b)	2.57	0.89	1.10

The three contracts differ sizably in the way they use the resources of the three departments. The percentage of total driver units in each department is:

Department	United Motors	Holden Motors	Leland Vehicle
Design	28%	51%	21%
Engineering	19	16	65
Production	3	70	27

The United Motors contract uses only 3% of total machines-hours in 2001, yet uses 28% of CAD design-hours and 19% of engineering hours. The result is that the plantwide rate, based on machine-hours, will greatly underestimate the cost of resources used on the United Motors contract. Hence, the 257% increase in indirect costs assigned to the United Motors contract when department rates are used.

In contrast, the Holden Motors contract uses less of design (51%) and engineering (16%) than of machine-hours (70%). Hence, department rates will report lower indirect costs than does a plantwide rate.

5-24 (30 min.) **ABC, product-costing at banks, cross-subsidization.**

1.

	Robinson	Skerrett	Farrel	Total
Revenues				
Spread revenue on annual basis				
(3% × ; $1,100, $800, $25,000)	$ 33	$ 24	$750.0	$ 807.0
Monthly fee charges				
($20 ×; 0, 12, 0)	0	240	0.0	240.0
Total revenues	33	264	750.0	1,047.0
Costs				
Deposit/withdrawal with teller				
$2.50 × 40; 50; 5	100	125	12.5	237.5
Deposit/withdrawal with ATM				
$0.80 × 10; 20; 16	8	16	12.8	36.8
Deposit/withdrawal on prearranged basis:				
$0.50 × 0; 12; 60	0	6	30.0	36.0
Bank checks written				
$8.00 × 9; 3; 2	72	24	16.0	112.0
Foreign currency drafts				
$12.00 × 4; 1; 6	48	12	72.0	132.0
Inquiries				
$1.50 × 10; 18; 9	15	27	13.5	55.5
Total costs	243	210	156.8	609.8
Operating income	$(210)	$ 54	$593.2	$ 437.2

The assumption that the Robinson and Farrel accounts exceed $1,000 every month and the Skerrett account is less than $1,000 each month means the monthly charges apply only to Skerrett.

One student with a banking background noted that in this solution 100% of the spread is attributed to the "borrowing side of the bank." He noted that often the spread is divided between the "borrowing side" and the "lending side" of the bank.

2.   Cross-subsidization across individual Premier Accounts occurs when profits made on some accounts are offset by losses on other accounts. The aggregate profitability on the three customers is $437.20. The Farrel account is highly profitable ($593.20), while the Robinson account is sizably unprofitable.

FIB should be very concerned about the cross-subsidization. Competition likely would "understand" that high-balance low-activity type accounts (such as Farrel) are highly profitable. Offering free services to these customers is not likely to retain these accounts if other banks offer higher interest rates. Competition likely will reduce the interest rate spread FIB can earn on the high-balance low-activity accounts they are able to retain.

5-24 (Cont'd.)

3. Possible changes FIB could make are:
   a. Offer higher interest rates on high-balance accounts to increase FIB's competitiveness in attracting and retaining these accounts.
   b. Introduce charges for individual services. The ABC study reports the cost of each service. FIB has to decide if it wants to price each service at cost, below cost, or above cost. If it prices above cost, it may use advertising and other means to encourage additional use of those services by customers.

5-26 (30 min.) **ABC, product-cost cross-subsidization.** (Continuation of 5-25)

1.

Direct costs		
Direct materials		$150,000
Indirect costs		
Product support		983,000
Total costs		$1,133,000

$$\text{Cost per pound of potato cuts (for either the retail or the institutional market}} = \frac{\$1,133,000}{1,000,000}$$

$$= \$1.133$$

2.

	Retail Potato Cuts		Institutional Potato Cuts	
Direct costs				
Direct materials	$135,000		$15,000	
Packaging	180,000	$ 315,000	8,000	$23,000
Indirect costs				
Cleaning				
$0.10 × 90% × 1,200,000	108,000			
$0.10 × 10% × 1,200,000			12,000	
Cutting				
$60 × 3,600 hours	216,000			
$60 × 250 hours			15,000	
Packaging				
$12 × 36,000	432,000			
$12 × 1,000	———	756,000	12,000	39,000
Total costs		$1,071,000		$62,000
Pounds produced		900,000		100,000
Costs per pound		$1.19		$0.62

Note: The total costs of $1,133,000 ($1,071,000 + $62,000) are the same as those in Requirement 1.

5-26 (Cont'd.)

3. There is much evidence of product-cost cross-subsidization.

	Retail	Institutional
Current system	$1.133	$1.133
ABC system	$1.190	$0.620

Assuming the ABC numbers are more accurate, retail is undercosted by approximate 5% ($1.133 ÷ $1.19 = 0.95), while institutional is overcosted by 83% ($1.133 ÷ $0.620 = 1.83).

The current system assumes each product uses all the activity areas in a homogeneous way. This is not the case. Institutional sales use sizably less resources in the cutting area and the packaging area. The percentage of total costs for each cost category are:

	Retail	Institutional	Total
Direct costs			
Direct materials	90.0%	10.0%	100.0%
Packaging	95.7	4.3	100.0
Indirect costs			
Cleaning	90.0	10.0	100.0
Cutting	93.5	6.5	100.0
Packaging	97.3	2.7	100.0
Units produced	90.0%	10.0%	100.0%

Idaho can use the revised cost information for a variety of purposes:

a. *Pricing/product emphasis decisions.* The sizable drop in the reported cost of institutional potatoes makes it possible that Idaho was overpricing potato products in this market. It lost the bid for a large institutional contract with a bid 30% above the winning bid. With its revised product cost dropping from $1.133 to $0.620, Idaho could have bid much lower and still made a profit. An increased emphasis on the institutional market appears warranted.

b. *Product design decisions.* ABC provides a road map as to how to reduce the costs of individual products. The relative components of costs are:

	Retail	Institutional
Direct costs		
Direct materials	12.6%	24.20 %
Packaging	16.8	12.90
Indirect costs		
Cleaning	10.1	19.35
Cutting	20.2	24.20
Packaging	40.3	19.35
Total costs	100.0%	100.00%

5-10

5-26 (Cont'd.)

Packaging-related costs constitute 57.1% (16.8% + 40.3%) of total costs of the retail product line. Design efforts that reduce packaging costs can have a big impact on reducing total unit costs for retail.

c.   *Process improvements.* Each activity area is now highlighted as a separate cost. The three indirect cost areas are over 60% of total costs for each product, indicating the upside from improvements in the efficiency of processes in these activity areas.

5-28   (20–25 min.)   Activity-based costing, job-costing system.

1.   An overview of the activity-based job-costing system is:

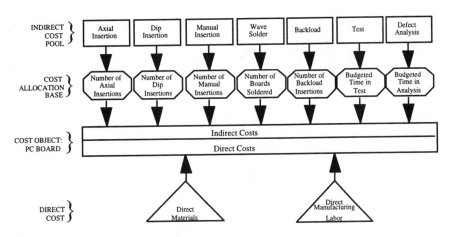

2.

	Activity Area	Indirect Manufacturing Costs Allocated		
1.	Axial insertion	$ 0.08	× 45	= $ 3.60
2.	Dip insertion	0.25	× 24	= 6.00
3.	Manual insertion	0.50	× 11	= 5.50
4.	Wave solder	3.50	× 1	= 3.50
5.	Backload	0.70	× 6	= 4.20
6.	Test	90.00	× .25	= 22.50
7.	Defect analysis	80.00	× .10	= 8.00
	Total			$53.30

Direct manufacturing costs:			
Direct materials	$75.00		
Direct manufacturing labor	15.00	$ 90.00	
Indirect manufacturing costs:			
Manufacturing overhead (see above)		53.30	
Total manufacturing costs		$143.30	

5-28 (Cont'd.)

3.   The manufacturing manager likely would find the ABC job-costing system useful in cost management. The seven indirect cost pools are systematically linked to the activity areas at the plant. Productivity measures can be developed that directly link to the management accounting system.

Marketing managers can use ABC information to price jobs as well as to advise customers about how selecting different product features will affect price.

5-30   (20-25 min.)   **Job costing with multiple direct-cost categories, single indirect-cost pool, law firm.** (Continuation of 5-29)

1.   Panel B of the Solution Exhibit 5-29/5-30/5-31 presents the costing overview for the multiple direct/single indirect (MD/SI) approach.

SOLUTION EXHIBIT 5-29/5-30/5-31
Alternative Job (Case)-Costing Approaches for Wigan Associates

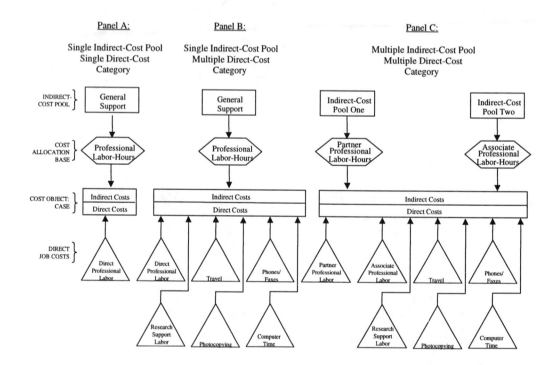

5-30 (Cont'd.)

2.   Indirect costs = $7,000
     Total professional labor-hours = 200 hours (104 hours on Widnes Coal + 96 hours on St. Helen's Glass)

     Indirect cost allocated per professional labor-hour = $7,000 ÷ 200 = $35 per hour

3.

	Widnes Coal	St. Helen's Glass	Total
Direct costs:			
Direct professional labor,			
$70 × 104; 96	$ 7,280	$ 6,720	$14,000
Research support labor	1,600	3,400	5,000
Computer time	500	1,300	1,800
Travel and allowances	600	4,400	5,000
Telephones/faxes	200	1,000	1,200
Photocopying	250	750	1,000
Total direct costs	10,430	17,570	28,000
Indirect costs allocated,			
$35 × 104; 96	3,640	3,360	7,000
Total costs to be billed	$14,070	$20,930	$35,000

4.

	Widnes Coal	St. Helen's Glass	Total
SD/SI			
Problem 5-29	$18,200	$16,800	$35,000
MD/SI			
Problem 5-30	14,070	20,930	35,000

The MD/SI (5-30) approach directly traces to the individual jobs $14,000 that is allocated in the SD/SI (5-29) approach on the basis of direct professional labor-hours. The averaging assumption implicit in the SD/SI (5-29) approach appears incorrect—for example, the St. Helen's Glass job has travel costs over seven times higher than the Widnes Coal case despite having lower direct professional labor-hours.

5-32 (30-40 min.) Activity-based costing, merchandising.

1.

	General Supermarket Chains	Drugstore Chains	Ma and Pa Single Stores	Total
Revenues[a]	$3,708,000	$3,150,000	$1,980,000	$8,838,000
Cost of goods sold[b]	3,600,000	3,000,000	1,800,000	8,400,000
Gross margin	$ 108,000	$ 150,000	$ 180,000	438,000
Other operating costs				301,080
Operating income				$ 136,920
Gross margin %	2.91%	4.76%	9.09%	

[a]($30,900 × 120); ($10,500 × 300); ($1,980 × 1,000)
[b]($30,000 × 120); ($10,000 × 300); ($1,800 × 1,000)

The gross margin of Figure Four Inc. was 4.96% ($438,000 ÷ $8,838,000). The operating income margin of Figure Four Inc. was 1.55% ($136,920 ÷ $8,838,000).

2. The per-unit cost driver rates are:

1. Customer purchase order processing, $80,000 ÷ 2,000   = $40 per order
2. Line item ordering, $63,840 ÷ 21,280   = $ 3 per line item
3. Store delivery, $71,000 ÷ 1,420   = $50 per delivery
4. Cartons shipped, $76,000 ÷ 76,000   = $ 1 per carton
5. Shelf-stocking, $10,240 ÷ 640   = $16 per hour

3. The activity-based costing of each distribution market for August 1999 is:

	General Supermarket Chains	Drugstore Chains	Ma and Pa Single Stores
1. Customer purchase order processing, ($40 × 140; 360; 1,500)	$ 5,600	$14,400	$ 60,000
2. Line item ordering, ($3 × (140 × 14; 360 × 12; 1,500 × 10))	5,880	12,960	45,000
3. Store delivery, ($50 × 120, 300, 1,000)	6,000	15,000	50,000
4. Cartons shipped, ($1 × (120 × 300; 300 ×80; 1,000 × 16))	36,000	24,000	16,000
5. Shelf-stocking, ($16 × (120 × 3; 300 × 0.6; 1,000 × 0.1))	5,760	2,880	1,600
	$59,240	$69,240	$172,600

5-32 (Cont'd.)

The revised operating income statement is:

	General Supermarket Chains	Drugstore Chains	Ma and Pa Single Stores	Total
Revenues	$3,708,000	$3,150,000	$1,980,000	$8,838,000
Cost of goods sold	3,600,000	3,000,000	1,800,000	8,400,000
Gross margin	108,000	150,000	180,000	438,000
Operating costs	59,240	69,240	172,600	301,080
Operating income	$ 48,760	$ 80,760	$ 7,400	$ 136,920
Operating income margin	1.31%	2.56%	0.37%	1.55%

The ranking of the three markets are:

Using Gross Margin
1. Ma and Pa Single Stores   9.09%
2. Drugstore Chains   4.76%
3. General Supermarket Chains   2.91%

Using Operating Income
1. Drugstore Chains   2.56%
2. General Supermarket Chains   1.31%
3. Ma and Pa Single Stores   0.37%

The activity-based analysis of costs highlights how the Ma and Pa Single Stores use a larger amount of Figure Four resources per revenue dollar than do the other two markets. The ratio of the operating costs to revenues across the three markets is:

General Supermarket Chains	1.60%	($59,240 ÷ $3,708,000)
Drugstore Chains	2.20%	($69,240 ÷ $3,150,000)
Ma and Pa Single Stores	8.72%	($172,600 ÷ $1,980,000)

This is a classic illustration of the maxim that "all revenue dollars are not created equal."

4. a. *Choosing the appropriate cost drivers for each area.* The case gives a cost driver for each chosen activity area. However, it is likely that over time further refinements in cost drivers would occur. For example, not all store deliveries are equally easy to make, depending on parking availability, accessibility of the storage/shelf space to the delivery point, etc. Similarly, not all cartons are equally easy to deliver—their weight, size, or likely breakage component are factors that can vary across carton types.

     b. *Developing a reliable data base on the chosen cost drivers.* For some items, such as the number of orders and the number of line items, this information likely would be available in machine readable form at a high level of accuracy. Unless the delivery personnel have hand-held computers that they use in a systematic way, estimates of shelf-stocking time are likely to be unreliable. Advances in information technology likely will reduce problems in this area over time.

5-32 (Cont'd.)

   c.   *Deciding how to handle costs that may be common across several activities.* For example, (3) store delivery and (4) cartons shipped to stores have the common cost of the same trip. Some organizations may treat (3) as the primary activity and attribute to (4) only incremental costs. Similarly, (1) order processing and (2) line item ordering may have common costs.

   d.   *Choice of the time period to compute cost rates per cost driver.* Flair calculates driver rates on a monthly basis (August 1999). He may want to consider using longer time periods that may be less affected by seasonal or random variations in demand.

   e.   *Behavioral factors are likely to be a challenge to Flair.* He must now tell those salespeople who specialize in Ma and Pa accounts that they have been less profitable than previously thought.

5-34 (30 min.) Plantwide versus department overhead cost rates.

1.

	Amounts (in thousands)			
	Molding	**Component**	**Assembly**	**Total**
Manufacturing department overhead	$21,000	$16,200	$22,600	$59,800
Service departments:				
Power				18,400
Maintenance				4,000
Total estimated plantwide overhead				$82,200
Estimated direct manufacturing labor hours (DMLH):				
Molding				500
Component				2,000
Assembly				1,500
Total estimated DMLH				4,000

$$\text{Plantwide overhead rate} = \frac{\text{Estimated plant wide overhead}}{\text{Estimated DMLH}}$$

$$= \frac{\$82,200}{4,000} = \$20.55 \text{ per DMLH}$$

2.   The department overhead cost rates are shown in Solution Exhibit 5-34

3.   MumsDay Corporation should use department rates to allocate plant overhead to its products. A plantwide rate is appropriate when all products pass through the same processes, and all departments are similar. Departmental rates are appropriate when the converse is true. MumsDay's departments are dissimilar in that the Molding Department is machine-intensive and the other two departments are labor-intensive. Department rates better capture cause-and-effect relationships at MumsDay than does a plantwide rate.

5-34 (Cont'd.)

SOLUTION EXHIBIT 5-34

	Departments (in thousands)				
	Service		Manufacturing		
	Power	Maintenance	Molding	Component	Assembly
Departmental overhead costs	$18,400	$ 4,000	$21,000	$16,200	$22,600
Allocation of maintenance costs (direct method) $4,000 × 90/125, 25/125, 10/125		(4,000)	2,880	800	320
Allocation of power costs $18,400 × 360/800, 320/800, 120/800	(18,400)	―	8,280	7,360	2,760
Total budgeted overhead of manufacturing departments	$ 0	$ 0	$32,160	$24,360	$25,680
Allocation Base			875 MH	2,000 DMLH	1,500 DMLH
Budgeted Rate (Budgeted overhead ÷ Base)			$36.75/MH	$12.18/DMLH	$17.12/DMLH

5-36 (30–40 min.) **Activity-based costing, product-cost cross-subsidization.**

The motivation for Problem 5-36 came from "ABC Minicase: Let them Eat Cake," *Cost Management Update* (Issue No. 31).

1. $$\text{Budgeted MOH rate in 2001} = \frac{\$210,800}{200,000 \text{ units}}$$

$$= \$1.054 \text{ per one-pound unit of cake}$$

	Raisin Cake		Layered Carrot Cake	
Unit direct manufacturing cost				
Direct materials	$0.600		$0.900	
Direct manufacturing labor	0.140	$0.740	0.200	$1.100
Unit indirect manufacturing cost				
Manufacturing overhead				
($1.054 × 1, 1)	$1.054	1.054	$1.054	1.054
Unit total manufacturing cost		$1.794		$2.154

5-36 (Cont'd.)

2. ABC costs for 120,000 pounds of raisin cake and 80,000 pounds of layered carrot cake in 2001 follow:

	Raisin Cake		Layered Carrot Cake	
	Total Costs (1)	Per Unit Cost (2) = (1) ÷ 120,000	Total Costs (3)	Per Unit Cost (4) = (3) ÷ 80,000
Direct costs				
Direct materials	$ 72,000	$0.60	$ 72,000	$0.90
Direct manufacturing labor	16,800	0.14	16,000	0.20
Total direct costs	88,800	0.74	88,000	1.10
Indirect costs				
Mixing				
$0.04 × 600,000	24,000	0.20		
$0.04 × 640,000			25,600	0.32
Cooking				
$0.14 × 240,000	33,600	0.28		
$0.14 × 240,000			33,600	0.42
Cooling				
$0.02 × 360,000	7,200	0.06		
$0.02 × 400,000			8,000	0.10
Creaming/Icing				
$0.25 × 0	0	0		
$0.25 × 240,000			60,000	0.75
Packaging				
$0.08 × 360,000	28,800	0.24		
$0.08 × 560,000			44,800	0.56
Total indirect costs	93,600	0.78	172,000	2.15
Total costs	$182,400	$1.52	$260,000	$3.25

Note that the significant shift in product mix will cause absorbed costs (based on budgeted rates and actual quantities of the cost-allocation base) to be different from the budgeted manufacturing overhead costs.

5-36 (Cont'd.)

3.　　The unit product costs in requirements 1 and 2 differ only in the assignment of indirect costs to individual products.

　　　The ABC system recognizes that indirect resources used per pound of layered carrot cake is 2.76 ($2.15 ÷ $0.78) times the indirect resources used per pound of raisin cake. The existing costing system erroneously assumes equal usage of activity areas by a pound of raisin cake and a pound of layered carrot cake.

4.　　Uses of activity-based cost numbers include:

a.　　Pricing decisions. BD can use the ABC data to decide preliminary prices for negotiating with its customers. Raisin cake is currently overcosted, while layered carrot cake is undercosted. Actual production of layered carrot cake is 100% more than budgeted. One explanation could be the underpricing of layered carrot cake.

b.　　Product emphasis. BD has more accurate product margins with ABC. BD can use this information for deciding which products to push (especially if there are production constraints).

c.　　Product design. ABC provides a road map on how a change in product design can reduce costs. The percentage breakdown of total indirect costs for each product is:

	Raisin Cake	**Layered Carrot Cake**
Mixing	25.6% ($0.20/$0.78)	14.9% ($0.32/$2.15)
Cooking	35.9	19.5
Cooling	7.7	4.7
Creaming/Icing	0.0	34.9
Packaging	30.8	26.0
	100.0%	100.0%

BD can reduce the cost of either cake by reducing its usage of each activity area. For example, BD can reduce raisin cake's cost by sizably reducing its cooking time or packaging time. Similarly, a sizable reduction in creaming/icing will have a marked reduction in layered carrot cake costs. Of course, BD must seek efficiency improvements without compromising quality.

d.　　Process improvements. Improvements in how activity areas are configured will cause a reduction in the costs of products that use those activity areas.

e.　　Cost planning and flexible budgeting. ABC provides a more refined model to forecast costs of BD and to explain why actual costs differ from budgeted costs.

5-38 (40–50 min.) **Activity-based job costing, unit-cost comparisons.**

An overview of the product-costing system is:

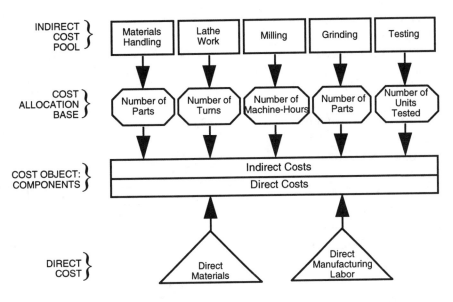

1.

	Job Order 410		Job Order 411	
Direct manufacturing costs:				
Direct materials	$9,700		$59,900	
Direct manufacturing labor,				
$30 × 25; 375	750	$10,450	11,250	$ 71,150
Indirect manufacturing costs,				
$115 × 25; 375		2,875		43,125
Total manufacturing costs		$13,325		$114,275
Number of units		÷ 10		÷ 200
Manufacturing costs per unit		$ 1,332.50		$ 571.375

5-38 (Cont'd.)

2.

	Job Order 410		Job Order 411	
Direct manufacturing costs:				
Direct materials	$9,700		$59,900	
Direct manufacturing labor,				
$30 × 25; 375	750	$10,450	11,250	$ 71,150
Indirect manufacturing costs:				
Materials handling,				
$0.40 × 500; 2,000	200		800	
Lathe work,				
$0.20 × 20,000; 60,000	4,000		12,000	
Milling,				
$20.00 × 150; 1,050	3,000		21,000	
Grinding,				
$0.80 × 500; 2,000	400		1,600	
Testing,				
$15.00 × 10; 200	150	7,750	3,000	38,400
Total manufacturing costs		$18,200		$109,550
Number of units per job		÷ 10		÷ 200
Unit manufacturing cost per job		$ 1,820		$ 547.75

3.

	Job Order 410	Job Order 411
Number of units in job	10	200
Costs per unit with prior costing system	$1,332.50	$571.375
Costs per unit with activity-based costing	1,820.00	547.75

Job order 410 has an increase in reported unit cost of 36.6% [($1,820 – $1,332.50) ÷ $1,332.50], while job order 411 has a decrease in reported unit cost of 4.1% [($547.75 – $571.375) ÷ $571.375].

A common finding when activity-based costing is implemented is that low-volume products have increases in their reported costs while high-volume products have decreases in their reported cost. This result is also found in requirements 1 and 2 of this problem. Costs such as materials-handling costs vary with the number of parts handled (a function of batches and complexity of products) rather than with direct manufacturing labor-hours, an output-unit level cost driver, which was the only cost driver in the previous job-costing system.

The product costs figures computed in requirements 1 and 2 differ because:
a. the job orders differ in the way they use each of five activity areas, and
b. the activity areas differ in their indirect cost allocation bases (specifically, each area does not use the direct labor-hours indirect cost allocation base).

The following table documents how the two job orders differ in the way they use each of the five activity areas included in indirect manufacturing costs:

5-38 (Cont'd.)

Activity Area	Usage Based on Analysis of Activity Area Cost Drivers		Usage Assumed with Direct Labor-Hours as Application Base	
	Job Order 410	Job Order 411	Job Order 410	Job Order 411
Materials handling	20.0%	80.0%	6.25%	93.75%
Lathe work	25.0	75.0	6.25	93.75
Milling	12.5	87.5	6.25	93.75
Grinding	20.0	80.0	6.25	93.75
Testing	4.8	95.2	6.25	93.75

The differences in product cost figures might be important to Tracy Corporation for product pricing and product emphasis decisions. The activity-based accounting approach indicates that job order 410 is being undercosted while job order 411 is being overcosted. Tracy Corporation may erroneously push job order 410 and deemphasize job order 411. Moreover, by its actions, Tracy Corporation may encourage a competitor to enter the market for job order 411 and take market share away from it.

4. Information from the ABC system can also help Tracy manage its business better in several ways.

a. *Product design*. Product designers at Tracy Corporation likely will find the numbers in the activity-based costing approach more believable and credible than those in the existing system. In a machine-paced manufacturing environment, it is unlikely that direct labor-hours would be the major cost driver. Activity-based costing provides more credible signals to product designers about the ways the costs of a product can be reduced—for example, use fewer parts, require fewer turns on the lathe, and reduce the number of machine-hours in the milling area.

b. *Cost management*. Tracy can reduce the cost of jobs both by making process improvements that reduce the activities that need to be done to complete jobs and by reducing the costs of doing the activities.

c. *Cost planning*. ABC provides a more refined model to forecast costs and to explain why actual costs differ from budgeted costs.

5-40 (40–60 min.) **Activity-based costing, cost hierarchy.**

This solution is adapted from the CMA suggested solution.

1. a.
$$\text{Budgeted manufacturing overhead rate} = \frac{\text{Budgeted manufacturing overhead}}{\text{Budgeted direct labor cost}}$$

$$= \frac{\$3,000,000}{\$600,000}$$

$$= \$5 \text{ per direct labor-dollar}$$

b.

	Mona Loa	**Malaysian**
Direct costs		
Direct materials	$4.20	$3.20
Direct labor	0.30	0.30
	4.50	3.50
Indirect costs		
Manufacturing overhead		
(0.30 × $5.00)	1.50	1.50
Total costs	$6.00	$5.00

Budgeted selling prices per pound:

Mona Loa ($6.00 × 1.30)	=	$7.80
Malaysian ($5.00 × 1.30)	=	$6.50

2. The cost per driver unit is:

Activity	Cost Driver	Budgeted Cost	Budgeted Activity	Unit Cost
Purchasing	Purchase orders	$579,000	1,158	$500
Material handling	Number of setups	720,000	1,800	400
Quality control	Number of batches	144,000	600	240
Roasting	Roasting hours	961,000	96,100	10
Blending	Blending hours	336,000	33,600	10
Packaging	Packaging hours	260,000	26,000	10

5-40 (Cont'd)

The budgeted unit cost per pound are:

Mona Loa Coffee				Malaysian Coffee		
Direct unit costs				Direct unit costs		
Direct materials	$4.20			Direct materials	$3.20	
Direct labor	0.30	$4.50		Direct labor	0.30	$3.50
Indirect unit costs				Indirect unit costs		
Purchasing				Purchasing		
(4[a] orders × $500 ÷ 100,000 lbs.)	0.02			(4[b] orders × $500 ÷ 2,000 lbs.)	1.00	
Material handling				Material handling		
(30[c] setups × $400 ÷ 100,000 lbs.)	0.12			(12[d] setups × $400 ÷ 2,000 lbs.)	2.40	
Quality control				Quality control		
(10 batches × $240 ÷ 100,000 lbs.)	0.02			(4 batches × $240 ÷ 2,000 lbs.)	0.48	
Roasting				Roasting		
(1,000 hours × $10 ÷ 100,000 lbs.)	0.10			(20 hours × $10 ÷ 2,000 lbs.)	0.10	
Blending				Blending		
(500 hours × $10 ÷ 100,000 lbs.)	0.05			(10 hours × $10 ÷ 2,000 lbs.)	0.05	
Packaging				Packaging		
(100 hours × $10 ÷ 100,000 lbs.)	0.01	0.32		(2 hours × $10 ÷ 2,000 lbs.)	0.01	4.04
Total unit cost		$4.82		Total unit cost		$7.54

[a] 100,000 lbs ÷ 25,000 lbs   [b] 2,000 lbs ÷ 500 lbs

[c] 100,000 lbs ÷ 10,000 pounds/batch × 3 setups/batch   [d] 2,000 lbs ÷ 500 lbs/batch × 3 setups/batch

The comparative cost numbers are:

	Mona Loa	Malaysian
Requirement 1	$6.00	$5.00
Requirement 2	4.82	7.54

The ABC system in requirement 2 reports a decreased cost for the high-volume Mona Loa and an increased cost for the low-volume Malaysian.

3.   Three of the indirect cost items can be classified as output-unit driven:

	Mona Loa Unit Cost	Malaysian Unit Cost
Roasting	$0.10	$0.10
Blending	0.05	0.05
Packaging	0.01	0.01

5-40 (Cont'd.)

The other three indirect cost items are batch-level driven:

	Mona Loa Unit Cost	Malaysian Unit Cost
Purchasing	$0.02	$1.00
Material handling	0.12	2.40
Quality control	0.02	0.48

Malaysian coffee has a greater number of setups per output unit than does Mona Loa coffee. The result is that the unit cost of the lower-volume coffee is much higher than that of the higher-volume coffee.

4. The traditional costing approach leads to cross-subsidization between the two products:

	Mona Loa	Malaysian
Traditional	$6.00	$5.00
ABC	4.82	7.54

With the traditional approach, the high-volume Mona Loa is overcosted, while the low-volume Malaysian is undercosted. The ABC system indicates that Mona Loa is profitable and should be emphasized.

Pricing of Mona Loa can be reduced to make it more competitive. In contrast, Malaysian should be priced at a much higher level if the strategy is to cover the current period's cost. Coffee Bean may wish to have lower margins with its low-volume products in an attempt to build up volume.

CHAPTER 6
MASTER BUDGET AND RESPONSIBILITY ACCOUNTING

6-2   The *master budget* is a comprehensive expression of management's operating and financial plans for a future time period (usually a year) that is summarized in a set of budgeted financial statements. It embraces the impact of both *operating* decisions and *financing* decisions.

6-4   Budgeted performance is better than past performance for judging managers. Why? Mainly because inefficiencies included in past results can be detected and eliminated in budgeting. Also, new opportunities in the future, which did not exist in the past, may be ignored if past performance is used.

6-6   A company that shares its own internal budget information with other companies can gain multiple benefits. One benefit is better coordination with suppliers, which can reduce the likelihood of supply shortages. Better coordination with customers can result in increased sales as demand by customers is less likely to exceed supply. Better coordination across the whole supply chain can also help a company reduce inventories and thus reduce the costs of holding inventories.

6-8   A *rolling budget* is a budget or plan that is always available for a specified future period by adding a month, quarter, or year in the future as the month, quarter, or year just ended is dropped. *Pro forma statements* are budgeted or forecasted financial statements.

6-10 The sales forecast is typically the cornerstone for budgeting, because production (and, hence, costs) and inventory levels generally depend on the forecasted level of sales.

6-12 Factors reducing the effectiveness of budgeting of companies include:
1.   Lack of a well-defined strategy,
2.   Lack of a clear linkage of strategy to operational plans,
3.   Lack of individual accountability for results, and
4.   Lack of meaningful performance measures.

6-14 Nonoutput-based cost drivers can be incorporated into budgeting by the use of activity-based budgeting (ABB). ABB focuses on the budgeted cost of activities necessary to produce and sell products and services. Nonoutput-based cost drivers, such as the number of part numbers, number of batches, and number of new products can be used with ABB.

6-16 (15 min.) **Production budget (in units), fill in the missing numbers.**

	Model 101	Model 201	Model 301
Budgeted sales	180^G	193^c	867^G
Add target ending FGI	14^a	6^G	33^G
Total requirements	194^G	199^G	900^e
Deduct beginning FGI	11^G	8^G	45^f
Units to be produced	183^b	191^d	855^G

^{a} 194 − 180 = 14 ^{d} 199 − 8 = 191   G = given
^{b} 194 − 11 = 183 ^{e} 867 + 33 = 900
^{c} 199 − 6 = 193 ^{f} 900 − 855 = 45

6-18 (5 min.) **Direct materials purchases budget.**

Direct materials to be used in production (bottles)	1,500,000
Add target ending direct materials inventory (bottles)	50,000
Total requirements (bottles)	1,550,000
Deduct beginning direct materials inventory (bottles)	20,000
Direct materials to be purchased (bottles)	1,530,000

6-20 (30 min.) **Sales and production budget.**

1.

	Selling Price	Units Sold	Total Revenues
12-ounce bottles	$0.25	4,800,000^a	$1,200,000
4-gallon units	1.50	1,200,000^b	1,800,000
			$3,000,000

a. 400,000 × 12 months = 4,800,000
b. 100,000 × 12 months = 1,200,000

2.

Budgeted unit sales (12-ounce bottles)	4,800,000
Add target ending finished goods inventory	600,000
Total requirements	5,400,000
Deduct beginning finished goods inventory	900,000
Units to be produced	4,500,000

3. $\dfrac{\text{Beginning}}{\text{Inventory}} = \dfrac{\text{Budgeted}}{\text{Sales}} + \dfrac{\text{Target}}{\text{ending inventory}} - \dfrac{\text{Budgeted}}{\text{production}}$

= 1,200,000 + 200,000 − 1,300,000
= 100,000 4-gallon units

6-22 (15-20 min.) **Revenue, production, and purchases budget.**

1. 800,000 motorcycles × 400,000 yen = 320,000,000,000 yen

2.
Budgeted sales (units)	800,000
Add target ending finished goods inventory	100,000
Total requirements	900,000
Deduct beginning finished goods inventory	120,000
Units to be produced	780,000

3.
Direct materials to be used in production, 780,000 × 2	1,560,000
Add target ending direct materials inventory	30,000
Total requirements	1,590,000
Deduct beginning direct materials inventory	20,000
Direct materials to be purchased	1,570,000
Cost per wheel in yen	16,000
Direct materials purchase cost in yen	25,120,000,000

Note the relatively small inventory of wheels. In Japan, suppliers tend to be located very close to the major manufacturer. Inventories are controlled by just-in-time and similar systems. Indeed, some direct materials inventories are almost nonexistent.

6-24 (20-30 min.) **Activity-based budgeting.**

1. This question links to the ABC example used in the Problem for Self-Study in Chapter 5 and to Question 5-23 (ABC, retail product-line profitability).

Activity	Cost Hierarchy	Soft Drinks	Fresh Produce	Packaged Food	Total
Ordering $90 × 14; 24; 14	Batch-level	$1,260	$ 2,160	$1,260	$ 4,680
Delivery $82 × 12; 62; 19	Batch-level	984	5,084	1,558	7,626
Shelf-stocking $21 × 16; 172; 94	Output-unit-level	336	3,612	1,974	5,922
Customer support $0.18 × 4,600; 34,200; 10,750	Output-unit-level	828	6,156	1,935	8,919
Total budgeted costs		$3,408	$17,012	$6,727	$27,147

6-24 (Cont.)

2.   An ABB approach recognizes how different products require different mixes of support activities. The relative percentage of how each product area uses the cost driver at each activity area is:

Activity	Cost Hierarchy	Soft Drinks	Fresh Produce	Packaged Food	Total
Ordering	Batch-level	26.9	46.2	26.9	100.0%
Delivery	Batch-level	12.9	66.7	20.4	100.0
Shelf-stocking	Output-unit-level	5.7	61.0	33.3	100.0
Customer support	Output-unit-level	9.3	69.0	21.7	100.0

By recognizing these differences, FS managers are better able to budget for different unit sales levels and different mix of individual product-line items sold. Using a single cost driver (such as COGS) assumes homogeneity across product lines which does not occur at FS. Other benefits cited by managers include: (1) better identification of resource needs, (2) clearer linking of costs with staff responsibilities, and (3) identification of budgetary slack.

6-26 (20 min.)   Budgeting and human behavior.

1. (a) Gain additional insight into the strategy of an organization. Exhibit 6-1 (p. 179) shows arrows pointing both ways between strategy analysis, long-run planning, and short-run planning. Detailed analysis for budgeting can sometimes highlight strategy assumptions (such as cost levels and demand levels) that are not likely to hold.
   (b) Anticipate resource demands in a timely way. Budgeting can highlight working capital shortages, cash shortages, personnel shortages, and so on. Early warning signals can enable a company to take action to avoid small problems becoming large problems.
   (c) Improve the communication level in an organization. The budgeting process itself can assist in diverse groups gaining a better understanding of how other groups affect their performance. Sharing budgets across organizations in a supply chain can assist a company better meet end-point customer demand. Communication with suppliers can reduce parts shortages.

2. Factors to consider when preparing sales forecasts include:
   (a) Any constraining variables on sales. For example, if demand outstrips available productive capacity or a key component is in short supply, the sales forecast should be based on the maximum units that could be produced.
   (b) Information from customers about their new product developments and advertising plans. Chapter 6 (p. 180) gives the example of Pace, a manufacturer of decoder boxes for cable television. Pace is able to make better sales forecasts by coordinating with BSKYB about BSKYB's planned launch of a new digital satellite service.
   (c) Feedback from customers about satisfaction with a company's products vis-à-vis satisfaction levels for the products of competitors.
   (d) Likely new product releases by competitors or new entrants into a market.

6-28 (40 min.) Budget schedules for a manufacturer.

a. Sales or Revenue Budget

	Executive Line	Chairman Line	Total
Units sold	740	390	
Unit selling price	$ 1,020	$ 1,600	
Budgeted revenue	$754,800	$624,000	$1,378,800

b. Production Budget in Units

	Executive Line	Chairman Line
Budgeted sales	740	390
Add budgeted ending f.g. inventory	30	15
Total requirements	770	405
Deduct beginning f.g. inventory	20	5
Budgeted production	750	400

c. Direct Materials Usage Budget (units):

	Oak	Red Oak	Oak Legs	Red Oak Legs	Total
Executive Line:					
1. Budgeted input per f.g. unit	16	–	4	–	
2. Budgeted production	750	–	750	–	
3. Budgeted usage	12,000	–	3,000	–	
Chairman Line:					
4. Budgeted input per f.g. unit	–	25	–	4	
5. Budgeted production	–	400	–	400	
6. Budgeted usage	–	10,000	–	1,600	
Total direct materials usage (3+6)	12,000	10,000	3,000	1,600	
1. Beginning inventory	320	150	100	40	
2. Unit price (FIFO)	$18	$23	$11	$17	
3. Cost of DM used from beginning inventory	$5,760	$3,450	$1,100	$680	$10,990
4. Materials to be used from purchases	11,680	9,850	2,900	1,560	
5. Cost of DM in March	$20	$25	$12	$18	
6. Cost of DM purchased and used in March	$233,600	$246,250	$34,800	$28,080	542,730
Direct materials used (3+6)	$239,360	$249,700	$35,900	$28,760	$553,720

6-28 (Cont'd.)

Direct Materials Purchases
    Budget:

	Oak	Red Oak	Oak Legs	Red Oak Legs	Total
Budgeted usage	12,000	10,000	3,000	1,600	
Add ending inventory	192	200	80	44	
Total requirements	12,192	10,200	3,080	1,644	
Deduct beginning inventory	320	150	100	40	
Total DM purchases	11,872	10,050	2,980	1,604	
Purchase price (March)	$20	$25	$12	$18	
Total purchases	$237,440	$251,250	$35,760	$28,872	$553,322

d.   Direct manufacturing labor budget

	Output Units Produced	Direct Manu. Labor-Hours per Output Unit	Total Hours	Hourly Rate	Total
Executive Line	750	3	2,250	$30	$ 67,500
Chairman Line	400	5	2,000	$30	60,000
			4,250		$127,500

e.   Manufacturing overhead budget
    Variable manufacturing overhead costs

(4,250 × $35)	$148,750
Fixed manufacturing overhead costs	42,500
Total manufacturing overhead costs	$191,250

Total manufacturing overhead cost per hour

$$= \frac{\$191,250}{4,250} = \$45 \text{ per direct manufacturing labor-hour}$$

Fixed manufacturing overhead cost per hour

$$= \frac{\$42,500}{4,250} = \$10 \text{ per direct manufacturing labor-hour}$$

f.   Computation of unit costs of finished goods:

	Executive Line	Chairman Line
Direct materials		
Oak top ($20 × 16, 0)	$320	$ 0
Red oak ($25 × 0, 25)	0	625
Oak legs ($12 × 4, 0)	48	0
Red oak legs ($18 × 0, 4)	0	72
Direct manufacturing labor ($30 × 3, 5)	90	150
Manufacturing overhead		
Variable ($35 × 3, 5)	105	175
Fixed ($10 × 3, 5)	30	50
Total manufacturing cost	$593	$1,072

6-28 (Cont'd.)

Ending Inventory Budget

	Cost per Unit	Units	Total
Direct Materials			
Oak top	$ 20	192	$ 3,840
Red oak top	25	200	5,000
Oak legs	12	80	960
Red oak legs	18	44	792
			10,592
Finished Goods			
Executive	593	30	17,790
Chairman	1,072	15	16,080
			33,870
Total			$44,462

g. Cost of goods sold budget

Budgeted finished goods inventory, March 1, 2002 ($10,480 + $4,850)		$ 15,330
Direct materials used	$553,720	
Direct manufacturing labor	127,500	
Manufacturing overhead	191,250	
Cost of goods manufactured		872,470
Cost of goods available for sale		887,800
Deduct ending finished goods inventory, March 31, 2002		33,870
Cost of goods sold		$853,930

6-28 (Cont'd.)

2.   Areas where continuous improvement might be incorporated into the budgeting process:
(a)   Direct materials. Either an improvement in usage or price could be budgeted. For example, the budgeted usage amounts could be related to the maximum improvement (current usage – minimum possible usage) of 1 square foot for either desk:
- Executive: 16 square feet – 15 square feet minimum = 1 square foot
- Chairman: 25 square feet – 24 square feet minimum = 1 square foot

Thus, a 1% reduction target per month could be:
- Executive: 15 square feet + (0.99 × 1) = 15.99
- Chairman: 24 square feet + (0.99 × 1) = 24.99

Some students suggested the 1% be applied to the 16 and 25 square-foot amounts. This is incorrect as, after several improvement cycles, the budgeted amount would be less than the minimum desk requirements

(b)   Direct manufacturing labor. The budgeted usage of 3 hours/5 hours could be continuously revised on a monthly basis. Similarly, the manufacturing labor cost per hour of $30 could be continuously revised down. The former appears more feasible than the latter.

(c)   Variable manufacturing overhead. By budgeting more efficient use of the allocation base, a signal is given for continuous improvement. A second approach is to budget continuous improvement in the budgeted variable overhead cost per unit of the allocation base.

(d)   Fixed manufacturing overhead. The approach here is to budget for reductions in the year-to-year amounts of fixed overhead. If these costs are appropriately classified as fixed, then they are more difficult to adjust down on a monthly basis.

6-30 (30-40 min.) **Revenue and production budgets.**

This is a routine budgeting problem. The key to its solution is to compute the correct *quantities* of finished goods and direct materials. Use the following general formula:

$$\begin{pmatrix} \text{Budgeted} \\ \text{production} \\ \text{or purchases} \end{pmatrix} = \begin{pmatrix} \text{Target} \\ \text{ending} \\ \text{inventory} \end{pmatrix} + \begin{pmatrix} \text{Budgeted} \\ \text{sales or} \\ \text{materials used} \end{pmatrix} - \begin{pmatrix} \text{Beginning} \\ \text{inventory} \end{pmatrix}$$

1.

Scarborough Corporation
Revenue Budget for 2003

	Units	Price	Total
Thingone	60,000	$165	$ 9,900,000
Thingtwo	40,000	250	10,000,000
Projected sales			$19,900,000

2.

Scarborough Corporation
Production Budget (in units) for 2003

	Thingone	Thingtwo
Budgeted sales in units	60,000	40,000
Add target finished goods inventories, December 31, 2003	25,000	9,000
Total requirements	85,000	49,000
Deduct finished goods inventories, January 1, 2003	20,000	8,000
Units to be produced	65,000	41,000

3.

Scarborough Corporation
Direct Materials Purchases Budget (in quantities) for 2003

	Direct Materials		
	A	B	C
Direct materials to be used in production			
• Thingone (budgeted production of 65,000 units times 4 lbs. of A, 2 lbs. of B)	260,000	130,000	--
• Thingtwo (budgeted production of 41,000 units times 5 lbs. of A, 3 lbs. of B, 1 lb. of C)	205,000	123,000	41,000
Total	465,000	253,000	41,000
Add target ending inventories, December 31, 2003	36,000	32,000	7,000
Total requirements in units	501,000	285,000	48,000
Deduct beginning inventories, January 1, 2003	32,000	29,000	6,000
Direct materials to be purchased (units)	469,000	256,000	42,000

4.

Scarborough Corporation
Direct Materials Purchases Budget (in dollars) for 2003

	Budgeted Purchases (Units)	Expected Purchase Price per unit	Total
Direct material A	469,000	$12	$5,628,000
Direct material B	256,000	5	1,280,000
Direct material C	42,000	3	126,000
Budgeted purchases			$7,034,000

5.

Scarborough Corporation
Direct Manufacturing Labor Budget (in dollars) for 2003

	Budgeted Production (Units)	Direct Manufacturing Labor-Hours per Unit	Total Hours	Rate per Hour	Total
Thingone	65,000	2	130,000	$12	$1,560,000
Thingtwo	41,000	3	123,000	16	1,968,000
Total					$3,528,000

6.

Scarborough Corporation
Budgeted Finished Goods Inventory
At December 31, 2003

Thingone:
　　Direct materials costs:
　　　　A, 4 pounds at $12 .... $48
　　　　B, 2 pounds at $5 .... 10 　$ 58
　　Direct manufacturing labor costs,
　　　　2 hours at $12 24
　　Manufacturing overhead costs at $20 per direct
　　　　manufacturing labor-hour (2 hours) 40
　　Budgeted manufacturing costs per unit $122
　　Finished goods inventory of Thingone
　　　　$122 × 25,000 units $3,050,000
Thingtwo:
　　Direct materials costs:
　　　　A, 5 pounds at $12 .... $60
　　　　B, 3 pounds at $5 15
　　　　C, 1 each at $3 .... 3 　$ 78
　　Direct manufacturing labor costs,
　　　　3 hours at $16 48
　　Manufacturing overhead costs at $20 per direct
　　　　manufacturing labor-hour (3 hours) 60
　　Budgeted manufacturing costs per unit $186
　　Finished goods inventory of Thingtwo
　　　　$186 × 9,000 units 1,674,000
Budgeted finished goods inventory, December 31, 2003 　$4,724,000

6-32 (60 min.) **Comprehensive operating budget.**

1. **Schedule 1: Revenue Budget**
   for the Year Ended December 31, 2001

	Units	Selling Price	Total Revenues
Snowboards	1,000	$450	$450,000
Total			

2. **Schedule 2: Production Budget (in Units)**
   for the Year Ended December 31, 2001

	Snowboards
Budgeted unit sales (Schedule 1)	1,000
Add target ending finished goods inventory	200
Total requirements	1,200
Deduct beginning finished goods inventory	100
Units to be produced	1,100

3. **Schedule 3A: Direct Materials Usage Budget**
   for the Year Ended December 31, 2001

	Wood	Fiberglass	Total
Physical Budget			
To be used in production	5,500		
(Wood: 1,100 × 5.00 b.f.			
Fiberglass: 1,100 × 6.00 yards)		6,600	
	5,500	6,600	
Cost Budget			
Available from beginning inventory			
(Wood: 2,000 b.f. × $28.00	56,000		
Fiberglass: 1,000 b.f. × 4.80)		4,800	
To be used from purchases this period			
(Wood: (5,500 – 2,000) × $30.00	105,000		
Fiberglass: (6,600 – 1,000) × $5.00)		28,000	
Total cost of direct materials to be used	$161,000	$32,800	$193,800

6-32 (Cont'd.)

Schedule 3B: Direct Materials Purchases Budget
For the Year Ended December 31, 2001

	Wood	Fiberglass	Total
Physical Budget			
Production usage (from Schedule 3A)	5,500	6,600	
Add target ending inventory	1,500	2,000	
Total requirements	7,000	8,600	
Deduct beginning inventory	2,000	1,000	
Purchases	5,000	7,600	
Cost Budget			
(Wood: 5,000 × $30.00	$150,000		
Fiberglass: 7,600 × $5.00)		$38,000	
	$150,000	$38,000	$188,000

4. **Schedule 4: Direct Manufacturing Labor Budget**
   for the Year Ended December 31, 2001

Labor Category	Cost Driver Units	DML Hours per Driver Unit	Total Hours	Wage Rate	Total
Manufacturing Labor	1,100	5.00	5,500	$25.00	$137,500

5. **Schedule 5: Manufacturing Overhead Budget**
   for the Year Ended December 31, 2001

	At Budgeted Level of 5,500 Direct Manufacturing Labor-Hours
Variable manufacturing overhead costs ($7.00 × 5,500)	$ 38,500
Fixed manufacturing overhead costs	66,000
Total manufacturing overhead costs	$104,500

6.

Budgeted manufacturing overhead rate: $\dfrac{\$104,500}{5,500} = \$19.00$ per hour

7.

Budgeted manufacturing overhead cost per output unit: $\dfrac{\$104,500}{1,100} = \$95.00$ per output unit

6-32 (Cont'd.)

8. Schedule 6A: Computation of Unit Costs of Manufacturing Finished Goods in 2001

	Cost per Unit of Input[a]	Inputs[b]	Total
Direct materials			
Wood	$30.00	5.00	$150.00
Fiberglass	5.00	6.00	30.00
Direct manufacturing labor	25.00	5.00	125.00
Total manufacturing overhead			95.00
			$400.00

[a] cost is per board foot, yard or per hour

[b] inputs is the amount of input per board

9. **Schedule 6B: Ending Inventory Budget**
    December 31, 2001

	Units	Cost per Unit	Total
Direct materials			
Wood	1,500	$ 30.00	$ 45,000
Fiberglass	2,000	5.00	10,000
Finished goods			
Snowboards	200	400.00	80,000
Total Ending Inventory			$135,000

10. **Schedule 7: Cost of Goods Sold Budget**
    for the Year Ended December 31, 2001

	From Schedule		Total
Beginning finished goods inventory January 1, 2001	Given		$ 37,480
Direct materials used	3A	$193,800	
Direct manufacturing labor	4	137,500	
Manufacturing overhead	5	104,500	
Cost of goods manufactured			435,800
Cost of goods available for sale			473,280
Deduct ending finished goods inventory, December 31, 2001	6B		80,000
Cost of goods sold			$393,280

6-32 (Cont'd.)

11. **Budgeted Income Statement for Slopes**
    for the Year Ended December 31, 2001

Revenues	Schedule 1	$450,000
Costs		
Cost of goods sold	Schedule 7	393,280
Gross margin		56,720
Operating costs		
Marketing costs ($250 × 30)	$ 7,500	
Other costs	30,000	37,500
Operating income		$ 19,220

6-34   (15 min.) **Responsibility of purchasing agent.**

The time lost in the plant should be charged to the purchasing department. The plant manager probably should not be asked to underwrite a loss due to failure of delivery over which he had no supervision. Although the purchasing agent may feel that he has done everything he possibly could, he must realize that, in the whole organization, he is *the one* who is in the best position to evaluate the situation. He receives an assignment. He may accept it or reject it. But if he accepts, he must perform. If he fails, the damage is evaluated. Everybody makes mistakes. The important point is to avoid making too many mistakes and also to understand fully that the extensive control reflected in responsibility accounting is the necessary balance to the great freedom of action that individual executives are given.

Discussions of this problem have again and again revealed a tendency among students (and among accountants and managers) to "fix the blame"—as if the variances arising from a responsibility accounting system should pinpoint misbehavior and provide answers. The point is that no accounting system or variances can provide answers. However, variances can lead to questions. In this case, in deciding where the penalty should be assigned, the student might inquire who should be asked—not who should be blamed.

Classroom discussions have also raised the following diverse points:
(a) Is the railroad company liable?
(b) Costs of idle time are usually routinely charged to the production department. Should the information system be fine-tuned to reallocate such costs to the purchasing department?
(c) How will the purchasing managers behave in the future regarding willingness to take risks?
    The text emphasizes the following: Beware of overemphasis on controllability. For example, a time-honored theme of management is that responsibility should not be given without accompanying authority. Such a guide is a useful first step, but responsibility accounting is more far-reaching. The basic focus should be on information or knowledge, not on control. The key question is: Who is the best informed? Put another way, "Who is the person who can tell us the most about the specific item, regardless of ability to exert personal control?"

6-36 (30 min.) Cash budget, fill in the blanks, chapter appendix.

| | Quarters | | | | |
	I	II	III	IV	Year as a Whole
Cash balance, beginning	$ 15,000	$ 32,000	$ 15,000	$ 50,000	$ 15,000
Add receipts					
Collections from customers	385,000	315,000	295,000	365,000	1,360,000
Total cash available for needs	400,000	347,000	310,000	415,000	1,375,000
Deduct disbursements					
Direct materials	175,000	125,000	110,000	155,000	565,000
Payroll	125,000	110,000	95,000	118,000	448,000
Other costs	50,000	45,000	40,000	49,000	184,000
Interest expense (LT debt)	3,000	3,000	3,000	3,000	12,000
Machinery purchase	0	85,000	0	0	85,000
Income taxes	15,000	14,000	12,000	20,000	61,000
Total disbursements	368,000	382,000	260,000	345,000	1,355,000
Minimum cash balance desired	15,000	15,000	15,000	15,000	15,000
Total cash needed	383,000	397,000	275,000	360,000	1,370,000
Cash excess (deficiency)	17,000	(50,000)	35,000	55,000	5,000
Financing					
Borrowing (at beginning)	0	50,000	0	0	50,000
Repayment (at end)	0	0	0	(50,000)	(50,000)
Interest (at 12% per annum)	0	0	0	(4,500)	(4,500)
Total effects of financing	0	50,000	0	(54,500)	(4,500)
Cash balance, ending	$ 32,000	$ 15,000	$ 50,000	$ 15,500	$ 15,500

6-38 (60-75 min.) **Comprehensive budget; fill in schedules.**

1. Schedule A: Budgeted Monthly Cash Receipts

Item	September	October	November	December
Total sales	$40,000*	$48,000*	$60,000*	$80,000*
Credit sales (25%)	10,000*	12,000*	15,000	20,000
Cash sales (75%)	$30,000	$36,000	$45,000	$60,000
Receipts:				
Cash sales		$36,000*	$45,000	$60,000
Collections on accounts receivable		10,000*	12,000	15,000
Total		$46,000*	$57,000	$75,000

*Given.

2. Schedule B: Budgeted Monthly Cash Disbursements for Purchases

Item	October	November	December	4th Quarter
Purchases	$42,000*	$56,000	$25,200	$123,200
Deduct 2% cash discount	840*	1,120	504	2,464
Disbursements	$41,160*	$54,880	$24,696	$120,736

*Given. Note that purchases are 70.0% of next month's sales given a gross margin of 30%.

3. Schedule C: Budgeted Monthly Cash Disbursements for Operating Costs

Item	October	November	December	4th Quarter
Salaries and wages (15% of sales)	$ 7,200*	$ 9,000	$12,000	$28,200
Rent (5% of sales)	2,400*	3,000	4,000	9,400
Other cash operating costs (4% of sales)	1,920*	2,400	3,200	7,520
Total	$11,520*	$14,400	$19,200	$45,120

*Given.

4. Schedule D: Budgeted Total Monthly Cash Disbursements

Item	October	November	December	4th Quarter
Purchases	$41,160*	$54,880	$24,696	$120,736
Cash operating costs	11,520*	14,400	19,200	45,120
Light fixtures	600*	400	--	1,000
Total	$53,280*	$69,680	$43,896	$166,856

*Given.

5. Schedule E: Budgeted Cash Receipts and Disbursements

Item	October	November	December	4th Quarter
Receipts	$46,000*	$57,000	$75,000	$178,000
Disbursements	53,280*	69,680	43,896	166,856
Net cash increase			$31,104	$ 11,144
Net cash decrease	$ 7,280*	$12,680		

*Given

6-38 (Cont'd.)

6. Schedule F: Financing Required

Item	October	November	December	4th Quarter
Beginning cash balance	$12,000*	$ 8,720*	$ 8,040	$12,000
Net cash increase			31,104	11,144
Net cash decrease	7,280*	12,680		
Cash position before borrowing (a)	4,720*	(3,960)	39,144	23,144
Minimum cash balance required	8,000*	8,000	8,000	8,000
Excess (Deficiency)	(3,280)*	(11,960)	31,144	15,144
Borrowing required (b)	4,000*	12,000		16,000
Interest payments (c)			540	540
Borrowing repaid (d)			(16,000)	(16,000)
Ending cash balance (a+b–c–d)	$ 8,720*	$ 8,040	$22,604	$22,604

*Given.

Interest computation:

$ 4,000 @ 18% for 3 months	=	$180
$12,000 @ 18% for 2 months	=	360
Total interest expense		$540

7. Short-term, self-liquidating financing is best. The schedules clearly demonstrate the mechanics of a self-liquidating loan. The need for such a loan arises because of the seasonal nature of many businesses. When sales soar, the payroll and suppliers must be paid in cash. The basic source of cash is proceeds from sales. However, the credit extended to customers creates a lag between the sale and the collection of cash. When the cash is collected, it in turn may be used to repay the loan. The amount of the loan and the timing of the repayment are heavily dependent on the credit terms that pertain to both the purchasing and selling functions of the business. Somewhat strangely, in seasonal businesses, the squeeze on cash is often heaviest in the months of peak sales and is lightest in the months of low sales.

8.

Newport Stationery Store
Budgeted Income Statement
For the Quarter Ending December 31, 2001

Revenues—Schedule A		$188,000
Cost of goods sold (70% of sales)		131,600*
Gross margin		56,400
Operating costs		
Salaries and wages—Schedule C	$28,200	
Rent—Schedule C	9,400	
Other cash operating costs—Schedule C	7,520	
Depreciation ($1,000 × 3 months)	3,000	48,120
Operating income		8,280
Deduct interest expense— Schedule F		540
Add purchase discounts— Schedule B		2,464
Net income (before taxes)		$ 10,204
*Note: Ending inventory and proof of cost of goods sold:		
Inventory, September 30	$ 63,600	
Add purchases—Schedule B	123,200	$186,800
Deduct inventory, December 31:		
Basic inventory	30,000	
December purchases—Schedule B	25,200	55,200
Cost of goods sold		$131,600

6-38 (Cont'd.)

Newport Stationery Store
Budgeted Balance Sheet
December 31,

Assets:
  Current assets:
    Cash—Schedule F $ 22,604
    Accounts receivable
      December credit sales—Schedule A   20,000
    Inventory (see Note above)   55,200
      Total current assets   97,804
  Equipment and fixtures:
    Equipment—net ($100,000 – $3,000 depreciation) $97,000
    Fixtures—Schedule D   1,000   98,000
    Total $195,804

Liabilities and Owners' Equity:
  Liabilities   None
  Owners' equity $195,804*
  Total $195,804

*Owners' equity, September 30:
  $12,000 + $63,600 + $10,000 + $100,000 (Given) $185,600
  Net income, quarter ended December 31   10,204
  Owners' equity, December 31 $195,804

9.   All of the transactions have been simplified–for example, no bad debts are considered. Also, many businesses face wide fluctuation of cash flows within a month. For example, perhaps customer receipts lag and are bunched together near the end of a month, and disbursements are due evenly throughout the month, or are bunched near the beginning of the month. Cash needs would then need to be evaluated on a weekly and, perhaps, daily basis rather than on a monthly basis.

6-40 (60 min.) Athletic department of a university, budget revision options.

This exercise illustrates the difficulty of budgeting issues in universities. There are multiple stakeholders—student-athletes, student non-athletes, coaches, sports administrators, university faculty, university administrators, and alumni. Actions that benefit one type of stakeholder can "gore the ox" of other stakeholders.

The general options that groups could examine are outlined below:

Increasing Revenues

There are at least two approaches to "increase" revenues:

(a)   Increase revenues from outside sources. For example, sell more tickets to football, basketball, etc. This is heavily driven by success. Reddy's concerns about academic standards likely will constrain Connolly's flexibility to recruit any athlete he believes to be a major star.

Some universities have been innovative in terms of increasing cable television revenues from coverage of college sporting games.

The tax status of universities needs to be considered in any revenue-increasing strategy. For example, holding non-university-related events at athletic facilities (e.g., a SuperBowl) can endanger the tax-exempt status of a university.

Connolly could propose direct fundraising for the Athletic Department. This could run into problems with Reddy, as she may require all fundraising to be coordinated at the University level.

(b)   Increase the "revenues" attributed to the Athletic Department. Connolly could argue that a successful athletic program has many positive externalities for Pacific University, many of which increase PU revenues.

- Alumni are more likely to give money and other contributions when they are stimulated by being on campus to watch a nationally-ranked team or viewing a successful PU team on television. Many universities use tickets to athletic events and invitations to related social functions as a thank-you to major donors.
- Athletic officials (especially nationally prominent coaches) are expected to assist Reddy and her senior officers in promoting PU to potential donors, parents of future students, etc. For example, the coach of a number-one-ranked football team may attend over 50 dinners/functions a year on behalf of the university. Some of these dinners are "one-on-one" with potential large donors.
- Merchandising revenue sold to alumni and other supporters is likely to increase when PU's athletic teams achieve national success. These include sweaters, towels, and rings.

The current budgeting process gives zero recognition to these externalities, which may well exceed the projected $3.010 million deficit.

6-40 (Cont'd.)

Decreasing Costs

     Connolly can always cut costs to meet any level Reddy may impose. However, the ways to achieve any substantive reduction will be relatively painful.

(a)   Reduce scholarships (either number or amount) to students. This can take time to achieve bottom-line reductions, as existing students may have three more years of scholarship remaining. Unless Connolly cuts existing scholarships, he is restricted to cutting back on scholarships to new students. This option will be very painful. One consequence will be lower-quality levels of student athletes which will have implications for the sporting competitiveness of PU. The option of cutting back on already committed existing scholarships would be traumatic (but it has occurred).

     Connolly could undertake across-the-board cuts or target the reductions to some sports. For example, sports that do not draw sizable crowds may be candidates for reduction. One difficulty here is that Connolly is faced with both reducing total costs *and* increasing the relative percentage of scholarships to women. The scholarship breakdown is:

	Men's Program	Woman's Program	Total
Football	37	–	37
Basketball	21	11	32
Swimming	6	4	10
Other	4	2	6
Total	68	17	85

The largest percentages of scholarships are for the two highly successful programs—men's football (37/85 = 44%) and men's basketball (21/85 = 25%). There is little room for cutbacks in the second-tier sports at PU.

(b)   Reduce sports sponsored by the athletic department. Cut out support for all but a few targeted sporting programs. This will cause morale problems for students in these sporting programs (such as rugby, soccer, and volleyball).

(c)   Reduce salaries and other costs of the athletic department. The salary for Bill Madden is an obvious target for Connolly's cost reduction. However, Madden may have a multi-year contract that leaves PU little room for cost reduction. Moreover, if cost reduction is attempted, Madden may leave, which could have negative general effects on morale and university finances. Connolly could approach alumni or sponsors to cover Madden's salary and other costs. This would address Reddy's budget balance concerns but not her concern as to the level of Madden's salary vis-a-vis leading academics.

     Cost reductions could be achieved by reducing the number of assistant coaches, and the number of support officials. The effect of these reductions on student morale and PU athletic achievements is difficult to measure.

6-40 (Cont'd.)

Gender Issues

Based on dollar expenditures and scholarships, Reddy has evidence to support her concerns. The men's programs get the "lion's share" of the expenditures and student scholarships.

	Men's Program	Woman's Program
Costs	$11.040 million	$2.800 million
Full student scholarships	68	17

Connolly could respond by noting that the men's programs have a lower deficit based on revenues minus assigned costs (in millions):

	Men's Program	Woman's Program
Revenues	$10.350	$0.780
Assigned costs	11.040	2.800
Contribution	$(0.690)	$(2.020)

This lower deficit reflects, in part, the large revenue-drawing capacity of their successful men's football and athletic departments.

Reddy's demands for a balanced budget, more gender equality, and higher academic standards leaves Connolly in an unenviable position.

CHAPTER 7
FLEXIBLE BUDGETS, VARIANCES, AND
MANAGEMENT CONTROL: I

7-2 Sources of information about budgeted amounts include (a) past amounts, and (b) detailed engineering studies.

7-4 The key difference is the output level used to set the budget. A *static budget* is based on the level of output planned at the *start of the budget period*. A *flexible budget* is developed using budgeted revenues or cost amounts based on the level of output actually achieved in the budget period. The actual level of output is not known until the *end of the budget period*.

7-6 The steps in developing a flexible budget are:

Step 1: Determine budgeted selling price, budgeted variable costs per unit, and budgeted fixed costs.

Step 2: Determine the actual quantity of output.

Step 3: Determine the flexible budget for revenues based on budgeted selling price and actual quantity of output.

Step 4: Determine the flexible budget for costs based on budgeted variable costs per output unit, actual quantity of output, and budgeted fixed costs.

7-8 A manager should decompose the flexible-budget variance for direct materials into a price variance and an efficiency variance. The individual causes of these variances can then be investigated, recognizing possible interdependencies across these individual causes.

7-10 Direct materials price variances are often computed at the time of purchase, while direct materials efficiency variances are often computed at the time of usage. Purchasing managers are typically responsible for price variances, while production managers are typically responsible for usage variances.

7-12 An individual business function, such as production, is interdependent with other business functions. Factors outside of production can explain why variances arise in the production area. For example:

- poor design of products or processes can lead to a sizable number of defects, and
- marketing personnel making promises for delivery times that require a large number of rush orders can create production-scheduling difficulties.

7-14 Variances can be calculated at the activity level as well as at the company level. For example, a price variance and an efficiency variance can be computed for an activity area.

7-16 (20-30 min.)   **Flexible budget.**

	Actual Results (1)	Flexible-Budget Variances (2) = (1) – (3)	Flexible Budget (3)	Sales-Volume Variances (4) =(3)–(5)	Static Budget (5)
Units sold	2,800[G]	—	2,800		3,000[G]
Revenues	$313,600[a]	$ 5,600 F	$ 308,000[b]	$22,000 U	$330,000[c]
Variable costs	229,600[d]	22,400 U	207,200[e]	14,800 F	222,000[f]
Contribution margin	84,000	16,800 U	100,800	7,200 U	108,000
Fixed costs	50,000[G]	4,000 F	54,000[G]	0	54,000[G]
Operating income	$ 34,000	$12,800 U	$ 46,800	$ 7,200 U	$ 54,000

$12,800 U → Total flexible-budget variance $ 7,200 U → Total sales-volume variance

$20,000 U

Total static-budget variance

[a] $112 × 2,800 = $313,600
[b] $110 × 2,800 = $308,000
[c] $110 × 3,000 = $330,000
[d] Given. Unit variable cost = $229,600 ÷ 2,800 = $82 per tire
[e] $74 × 2,800 = $207,200
[f] $74 × 3,000 = $222,000
[G] Given

2.   The key information items are:

	Actual	Budgeted
Units	2,800	3,000
Unit selling price	$ 112	$ 110
Unit variable cost	$ 82	$ 74
Fixed costs	$50,000	$54,000

The total static-budget variance in operating income is $20,000 U. There is both an unfavorable total flexible-budget variance ($12,800) and an unfavorable sales-volume variance ($7,200).

The unfavorable sales-volume variance arises solely because actual units manufactured and sold were 200 less than the budgeted 3,000 units. The unfavorable flexible-budget variance of $12,800 in operating income is due primarily to the $8 increase in unit variable costs. This increase in unit variable costs is only partially offset by the $2 increase in unit selling price and the $4,000 decrease in fixed costs.

7-18 (10 min.)   **Flexible budget**

1.

Static-budget variance	=	Actual results	−	Static-budget amount
	=	$6,556,000	−	$3,150,000
	=	$3,406,000 F		

2.

Flexible-budget variance	=	Actual results	−	Flexible-budget amount
	=	$6,556,000	−	$6,930,000
	=	$ 374,000 U		

Sales-volume variance	=	Flexible-budget amount	−	Static-budget amount
	=	$6,930,000	−	$3,150,000
	=	$3,780,000 F		

3.

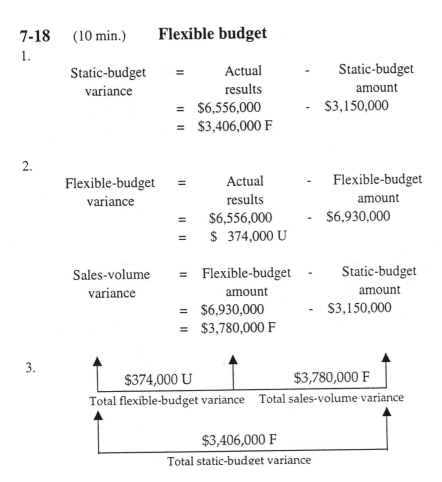

$374,000 U	$3,780,000 F
Total flexible-budget variance	Total sales-volume variance

$3,406,000 F

Total static-budget variance

The total flexible-budget variance is $374,000 unfavorable. This arises because for the actual output level: (a) selling prices were lower than budgeted, or (b) variable costs were higher than budgeted, or (c) fixed costs were higher than budgeted, or (d) some combination of (a), (b), and (c).

7-20 (15 min.) **Materials and manufacturing labor variances.**

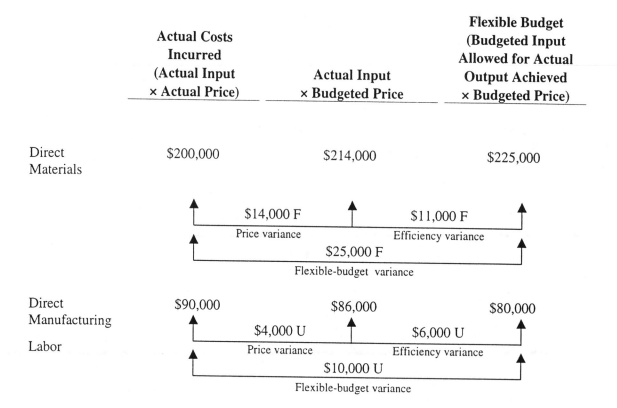

7-22 (30-40 min.) **Flexible budgets, variance analysis.**

1. Variance Analysis of Flanagan Company for May 20_X

Level 0 Analysis

Actual operating income	$ 49,000
Budgeted operating income	100,000
Static-budget variance of operating income	$ 51,000 U

Level 1 Analysis

	Actual Results (1)	Static-Budget Variances (2) = (1) – (3)	Static Budget (3)
Units sold	23,000	3,000 F	20,000
Revenues	$874,000	$ 74,000 F	$800,000
Variable costs	630,000	130,000 U	500,000
Contribution margin	244,000	56,000 U	300,000
Fixed costs	195,000	5,000 F	200,000
Operating income	$ 49,000	$ 51,000 U	$100,000

$51,000 U
Total static-budget variance

Level 2 Analysis

	Actual Results (1)	Flexible-Budget Variances (2) =(1) – (3)	Flexible Budget (3)	Sales-Volume Variances (4) = (3) – (5)	Static Budget (5)
Units sold	23,000	0	23,000	3,000 F	20,000
Revenue	$874,000	$ 46,000 U	$920,000	$120,000 F	$800,000
Variable costs	630,000	55,000 U	575,000	75,000 U	500,000
Contribution margin	244,000	101,000 U	345,000	45,000 F	300,000
Fixed costs	195,000	5,000 F	200,000	0	200,000
Operating income	$ 49,000	$ 96,000 U	$145,000	$ 45,000 F	$100,000

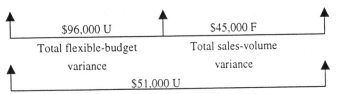

$96,000 U
Total flexible-budget variance

$45,000 F
Total sales-volume variance

$51,000 U
Total static-budget variance

2. The actual selling price per unit is $38 ($874,000 ÷ 23,000) compared to a budgeted $40 per unit. This reduction in selling price may explain the 15% increase in unit sales (23,000 versus the budgeted 20,000).

Variable costs may have exceeded the budget for many reasons, including individual price increases in materials and supplies and possible inefficiencies because of the 15% spurt in production.

Fixed cost could be less than the budget because of delays in planned salary increases, adjustments in insurance coverage, or other reasons.

7-24   (30 min.)   Flexible budget, working backward.

1.

	Actual Results (1)	Flexible-Budget Variances (2)=(1)-(3)	Flexible Budget (3)	Sales-Volume Variances (4)=(3)-(5)	Static Budget (5)
Units Sold	650,000	0	650,000	50,000 F	600,000
Revenues	$3,575,000	$1,300,000 F	$2,275,000[a]	$175,000 F	$2,100,000
Variable costs	2,575,000	1,275,000 U	1,300,000[b]	100,000 U	1,200,000
Contribution margin	1,000,000	25,000 F	975,000	75,000 F	900,000
Fixed costs	700,000	100,000 U	600,000	0	600,000
Operating income	$ 300,000	$ 75,000 U	$ 375,000	$ 75,000 F	$ 300,000

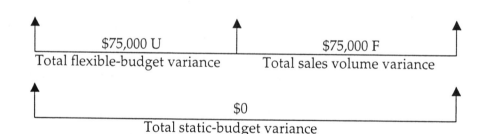

$75,000 U
Total flexible-budget variance

$75,000 F
Total sales volume variance

$0
Total static-budget variance

a. 650,000 × $3.50 = $2,275,000
b. 650,000 × $2.00 = 1,300,000

2. Actual selling price: $3,575,000 ÷ 650,000   = $5.50
    Budgeted selling price: 2,100,000 ÷ 600,000   =   3.50
    Actual variable cost per unit: 2,575,000 ÷ 650,000   =   3.96
    Budgeted variable cost per unit: 1,200,000 ÷ 600,000   =   2.00

3. The CEO's reaction was inappropriate. A nil total static-budget variance may be due to offsetting total flexible-budget and total sales-volume variances. In this case, these two variances exactly offset each other:

7-24 (Cont'd.)

Total flexible-budget variance	$75,000 Unfavorable
Total sales-volume variance	$75,000 Favorable

A closer look at the variance components reveals some major deviations from plan. Actual variable costs increased from $2.00 to $3.96, causing an unfavorable flexible-budget variable cost variance of $1,275,000. Such an increase could be a result of, for example, a jump in platinum prices. Specialty Balls was able to pass most of the increase in costs onto their customers – average selling price went up about 57%, bringing about an offsetting favorable flexible-budget variance in the amount of $1,300,000. An increase in the actual number of units sold also contributed to more favorable results. Although such an increase in quantity in the face of a price increase may appear counter-intuitive, customers may have forecast higher future platinum prices and therefore decided to stock up.

4. The most important lesson learned here is that a superficial examination of summary level data (Levels 0 and 1) may be insufficient. It is imperative to scrutinize data at a more detailed level (Level 2). Had Specialty Balls not been able to pass costs on to customers, losses would have been considerable.

7-26 (30 min.) Finance function activities, benchmarking.

1. The Hackett benchmark data are attention-directing inputs. The key new insight is how Flowers.net compares with world-class organizations. At face value, there is much room for improvement. The per unit cost differences are dramatic:

| | Flowers.net | | |
	2001 Budgeted	2001 Actual	World-Class Cost Performance
Payables	$2.900	$2.80	$0.71 per invoice
Receivables	0.639	0.75	0.10 per remittance
Travel	7.600	7.40	$1.58 per expense report

2. Chase should first examine whether there is an "apples to apples" comparison with these figures. Are costs of the finance department activities measured the same across Flowers.net and the company with "world-class cost performance"? Is the unit of activity measured the same? Suppose Flowers.net allocates other costs into the finance area (such as the President's salary), while the $1.58 per expense report figure is for finance department costs only. Will Chase either adjust the $1.58 figure upwards or exclude non-finance department costs in Flowers.net's cost figures?

Chase should also gain information on why the large cost differences occur. For example, is it because the "world-class performer" is more aggressive in using new technology in the finance area. For example, some companies are reducing financing department costs by the use of web-based reporting procedures. A related issue is whether Chase is willing to invest in new technologies in the same way that world-class finance function organizations do. If not, then the $1.58 benchmark could be unattainable, no matter how hard and smart the travel expense reporting group performs.

7-28 (20 min.) Continuous improvement. (continuation of 7-27)

1. Standard quantity input amounts per output unit are:

	Direct Materials	Direct Manufacturing Labor
January	10.0000	0.5000
February (Jan. × 0.997)	9.9700	0.4985
March (Feb. × 0.997)	9.9400	0.4970

7-28 (Cont'd.)

2. The answer to requirement 1 of Question 7-27 is identical except for the flexible- budget amount.

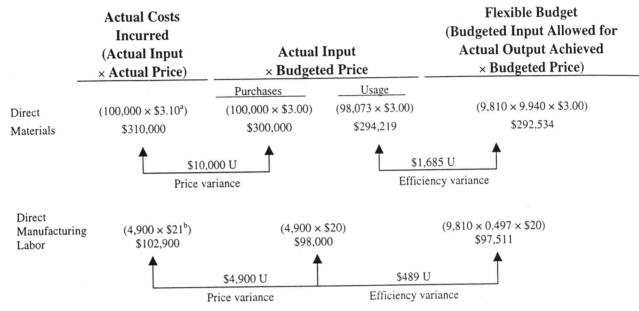

	Actual Costs Incurred (Actual Input × Actual Price)	Actual Input × Budgeted Price		Flexible Budget (Budgeted Input Allowed for Actual Output Achieved × Budgeted Price)
		Purchases	Usage	
Direct Materials	(100,000 × $3.10ᵃ) $310,000	(100,000 × $3.00) $300,000	(98,073 × $3.00) $294,219	(9,810 × 9.940 × $3.00) $292,534
		$10,000 U Price variance	$1,685 U Efficiency variance	
Direct Manufacturing Labor	(4,900 × $21ᵇ) $102,900	(4,900 × $20) $98,000		(9,810 × 0.497 × $20) $97,511
		$4,900 U Price variance	$489 U Efficiency variance	

a. $310,000 ÷ 100,000 = $3.10
b. $102,900 ÷ 4,900 = $21

Using continuous improvement standards sets a tougher benchmark. The efficiency variances for January (from Exercise 7-27) and March (from Exercise 7-28) are:

	January	March
Direct materials	$ 81 F	$1,685 U
Direct manufacturing labor	$100 F	$ 489 U

Note that the question assumes the continuous improvement applies only to quantity inputs. An alternative approach is to have continuous improvement apply to budgeted input cost per output unit ($30 for direct materials in January and $10 for direct manufacturing labor in January). This approach is more difficult to incorporate in a Level 2 variance analysis, as Level 2 requires separate amounts for quantity inputs and the cost per input.

7-30 (15–25 min.)   **Journal entries and T-accounts.**
(continuation of 7-29)

a. Work in Process Control   400,000
    Direct Materials Price Variance   7,400
        Direct Materials Efficiency Variance   30,000
        Materials Control   377,400
    To record direct materials used

b. Work in Process Control   200,000
        Direct Manufacturing Labor Price Variance   3,600
        Direct Manufacturing Labor Efficiency Variance   20,000
        Wages Payable Control   176,400
    To record liability and allocation of direct labor costs

Materials Control		Direct Materials Price Variance		Direct Materials Efficiency Variance	
	(a) 377,400	(a) 7,400			(a) 30,000

Work in Process Control		Direct Manufacturing Labor Price Variance		Direct Manufacturing Labor Efficiency Variance	
(a) 400,000			(b) 3,600		(b) 20,000
(b) 200,000					

Wages Payable Control	
	(b) 176,400

7-28 (Cont'd.)

2. The answer to requirement 1 of Question 7-27 is identical except for the flexible- budget amount.

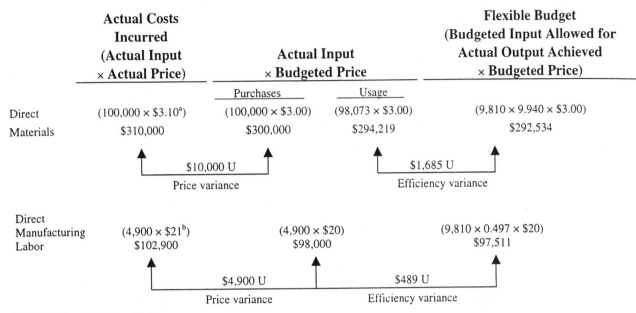

	Actual Costs Incurred (Actual Input × Actual Price)	Actual Input × Budgeted Price		Flexible Budget (Budgeted Input Allowed for Actual Output Achieved × Budgeted Price)
		Purchases	Usage	
Direct Materials	(100,000 × $3.10ª) $310,000	(100,000 × $3.00) $300,000	(98,073 × $3.00) $294,219	(9,810 × 9.940 × $3.00) $292,534

$10,000 U — Price variance $1,685 U — Efficiency variance

| Direct Manufacturing Labor | (4,900 × $21ᵇ) $102,900 | (4,900 × $20) $98,000 | | (9,810 × 0.497 × $20) $97,511 |

$4,900 U — Price variance $489 U — Efficiency variance

ª $310,000 ÷ 100,000 = $3.10
ᵇ $102,900 ÷ 4,900 = $21

Using continuous improvement standards sets a tougher benchmark. The efficiency variances for January (from Exercise 7-27) and March (from Exercise 7-28) are:

	January	March
Direct materials	$ 81 F	$1,685 U
Direct manufacturing labor	$100 F	$ 489 U

Note that the question assumes the continuous improvement applies only to quantity inputs. An alternative approach is to have continuous improvement apply to budgeted input cost per output unit ($30 for direct materials in January and $10 for direct manufacturing labor in January). This approach is more difficult to incorporate in a Level 2 variance analysis, as Level 2 requires separate amounts for quantity inputs and the cost per input.

7-30 (15–25 min.)　　**Journal entries and T-accounts.**
　　　　　　　　　　　　　(continuation of 7-29)

a.	Work in Process Control	400,000	
	Direct Materials Price Variance	7,400	
	Direct Materials Efficiency Variance		30,000
	Materials Control		377,400
	To record direct materials used		
b.	Work in Process Control	200,000	
	Direct Manufacturing Labor Price Variance		3,600
	Direct Manufacturing Labor Efficiency Variance		20,000
	Wages Payable Control		176,400
	To record liability and allocation of direct labor costs		

Materials Control	Direct Materials Price Variance	Direct Materials Efficiency Variance
(a) 377,400	(a) 7,400	(a) 30,000

Work in Process Control	Direct Manufacturing Labor Price Variance	Direct Manufacturing Labor Efficiency Variance
(a) 400,000	(b) 3,600	(b) 20,000
(b) 200,000		

Wages Payable Control
(b) 176,400

7–30 (Cont'd.)

The following journal entries pertain to the measurement of price variances when materials are purchased:

a1.	Materials Control	600,000	
	Direct Materials Price Variance	12,000	
	Accounts Payable Control		612,000
	To record direct materials purchased		

a2.	Work in Process Control	400,000	
	Materials Control		370,000
	Direct Materials Efficiency Variance		30,000
	To record direct materials used		

Materials Control	
(a1) 600,000	(a2) 370,000

Direct Materials Price Variance	
(a1) 12,000	

Accounts Payable Control	
	(a1) 612,000

Work in Process Control	
(a2) 400,000	

Direct Materials Efficiency Variance	
	(a2) 30,000

The difference between standard costing and normal costing for direct cost items is:

	Standard Costs	**Normal Costs**
Direct Costs	Standard price(s) × Standard input allowed for actual outputs achieved	Actual price(s) × Actual input

These journal entries differ from the _normal costing_ entries because Work in Process Control is no longer carried at "actual" costs. Furthermore, Materials Control can also be carried at standard unit prices rather than actual unit prices. Finally, variances appear for direct materials and direct manufacturing labor under _standard costing_ but not under _normal costing_.

7-32 (30 min.) **Flexible budget preparation, service sector.**

1. • Budgeted selling price (revenue per loan application)

   $0.5\% \times$ budgeted average loan amount $= 0.5\% \times \$200,000 = \$1,000$

   • Budgeted variable costs per output unit are:

Professional labor (6 × $40)	$240
Loan filing fees	100
Credit-worthiness checks	120
Courier mailings	50
Budgeted variable costs	$510

   • Budgeted fixed costs = $31,000 per month.

   The static budget for the 90 loan applicant level (and the flexible budget for the 120 loan application level in Requirement 2) are:

	Requirement 1 90 Loan Applications	Requirement 2 120 Loan Applications
Budgeted revenue (90, 120 × $1,000)	$90,000	$120,000
Budgeted variable costs (90, 120 × $510)	45,900	61,200
Contribution margin	44,100	58,800
Fixed costs	31,000	31,000
Operating income	$13,100	$ 27,800

7-32 (Cont'd)

2. The actual results are:

Revenue (120 × 0.5% × $224,000)		$134,400
Variable costs:		
Professional labor (120 × 7.2 × $42)	$36,288	
Loan filing fees (120 × $100)	12,000	
Credit-worthiness checks (120 × $125)	15,000	
Courier mailings (120 × $54)	6,480	69,768
Contribution margin		64,632
Fixed costs		33,500
Operating income		$ 31,132

These actual results can be analyzed in a Level 2 variance analysis.

Level 2 Analysis

	Actual Results (1)	Flexible-Budget Variances (2) = (1) – (3)	Flexible Budget (3)	Sales-Volume Variances (4) = (3) – (5)	Static Budget (5)
Units sold	120	0	120	30 F	90
Revenue	$134,400	$14,400 F	$120,000	$30,000 F	$90,000
Variable costs	69,768	8,568 U	61,200	15,300 U	45,900
Contribution margin	64,632	5,832 F	58,800	14,700 F	44,100
Fixed costs	33,500	2,500 U	31,000	0	31,000
Operating income	$ 31,132	$ 3,332 F	$ 27,800	$14,700 F	$13,100

$3,332 F \qquad\qquad $14,700 F

Total flexible-budget variance \qquad Total sales-volume variance

$18,032 F

Total static-budget variance

    Note that the $18,032 favorable static-budget variance is largely the result of an increase in loan applications from a budgeted 90 to an actual 120. In addition, the average size of a loan increased from a budgeted $200,000 to $224,000, which explains the flexible-budget variance of $14,400 F for revenues (0.5% × $24,000 × 120 = $14,400).

    One possible explanation is a rapid decrease in interest rates leading to an increase in demand for loan refinancing.

7-34   (60 min.)   **Comprehensive variance analysis, responsibility issues**

1. (a)   Actual selling price = $82.00
          Budgeted selling price = $80.00
          Actual sales volume = 4,850 units
          Selling price variance = (Actual Sales Price - Budgeted Sales Price) × Actual Units
                              = ($82 - $80) × 4,850 = $9,700 Favorable
    (b)   Development of Flexible Budget

		Budgeted Unit Amounts	Actual Volume	Flexible Budget Amount
Revenues		$80.00	4,850	$388,000
Variable costs				
DM–Frames	$ 2.20 × 3.00	6.60	4,850	32,010
DM–Lenses	3.10 × 6.00	18.60	4,850	90,210
Direct Labor	15.00 × 1.20	18.00	4,850	87,300
Total variable manufacturing costs				$209,520
Fixed manufacturing costs				75,000
Total manufacturing cost				284,520
Gross margin				$103,480

	Actual Results (1)	Flexible-Budget Variances (2)=(1)-(3)	Flexible Budget (3)	Sales - Volume Variance (4)=(3)-(5)	Static Budget (5)
Units sold	4,850		4,850		5,000
Revenues	$397,700	$ 9,700 F	$388,000	$ 12,000 U	$400,000
Variable costs					
DM–frames	37,248	5,238 U	32,010	990 F	33,000
DM–lens	100,492	10,282 U	90,210	2,790 F	93,000
Direct labor	96,903	9,603 U	87,300	2,700 F	90,000
Total variable costs	234,643	25,123 U	209,520	6,480 F	216,000
Fixed manuf. costs	72,265	2,735 F	75,000	0	75,000
Total costs	306,908	22,388 U	284,520	6,480 F	291,000
Gross margin	$ 90,792	$12,688 U	$103,480	$ 5,520 U	$109,000

7-34 (Cont'd.)

(c) **Price and Efficiency Variances**

DM—Frames—Actual ounces used = 3.20 per unit × 4,850 units = 15,520 oz.
Price per oz = $37,248/15,520 = $2.40
DM—Lenses—Actual ounces used = 7.00 per unit × 4,850 units = 33,950 oz.
Price per oz = $100,492/33,950 = $2.96
Direct Labor—Actual labor hours = $96,903/14.80 = 6,547.5 hours
Labor hours per unit = 6,547.5/4,850 units = 1.35 hours per unit

	Actual Costs Incurred (Actual Input × Actual Price) **(1)**	**Actual Input × Budgeted Price** **(2)**	**Flexible Budget (Budgeted Input Allowed for Actual Output × Budgeted Price)** **(3)**
Direct Materials: Frames	(4,850 × 3.2 × $2.40) $37,248	(4,850 × 3.2 × $2.20) $34,144	(4,850 × 3.00 × $2.20) $32,010

‖ $3,104 U ‖ $2,134 U ‖
Price variance   Efficiency variance

Direct Materials: Lenses	(4,850 × 7.0 × $2.96) $100,492	(4,850 × 7.0 × $3.10) $105,245	(4,850 × 6.00 × $3.10) $90,210

‖ $4,753 F ‖ $15,035 U ‖
Price variance   Efficiency variance

Direct Manufacturing Labor	(4,850 × 1.35 × $14.80) $96,903	(4,850 × 1.35 × $15.00) $98,212.50	(4,850 × 1.20 × $15.00) $87,300

‖ $1,309.50 F ‖ $10,912.50 U ‖
Price variance   Efficiency variance

7-34 (Cont'd.)

Possible explanations for price variance of $4,753 F:
  (a) Astute negotiations in purchasing.
  (b) Lower quality lenses purchased at lower price.
  (c) Standards were set incorrectly.

Possible explanations for efficiency variance of $15,035 U:
  (a) Higher materials usage due to lower quality lenses purchased at lower price.
  (b) Lesser trained workers hired at lower rates result in higher materials usage.
  (c) Standards were set incorrectly.

7-36 (30 min.) **Level 2 variance analysis, solve for unknowns.**

1. Budgeted selling price $= \dfrac{\$4,800,000}{600,000} = \$\ 8.00$ per cap

   Actual selling price $= \dfrac{\$5,000,000}{500,000} = \$10.00$ per cap

2. Budgeted variable cost per unit $= \dfrac{\$1,800,000}{600,000} = \$3.00$ per unit

   Actual variable cost per unit $= \dfrac{\$1,400,000}{500,000} = \$2.80$ per unit

3, 4, 5 and 6.

	Actual Results (1)	Flexible-Budget Variances (2)=(1)−(3)	Flexible Budget (3)	Sales - Volume Variance (4)=(3)−(5)	Static Budget (5)
Units sold	500,000	0	500,000	100,000 U	600,000
Revenues (sales)	$5,000,000	$1,000,000 F	$4,000,000	$800,000 U	$4,800,000
Variable costs	1,400,000	100,000 F	1,500,000	300,000 F	1,800,000
Contribution margin	3,600,000	1,100,000 F	2,500,000	500,000 U	3,000,000
Fixed costs	1,150,000	150,000 U	1,000,000	0	1,000,000
Operating income	$2,450,000	$950,000 F	$1,500,000	$500,000 U	$2,000,000

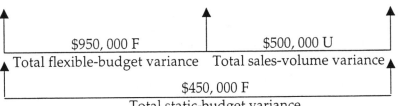

$950,000$ F $500,000$ U

Total flexible-budget variance   Total sales-volume variance

$450,000$ F

Total static-budget variance

Total flexible-budget variance = $950,000 F

Total sales-volume variance = $500,000 U

Total static-budget variance = $450,000 F

7-38   (60 min.)   **Comprehensive variance analysis review.**

1. **Actual Results:**

Units sold	1,200,000
Selling price per unit	$3.70
Revenues	$4,440,000
Direct materials purchased and used:	
Total direct materials cost	$960,000
Direct materials per unit	$0.80
Direct manufacturing labor:	
Total direct manufacturing labor costs	$72,000
Manufacturing labor-hours of input	4,800
Labor productivity per hour	250
Actual manufacturing rate per hour	$15
Direct marketing labor:	
Total direct marketing costs	$360,000
Direct marketing cost per unit	$0.30
Fixed costs	$870,000

Static Budgeted Amounts

Units sold	1,500,000
Selling price per unit	$4.00
Revenues	$6,000,000
Direct materials purchased and used:	
Direct materials per unit	$0.85
Total direct materials costs	$1,275,000
Direct manufacturing labor:	
Direct manufacturing rate per hour	$15.00
Labor productivity per hour	300
Manufacturing labor-hours of input	5,000
Total direct manufacturing labor cost	$75,000
Direct marketing labor	
Direct marketing cost per unit	$0.30
Total direct marketing cost	$450,000
Fixed costs	$900,000

7-38 (Cont'd)

2.

	Actual Results	Static-Budgeted Amount
Revenues	$4,440,000	$6,000,000
Variable costs		
Direct materials	960,000	1,275,000
Direct manufacturing labor	72,000	75,000
Direct marketing labor	360,000	450,000
Total variable costs	1,392,000	1,800,000
Contribution margin	3,048,000	4,200,000
Fixed costs	870,000	900,000
Operating income	$2,178,000	$3,300,000

Actual operating income	$2,178,000
Static-budget operating income	3,300,000
Total static-budget variance	$1,122,000 U

7-38 (Cont'd.)

3, 4, and 5.

	Actual Results	Flexible-Budget Variances	Flexible Budget	Sales-Volume Variances	Static Budget
Units sold	1,200,000	-	1,200,000	-	1,500,000
Revenues	$4,440,000	$360,000 U	$4,800,000	$1,200,000 U	$6,000,000
Variable costs					
Direct materials	960,000	60,000 F	1,020,000	255,000 F	1,275,000
Direct manuf. labor	72,000	12,000 U	60,000	15,000 F	75,000
Direct marketing labor	360,000	0	360,000	90,000 F	450,000
Total variable costs	1,392,000	48,000 F	1,440,000	360,000 F	1,800,000
Contribution margin	3,048,000	312,000 U	3,360,000	840,000 U	4,200,000
Fixed costs	870,000	30,000 F	900,000	0	900,000
Operating income	$2,178,000	$282,000 U	$2,460,000	$840,000 U	$3,300,000

$282,000 U
Total flexible-budget variance

$840,000 U
Total sales-volume variance

$1,122,000 U
Total static-budget variance

6.

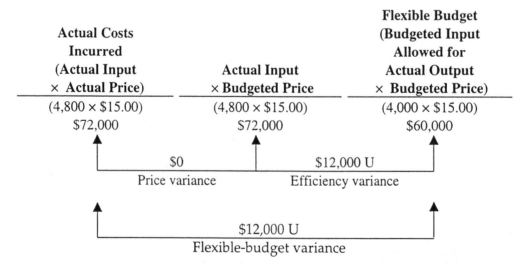

Actual Costs Incurred (Actual Input × Actual Price)	Actual Input × Budgeted Price	Flexible Budget (Budgeted Input Allowed for Actual Output × Budgeted Price)
(4,800 × $15.00)	(4,800 × $15.00)	(4,000 × $15.00)
$72,000	$72,000	$60,000

$0
Price variance

$12,000 U
Efficiency variance

$12,000 U
Flexible-budget variance

The unfavorable efficiency variance arises because of the decline in productivity from the budgeted 300 diskettes per hour to the actual 250 diskettes per hour.

7-40   (30 min.)   **Comprehensive variance analysis.**

1.   Computing unit selling prices and unit costs of inputs:
      Actual selling price   = $3,555,000 ÷ 450,000
                                   = $7.90
      Budgeting selling price   = $3,200,000 ÷ 400,000
                                   = $8.00
      Selling-price   = $\left(\begin{array}{c}\text{Actual} \\ \text{selling price}\end{array} - \begin{array}{c}\text{Budgeted} \\ \text{selling price}\end{array}\right) \times \begin{array}{c}\text{Actual} \\ \text{units sold}\end{array}$
          variance
                                  =   ($7.90 – $8.00) × 450,000
                                  = $45,000 U

2., 3. and 4.
      The actual and budgeted unit costs are:

	Actual	Budgeted
Direct materials		
Cookie mix	$0.02	$0.02
Milk chocolate	0.20	0.15
Almonds	0.50	0.50
Direct labor		
Mixing	14.40	14.40
Baking	18.00	18.00

The actual output achieved is 450,000 pounds of chocolate nut supreme.

7-40 (Cont'd.)

The direct cost price and efficiency variances are:

	Actual Costs Incurred (Actual Input × Actual Price) (1)	Price Variance (2)=(1)–(3)	Actual Input × Budgeted Prices (3)	Efficiency Variance (4)=(3)–(5)	Flex. Budget (Budgeted Input Allowed for Actual Output × Budgeted Price) (5)
Direct materials					
Cookie mix	$ 93,000	$ 0	$ 93,000[a]	$ 3,000 U	$ 90,000[h]
Milk chocolate	532,000	133,000 U	399,000[b]	61,500 U	337,500[i]
Almonds	240,000	0	240,000[c]	15,000 U	225,000[j]
	$865,000	$133,000 U	$732,000	$79,500 U	$652,500
Direct labor costs					
Mixing	$108,000	$ 0	$108,000[d]	$ 0	$108,000[k]
Baking	240,000	0	240,000[e]	30,000 F	270,000[l]
	$348,000	$ 0	$348,000	$30,000 F	$378,000

[a] $0.02 × 4,650,000 = $93,000

[b] $0.15 × 2,660,000 = $399,000

[c] $0.50 × 480,000 = $240,000

[d] $14.40 × (450,000 ÷ 60) = $108,000

[e] $18.00 × (800,000 ÷ 60) = $240,000

[h] $0.02 × 10 × 450,000 = $90,000

[i] $0.15 × 5 × 450,000 = $337,500

[j] $0.50 × 1 × 450,000 = $225,000

[k] $14.40 × (450,000 ÷ 60) = $108,000

[l] $18.00 × (450,000 ÷ 30) = $270,000

7-40 (Cont'd.)

Comments on the variances include:

- Selling price variance. This may arise from a proactive decision to reduce price to expand market share or from a reaction to a price reduction by a competitor. It could also arise from unplanned price discounting by salespeople.

- Material price variance. The $0.05 increase in the price per ounce of milk chocolate could arise from uncontrollable market factors or from poor contract negotiations by Aunt Molly's.

- Material efficiency variance. For all three material inputs, usage is greater than budgeted. Possible reasons include lower quality inputs, use of lower quality workers, and the mixing and baking equipment not being maintained in a fully operational mode.

- Labor efficiency variance. The favorable efficiency variance for baking could be due to workers eliminating non value-added steps in production.

7-42 (30 min.) **Activity-based costing, variance analysis.**

1. Budgeted batch size = 55
   Budgeted number of batches to produce 330,000 cakes
   $$= 330,000 \div 6,000 = 55 \text{ batches}$$
   Budgeted number of cleaning hours to produce 330,000 cakes
   $$= 55 \text{ batches} \times 20 \text{ hours} = 1,100 \text{ hours}$$

$$\begin{array}{c} \text{Flexible - budget} \\ \text{variance} \end{array} = \begin{array}{c} \text{Actual} \\ \text{costs} \end{array} - \begin{array}{c} \text{Flexible - budget} \\ \text{costs} \end{array}$$

$$= \left[\left(\frac{330,000}{10,000} \right) \times 24 \times \$21 \right] - (1,100 \times \$20)$$
$$= (33 \times 24 \times \$21) - (1,100 \times \$20)$$
$$= \$16,632 - \$22,000$$
$$= \$5,368 \text{ F}$$

2. $$\begin{array}{c} \text{Price} \\ \text{variance} \end{array} = \left(\begin{array}{c} \text{Actual price} \\ \text{of input} \end{array} - \begin{array}{c} \text{Budgeted price} \\ \text{of input} \end{array} \right) \times \begin{array}{c} \text{Actual quantity} \\ \text{of input} \end{array}$$

$$= (\$21 - \$20) \times (33 \times 24)$$
$$= \$792 \text{ U}$$

$$\begin{array}{c} \text{Efficiency} \\ \text{variance} \end{array} = \left(\begin{array}{c} \text{Actual} \\ \text{quantity of} \\ \text{input used} \end{array} - \begin{array}{c} \text{Budgeted quantity} \\ \text{of input allowed} \\ \text{for actual output} \end{array} \right) \times \begin{array}{c} \text{Budgeted} \\ \text{price} \\ \text{of input} \end{array}$$

$$= [(33 \times 24) - (55 \times 20)] \times \$20$$
$$= (792 - 1,100) \times \$20$$
$$= \$6,160 \text{ F}$$

The favorable flexible budget variance of $5,368 is comprised of two offsetting amounts:
• Price variance of $792 U due to the actual changeover labor cost of $21 per hour exceeding the $20 budgeted rate.
• Efficiency variance of $6,160 F due to the actual batch size (10,000) being sizably above the budgeted size (6,000), thus requiring less batches to produce 330,000 cakes.

7-42 (Cont'd.)

1. Explanations for the price variance of $792 U include:
    - More highly trained workers hired to make changeovers
    - Change in labor market requires unexpected increase in labor rates to retain workers
    - Budgeted amounts set without adequate analysis.

Explanations for the efficiency variance of $6,160 F include:
    - More highly trained workers are able to produce longer batch sizes
    - More automated machinery acquired
    - Budgeted amounts set without adequate analysis

7-44 (30 min.) **Price and efficiency variances, problems in standard setting, benchmarking.**

1. Budgeted materials input per shirt = 0.10 roll of cloth
    Budgeted manufacturing labor hours per shirt = 0.25 hours
    Budgeted materials cost = $50 per roll
    Budgeted manufacturing labor cost per hour = $18 per hour
    Actual output achieved = 4,488 shirts.

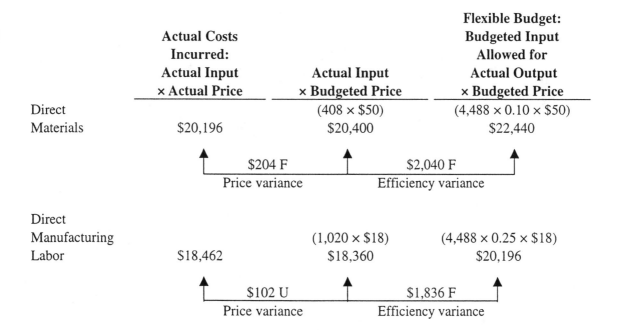

	Actual Costs Incurred: Actual Input × Actual Price	**Actual Input × Budgeted Price**	**Flexible Budget: Budgeted Input Allowed for Actual Output × Budgeted Price**
Direct Materials	$20,196	(408 × $50) $20,400	(4,488 × 0.10 × $50) $22,440
		↑ $204 F ↑	↑ $2,040 F ↑
		Price variance	Efficiency variance
Direct Manufacturing Labor	$18,462	(1,020 × $18) $18,360	(4,488 × 0.25 × $18) $20,196
		↑ $102 U ↑	↑ $1,836 F ↑
		Price variance	Efficiency variance

2.   Actions employees may have taken include:
(a)   Adding steps that are not necessary in working on a shirt.
(b)   Taking more time on each step than is necessary.
(c)   Creating problem situations so that the budgeted amount of average downtime will be overstated.
(d)   Creating defects in shirts so that the budgeted amount of average rework will be overstated.

7-44 (Cont'd.)

Employees may take these actions for several possible reasons.
(a)   They may be paid on a piece-rate basis with incentives for above-budgeted production.
(b)   They may want to create a relaxed work atmosphere, and less demanding standards can reduce stress.
(c)   They may have a "them vs. us" mentality rather than a partnership perspective.

This behavior is unethical if it is deliberately designed to undermine the credibility of the standards used at Winston Fabrics.

7-44 (Cont'd.)

3.   Savannah could use Benchmarking Clearing House information in several ways:

(a)   For pricing and product emphasis purposes. Savannah should avoid getting into a pricing war with a competitor who has a sizably lower cost structure.

(b)   As indicators of areas where Savannah is either highly cost-competitive or highly cost-noncompetitive.

(c)   As performance targets for motivating and evaluating managers.

4.   Main pros of Benchmarking Clearing House information:

(a)   Highlights to Savannah in a direct way how it may or may not be cost-competitive.

(b)   Provides a "reality check" to many internal positions about efficiency or effectiveness.

Main cons are:

(a)   Savannah may not be comparable to companies in the data base.

(b)   Data about other company's costs may not be reliable.

(c)   Cost of Benchmarking Clearing House reports.

CHAPTER 8
FLEXIBLE BUDGETS, VARIANCES,
AND MANAGEMENT CONTROL: II

8-2 At the start of an accounting period, a larger percentage of fixed overhead costs are locked-in than is the case with variable overhead costs.

8-4 Steps in developing a budgeted variable-overhead cost rate are:
1. Choose the time period used to compute the budget,
2. Select the cost-allocation bases to use in allocating variable overhead to the cost object(s),
3. Identify the variable overhead costs associated with each cost-allocation base, and
4. Compute the rate per unit of each cost-allocation base used to allocate variable overhead costs to the cost objects.

8-6 Reasons for a $25,000 favorable variable-overhead efficiency variance are:
- Workers more skillful in using machines than budgeted,
- Production scheduler was able to schedule jobs better than budgeted, resulting in lower-than-budgeted machine-hours,
- Machines operated with fewer slowdowns than budgeted, and
- Machine time standards set with padding built in by machine-workers.

8-8 Steps in developing a budgeted fixed-overhead rate are:
1. Choose the time period used to compute the budget,
2. Select the cost-allocation base to use in allocating fixed overhead costs to the cost object(s),
3. Identify the fixed-overhead costs associated with each cost-allocation base, and
4. Compute the rate per unit of each cost-allocation base used to allocate fixed overhead costs to the cost object(s).

8-10 An important caveat is what change in selling price might have been necessary to attain the level of sales assumed in the denominator of the fixed manufacturing overhead rate. For example, the entry of a new low-price competitor may have reduced demand below the denominator level if the budgeted selling price was maintained. An unfavorable production-volume variance may be small relative to the selling-price variance had prices been dropped to attain the denominator level of unit sales.

8-12 Fixed manufacturing costs represent resources sacrificed in acquiring capacity that cannot be decreased if the resources needed are less than the resources acquired. A lump-sum amount of fixed costs will be unaffected by the degree of operating efficiency in a given budget period.

8-14 For planning and control purposes, fixed overhead costs are a lump sum amount that is not controlled on a per-unit basis. In contrast, for inventory costing purposes, fixed overhead costs are allocated to products on a per-unit basis.

8-16 (20 min.)   **Variable manufacturing overhead, variance analysis.**

1.

Actual Costs Incurred (1)	Actual Inputs x Budgeted Rate (2)	Flexible Budget : Budgeted Input Allowed for Actual Output Achieved x Budgeted Rate (3)	Allocated: Budgeted Input Allowed for Actual Output x Budgeted Rate (4)
(4,536 x $11.50)	(4,536 x $12)	(4 x 1,080 x $12)	(4 x 1,080 x $12)
$52,164	$54,432	$51,840	$51,840

$2,268 F   Spending variance $2,592 U   Efficiency variance   Never a variance

$324 U   Flexible-budget variance   Never a variance

2. Esquire had a favorable spending variance of $2,268 because the actual variable overhead rate was $11.50 per direct manufacturing labor-hour versus $12 budgeted. It had an unfavorable efficiency variance of $2,592 U because each suit averaged 4.2 labor-hours versus 4.0 budgeted.

8-18 (30 min.)   **Variable manufacturing overhead variance analysis.**

1.   Denominator level=
   (3,200,000 x 0.02 hours) = 64,000 hours

	Actual Results	Flexible Budget Amount
1. Output units (baguettes)	2,800,000	2,800,000
2. Direct labor-hours	50,400	56,000[a]
3. Labor-hours per output unit (2 ÷ 1)	0.018	0.020
4. Variable MOH costs	$680,400	$560,000
5. Variable MOH per labor-hour (4 ÷ 2)	$13.50	$10
6. Variable MOH per output unit (4 ÷ 1)	$0.243	$0.200

8-18 (Cont.)

a. 2,800,000 x 0.020= 56,000 hours

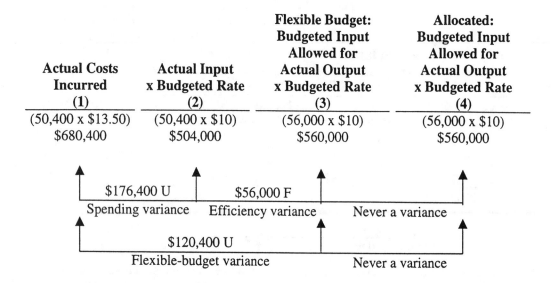

Actual Costs Incurred (1)	Actual Input x Budgeted Rate (2)	Flexible Budget: Budgeted Input Allowed for Actual Output x Budgeted Rate (3)	Allocated: Budgeted Input Allowed for Actual Output x Budgeted Rate (4)
(50,400 x $13.50) $680,400	(50,400 x $10) $504,000	(56,000 x $10) $560,000	(56,000 x $10) $560,000

$176,400 U — Spending variance
$56,000 F — Efficiency variance
Never a variance

$120,400 U — Flexible-budget variance
Never a variance

3. Spending variance of $176,400 U. It is unfavorable because variable manufacturing overhead was 35% higher than planned. A possible explanation could be an increase in energy rates relative to the rate per standard labor-hour assumed in the flexible budget.

Efficiency variance of $56,000 F. It is favorable because the actual number of direct manufacturing labor-hours required was lower than the number of hours budgeted. Labor was more efficient in producing the baguettes than management had anticipated in the budget. This could occur because of improved morale in the company, which could result from an increase in wages or an improvement in the compensation scheme.

Flexible-budget variance. It is unfavorable because the favorable efficiency variance was not large enough to compensate for the large unfavorable spending variance.

8-20 (30-40 min.) **Manufacturing overhead, variance analysis.**

1.   The summary analysis is:

	Spending Variance	Efficiency Variance	Production-Volume Variance
Variable Manufacturing Overhead	$40,700 F	$59,200 U	Never a variance
Fixed- Manufacturing Overhead	$23,420 U	Never a variance	$36,000 U

Variable Manufacturing Overhead

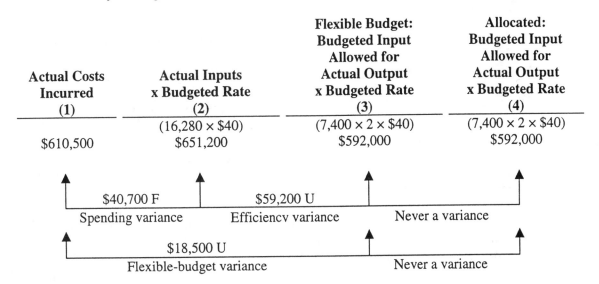

Actual Costs Incurred (1)	Actual Inputs x Budgeted Rate (2)	Flexible Budget: Budgeted Input Allowed for Actual Output x Budgeted Rate (3)	Allocated: Budgeted Input Allowed for Actual Output x Budgeted Rate (4)
	(16,280 × $40)	(7,400 × 2 × $40)	(7,400 × 2 × $40)
$610,500	$651,200	$592,000	$592,000

$40,700 F ——— Spending variance

$59,200 U ——— Efficiency variance

Never a variance

$18,500 U ——— Flexible-budget variance

Never a variance

Fixed-Manufacturing Overhead

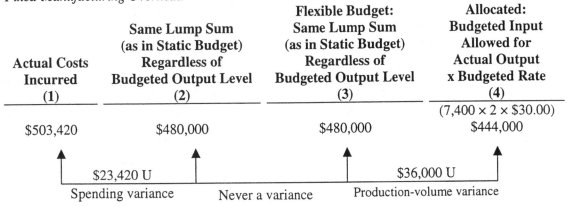

Actual Costs Incurred (1)	Same Lump Sum (as in Static Budget) Regardless of Budgeted Output Level (2)	Flexible Budget: Same Lump Sum (as in Static Budget) Regardless of Budgeted Output Level (3)	Allocated: Budgeted Input Allowed for Actual Output x Budgeted Rate (4)
			(7,400 × 2 × $30.00)
$503,420	$480,000	$480,000	$444,000

$23,420 U ——— Spending variance

Never a variance

$36,000 U ——— Production-volume variance

8-20 (Cont'd.)

Summary information is:

	Actual	Flexible Budget
Output units	7,400	7,400
Allocation base (hours)	16,280	14,800[a]
Allocation base per output unit	2.20	2.00
Variable MOH	$610,500	$592,000[b]
Variable MOH per hour	$37.50[c]	$40.00
Fixed MOH	$503,420	$480,000
Fixed MOH per hour	$30.92[d]	–

[a] 7,400 x 2.00 = 14,800   [c] $610,500 ÷ 16,280 hours = $37.50 per hour

[b] 7,400 x 2 x $40 = $592,000   [d] $503,420 ÷ 16,280 hours $\simeq$ $30.92 per hour

The budget fixed manufacturing overhead rate is $30.00 for assembly by hour:

$$\frac{\$480,000}{8,000 \times 2 \text{ hours}} = \$30.00 \text{ per assembly hour}$$

2. Zyton produces 600 less CardioX units than were budgeted. The variable manufacturing overhead cost efficiency variance of $59,200 U arises because more assembly-time-hours per output unit (16,280 ÷ 7,400 = 2.2 hours) were used than the budgeted 2.0 hours per unit. The variable manufacturing overhead cost spending variance of $40,700 F indicates one or more of the following probably occurred—(i) actual prices of individual items included in variable overhead differ from their budgeted prices, or (ii) actual usage of individual items included in variable overhead differs from their budgeted usage.

The fixed manufacturing overhead cost spending variance of $23,420 U means fixed overhead was above that budgeted. For example, it could be due to an unexpected increase in plant leasing costs. The unfavorable production-volume variance of $36,000 arises because actual output of 7,400 units is below the 8,000 units used in determining the $30.00 per assembly-hour budgeted rate.

3. Planning and control of *variable* manufacturing overhead costs has both a long-run and a short-run focus. It involves Zyton planning to undertake only value-added overhead activities (a long-run view) and then managing the cost drivers of those activities in the most efficient way (a short-run view). Planning and control of *fixed* manufacturing overhead costs at Zyton have primarily a long-run focus. It involves undertaking only value-added fixed-overhead activities for a budgeted level of output. Zyton makes most of the key decisions that determine the level of fixed-overhead costs at the start of the accounting period.

8-22 (20–25 min.) **Spending and efficiency overhead variances, distribution.**

1. Budgeted variable overhead rate   = \$2 per hour of delivery time

$$\text{Budgeted fixed overhead rate} = \frac{\$120,000}{100,000 \times 0.25} = \frac{\$120,000}{25,000}$$

= \$4.80 per hour of delivery time

A detailed comparison of actual and flexible budgeted amounts is:

	Actual	**Flexible Budget**
Output units (deliveries)	96,000	96,000
Allocation base (hours)	28,800	24,000[a]
Allocation base per output unit	0.30[b]	0.25
Variable MOH	\$60,000	\$48,000[c]
Variable MOH per hour	\$2.08[d]	\$2.00
Fixed MOH	\$128,400	\$120,000
Fixed MOH per hour	\$4.46[e]	–

[a] 96,000 x 0.25 = 24,000
[b] 28,800 ÷ 96,000 = 0.30
[c] 96,000 x 0.25 x \$2.00 = \$48,000
[d] \$60,000 ÷ 28,800 = \$2.08
[e] \$128,400 ÷ 28,800 = \$4.46

The required variances are:

	Spending Variance	**Efficiency Variance**
Variable overhead	\$2,400 U	\$ 9,600 U
Fixed overhead	\$8,400 U	—

These variances are computed as follows.

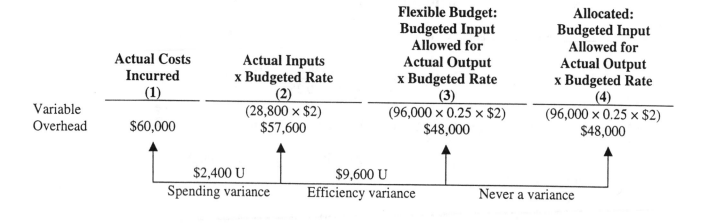

	Actual Costs Incurred (1)	Actual Inputs x Budgeted Rate (2)	Flexible Budget: Budgeted Input Allowed for Actual Output x Budgeted Rate (3)	Allocated: Budgeted Input Allowed for Actual Output x Budgeted Rate (4)
Variable Overhead	$60,000	(28,800 × $2) $57,600	(96,000 × 0.25 × $2) $48,000	(96,000 × 0.25 × $2) $48,000

$2,400 U ← Spending variance → $9,600 U ← Efficiency variance → Never a variance

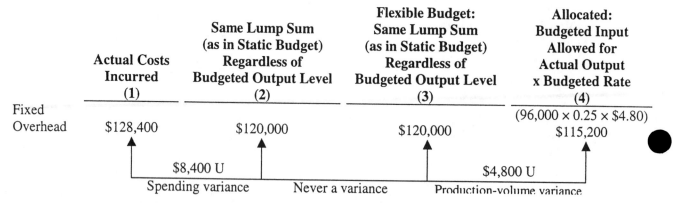

	Actual Costs Incurred (1)	Same Lump Sum (as in Static Budget) Regardless of Budgeted Output Level (2)	Flexible Budget: Same Lump Sum (as in Static Budget) Regardless of Budgeted Output Level (3)	Allocated: Budgeted Input Allowed for Actual Output x Budgeted Rate (4)
Fixed Overhead	$128,400	$120,000	$120,000	(96,000 × 0.25 × $4.80) $115,200

$8,400 U ← Spending variance → Never a variance → $4,800 U ← Production-volume variance

The spending variances for variable and fixed overhead are both unfavorable. This means that PPS had increases in either or both the cost of individual items (such as gasoline and truck maintenance) or higher-than-budgeted usage of these individual items per unit of the allocation base (delivery time). The unfavorable efficiency variance for variable overhead results from less efficient use of the cost allocation base—each delivery takes 0.30 hours versus a budgeted 0.25 hours.

2.   The single direct cost category is delivery driver payments. The major problem in managing these costs is to restrain the rate of increase in the rate paid to drivers per delivery. PPS faces the challenge of having a low-cost delivery infrastructure. For example, purchasing delivery trucks with low fuel consumption will help reduce variable overhead costs. Purchasing vehicles with low annual maintenance will help reduce fixed overhead costs. Variable overhead costs are controlled, well prior to their incurrence, by both cost planning and day-to-day decisions. In contrast, most fixed overhead cost items are controlled by planning decisions made prior to the start of the year.

8-24 (20-30 min.) Straightforward 4-variance overhead analysis.

1. The budget for fixed manufacturing overhead is 4,000 X 6 X $15 = $360,000.

An overview of the 4-variance analysis is:

4-Variance Analysis	Spending Variance	Efficiency Variance	Production-Volume Variance
Variable Manufacturing Overhead	$17,800 U	$16,000 U	Never a Variance
Fixed Manufacturing Overhead	$13,000 U	Never a Variance	$36,000 F

Solution Exhibit 8-24 has details of these variances.
A detailed comparison of actual and flexible budgeted amounts is:

	Actual	Flexible Budget
Output units (auto parts)	4,400	4,400
Allocation base (machine-hours)	28,400	26,400[a]
Allocation base per output unit	6.45[b]	6.00
Variable MOH	$245,000	$211,200[c]
Variable MOH per hour	$8.63[d]	$8.00
Fixed MOH	$373,000	$360,000[e]
Fixed MOH per hour	$13.13[f]	–

[a] 4,400 x 6.00 = 26,400
[b] 28,400 ÷ 4,400 = 6.45
[c] 4,400 x 6.00 x $8.00 = $211,200
[d] $245,000 ÷ 28,400 = $8.63
[e] 4,000 x 6.00 x $15 = $360,000
[f] $373,000 ÷ 28,400 = $13.13

8-24 (Cont'd.)

2.	Variable Manufacturing Overhead Control	245,000	
	Accounts Payable Control and other accounts		245,000
	Work-in-Process Control	211,200	
	Variable Manufacturing Overhead Allocated		211,200
	Fixed Manufacturing Overhead Control	373,000	
	Wages Payable Control, Accumulated Depreciation		
	Control, etc.		373,000
	Work-in-Process Control	396,000	
	Fixed Manufacturing Overhead Allocated		396,000

3.   The control of variable manufacturing overhead requires the identification of the cost drivers for such items as energy, supplies, and repairs. Control often entails monitoring nonfinancial measures that affect each cost item, one by one. Examples are kilowatts used, quantities of lubricants used, and repair parts and hours used. The most convincing way to discover why overhead performance did not agree with a budget is to investigate possible causes, line item by line item.

Individual fixed manufacturing overhead items are not usually affected very much by day-to-day control. Instead, they are controlled periodically through planning decisions and budgeting procedures that may sometimes have horizons covering six months or a year (for example, management salaries) and sometimes covering many years (for example, long-term leases and depreciation on plant and equipment).

SOLUTION EXHIBIT 8-24

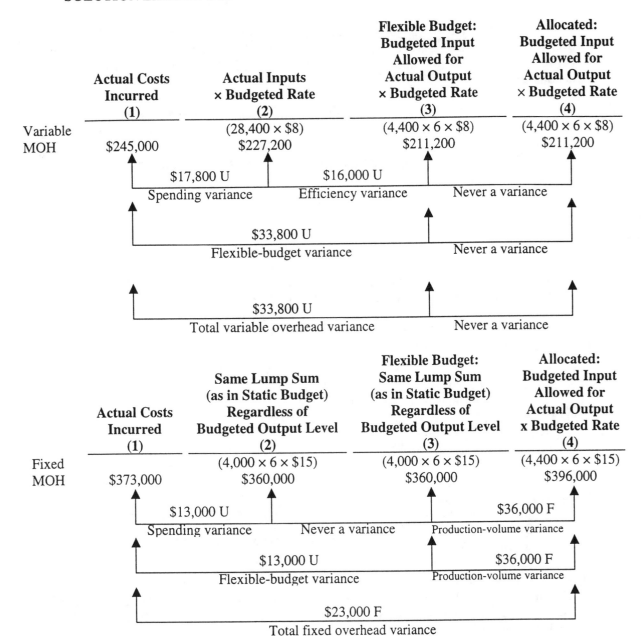

8-26 (35–50 min.) **Total overhead, 3-variance analysis.**

1. This problem has two major purposes: (a) to give experience with data allocated on a total overhead basis instead of on separate variable and fixed bases and (b) to reinforce distinctions between actual hours of input, budgeted (standard) hours allowed for actual output, and denominator level.

An analysis of direct manufacturing labor will provide the data for actual hours of input and standard hours allowed. One approach is to plug the known figures (designated by asterisks) into the analytical framework and solve for the unknowns. The direct manufacturing labor efficiency variance can be computed by subtracting $9,640 from $14,440. The complete picture is:

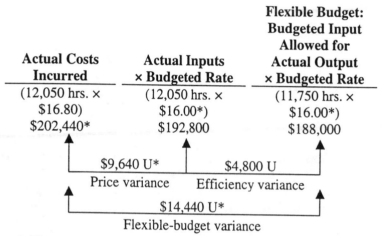

Actual Costs Incurred	Actual Inputs × Budgeted Rate	Flexible Budget: Budgeted Input Allowed for Actual Output × Budgeted Rate
(12,050 hrs. × $16.80)	(12,050 hrs. × $16.00*)	(11,750 hrs. × $16.00*)
$202,440*	$192,800	$188,000

$9,640 U* Price variance $4,800 U Efficiency variance

$14,440 U* Flexible-budget variance

* Given

Manufacturing Overhead

Variable overhead rate = $64,000* ÷ 8,000* hrs. = $8.00 per standard labor-hour

Budgeted fixed overhead costs = $197,600* − 10,000*($8.00) = $117,600

If total manufacturing overhead is allocated at 120% of direct standard manufacturing labor-hours, the single overhead rate must be 120% of $16.00, or $19.20 per hour. Therefore, the fixed overhead component of the rate must be $19.20 − $8.00, or $11.20 per direct standard manufacturing labor-hour.

Let D = denominator level in input units

$$\text{Budgeted fixed overhead rate per input unit} = \frac{\text{Budgeted fixed overhead costs}}{\text{Denominator level in input units}}$$

$$\$11.20 = \frac{\$117,600}{D}$$

$$D = 10,500 \text{ standard direct manufacturing labor-hours}$$

8-26 (Cont'd.)

A summary 3-variance analysis for October follows:

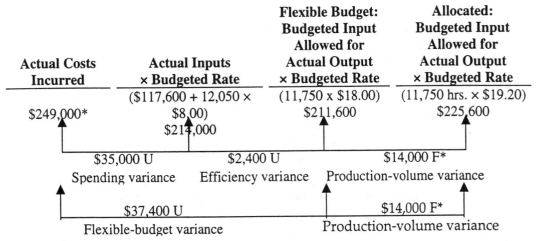

	Actual Costs Incurred	Actual Inputs × Budgeted Rate	Flexible Budget: Budgeted Input Allowed for Actual Output × Budgeted Rate	Allocated: Budgeted Input Allowed for Actual Output × Budgeted Rate
	$249,000*	($117,600 + 12,050 × $8.00) $214,000	(11,750 x $18.00) $211,600	(11,750 hrs. × $19.20) $225,600

$35,000 U — Spending variance

$2,400 U — Efficiency variance

$14,000 F* — Production-volume variance

$37,400 U — Flexible-budget variance

$14,000 F* — Production-volume variance

* Known figure

An overview of the 3-variance analysis using the block format in the text is:

3-Variance Analysis	Spending Variance	Efficiency Variance	Production–Volume Variance
Total Manufacturing Overhead	$35,000 U	$2,400 U	$14,000 F

2. The control of variable manufacturing overhead requires the identification of the cost drivers for such items as energy, supplies, equipment, and maintenance. Control often entails monitoring nonfinancial measures that affect each cost item, one by one. Examples are kilowatts used, quantities of lubricants used, and equipment parts and hours used. The most convincing way to discover why overhead performance did not agree with a budget is to investigate possible causes, line item by line item.

Individual fixed manufacturing overhead items are not usually affected very much by day-to-day control. Instead, they are controlled periodically through planning decisions and budgeting that may sometimes have horizons covering six months or a year (for example, management salaries) and sometimes covering many years (for example, long-term leases and depreciation on plant and equipment).

8-28 (40 min.) Flexible-budget variances, review of Chapters 7 and 8.

1. A summary of the variances for the four categories of cost is:

Flexible-Budget Variances

Direct materials	$32,640 U
Direct labor	2,112 U
Variable indirect	64 F
Fixed indirect	7,000 U

Price-Spending Variances		*Efficiency Variances*	
Direct materials	$17,280 U	Direct materials	$15,360 U
Direct labor	1,728 F	Direct labor	3,840 U
Variable indirect	5,184 F	Variable indirect	5,120 U
Fixed indirect	7,000 U	Fixed indirect	–

In addition, there is a production-volume variance of $6,000 F for fixed indirect costs.
Direct Cost Variances

The key items for computing the flexible-budget, price, and efficiency for direct cost items are:

	Actual Quantity of Inputs (1)	Actual Unit Cost of Inputs (2)	Actual Cost of Inputs (3) = (1) × (2)	Budgeted Unit Cost of Inputs (4)	Actual Inputs x Budgeted Cost per Inputs (5) = (1) × (4)
Direct materials	17,280,000 pages	$ 0.0130[b]	$224,640	$ 0.0120[d]	$207,360
Direct labor costs	1,728 hours[a]	$29.00[c]	$ 50,112	$30.00[e]	$ 51,840

[a] $17,280,000 ÷ 10,000 = 1,728 hours
[b] $224,640 ÷ 17,280,000 = $0.0130 per page
[c] $50,112 ÷ 1,728 = $29.00 per hour
[d] $180,000 ÷ 15,000,000 (300,000 copies x 50 pages) = $0.0120 per page
[e] $$45,000 ÷ 1,500(15,000,000 ÷ 10,000) = $30.00 per hour

8-28 (Cont'd.)

	Budgeted Inputs Allowed per Output Unit (1)	Actual Output Achieved (2)	Budgeted Unit Cost of Inputs (3)	Flexible Budget (4) = (1) x (2) x (3)
Direct materials	50	320,000	$ 0.0120	$192,000
Direct labor costs	.005[f]	320,000	$30.00	48,000

[f] Budgeted 10,000 pages produced per labor-hour yields budgeted output of 200 newspapers (50 pages each) per hour. Thus, each output unit is budgeted to require 0.005 units of a direct labor-hour.

The price and efficiency variances for direct materials and direct labor are:

	Actual Costs Incurred (Actual Input x Actual Price)	Price Variance	Actual Inputs x Budgeted Prices	Efficiency Variance	Flexible Budget: Budgeted Input Allowed for Actual Output x Budgeted Price
Direct materials	$224,640	$ 17,280 U	$207,360	$15,360 U	$192,000
Direct labor costs	50,112	1,728 F	51,840	3,840 U	48,000

Indirect Cost Variances

A summary of the information is:

	Actual	Flexible Budget
Output units (papers)	320,000	320,000
Allocation base (printed paper)	17,280,000	16,000,000[a]
Allocation base per output unit	54	50
Variable MOH	$63,936	$64,000[b]
Variable MOH per printed page	$0.0037	$0.0040
Fixed MOH	$97,000	$90,000
Fixed MOH per printed page	$0.0056[c]	–

[a] 320,000 x 50 = 16,000,000

[b] $320,000 x 50 x $0.0040 = $64,000

[c] $97,000 ÷ 17,280,000 = $0.0056 per printed page

8-28 (Cont'd.)

The spending and efficiency variances for variable indirect costs are:

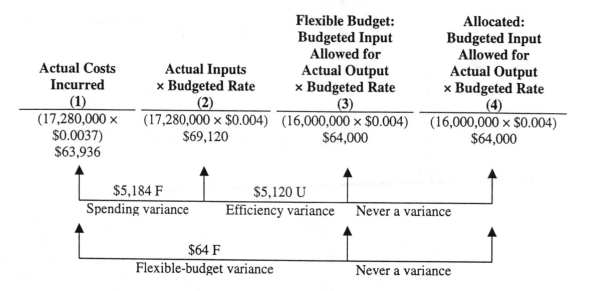

Actual Costs Incurred (1)	Actual Inputs × Budgeted Rate (2)	Flexible Budget: Budgeted Input Allowed for Actual Output × Budgeted Rate (3)	Allocated: Budgeted Input Allowed for Actual Output × Budgeted Rate (4)
(17,280,000 × $0.0037) $63,936	(17,280,000 × $0.004) $69,120	(16,000,000 × $0.004) $64,000	(16,000,000 × $0.004) $64,000

$5,184 F — Spending variance

$5,120 U — Efficiency variance

Never a variance

$64 F — Flexible-budget variance

Never a variance

The spending and production-volume variances for fixed indirect costs are:

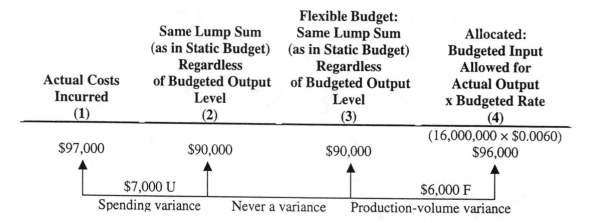

Actual Costs Incurred (1)	Same Lump Sum (as in Static Budget) Regardless of Budgeted Output Level (2)	Flexible Budget: Same Lump Sum (as in Static Budget) Regardless of Budgeted Output Level (3)	Allocated: Budgeted Input Allowed for Actual Output x Budgeted Rate (4)
$97,000	$90,000	$90,000	(16,000,000 × $0.0060) $96,000

$7,000 U — Spending variance

Never a variance

$6,000 F — Production-volume variance

8-28 (Cont'd.)

2.   The largest individual variance category is for direct materials—comprising a $17,280 U price variance (the actual cost per page of $0.013 exceeds the budgeted $0.012 per page) and a $15,360 U efficiency variance (the 1,280,000 unusable pages × $0.012 budgeted cost).

The direct labor price variance ($1,728 F) is due to the actual labor rate being $29.00 per hour compared to the budgeted $30.00 per hour.

The unfavorable variable indirect costs efficiency variance of $5,120 U is due to 1,280,000 extra pages being used (the cost allocation base) over that budgeted.

The spending variance for fixed indirect costs is due to actual costs being $7,000 above the budgeted $90,000. An analysis of the line items in this budget would help assist in determining the causes of this variance.

The production-volume variance of $6,000 F arises because the denominator used to allocate the $90,000 of fixed indirect costs is 17,280,000 printed pages rather than the 16,000,000 budgeted. This increase arose due to both an increase in the production run (320,000 newspapers vs. 300,000 budgeted) and an increase in the size per newspaper (54 pages vs. 50 pages budgeted).

8-30 (60 min.)   Journal entries (continuation of 8-29).

1. Key information underlying the computation of variances is:

	Actual Results	Flexible Budget Amount	Static-Budget Amount
1. Output units (panels)	19,200	19,200	17,760
2. Machine-hours	36,480	38,400	35,520
3. Machine-hours per panel	1.90	2.00	2.00
4. Variable MOH costs	$1,532,160	$1,536,000	$1,420,800
5. Variable MOH costs per machine-Hour (4/2)	$42.00	$40.00	$40.00
6. Variable MOH costs per unit (4/1)	$79.80	$80.00	$80.00
7. Fixed MOH costs	$7,004,160	$6,961,920	$6,961,920
8. Fixed MOH costs per machine-Hour (7/2)	$192.00	$181.30	$196.00
9. Fixed MOH costs per unit (7/1)	$364.80	$362.60	$392.00

Solution Exhibit 8-30 as the computation of the variances.

8-30 (Cont'd.)

1. **Journal entries for variable MOH, year ended December 31, 2000:**

Variable MOH Control	1,532,160	
Accounts Payable Control and Other Accounts		1,532,160
Work-in-Process Control	1,536,000	
Variable MOH Allocated		1,536,000
Variable MOH Allocated	1,536,000	
Variable MOH Spending Variance	72,960	
Variable MOH Control		1,532,160
Variable MOH Efficiency Variance		76,800

Journal entries for fixed MOH, year ended December 31, 2000:

Fixed MOH Control	7,004,160	
Wages Payable, Accumulated Depreciation, etc.		7,004,160
Work-in-Process Control	7,526,400	
Fixed MOH Allocated		7,526,400
Fixed MOH Allocated	7,526,400	
Fixed MOH Spending Variance	42,240	
Fixed MOH Control		7,004,160
Fixed MOH Production-Volume Variance		564,480

2. **Adjustment of COGS**

Cost of Goods Sold		526,080
Variable MOH Efficiency Variance	76,800	
Fixed MOH Production-Volume Variance	564,480	
Variable MOH Spending Variance		72,960
Fixed MOH Spending Variance		42,240

8-30 (Cont'd.)

SOLUTION EXHIBIT 8-30

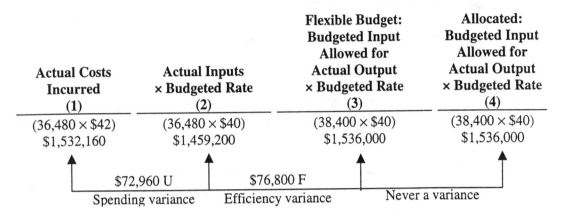

Actual Costs Incurred (1)	Actual Inputs × Budgeted Rate (2)	Flexible Budget: Budgeted Input Allowed for Actual Output × Budgeted Rate (3)	Allocated: Budgeted Input Allowed for Actual Output × Budgeted Rate (4)
(36,480 × $42) $1,532,160	(36,480 × $40) $1,459,200	(38,400 × $40) $1,536,000	(38,400 × $40) $1,536,000

$72,960 U — Spending variance $76,800 F — Efficiency variance   Never a variance

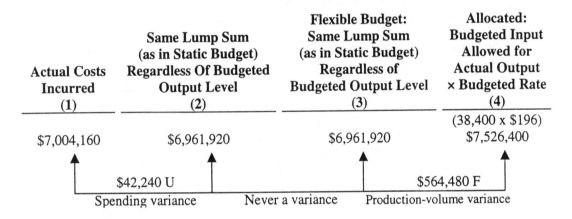

Actual Costs Incurred (1)	Same Lump Sum (as in Static Budget) Regardless Of Budgeted Output Level (2)	Flexible Budget: Same Lump Sum (as in Static Budget) Regardless of Budgeted Output Level (3)	Allocated: Budgeted Input Allowed for Actual Output × Budgeted Rate (4)
$7,004,160	$6,961,920	$6,961,920	(38,400 x $196) $7,526,400

$42,240 U — Spending variance   Never a variance $564,480 F — Production-volume variance

8-32 (20–30 min.) **Journal entries (continuation of 8-31).**

a.	Variable Manufacturing Overhead Control	36,100,000	
	Accounts Control Payable and other accounts		36,100,000
	Fixed Manufacturing Overhead Control	72,200,000	
	Wages Payable Control, Accumulated		
	Depreciation Control, etc.		72,200,000

(Note: Detailed postings of fixed overhead items such as salaries, property taxes, and insurance would be made to the department overhead records in the subsidiary ledger for Fixed Manufacturing Overhead Control.)

b.	Work-in-Process Control	31,500,000	
	Variable Manufacturing Overhead Allocated		31,500,000
	Work-in-Process Control	63,000,000	
	Fixed Manufacturing Overhead Allocated		63,000,000

c.

Variable Manufacturing Overhead Allocated	31,500,000	
Variable Manufacturing Overhead Spending Variance	1,900,000	
Variable Manufacturing Overhead Efficiency Variance	2,700,000	
Variable Manufacturing Overhead Control		36,100,000
Fixed Manufacturing Overhead Allocated	63,000,000	
Fixed Manufacturing Overhead Spending Variance	200,000	
Fixed Manufacturing Prodn.-Volume Overhead Variance	9,000,000	
Fixed Manufacturing Overhead Control		72,200,000
Cost of Goods Sold	4,600,000	
Variable Manufacturing Overhead Efficiency Variance		2,700,000
Variable Manufacturing Overhead Spending Variance		1,900,000
Cost of Goods Sold	9,200,000	
Fixed Manuf. Overhead Spending Variance		200,000
Fixed Manuf. Prodn.-Volume Overhead Variance		9,000,000

Of course, rather than being closed directly to Cost of Goods Sold, in certain cases the overhead variances may be prorated at year end.

8-34 (15–25 min.)   **Flexible budgets, 4-variance analysis.**

1.
$$\text{Budgeted hours allowed per unit of output} = \frac{\text{Budgeted DLH}}{\text{Budgeted actual output}}$$
$$= \frac{3,600,000}{720,000} = 5 \text{ hours}$$

Budgeted DLH allowed for May output = 66,000 units × 5 = 330,000
Allocated total MOH = 330,000 × Total MOH rate per hour
= 330,000 x $1.20 = $396,000

2, 3, 4, 5. See Solution Exhibit 8-34

Variable overhead rate per DLH = $0.25 + $0.34 = $0.59
Fixed overhead rate per DLH = $0.18 + $0.15 + $0.28 = $0.61
Fixed overhead budget for May = ($648,000 + $540,000 + $1,008,000)
÷ 12
= $2,196,000 ÷ 12 = $183,000

Using the format of Exhibit 8-3 (p. 263 in text) for variable overhead and then fixed overhead:

Actual variable overhead: $75,000 + $111,000 = $186,000
Actual fixed overhead: $51,000 + $54,000 + $84,000 = $189,000

An overview of the 4-variance analysis using the block format of the text is:

4-Variance Analysis	Spending Variance	Efficiency Variance	Production-Volume Variance
Variable Manufacturing Overhead	$150 U	$8,850 F	Never a variance
Fixed Manufacturing Overhead	$6,000 U	Never a variance	$18,300 F

8–34 (Cont'd.)

SOLUTION EXHIBIT 8-34

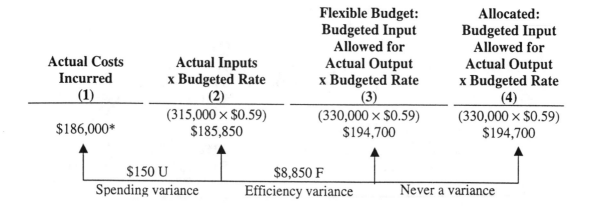

	Actual Costs Incurred (1)	Actual Inputs x Budgeted Rate (2)	Flexible Budget: Budgeted Input Allowed for Actual Output x Budgeted Rate (3)	Allocated: Budgeted Input Allowed for Actual Output x Budgeted Rate (4)
	$186,000*	(315,000 × $0.59) $185,850	(330,000 × $0.59) $194,700	(330,000 × $0.59) $194,700

$150 U — Spending variance $8,850 F — Efficiency variance Never a variance

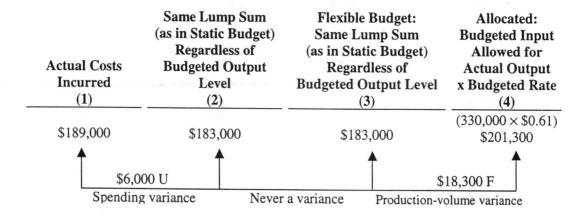

	Actual Costs Incurred (1)	Same Lump Sum (as in Static Budget) Regardless of Budgeted Output Level (2)	Flexible Budget: Same Lump Sum (as in Static Budget) Regardless of Budgeted Output Level (3)	Allocated: Budgeted Input Allowed for Actual Output x Budgeted Rate (4)
	$189,000	$183,000	$183,000	(330,000 × $0.61) $201,300

$6,000 U — Spending variance   Never a variance $18,300 F — Production-volume variance

Alternate computation of the production volume variance:

$$= \left[\left(\begin{array}{c} \text{Budgeted hours} \\ \text{allowed for actual} \\ \text{output achieved} \end{array} \right) - \left(\begin{array}{c} \text{Denominator} \\ \text{hours} \end{array} \right) \right] \times \left[\begin{array}{c} \text{Budgeted} \\ \text{fixed} \\ \text{overhead} \\ \text{rate} \end{array} \right]$$

$$= \left[(330,000) - \left(\frac{3,600,000}{12} \right) \right] \times \$0.61$$

$$= (330,000 - 300,000) \times \$0.61 = \$18,300 \text{ F}$$

8-36 (40 min.)   **Activity-based costing, variance analysis.**

	Static-Budget Amounts	Actual Amounts
1. Units of TGC produced and sold	30,000	22,500
2. Batch size	250	225
3. Number of batches (1 ÷ 2)	120	100
4. Setup-hours per batch	5	5.25
5. Total setup-hours (3 x 4)	600	525
6. Variable overhead cost per setup-hour	$25	$24
7. Variable setup overhead costs (5 x 6)	$15,000	$12,600
8. Total fixed setup overhead costs	$18,000	$17,535
9. Fixed overhead cost per setup-hour (8 ÷ 5)	$30	$33.40

The flexible-budget is based on the budgeted number of setups for the actual output achieved:

$$22,500 \div 250 = 90 \text{ batches}$$

Computation of variable setup overhead cost variances follows:

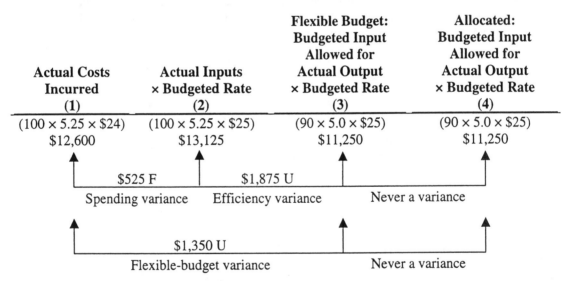

The favorable variance is due to the actual variable overhead cost per setup-hour declining from the budgeted $25 per hour to the actual rate of $24 per hour. The unfavorable efficiency variance is due to the actual output of 22,500 units requiring more setups (100) than the budgeted amount (90) and each setup taking longer time (5.25 hours) than the budgeted time (5.0 hours). The flexible-budget variance of $1,350 U reflects the larger unfavorable efficiency variance not being offset by the favorable spending variance.

8–36 (Cont'd.)

2. Computation of the fixed setup overhead cost variances follows:

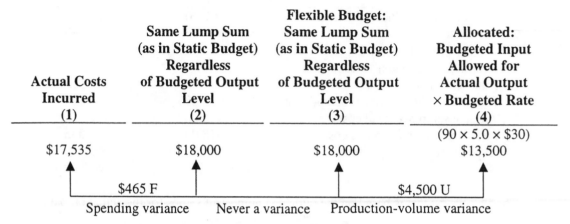

Actual Costs Incurred (1)	Same Lump Sum (as in Static Budget) Regardless of Budgeted Output Level (2)	Flexible Budget: Same Lump Sum (as in Static Budget) Regardless of Budgeted Output Level (3)	Allocated: Budgeted Input Allowed for Actual Output × Budgeted Rate (4)
			$(90 \times 5.0 \times \$30)$
$17,535	$18,000	$18,000	$13,500

$465 F — Spending variance   Never a variance $4,500 U — Production-volume variance

The fixed setup overhead cost spending variance is $465 F because the actual costs were lower than the budgeted $18,000. For example, the plant insurance costs allocated to the setup area may be lower due to the insurance company unexpectedly reducing its premiums. The production-volume variance is $4,500 U because the reduction in units of TGC produced and sold is budgeted to require a lower number of batches.

8-38 (30–40 min.) **Comprehensive review of Chapters 7 and 8, working backward from given variances.**

1. Solution Exhibit 8-38 outlines the Chapter 7 and 8 framework underlying this solution.
   (a) $176,000 ÷ $1.10 = 160,000 pounds
   (b) $69,000 ÷ $11.50 = 6,000 pounds
   (c) $10,350 – $18,000 = $7,650 F
   (d) Standard direct manufacturing labor rate

   = $800,000 ÷ 40,000 hours
   = $20 per hour

   Actual direct manufacturing labor rate = $20 + $0.50 = $20.50
   Actual direct manufacturing labor hours = $522,750 ÷ $20.50
   = 25,500 hours

   (e) Standard variable manufacturing overhead rate = $480,000 ÷ 40,000
   = $12 per direct manufacturing labor-hour

   Variable manufacturing overhead efficiency
   variance of $18,000 ÷ $12 = 1,500 excess hours
   Actual hours – Excess hours = Standard hours allowed
   25,500 – 1,500 = 24,000 hours

   (f) Budgeted fixed manufacturing overhead rate = $640,000 ÷ 40,000 hours
   = $16 per direct manufacturing labor-hour

   Fixed manufacturing overhead allocated = $16 x 24,000 hours
   = $384,000

   Production-volume variance = $640,000 – $384,000
   = $256,000 U

2. The control of variable manufacturing overhead requires the identification of the cost drivers for such items as energy, supplies, and repairs. Control often entails monitoring nonfinancial measures that affect each cost item, one by one. Examples are kilowatts used, quantities of lubricants used, and repair parts and hours used. The most convincing way to discover why overhead performance did not agree with a budget is to investigate possible causes, line item by line item.

Individual fixed overhead items are not usually affected very much by day-to-day control. Instead, they are controlled periodically through planning decisions and budgeting procedures that may sometimes have planning horizons covering six months or a year (for example, management salaries) and sometimes covering many years (for example, long-term leases and depreciation on plant and equipment).

8–38 (Cont'd)

SOLUTION EXHIBIT 8-38

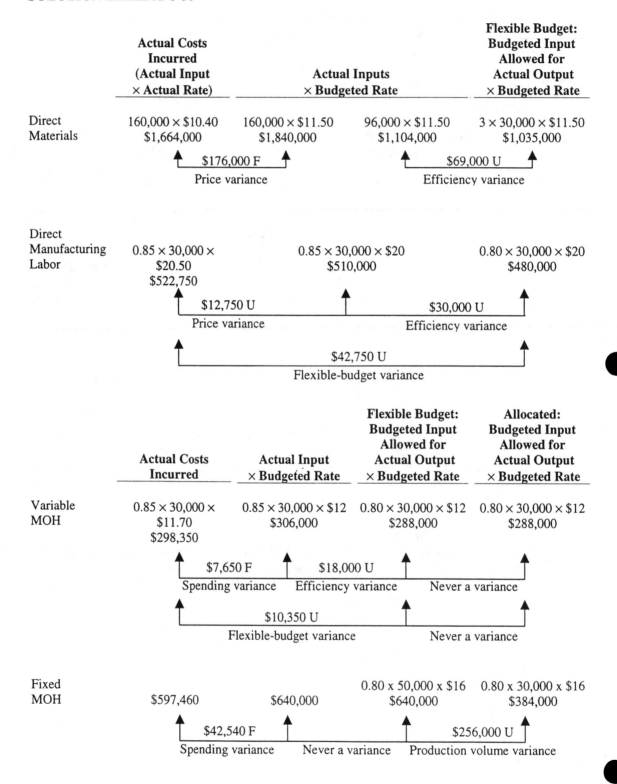

	Actual Costs Incurred (Actual Input × Actual Rate)	**Actual Inputs × Budgeted Rate**		**Flexible Budget: Budgeted Input Allowed for Actual Output × Budgeted Rate**
Direct Materials	160,000 × $10.40 $1,664,000	160,000 × $11.50 $1,840,000	96,000 × $11.50 $1,104,000	3 × 30,000 × $11.50 $1,035,000

$176,000 F Price variance $69,000 U Efficiency variance

| Direct Manufacturing Labor | 0.85 × 30,000 × $20.50 $522,750 | 0.85 × 30,000 × $20 $510,000 | | 0.80 × 30,000 × $20 $480,000 |

$12,750 U Price variance $30,000 U Efficiency variance

$42,750 U Flexible-budget variance

	Actual Costs Incurred	**Actual Input × Budgeted Rate**	**Flexible Budget: Budgeted Input Allowed for Actual Output × Budgeted Rate**	**Allocated: Budgeted Input Allowed for Actual Output × Budgeted Rate**
Variable MOH	0.85 × 30,000 × $11.70 $298,350	0.85 × 30,000 × $12 $306,000	0.80 × 30,000 × $12 $288,000	0.80 × 30,000 × $12 $288,000

$7,650 F Spending variance $18,000 U Efficiency variance   Never a variance

$10,350 U Flexible-budget variance   Never a variance

| Fixed MOH | $597,460 | $640,000 | 0.80 x 50,000 x $16 $640,000 | 0.80 x 30,000 x $16 $384,000 |

$42,540 F Spending variance   Never a variance $256,000 U Production volume variance

8-40 (30 min.) **Hospital overhead variances, 4-variance analysis, ethics.**

1. Solution Exhibit 8-40 shows the summary results:
* denotes given.

a.   Favorable VOH efficiency   = (Budgeted hours allowed − Actual hours) × \$10

$$\$2,000^* = (1,800\ ^*-\ A)\ \$10^*$$
$$\$2,000 = \$18,000 - \$10A$$
$$\$10A = \$16,000$$
$$A = 1,600$$

b.   Budgeted total MOH = Budgeted fixed MOH + Budgeted variable MOH

$$\$22,500^* = \text{B.F. MOH} + (1,800^* \times \$10^*)$$
$$\text{Budgeted fixed MOH} = \$4,500$$

c.   Answer (b) + \$900, or:

Fixed MOH overhead allocated = Budgeted fixed MOH +
                                        Favorable production-volume variance
$$= \$4,500 + \$900^*$$
$$= \$5,400$$

d.   Answer (c) ÷ 1,800 hours = Fixed MOH rate

$$\$5,400 \div 1,800^* = \$3.00$$

e.   Favorable production-volume variance $= \left(\begin{array}{ccc}\text{Budgeted} & & \text{Denominator}\\ \text{hours} & - & \text{level}\\ \text{allowed} & & \text{hours}\end{array}\right) \times \left(\begin{array}{c}\text{Budgeted}\\ \text{fixed}\\ \text{MOH}\\ \text{rate}\end{array}\right)$

$$\$900^* = (1,800^* - D)\ \$3$$
$$\$900 = \$5,400 - \$3D$$
$$-\$4,500 = -\$3D$$
$$D = 1,500 \text{ hours}$$

Alternatively,

$$\text{Budgeted Fixed MOH Rate} = \frac{\text{Budgeted Fixed MOH}}{\text{Denominator level}}$$
$$\$3.00 = \frac{\$4,500}{D}$$
$$D = 1,500 \text{ hours}$$

8-40 (Cont'd.)

SOLUTION EXHIBIT 8-40

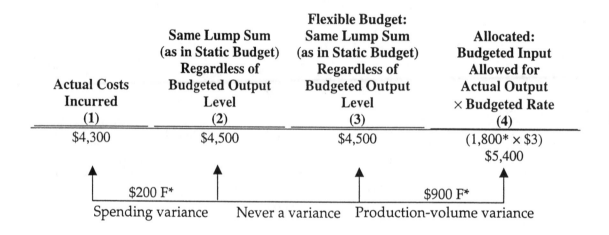

Actual Costs Incurred (1)	Actual Input x Budgeted Rate (2)	Flexible Budget: Budgeted Input Allowed for Actual Output × Budgeted Rate (3)	Allocated: Budgeted Input Allowed for Actual Output × Budgeted Rate (4)
(1,600 × $11.25)	(1,600 × $10*)	(1,800* × $10*)	(1,800* × $10*)
$18,000	$16,000	$18,000	$18,000

$2,000 U* $2,000 F*
Spending variance   Efficiency variance   Never a variance

Actual Costs Incurred (1)	Same Lump Sum (as in Static Budget) Regardless of Budgeted Output Level (2)	Flexible Budget: Same Lump Sum (as in Static Budget) Regardless of Budgeted Output Level (3)	Allocated: Budgeted Input Allowed for Actual Output × Budgeted Rate (4)
$4,300	$4,500	$4,500	(1,800* × $3)
			$5,400

$200 F* $900 F*
Spending variance   Never a variance   Production-volume variance

2. a. Padding of standard costs and standard amounts for a billing operation can arise from:

(i) Deliberately taking longer time to process the bills when standards are being set.

(ii) Deliberately not taking advantage of information technology in the standard-setting period and then exploiting that technology later on.

(iii) Creating problems in billing for which solutions have already been worked out and using only those solutions in the non-standard-setting period.

(iv) Not purchasing items in the most economic way during the standard- setting period.
   Reasons for padding include:

(i) Individual performance evaluation—individuals wish to look "good" for bonuses, promotion, etc. purposes.

(ii) Department performance evaluation—departments wish to retain autonomy, which is more likely with favorable variances.

(iii) Defying authority and control systems—some individuals have an inherent opposition to "standards" and "controls"

b. Stone can operate at several levels:

(i) Best practice observation—MEG's report should be a catalyst to Sharon examining what other companies in the survey are doing and then using this best practice internally. MEG may be hired to facilitate field visits to other more efficient companies.

(ii) Operations—make flow charts of how billing occurs at Sharon, and eliminate all unnecessary steps.

(iii) Incentive systems—provide economic and other incentives to Sharon employees to implement efficiency and effectiveness improvements. The emphasis here should be on accuracy and timeliness of billing as well as the cost of billing.

(iv) Corporate culture—Sharon should emphasize that "padding" and the deliberate misrepresentation it entails is unacceptable. This could be done via in-house programs on ethics and culture or by making "examples" of those found deliberately undermining a culture of honesty and teamwork for Sharon.

CHAPTER 9
INVENTORY COSTING AND CAPACITY ANALYSIS

9-2 The term **direct costing** is a misnomer for variable costing for two reasons:
a. Variable costing does not include all direct costs as inventoriable costs. Only variable direct manufacturing costs are included. Any fixed direct manufacturing costs, and any direct nonmanufacturing costs, (either variable or fixed) are excluded from inventoriable costs.
b. Variable costing includes as inventoriable costs not only direct manufacturing costs but also some indirect costs (variable indirect manufacturing costs).

9-4 The main issue between variable costing and absorption costing is the proper timing of the release of fixed manufacturing costs as costs of the period:
    a. at the time of incurrence, or
    b. at the time the finished units to which the fixed overhead relates are sold.
Variable costing uses (a) and absorption costing uses (b).

9-6 Variable costing does not view fixed costs as unimportant or irrelevant, but it maintains that the distinction between behaviors of different costs is crucial for certain decisions. The planning and management of fixed costs is critical, irrespective of what inventory costing method is used.

9-8 (a) The factors that affect the breakeven point under variable costing are:

    1.   Fixed costs,
    2.   Unit contribution margin, and
    3.   Sales level in units.

(b) The factors that affect the breakeven point under absorption costing are:

    1.   Fixed costs,
    2.   Unit contribution margin,
    3.   Sales level in units,
    4.   Production level in units, and
    5.   Denominator level chosen to set the fixed manufacturing costs rate.

9-10 Approaches used to reduce the negative aspects associated with using absorption costing include:
a. Change the accounting system:
    • Adopt either variable or throughput costing, both of which reduce the incentives of managers to build for inventory.
    • Adopt an inventory holding charge for managers who tie up funds in inventory.
b. Extend the time period used to evaluate performance. By evaluating performance over a longer time period (say, 3 to 5 years), the incentive to take short-run actions that reduce long-term income is lessened.
c. Include nonfinancial as well as financial variables in the measures used to evaluate performance.

9-12 The *downward demand spiral* is the continuing reduction in demand that occurs when the prices of competitors are not met and demand drops, resulting in even higher unit costs and even more reluctance to meet the prices of competitors. Pricing decisions need to consider competitors and customers as well as costs.

9-14 For tax reporting in the U.S., the IRS requires companies to use the practical capacity concept. At year end, proration of any variances between inventories and cost of goods sold is required (unless the variance is immaterial in amount).

9-16 (30 min.) Variable and absorption costing, explaining operating income differences.

1. Key inputs for income statement computations are:

	April	May
Beginning inventory	0	150
Production	500	400
Goods available for sale	500	550
Units sold	350	520
Ending inventory	150	30

The unit fixed and total manufacturing costs per unit under absorption costing are:

		April	May
(a)	Fixed manufacturing costs	$2,000,000	$2,000,000
(b)	Units produced	500	400
(c)=(a)÷(b)	Unit fixed manufacturing costs	$4,000	$5,000
(d)	Unit variable manufacturing costs	$10,000	$10,000
(e)=(c)+(d)	Unit total manufacturing costs	$14,000	$15,000

9-16 (Cont'd.)

(a) Variable costing

	April 19_7		May 19_7	
Revenues[a]		$8,400,000		$12,480,000
Variable costs				
Beginning inventory	$ 0		$1,500,000	
Variable cost of goods manufactured[b]	5,000,000		4,000,000	
Cost of goods available for sale	5,000,000		5,500,000	
Ending inventory[c]	1,500,000		300,000	
Variable manufacturing cost of goods sold	3,500,000		5,200,000	
Variable marketing costs	1,050,000		1,560,000	
Total variable costs		4,550,000		6,760,000
Contribution margin		3,850,000		5,720,000
Fixed costs				
Fixed manufacturing costs	2,000,000		2,000,000	
Fixed marketing costs	600,000		600,000	
Total fixed costs		2,600,000		2,600,000
Operating income		$1,250,000		$3,120,000

[a] $24,000 × 350; 520

[b] $10,000 × 500; 400

[c] $10,000 × 150; 30

9-16 (Cont'd.)

(b) Absorption costing

	April 19_7		May 19_7	
Revenues[a]		$8,400,000		$12,480,000
Cost of goods sold				
Beginning inventory	0		$2,100,000	
Variable manufacturing costs[b]	$5,000,000		4,000,000	
Fixed manufacturing costs[c]	2,000,000		2,000,000	
Cost of goods available for sale	7,000,000		8,100,000	
Ending inventory[d]	2,100,000		450,000	
Cost of goods sold		4,900,000		7,650,000
Gross margin		3,500,000		4,830,000
Marketing costs				
Variable marketing costs[e]	1,050,000		1,560,000	
Fixed marketing costs	600,000		600,000	
Total marketing costs		1,650,000		2,160,000
Operating income		$1,850,000		$ 2,670,000

[a] $24,000 × 350; 520

[b] $10,000 × 500; 400

[c] ($4,000 × 500); ($5,000 × 400)

[d] ($14,000 × 150; $15,000 × 30)

[e] ($3,000 × 350; $3,000 × 520)

9-16 (Cont'd.)

2. $\begin{pmatrix} \text{Absorption-Costing} \\ \text{operating income} \end{pmatrix} - \begin{pmatrix} \text{Variable-costing} \\ \text{operating income} \end{pmatrix} = \begin{pmatrix} \text{Fixed manufacturing} \\ \text{costs in} \\ \text{ending inventory} \end{pmatrix} - \begin{pmatrix} \text{Fixed manufacturing} \\ \text{costs in} \\ \text{beginning inventory} \end{pmatrix}$

April:

$$\begin{aligned} \$1,850,000 - \$1,250,000 &= (\$4,000 \times 150) - (\$0) \\ \$600,000 &= \$600,000 \end{aligned}$$

May:

$$\begin{aligned} \$2,670,000 - \$3,120,000 &= (\$5,000 \times 30) - (\$4,000 \times 150) \\ -\$450,000 &= \$150,000 - \$600,000 \\ -\$450,000 &= -\$450,000 \end{aligned}$$

The difference between absorption and variable costing is due solely to moving fixed manufacturing costs into inventories as inventories increase (as in April) and out of inventories as they decrease (as in May).

9-18 (40 min.) Variable and absorption costing, explaining operating income differences.

1. Key inputs for income statement computations are:

	January	February	March
Beginning inventory	0	300	300
Production	1,000	800	1,250
Goods available for sale	1,000	1,100	1,550
Units sold	700	800	1,500
Ending inventory	300	300	50

The unit fixed and total manufacturing costs per unit under absorption costing are:

		January	February	March
(a)	Fixed manufacturing costs	$400,000	$400,000	$400,000
(b)	Units produced	1,000	800	1,250
(c)=(a)÷(b)	Unit fixed manufacturing costs	$400	$500	$320
(d)	Unit variable manufacturing costs	$900	$900	$900
(e)=(c)+(d)	Unit total manufacturing costs	$1,300	$1,400	$1,220

9-18 (Cont'd.)

(a) Variable Costing

	January 19_8	February 19_8	March 19_8
Revenues[a]	$1,750,000	$2,000,000	$3,750,000
Variable costs			
Beginning inventory[b]	$ 0	$270,000	$ 270,000
Variable cost of goods manufactured[c]	900,000	720,000	1,125,000
Cost of goods available for sale	900,000	990,000	1,395,000
Ending inventory[d]	270,000	270,000	45,000
Variable manufacturing cost of goods sold	630,000	720,000	1,350,000
Variable marketing costs[e]	420,000	480,000	900,000
Total variable costs	1,050,000	1,200,000	2,250,000
Contribution margin	700,000	800,000	1,500,000
Fixed costs			
Fixed manufacturing costs	400,000	400,000	400,000
Fixed marketing costs	140,000	140,000	140,000
Total fixed costs	540,000	540,000	540,000
Operating income	$ 160,000	$ 260,000	$ 960,000

[a] $2,500 × 700; 800; 1,500
[b] $? × 0; $900 × 300; $900 × 300
[c] $900 × 1,000; 800; 1,250
[d] $900 × 300; 300; 50
[e] $600 × 700; 800; 1,500

9-18 (Cont'd.)

(b)   Absorption Costing

	January 19_8	February 19_8	March 19_8
Revenues[a]	$1,750,000	$2,000,000	$3,750,000
Cost of goods sold			
Beginning inventory[b]	$ 0	$ 390,000	$ 420,000
Variable manufacturing costs[c]:	900,000	720,000	1,125,000
Fixed manufacturing costs[d]:	400,000	400,000	400,000
Cost of goods available for sale	1,300,000	1,510,000	1,945,000
Ending inventory[e]	390,000	420,000	61,000
Cost of goods sold	910,000	1,090,000	1,884,000
Gross margin	840,000	910,000	1,866,000
Marketing costs			
Variable marketing costs[f]	420,000	480,000	900,000
Fixed marketing costs	140,000	140,000	140,000
Total marketing costs	560,000	620,000	1,040,000
Operating income	$ 280,000	$ 290,000	$ 826,000

[a] $2,500 × 700; 800; 1,500
[b] ($?× 0; $1,300 × 300; $1,400 × 300)
[c] $900 × 1,000, 800, 1,250
[d] ($400 × 1,000); ($500 × 800); ($320 × 1,250)
[e] ($1,300 × 300); ($1,400 × 300); ($1,220 × 50)
[f] $600 × 700; 800; 1,500

9-8

9-18 (Cont'd.)

2. $$\begin{pmatrix} \text{Absorption-costing} \\ \text{operating income} \end{pmatrix} - \begin{pmatrix} \text{Variable costing} \\ \text{operating income} \end{pmatrix} = \begin{pmatrix} \text{Fixed manufacturing} \\ \text{costs in} \\ \text{ending inventory} \end{pmatrix} - \begin{pmatrix} \text{Fixed manufacturing} \\ \text{costs in} \\ \text{beginning inventory} \end{pmatrix}$$

January:
$$\$280,000 - \$160,000 \; = \; \$120,000 - \$0$$
$$\$120,000 \; = \; \$120,000$$

February:
$$\$290,000 - \$260,000 \; = \; \$150,000 - \$120,000$$
$$\$30,000 \; = \; \$30,000$$

March:
$$\$826,000 - \$960,000 \; = \; \$16,000 - \$150,000$$
$$-\$134,000 \; = \; -\$134,000$$

The difference between absorption and variable costing is due solely to moving fixed manufacturing costs into inventories as inventories increase (as in January) and out of inventories as they decrease (as in March).

9-20 (40 min) **Variable vs. absorption costing.**

1.

Beginning inventory, January 1, 2001	85,000 units
Ending inventory, December 31, 2001	34,500 units
Sales	345,400 units
Selling price (to distributor)	$22.00 per unit
Variable manufacturing cost per unit	$5.10
Variable marketing cost per unit sold	$1.10 per unit sold
Fixed manufacturing overhead	$1,440,000
Denominator level machine hours	6,000 machine hours
Standard production rate	50 units per machine-hour
Fixed marketing and SG&A costs	$1,080,000

Income Statement for the Zwatch Company, Variable Costing
for the year ended December, 31, 2001

Revenues: $22 × 345,400		$7,598,800
Variable costs		
Beginning inventory: $5.10 × 85,000	$ 433,500	
Variable manufacturing costs: $5.10 × 294,900	1,503,990	
Cost of good available for sale	1,937,490	
Ending inventory: $5.10 × 34,500	175,950	
Variable cost of goods sold	1,761,540	
Variable marketing and SG&A costs: $1.10 × 345,400	379,940	
Total variable costs (at standard costs)	2,141,480	
Adjustment for variances	0	
Total variable costs		2,141,480
Contribution Margin		5,457,320
Fixed Costs		
Fixed manufacturing overhead costs	1,440,000	
Fixed marketing and SG&A costs	1,080,000	
Adjustment for variances	0	
Total fixed costs		2,520,000
Operating income		$2,937,320

9-20 (Cont'd.)

Absorption Costing Data

Fixed manufacturing overhead allocation rate =
Fixed manufacturing overhead/Denominator level machine hours =
$1,440,000/6,000 = $240 per machine hour

Fixed manufacturing overhead allocation rate per unit =
Fixed manufacturing overhead allocation rate/standard production rate =
$240/50 = $4.80 per unit

Income Statement for the Zwatch Company, Absorption Costing
For the year ended December 31, 2001

Revenues: $22 × 345,400		$7,598,800
Cost of goods sold		
Beginning inventory ($5.10 + $4.80) × 85,000	$ 841,500	
Variable manuf. costs: $5.10 × 294,900	1,503,990	
Fixed manuf. costs: $4.80 × 294,900	1,415,520	
Cost of goods available for sale	$3,761,010	
Ending inventory: ($5.10 + $4.80) × 34,500	341,550	
Adjust for manuf. variances ($4.80 × 5,100)[a]	24,480	
Cost of goods sold		3,443,940
Gross margin		4,154,860
Operating costs		
Variable marketing costs: $1.10 × 345,400	$ 379,940	
Fixed marketing costs	1,080,000	
Adjust for operating cost variances	0	
Total operating costs		1,459,940
Operating income		$2,694,920

[a] Production volume variance
$$= [(6{,}000 \text{ hours} \times 50) - 294{,}900] \times \$4.80$$
$$= (300{,}000 - 294{,}900) \times \$4.80$$
$$= \$24{,}480$$

2. Zwatch's pre-tax profit margins –

Under variable costing:

Revenues	$7,598,800
Operating income	2,937,32
Pre-tax profit margin	38.7%

Under absorption costing:

Revenues	$7,598,800
Operating income	2,694,92
Pre-tax profit margin	35.5%

9-20 (Cont'd.)

3. Operating income using variable costing is about nine percent higher than operating income calculated using absorption costing.

Variable costing operating income – Absorption costing operating income =
$$\$2,937,320 - \$2,694,920 = \$242,400$$

Fixed manufacturing costs in beginning inventory under absorption costing –
Fixed manufacturing costs in ending inventory under absorption costing =
$$(\$4.80 \times 85,000) - (\$4.80 \times 34,500) = \$242,400$$

4. The factors the CFO should consider include:
    (a) Effect on managerial behavior, and
    (b) Effect on external users of financial statements.

Absorption costing has many critics. However, the dysfunctional aspects associated with absorption costing can be reduced by:

- Careful budgeting and inventory planning,
- Adding a capital charge to reduce the incentives to build up inventory, and
- Monitoring nonfinancial performance measures.

9-22 (40 min) Absorption vs. variable costing.

1. The number of Mimic™ pills sold in 2001 is:
44,800 × 365 × 3 = 49,056,000 pills

Ending inventory on December 31, 2000 is 5,694,000 pills:

Unit data

Beginning inventory	0
Production	54,750,000
Sales	49,056,000
Ending inventory	5,694,000

Variable cost data

Manufacturing costs per pill produced

Direct materials	$0.05
Direct manufacturing labor	0.04
Manufacturing overhead	0.11
Total variable manufacturing costs	$0.20

Fixed cost data

Manufacturing costs	$ 7,358,400
R&D	4,905,600
SG&A	19,622,400

Wholesale selling price per pill	$1.20
Fixed manufacturing costs allocation rate per pill	$0.15

2. Variable costing:

Revenues: $1.20 × 49,056,000		$58,867,200
Variable costs		
Beginning inventory	$ 0	
Variable manuf. cost: $0.20 × 54,750,000	10,950,000	
Cost of goods available for sale	10,950,000	
Ending inventory: $0.20 × 5,694,000	1,138,800	
Variable cost of goods sold	9,811,200	
Variable marketing costs: $0.07 × 49,056,000	3,433,920	
Adjust for variable-cost variance	0	
Total variable cost		13,245,120
Contribution margin		45,622,080
Fixed costs		
Fixed manufacturing costs	7,358,400	
Fixed R&D	4,905,600	
Fixed marketing	19,622,400	
Total fixed costs		31,886,400
Operating income		$13,735,680

Absorption costing:

9–22 (Cont'd.)

Absorption costing:

Revenues: $1.20 \times 49{,}056{,}000$		$58,867,200
Costs of goods sold		
Beginning inventory	$ 0	
Variable manuf. cost: $0.20 \times 54{,}750{,}000$	10,950,000	
Fixed manuf. costs: $0.15 \times 54{,}750{,}000$	8,212,500	
Cost of goods available for sale	19,162,500	
Ending inventory: $0.35 \times 5{,}694{,}000$	1,992,900	
Adjust for manuf. variances	854,100	
Cost of goods sold		16,315,500
Gross margin		42,551,700
Operating costs		
Variable marketing costs: $0.07 \times 49{,}056{,}000$	3,433,920	
Fixed R&D	4,905,600	
Fixed marketing	19,622,400	
Adjustment for operating cost variances	0	
Total operating costs		27,961,920
Operating income		$14,589,780

3. The difference of $854,100 is due to:

$$= \left(\begin{array}{c} \text{Fixed manufacturing} \\ \text{costs in ending inventory} \\ \text{under absorption costing} \end{array} \right) - \left(\begin{array}{c} \text{Fixed manufacturing} \\ \text{costs in beginning inventory} \\ \text{under absorption costing} \end{array} \right)$$

$= \quad (\$0.15 \times 5{,}694{,}000) \quad - \quad \$0$

$= \quad \$854{,}100$

9-24 (20-30 min.) **Comparison of actual-costing methods.**

The numbers are simplified to ease computations. This problem avoids standard costing and its complications.

1. Variable-costing income statements:

	2000		2001	
	Sales 1,000 units		Sales 1,200 units	
	Production 1,400 units		Production 1,000 units	
Revenues ($3 per unit)		$3,000		$3,600
Variable costs:				
Beginning inventory	$ 0		$ 200	
Variable cost of goods manufactured	700		500	
Cost of goods available for sale	700		700	
Ending inventory[a]	200		100	
Variable manuf. cost of goods sold	500		600	
Variable marketing and admin. costs	1,000		1,200	
Variable costs:		1,500		1,800
Contribution margin		1,500		1,800
Fixed costs				
Fixed manufacturing costs	700		700	
Fixed marketing and admin. costs	400		400	
Fixed costs		1,100		1,100
Operating income		$ 400		$ 700

[a] Unit inventoriable costs:
    Year 1: $700 ÷ 1,400 = $0.50 per unit
    Year 2: $500 ÷ 1,000 = $0.50 per unit

9-24 (Cont'd.)

2. Absorption-costing income statements:

	2000		2001	
	Sales 1,000 units		Sales 1,200 units	
	Production 1,400 units		Production 1,000 units	
Revenues ($3 per unit)		$3,000		$3,600
Cost of goods sold:				
Beginning inventory	$ 0		$ 400	
Variable manufacturing costs	700		500	
Fixed manufacturing costs[a]	700		700	
Cost of goods available for sale	1,400		1,600	
Ending inventory[b]	400		240	
Cost of goods sold		1,000		1,360
Gross margin		2,000		2,240
Marketing and administrative costs:				
Variable marketing and admin. costs	1,000		1,200	
Fixed marketing and admin. costs	400		400	
Marketing and admin. costs		1,400		1,600
Operating income		$ 600		$ 640

[a] Fixed manufacturing costs:
    Year 1: $700 ÷ 1,400 = $0.50 per unit
    Year 2: $700 ÷ 1,000 = $0.70 per unit

[b] Unit inventoriable costs:
    Year 1: $1,400 ÷ 1,400 = $1.00 per unit
    Year 2: $1,200 ÷ 1,000 = $1.20 per unit

3.

	2000	**2001**
Variable Costing:		
Operating income	$400	$700
Ending inventory	200	100
Absorption Costing:		
Operating income	$600	$640
Ending inventory	400	240
Fixed manuf. overhead		
• in beginning inventory	0	200
• in ending inventory	200	140

$$\begin{pmatrix} \text{Absorption} & \text{Variable} \\ \text{costing} & \text{costing} \\ \text{operating} & ^{-}\text{operating} \\ \text{income} & \text{income} \end{pmatrix} = \begin{pmatrix} \text{Fixed} & \text{Fixed} \\ \text{manuf. costs} & \text{manuf. costs} \\ \text{in ending} & ^{-}\text{in beginning} \\ \text{inventory} & \text{inventory} \end{pmatrix}$$

$$
\begin{aligned}
\text{Year 1: } \$600 - \$400 &= \$200 - \$0 \\
&= \$200 \\
\text{Year 2: } \$640 - \$700 &= \$140 - \$200 \\
&= -\$60
\end{aligned}
$$

The difference in reported operating income is due the amount of fixed manufacturing overhead in the beginning and ending inventories. In Year I, absorption costing has a higher operating income of $200 due to ending inventory having $200 more in fixed manufacturing overhead than does beginning inventory. In Year 2, variable costing has a higher operating income of $60 due to ending inventory having $60 less in fixed manufacturing overhead than does ending inventory.

4.   a. Absorption costing is more likely to lead to inventory build-ups than variable costing. Under absorption costing, operating income in a given accounting period is increased, because some fixed manufacturing costs are accounted for as an asset (inventory) instead of a cost of the current period.

    b.   Although variable costing will counteract undesirable inventory build-ups, other measures can be used without abandoning absorption costing. Examples include budget targets and nonfinancial measures of performance such as maintaining specific inventory levels, inventory turnovers, delivery schedules, and equipment maintenance schedules.

9-26 (30 min.)   **Variable and absorption costing and breakeven points.**

1. Production = Sales + Ending Inventory - Beginning Inventory
   = 242,400 + 24,800 − 32,600
   = 234,600

2. Breakeven point in cases:
   a. Variable Costing:

$$QT = \frac{\text{Total Fixed Costs} + \text{Target Operating Income}}{\text{Contribution Margin Per Unit}}$$

$$QT = \frac{(\$3,753,600 + \$6,568,800) + \$0}{\$94 - (\$16 + \$10 + \$6 + \$14 + \$2)}$$

$$QT = \frac{\$10,322,400}{\$46}$$

$$QT = 224,400 \text{ cases}$$

   b. Absorption costing:

$$QT = \frac{\begin{array}{c}\text{Total Fixed} \\ \text{Cost}\end{array} + \begin{array}{c}\text{Target} \\ \text{IO}\end{array} + \left[\begin{array}{c}\text{Fixed Manuf.} \\ \text{Cost Rate}\end{array} \times \left(\begin{array}{c}\text{Breakeven} \\ \text{Sales in Units}\end{array} - \begin{array}{c}\text{Units} \\ \text{Produced}\end{array}\right)\right]}{\text{Contribution Margin Per Unit}}$$

$$QT = \frac{\$10,322,400 + \left[\$16\,(QT - 234,600)\right]}{\$46}$$

$$QT = \frac{\$10,322,400 + 16\,QT - 3,753,600}{\$46}$$

$$QT = \frac{\$6,568,800 + 16\,QT}{\$46}$$

$$46\,QT - 16\,QT = \$6,568,800$$

$$30\,QT = \$6,568,800$$

$$QT = 218,960 \text{ cases.}$$

9–26 (Cont'd.)

3. If grape prices increase by 25%, the cost of grapes per case will increase from $16 in 2001 to $20 in 2002. This will decrease the unit contribution margin from $46 in 2001 to $42 in 2002.

   a. Variable Costing:

$$QT = \frac{\$10,322,400}{\$42}$$

$$= 245,772 \text{ cases}$$

   b. Absorption Costing:

$$QT = \frac{\$6,568,800 + \$16\,QT}{\$42}$$

$$\$42\,QT = \$6,568,800 + \$16\,QT$$

$$\$26\,QT = \$6,568,800$$

$$QT = 252,647 \text{ cases}$$

9-28 (10-20 min.) **Breakeven under absorption costing (continuation of Problem 9-27).**

1.   The unit contribution margin is $5 – $3 – $1 = $1. Total fixed costs ($540,000) divided by the unit contribution margin ($1.00) equals 540,000 units. Therefore, under variable costing 540,000 units must be <u>sold</u> to break even.

2.   If there are no changes in inventory levels, the breakeven point can be the same, 540,000 units, under both variable costing and absorption costing. However, as the preceding problem demonstrates, under absorption costing, the breakeven point is not unique; operating income is a function of both sales and production. Some fixed overhead is "held back" when inventories rise (10,000 units × $0.70 = $7,000), so operating income is positive even though sales are at the breakeven level as commonly conceived.

$$\text{Breakeven sales in units} = \frac{\left(\begin{array}{c}\text{Total fixed}\\\text{costs}\end{array}\right) + \left(\begin{array}{c}\text{Target}\\\text{operating}\\\text{income}\end{array}\right) + \left[\left(\begin{array}{c}\text{Fixed manuf.}\\\text{overhead}\\\text{rate}\end{array}\right) \times \left(\begin{array}{c}\text{Breakeven}\\\text{sales in}\\\text{units}\end{array} - \begin{array}{c}\text{Units}\\\text{produced}\end{array}\right)\right]}{\text{Unit contribution margin}}$$

Let N   = Breakeven sales in units

$$N = \frac{\$540,000 + \$0 + \$0.70(N - 550,000)}{\$1.00}$$

$$N = \frac{\$540,000 + \$0.70N - \$385,000}{\$1.00}$$

$0.30N   = $155,000

N   =   516,667 units (rounded)

Therefore, under absorption costing, when 550,000 units are produced, 516,667 units must be sold for the income statement to report zero operating income.

Proof of 2001 breakeven point:

Gross margin, 516,667 units × ($5.00 – $3.70)		$671,667
Output level MOH variance, as before	$ 35,000	
Marketing and administrative costs:		
Variable, 516,667 units × $1.00	516,667	
Fixed	120,000	671,667
Operating income		$ 0

9-28 (Cont'd.)

3.   If no units are sold, variable costing will show an operating loss equal to the fixed manufacturing costs, $420,000 in this instance. In contrast, the company would break even under absorption costing, although nothing was sold to customers. This is an extreme example of what has been called "selling fixed manufacturing overhead to inventory."

A final note: We find it helpful to place the following comparisons on the board, keyed to the three parts of this problem:

    1. Breakeven = f (sales)
    2. Breakeven = f (sales and production)
    3. Breakeven = f (0 units sold and 540,000 units produced), an extreme case

9-30 (30 min.) The Semi-Fixed Company in 2001 (continuation of Problem 9-29).

1.   a. Variable-Costing Income Statements (in thousands):

		2000	2001	Together
Revenues		$300	$300	$600
Variable cost of sales		70	70	140
Contribution margin		230	230	460
Fixed manufacturing costs	$140			
Fixed marketing and admin. costs	40	180	180	360
Operating income		$ 50	$ 50	$100

    b.

	Absorption Statements (in thousands)					
	Alternative 1			Alternative 2		
	2000	2001	Together	2000	2001	Together
Revenues	$300	$300	$600	$300	$300	$600
Beginning inventory	--	140	--	--	210	--
Manufacturing costs	280	--	280	420	--	420
Available for sales	280	140	280	420	210	420
Ending inventory	140	--	--	210	--	--
Cost of goods sold	140	140	280	210	210	420
Underallocated overhead	--	140	140	--	140	--
Overallocated overhead	--	--	--	(140)	--	--
Marketing & administrative costs	40	40	80	40	40	80
Total costs	180	320	500	110	390	500
Operating income (loss)	$120	$ (20)	$100	$190	$ (90)	$100

Alternative 1:   Rate for fixed manufacturing overhead allocation based on 20,000 units: $140,000 ÷ 20,000 = $7.00 per ton.

Alternative 2: Rate for fixed manufacturing overhead allocation based on 10,000 units: $140,000 ÷ 10,000 = $14.00 per ton.

9-30 (Cont'd.)

2.   The Semi-Fixed Company has a positive operating income because some of its costs were variable. They could be avoided when the plant shut down for the second year. Variable costs can be "stored" as measures of assets, while fixed costs cannot. When the Semi-Fixed Co. paid $70,000 for direct materials, direct manufacturing labor, and variable manufacturing overhead to produce 10,000 additional tons of fertilizer during the first year for sale in the second year, it saved that amount of cost in the second year.

3.

	Variable Costing	Absorption Costing	
		20,000 Unit Base*	10,000 Unit Base*
Inventory, end of 2000	$70,000	$140,000	$210,000
Inventory, end of 2001	0	0	0

*Fixed manufacturing overhead rate is $7.00 when denominator level is 20,000 units and is $14.00 when denominator level is 10,000 units.

4.   Reported operating income is affected by both production <u>and</u> sales under absorption costing. Hence, most managers would prefer absorption costing because their performance in any given reporting period, at least in the short run, is influenced by how much production is scheduled near the end of a reporting period.

9-32 (25-30 min.) **Alternative denominator-level concepts.**

1.

Denominator-Level Concept	Budgeted Fixed Manufacturing Overhead per Period	Budgeted Denominator Level	Budgeted Fixed Manufacturing Overhead Cost Rate
Theoretical capacity	$42,000,000	5,256,000	$ 7.99
Practical capacity	42,000,000	3,500,000	12.00
Normal utilization	42,000,000	2,800,000	15.00
Master-budget utilization			
(a) Jan.–June 2000			
(b) July–Dec. 2000	21,000,000	1,120,000	18.75
	21,000,000	1,680,000	12.50

The differences arise for several reasons:

a. The theoretical and practical capacity concepts emphasize supply factors, while normal utilization and master-budget utilization emphasize demand factors.

b.   The two separate six-month rates for the master-budget utilization concept differ because of seasonal differences in budgeted production.

2.   Theoretical capacity--based on the production of output at maximum efficiency for 100% of the time.

Practical capacity--reduces theoretical capacity for unavoidable operating interruptions such as scheduled maintenance time, shutdowns for holidays and other days, and so on.

For each of the three determinants of capacity in Lucky Larger's plant, practical capacity is less than theoretical capacity:

	Barrels Per Hour (1)	Working Hours Per Day (2)	Working Days Per Yea (3)	Capacity (4)=(1) × (2) × (3)
Theoretical capacity	600	24	365	= 5,256,000
Practical capacity	500	20	350	= 3,500,000

3.   The smaller the denominator, the higher the amount of overhead costs capitalized for inventory units. Thus, if the plant manager wishes to be able to "adjust" plant operating income by building inventory, master-budget utilization or possibly normal utilization would be preferred.

9-34 (60 min.)   **Downward demand spiral and profitability assessment.**

1.

			Total overhead costs	$4,326,408
			Total labor-hours	60,089
			Allocation rate per labor hour	$72.00

	Duda	Rock	Funky	Iotera, Inc.
Product characteristics				
Direct labor-hours per 10 units	1	6	10	
Total units produced	123,190	72,600	4,210	200,000
Total labor-hours spent	12,319	43,560	4,210	60,089
Product costs				
Direct materials per unit	$16.20	$ 89.80	$184.60	
Direct labor per unit @ 18.00 per hour	1.80	10.80	18.00	
Allocated overhead per units	7.20	43.20	72.00	
Total product costs	$25.20	$143.80	$274.60	
Average selling price	$39.80	$159.00	$320.00	
Gross margin per unit	14.60	15.20	45.40	
Total revenues	$4,902,962	$11,543,400	$1,347,200	$17,793,562
Total costs	3,104,388	10,439,880	1,156,066	14,700,334
Operating income	$1,798,574	$ 1,103,520	$ 191,134	$ 3,093,228
Gross-margin percentage	36.68%	9.56%	14.19%	17.38%

Iotera, Inc. will discontinue the Rock product as its gross margin percentage of 9.56% is below the 10% minimum. It will redirect the available capacity freed-up to produce more of the most profitable product in total dollar terms. Duda is the most profitable product. The revised production schedule would be 195,790 of Duda (123,190 + 72,600 units freedup) and 4,210 of Funky.

9-34 (Cont'd.)

2.

Total overhead costs	$4,326,408	
Total labor-hours	23,789	
Allocation rate per labor hour	$181.87	

	Duda	Funky	Iotera, Inc.
Product characteristics			
Direct labor-hours per 10 units	1	10	
Total units produced	195,790	4,210	200,000
Total labor-hours spent	19,579	4,210	23,789
Product costs			
Direct materials per unit	$16.200	$184.60	
Direct labor per unit	1.800	18.00	
Allocated overhead per units	18.187	181.87	
Total product costs	$36.187	$384.47	
Average selling price	S 43.50	$390.00	
Gross margin	S 7.313	$5.53	
Total revenues	$8.516,865	$1,641,900	$10,158,765
Total costs	7.085,053	1,618,619	8,703,672
Operating income	$1,431,812	$ 23,281	1,455,093
Gross-margin percentage	16.81%	1.42%	14.32%

Iotera will discontinue the Funky product.

9-34(Cont'd.)

3.a.

Total overhead costs	$4,326,408
Total labor-hours	20,000
Allocation rate per labor hour	$216.32

	Duda (and Iotera)
Product characteristics	
Direct labor-hours per 10 units	1
Total units produced	200,000
Total labor hours spent	20,000
Product costs	
Direct materials per unit	$16.200
Direct labor per unit @ 18.00 per hour	1.800
Allocated overhead per units	21.632
	$39.632
Average selling price	$43.500
gross margin per unit	3.868
Total revenues	$8,700,000
Total costs	7,926,400
Operating income	$ 773,600
Gross-margin percentage	8.89%

b. Iotera would now drop its only remaining product (Duda) as it does not meet the 10% minimum requirement:

c.

With 3 products (requirement 1)	$ 72.00
With 2 products (requirement 2)	181.87
With 1 product (requirement 3)	216.32

d.

	Duda	Rock	Funky	Iotera
With 3 products (req. 1)	36.68%	9.56%	14.19%	17.38%
With 2 products (req. 2)	16.81%		1.42%	14.32%
With 1 product (req. 3)	8.89%	–	–	8.89%

9-34 (Cont'd.)

4. The current 10% discontinuance benchmark is an overly mechanical rule. It is appropriate to consider other factors such as future growth potential and demand externalities across products (will the discontinuance of one product affect the demand for its other products?).

The product-costing system includes the allocation of the $4,326,408 fixed costs. These costs are unaffected by any product discontinuance decisions. For short-run pricing decisions, a contribution margin (as in variable costing) approach would provide more useful cost signals.

9-36 (20 min.) **Cost allocation, downward demand spiral.**

1.
$$\text{Budgeted fixed costs per meal} = \frac{\text{Budgeted fixed costs}}{\text{Budgeted denominator level}}$$

$$\$1.50 = \frac{\$4,380,000}{\text{Budgeted denominator level}}$$

$$\text{Budgeted denominator level} = \frac{\$4,380,000}{\$1.50}$$
$$= 2,920,000 \text{ meals}$$

WHM is using budgeted usage as its denominator level for calculating the budgeted fixed costs per meal in 2001.

2. Alternative denominator levels include:

a. Capacity available. The question notes that the facility can serve 3,650,000 meals a year. With this denominator level, there will be budgeted unused capacity, which could be recorded as a separate line in the cost report for the Santa Monica facility.

b. Budgeted usage of capacity. With the 2001 budgeted usage of 2,920,000 meals, the fixed costs charge is $1.50 per meal. The marketplace is signaling that WHM's own central food-catering facility is not providing value for the costs charged. If Jenkins decides to raise prices to recover fixed costs from a declining demand base, he will likely encounter the downward demand spiral:

9-36 (Cont'd.)

Budgeted Denominator (1)	Variable Cost per Meal (2)	Fixed Cost per Meal $4,380,000 ÷ (1) (3)	Total Cost per Meal (4)
3,650,000	$3.80	$1.20	$5.00
2,920,000	3.80	1.50	5.30
2,550,000	3.80	1.72	5.52
2,000,000	3.80	2.19	5.99

Jenkins might adopt a contribution margin approach, which means viewing the $3.80 variable cost as the only per-unit cost and the $4,380,000 as a fixed cost.

3. Chapter 12 outlines three factors managers should consider in pricing decisions:
   a. Customers. Jenkins is facing customers who are dissatisfied with both the cost and the quality of the meal service. Three of the 10 hospitals have already elected to use an outside canteen service.
   b. Competitors. For the three hospitals terminating use of the Santa Monica facility, at least one competitor is more cost-effective. The seven remaining hospitals likely will be very interested in how this competitor performs at the 3 hospitals.
   c. Costs. Jenkins should consider ways to reduce both the variable costs per meal and the fixed costs.

9-38 (60 min.) Absorption, variable, and throughput costing.

1.

(a) Unit fixed manufacturing overhead cost $= \dfrac{\$7,500,000}{3,000 \text{ vehicles} \times 20 \text{ standard hours}}$

$= \dfrac{\$7,500,000}{60,000}$

$= \$125$ per standard assembly hour or $2,500 per vehicle

(b)

Direct materials per unit	$6,000
Direct manufacturing labor per unit	1,800
Variable manufacturing overhead per unit	2,000
Fixed manufacturing overhead per unit	2,500
Total manufacturing cost per unit	$12,300

2. Amounts in thousands.

	Absorption Costing		
	January	**February**	**March**
Revenues	$32,000	$46,400	$51,200
Cost of goods sold			
Beginning inventory	0	14,760	8,610
Variable manufacturing costs	31,360	23,520	37,240
Fixed manufacturing costs	8,000	6,000	9,500
Cost of goods available for sale	39,360	44,280	55,350
Ending inventory	14,760	8,610	15,990
Cost of goods sold (at standard cost)	24,600	35,670	39,360
Adjustment for variances	500 F	1,500 U	2,000 F
Total cost of goods sold	24,100	37,170	37,360
Gross margin	7,900	9,230	13,840
Marketing costs	0	0	0
Operating income	$ 7,900	$ 9,230	$13,840
Inventory Details (Units)			
Beginning inventory	0	1,200	700
Production	3,200	2,400	3,800
Goods available for sale	3,200	3,600	4,500
Sales	2,000	2,900	3,200
Ending inventory	1,200	700	1,300
Inventory Details ($12,300 per unit)			
Beginning inventory ($12,300 per unit)	$ 0	$14,760	$ 8,610
Ending inventory ($1,000s)	$14,760	$ 8,610	$15,990

Computation of Bonus	January	February	March
Operating income	$7,900,000	$9,230,000	$13,840,000
× 0.5%	$ 39,500	$46,150	$ 69,200

9-38 (Cont'd.)

3. Amounts in thousands

	Variable Costing		
	January	February	March
Revenues	$32,000	$46,400	$51,200
Variable Costs			
Beginning inventory	0	11,760	6,860
Variable cost of goods manufactured	31,360	23,520	37,240
Cost of goods available for sale	31,360	35,280	44,100
Ending inventory	11,760	6,860	12,740
Variable manuf. COGS	19,600	28,420	31,360
Variable marketing costs	0	0	0
Variable costs (at standard cost)	19,600	28,420	31,360
Adjustment for variances	0	0	0
Total variable costs	19,600	28,420	31,360
Contribution margin	12,400	17,980	19,840
Fixed costs			
Fixed manuf. overhead costs	7,500	7,500	7,500
Fixed marketing costs	0	0	0
Fixed costs (at standard cost)	7,500	7,500	7,500
Adjustment for variances	0	0	0
Total fixed costs	7,500	7,500	7,500
Operating income	$ 4,900	$10,480	$12,340
Inventory details ($9,800 per unit)			
Beginning inventory (units)	0	1,200	700
Ending inventory (units)	1,200	700	1,300
Beginning inventory ($000s)	$0	$11,760	$ 6,860
Ending inventory ($000s)	$11,760	$ 6,860	$12,740

Computation of Bonus	January	February	March
Operating income	$4,900,000	$10,480,000	$12,340,000
× 0.5%	$ 24,500	$ 52,400	$ 61,700

4.

	January	February	March	Total
Absorption-Costing Bonus	$39,500	$46,150	$69,200	$154,850
Variable-Costing Bonus	24,500	52,400	61,700	138,600
Difference	$15,000	$ (6,250)	$ 7,500	$16,250

The difference between absorption and variable costing arises because of differences in production and sales:

	January	February	March	Total
Production	3,200	2,400	3,800	9,400
Sales	2,000	2,900	3,200	8,100
□ in Inventory	1,200	(500)	600	1,300

By building for inventory, Hart can capitalize $2,500 of fixed manufacturing overhead costs per unit. This will provide a bonus payment of $12.50 per unit, as operating income under absorption costing will exceed that under variable costing when production is greater than sales. Over the three-month period, the inventory buildup is 1,300 units giving a difference of $16,250 in bonus payments.

5.   Amounts in thousands

	Throughput Costing		
	January	February	March
Revenues	$32,000	$46,400	$51,200
Variable direct materials costs			
Beginning inventory	0	7,200	4,200
Direct materials in goods manufactured	19,200	14,400	22,800
Cost of goods available for sale	19,200	21,600	27,000
Ending inventory	7,200	4,200	7,800
Total variable direct materials costs	12,000	17,400	19,200
Throughput contribution	20,000	29,000	32,000
Other costs			
Manufacturing[a]	19,660	16,620	21,940
Marketing	0	0	0
Total other costs	19,660	16,620	21,940
Operating income	$ 340	$12,380	$10,060

[a] ($3,800 × 3,200) + $7,500,000
    ($3,800 × 2,400) + $7,500,000
    ($3,800 × 3,800) + $7,500,000

Computation of Bonus	January	February	March
Operating income	$340,000	$12,380,000	$10,060,000
× 0.5%	$ 1,700	$ 61,900	$ 50,300

A summary of the bonuses paid is:

	January	February	March	Total
Absorption Costing	$39,500	$46,150	$69,200	$154,850
Variable Costing	24,500	52,400	61,700	138,600
Throughput Costing	1,700	61,900	50,300	113,900

6. Alternative approaches include:
   (a) Careful budgeting and inventory planning,
   (b) Use an alternative income computation approach to absorption costing (such as variable costing or throughput costing),
   (c) Use a financial charge for inventory buildup,
   (d) Change the compensation package to have a longer-term focus using either an external variable (e.g., stock options) or an internal variable (e.g., five-year average income), and
   (e) Adopt non-financial performance targets—e.g., attaining but not exceeding present inventory levels.

CHAPTER 10
DETERMINING HOW COSTS BEHAVE

10-2   Three alternative linear cost functions are:
1. Variable cost function—a cost function in which total costs change in proportion to the changes in the level of activity in the relevant range.
2. Fixed cost function—a cost function in which total costs do not change with changes in the level of activity in the relevant range.
3. Mixed cost function—a cost function that has both variable and fixed elements. Total costs change but not in proportion to the changes in the level of activity in the relevant range.

10-4   No. High correlation merely indicates that the two variables move together in the data examined. It is essential to also consider economic plausibility before making inferences about cause and effect. Without any economic plausibility for a relationship, it is less likely that a high level of correlation observed in one set of data will be similarly found in other sets of data.

10-6   The conference method develops cost estimates on the basis of analysis and opinions gathered from various departments of an organization (purchasing, process engineering, manufacturing, employee relations, etc.). Advantages of the conference method include:
1. The speed with which cost estimates can be developed.
2. The pooling of knowledge from experts across functional areas.
3. The improved credibility of the cost function to all personnel.

10-8   The six steps are:
1. Choose the dependent variable (the variable to be predicted, which is some type of cost).
2. Identify the cost driver(s) (independent variables).
3. Collect data on the dependent variable and the cost driver(s).
4. Plot the data.
5. Estimate the cost function.
6. Evaluate the estimated cost function.

Step 3 typically is the most difficult for a cost analyst.

10-10   Criteria important when choosing among alternative cost functions are:
1. Economic plausibility.
2. Goodness of fit.
3. Slope of the regression line.

10-12 Frequently encountered problems when collecting cost data on variables included in a cost function are:

1. The time period used to measure the dependent variable is not properly matched with the time period used to measure the cost driver(s).
2. Fixed costs are allocated as if they are variable.
3. Data are either not available for all observations or are not uniformly reliable.
4. Extreme values of observations occur.
5. A homogeneous relationship between the individual cost items in the dependent variable and the cost driver(s) does not exist.
6. The relationship between cost and the cost driver is not stationary.
7. Inflation has occurred in a dependent variable, a cost driver, or both.

10-14 No. A cost driver is any factor whose change causes a change in the total cost of a related cost object. A cause-and-effect relationship underlies selection of a cost driver. Some users of regression analysis include numerous independent variables in a regression model in an attempt to maximize goodness of fit, irrespective of the economic plausibility of the independent variables included. Some of the independent variables included may not be cost drivers.

10-16 (10 min.) **Estimating a cost function**

1. Slope coefficient $= \dfrac{\text{Difference in costs}}{\text{Difference in machine-hours}}$

$= \dfrac{\$3,900 - \$3,000}{7,000 - 4,000}$

$= \dfrac{\$900}{3,000} = \$0.30$ per machine-hour

Constant $=$ Total cost $-$ (Slope coefficient $\times$ Quantity of cost driver)
$= \$3,900 - (\$0.30 \times 7,000) = \$1,800$
$= \$3,000 - (\$0.30 \times 4,000) = \$1,800$

The cost function based on the two observations is:

Maintenance costs $= \$1,800 + \$0.30$ (machine-hours)

2. The cost function in requirement 1 is an estimate of how costs behave within the relevant range, not at cost levels outside the relevant range. If there are no months with zero machine-hours represented in the maintenance account, data in that account cannot be used to estimate the fixed costs at the zero machine-hours level. Rather, the constant component of the cost function provides the best available starting point for a straight line that approximates how a cost behaves within the relevant range.

10-18 (20 min.) **Various cost-behavior patterns.**

1. K
2. B
3. G
4. J   Note that A is incorrect because, although the cost per pound eventually equals a constant at $9.20, the total dollars of cost increases linearly from that point onward.
5. I   The total costs will be the same regardless of the volume level.
6. L
7. F   This is a classic step-cost function.
8. K
9. C

10-20 (20 min.) **Account analysis method.**

1.
<table>
<tr><td colspan="2">Variable costs:</td></tr>
<tr><td>Car wash labor</td><td>$240,000</td></tr>
<tr><td>Soap, cloth, and supplies</td><td>32,000</td></tr>
<tr><td>Water</td><td>28,000</td></tr>
<tr><td>Power to move conveyor belt</td><td>72,000</td></tr>
<tr><td>Total variable costs</td><td>$372,000</td></tr>
<tr><td colspan="2"></td></tr>
<tr><td colspan="2">Fixed costs:</td></tr>
<tr><td>Depreciation</td><td>$ 64,000</td></tr>
<tr><td>Supervision</td><td>30,000</td></tr>
<tr><td>Cashier</td><td>16,000</td></tr>
<tr><td>Total fixed costs</td><td>$110,000</td></tr>
</table>

Costs are classified as variable because the total costs in these categories change in proportion to the number of cars washed in Lorenzo's operation. Costs are classified as fixed because the total costs in these categories do not vary with the number of cars washed.

2.   Variable costs per car $= \dfrac{\$372,000}{80,000} = \$4.65$ per car

Total costs estimated for 90,000 cars $= \$110,000 + (\$4.65 \times 90,000) = \$528,500$

3.   Average cost in 2001 $= \dfrac{\$372,000 + \$110,000}{80,000} = \dfrac{\$482,000}{80,000} = \$6.025$

Average cost in 2002 $= \dfrac{\$528,500}{90,000} = \$5.87$

10-20 (Cont'd.)

Some students may assume that power costs of running the continuously moving conveyor belt is a fixed cost. In this case, the variable costs in 2001 will be $300,000 and the fixed costs $182,000.

The variable costs per car in 2001 = $300,000 ÷ 80,000 cars = $3.75 per car

Total costs for 90,000 cars in 2002 = $182,000 + ($3.75 × 90,000) = $519,500

The average cost of washing a car in 2002 = $519,500 ÷ 90,000 = $5.77

10-22 (20 min.) Estimating a cost function, high-low method.

1. See Solution Exhibit 10-22. There is a positive relationship between the number of service reports (a cost driver) and the customer-service department costs. This relationship is economically plausible.

2.

	Number of Service Reports	Customer-Service Department Costs
Highest observation of cost driver	436	$21,890
Lowest observation of cost driver	122	12,941
Difference	314	$ 8,949

Customer-service department costs = $a + b$ (number of service reports)

$$\text{Slope coefficient } (b) \quad = \frac{\$8,949}{314} = \$28.50 \text{ per service report}$$

$$\text{Constant } (a) \quad = \$21,890 - \$28.50\,(436) = \$9,464$$
$$= \$12,941 - \$28.50\,(122) = \$9,464$$

Customer-service
department costs $= \$9,464 + \$28.50$ (number of service reports)

3. Other possible cost drivers of customer-service department costs are:
   a. Number of products replaced with a new product (and the dollar value of the new products charged to the customer-service department).
   b. Number of products repaired and the time and cost of repairs.

10-22 (Cont'd.)

SOLUTION EXHIBIT 10-22
Plot of Number of Service Reports versus Customer-Service Dept. Costs for Capitol Products

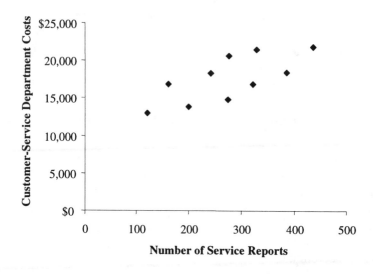

10-24 (20 min.) Cost-volume-profit and regression analysis.

1a. Average cost of manufacturing $= \dfrac{\text{Total manufacturing costs}}{\text{Number of bicycle frames}}$

$= \dfrac{\$900,000}{30,000} = \$30$ per frame

This cost is greater than the $28.50 per frame that Ryan has quoted.

1b. Garvin cannot take the average manufacturing cost in 1999 of $30 per frame and multiply it by 36,000 bicycle frames to determine the total cost of manufacturing 36,000 bicycle frames. The reason is that some of the $900,000 (or equivalently the $30 cost per frame) are fixed costs and some are variable costs. Without distinguishing fixed from variable costs, Garvin cannot determine the cost of manufacturing 36,000 frames. For example, if all costs are fixed, the manufacturing costs of 36,000 frames will continue to be $900,000. If, however, all costs are variable, the cost of manufacturing 36,000 frames would be $30 × 36,000 = $1,080,000. If some costs are fixed and some are variable, the cost of manufacturing 36,000 frames will be somewhere between $900,000 and $1,080,000.

10-24 (Cont'd.)

Some students could argue that another reason for not being able to determine the cost of manufacturing 36,000 bicycle frames is that not all costs are output unit-level costs. If some costs are, for example, batch-level costs, more information would be needed on the number of batches in which the 36,000 bicycle frames would be produced, in order to determine the cost of manufacturing 36,000 bicycle frames.

2. $\dfrac{\text{Expected cost to make}}{\text{36,000 bicycle frames}}$ $= \$432,000 + \$15 \times 36,000$

$\qquad\qquad\qquad\qquad\quad = \$432,000 + \$540,000 = \$972,000$

Purchasing bicycle frames from Ryan will cost $\$28.50 \times 36,000 = \$1,026,000$. Hence it will cost Garvin $\$1,026,000 - \$972,000 = \$54,000$ more to purchase the frames from Garvin rather than manufacture them in-house.

3.   Garvin would need to consider several factors before being confident that the equation in requirement 2 accurately predicts the cost of manufacturing bicycle frames.

   a.   Is the relationship between total manufacturing costs and quantity of bicycle frames economically plausible? For example, is the quantity of bicycles made the only cost driver or are there other cost-drivers (for example batch-level costs of setups, production-orders or material handling) that affect manufacturing costs?

   b.   How good is the goodness of fit? That is, how well does the estimated line fit the data?

   c.   Is the relationship between the number of bicycle frames produced and total manufacturing costs linear?

   d.   Does the slope of the regression line indicate that a strong relationship exists between manufacturing costs and the number of bicycle frames produced?

   e.   Are there any data problems such as, for example, errors in measuring costs, trends in prices of materials, labor or overheads that might affect variable or fixed costs over time, extreme values of observations, or a nonstationary relationship over time between total manufacturing costs and the quantity of bicycles produced?

10-26 (30–40 min.) **Regression analysis, activity-based costing, choosing cost drivers.**

1a.   Solution Exhibit 10-26A presents the plots and regression line of number of packaged units moved on distribution costs.

SOLUTION EXHIBIT 10-26A
Plots and Regression Line of Number of Packaged Units Moved on Distribution Costs

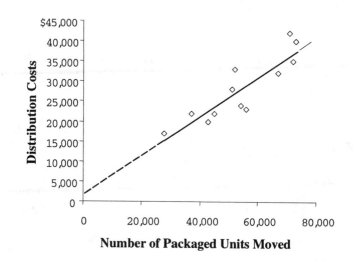

1b.   Solution Exhibit 10-26B presents the plots and regression line of number of shipments made on distribution costs.

SOLUTION EXHIBIT 10-26B
Plots and Regression Line of Number of Shipments Made on Distribution Costs

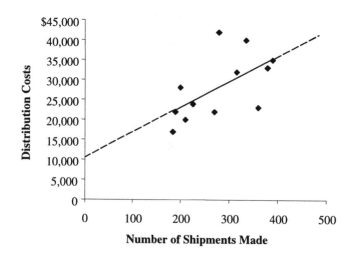

10-26 (Cont'd.)

Number of packaged units moved appears to be a better cost driver of distribution costs for the following reasons:

(i) *Economic plausibility.* Both number of packaged units moved and number of shipments are economically plausible cost drivers. Because the product is heavy, however, costs of freight are likely to be a sizable component of distribution costs. Thus, number of packaged units moved will affect distribution costs significantly because freight costs are largely a function of the number of units transported.

(ii) *Goodness of fit.* Compare Solution Exhibits 10-26A and 10-26B. Number of packaged units moved has a better goodness of fit with distribution costs than do number of shipments made. That is, the vertical differences between actual and predicted number of shipments made are smaller for the number of packaged units moved regression than for the number of shipments made regression.

(iii) *Slope of regression line.* Again, compare Solution Exhibits 10-26A and 10-26B. The number of packaged units moved regression line has a relatively steep slope indicating a strong relationship between number of packaged units moved and distribution costs. On average, distribution costs increase with the number of packaged units moved. The number of shipments made regression line is flatter and has more scatter of observations about the line indicating a weak relationship between number of shipments made and distribution costs. On average, the number of shipments made has a smaller effect on distribution costs.

2.   Using the preferred cost function,
Distribution costs = $1,349 + ($0.496 × Number of packaged units moved),
Flaherty would budget distribution costs of
          $1,349 + ($0.496 × 40,000) = $1,349 + 19,840 = $21,189

3.   Using the "other" cost function
          Distribution costs = $10,417 + ($63.77 × Number of shipments made),
                    Flaherty would budget distribution costs of
          $10,417 + ($63.77 × 220) = $10,417 + $14,029 = $24,446
The actual costs are likely to be lower than the prediction of $24,446 made using the number of shipments as the cost driver. The reason is that budgeted distribution costs are likely to be closer to the $21,189 predicted by the regression equation with number of packaged units moved as the cost driver. This regression equation provides a better explanation of the factors that affect distribution costs.

Choosing the "wrong" cost driver and estimating the incorrect cost function can have repercussions for pricing, cost management, and cost control. To the extent that Flaherty uses predicted costs of $24,446 for making pricing decisions, she may overprice the 40,000 packages she expects to move and could potentially lose business.

10-26 (Cont'd.)

To see the problems in cost management, suppose Saratoga moves 40,000 units in 220 shipments in the next month while incurring actual costs of $23,500. Compared to the budget of $24,446, management would consider this a good performance and seek ways to replicate it. In fact, on the basis of the preferred cost driver, the number of packaged units moved, actual distribution costs of $23,500 are higher than what they should be ($21,189)—a performance that management should seek to correct and improve rather than replicate.

10-28 (20 min.) Learning curve, incremental unit-time learning model.

1. The direct manufacturing labor-hours (DMLH) required to produce the first 2, 3, and 4 units, given the assumption of an incremental unit-time learning curve of 90%, is as follows:

Cumulative Number of Units (1)	Individual Unit Time for Xth Unit (2)	Cumulative Total Time (3)
1	3,000	3,000
2	2,700 (3,000 × 0.90)	5,700
3	2,539	8,239
4	2,430 (2,700 × 0.90)	10,669

Values in column 2 are calculated using the formula $y = pX^q$
where p = 3,000, X = 2, 3, or 4, and q = – 0.1520, which gives

when $X = 2$, $y = 3,000 \times 2^{-0.1520} = 2,700$

when $X = 3$, $y = 3,000 \times 3^{-0.1520} = 2,539$

when $X = 4$, $y = 3,000 \times 4^{-0.1520} = 2,430$

	Variable Costs of Producing		
	2 Units	3 Units	4 Units
Direct materials $80,000 × 2; 3; 4	$160,000	$240,000	$ 320,000
Direct manufacturing labor			
$25 × 5,700; 8,239; 10,669	142,500	205,975	266,725
Variable manufacturing overhead			
$15 × 5,700; 8,239; 10,669	85,500	123,585	160,035
Total variable costs	$388,000	$569,560	$746,760

2.

	Variable Costs of Producing	
	2 Units	4 Units
Incremental unit-time learning model (from requirement 1)	$388,000	$746,760
Cumulative average-time learning model (from Exercise 10-27)	376,000	708,800
Difference	$ 12,000	$ 37,960

10-28 (Cont'd.)

Total variable costs for manufacturing 2 and 4 units are lower under the cumulative average-time learning curve relative to the incremental unit-time learning curve. Direct manufacturing labor-hours required to make additional units decline more slowly in the incremental unit-time learning curve relative to the cumulative average-time learning curve assuming the same 90% factor is used for both curves. The reason is that, in the incremental unit-time learning curve, as the number of units double, only the last unit produced has a cost of 90% of the initial cost. In the cumulative average-time model, doubling the number of units causes the average cost of *all* the additional units produced (not just the last unit) to be 90% of the initial cost.

10-30   (30–40 min.)   High-low versus regression method.

1.   Solution Exhibit 10-30 presents the plots of advertising costs on revenues.

SOLUTION EXHIBIT 10-30
Plot and Regression Line of Advertising Costs on Revenues

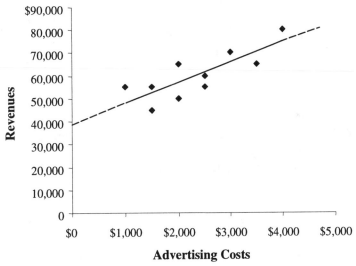

2.   Solution Exhibit 10-30 also shows the regression line of advertising costs on revenues. We evaluate the estimated regression equation using the criteria of economic plausibility, goodness of fit, and slope of the regression line.

Economic plausibility. Advertising costs appears to be a plausible cost driver of revenues. Restaurants frequently use newspaper advertising to promote their restaurants and increase their patronage.

Goodness of fit. The vertical differences between actual and predicted revenues appears to be reasonably small. This indicates that advertising costs are related to restaurant revenues.

Slope of regression line. The slope of the regression line appears to be relatively steep. This indicates that, on average, restaurant revenues increase with newspaper advertising.

10-30 (Cont'd.)

3. The high-low method would estimate the cost function as follows:

	Advertising Costs	Revenues
Highest observation of cost driver	$4,000	$80,000
Lowest observation of cost driver	1,000	55,000
Difference	$3,000	$25,000

$$\text{Revenues} = a + (b \times \text{advertising costs})$$

$$\text{Slope coefficient } (b) = \frac{\$25,000}{\$3,000} = 8.333$$

$$
\begin{aligned}
\text{Constant } (a) &= \$80,000 - (\$4,000 \times 8.333) \\
&= \$80,000 - 33,332 = \$46,668
\end{aligned}
$$

$$
\begin{aligned}
\text{or} \quad \text{Constant } (a) &= \$55,000 - (\$1,000 \times 8.333) \\
&= \$55,000 - 8,333 = \$46,667
\end{aligned}
$$

$$\text{Revenues} = \$46,667 + (8.333 \times \text{Advertising costs})$$

4. The increase in revenues for each $1,000 spent on advertising within the relevant range is
    a. Using the regression equation, $8.723 \times \$1,000 = \$8,723$
    b. Using the high-low equation, $8.333 \times \$1,000 = \$8,333$

5. The high-low equation does fairly well in estimating the relationship between advertising costs and revenues. However, Martinez and Brown should use the regression equation. The reason is that the regression equation uses information from all observations whereas the high-low method relies only on the observations that have the highest and lowest values of the cost driver. These observations are generally not representative of all the data.

10-32 (30–40 min.) **Cost estimation, cumulative average-time learning curve.**

1. Cost to Produce the Second through the Eighth Troop Deployment Boats:

Direct materials, 7 × $100,000	$ 700,000
Direct manufacturing labor, 39,130* × $30	1,173,900
Variable manufacturing overhead, 39,130 × $20	782,600
Other manufacturing overhead, 25% of $1,173,900	293,475
Total costs	$2,949,975

*The direct manufacturing labor-hours to produce the second to eighth boats can be calculated in several ways, given the assumption of a cumulative average-time learning curve of 85%:

a. Use of Table Format:

Cumulative Number of Units	Cumulative Average-Time per Unit	Cumulative Total Time
1	10,000.00	10,000
2	8,500.00 (10,000 × 0.85)	17,000
4	7,225.00 (8,500 × 0.85)	28,900
8	6,141.25 (7,225 × 0.85)	49,130

The direct labor-hours required to produce the second through the eighth boats is 49,130 – 10,000 = 39,130 hours.

b. Use of Formula:

$$y = pX^q$$

where p = 10,000, X = 8, and q = – 0.2345
$$y = 10,000 \times 8^{-0.2345} = 6,141 \text{ hours (rounded)}$$

The total direct labor-hours for 8 units is $6,141 \times 8$ = 49,128 hours

The direct labor-hours required to produce the second through the eighth boats is 49,128 – 10,000 = 39,128 hours. (By taking the q factor to 6 decimal digits, an estimate of 49,130 hours would result.)

Note: Some students will debate the exclusion of the tooling cost. The question specifies that the tooling "cost was assigned to the first boat." Although Nautilus may well seek to ensure its total revenue covers the $725,000 cost of the first boat, the concern in this question is only with the cost of producing seven more PT109s.

10-32 (Cont'd.)

2. Cost to Produce the Second through the Eighth Boats Assuming Linear Function for Direct Labor-Hours and Units Produced:

Direct materials, 7 × $100,000	$ 700,000
Direct manufacturing labor, 7 ×10,000 hours × $30	2,100,000
Variable manufacturing overhead, 7 × 10,000 hours × $20	1,400,000
Other manufacturing overhead, 25% of $2,100,000	525,000
Total costs	$4,725,000

The difference in predicted costs is:

Predicted cost in requirement 2	
(based on linear cost function)	$4,725,000
Predicted cost in requirement 1	
(based on an 85% learning curve)	2,949,975
Difference	$1,775,025

10-34 (30 min.) Promotion of a new product, simple and multiple regression analysis.

1. The t-value (value of the coefficient ÷ standard error of the coefficient) of the coefficients in each of the regressions follow. A t-value greater than 2 indicates that the coefficient is significantly different from zero.

Regression 1: t-value of coefficient of X_1 = $3.45 ÷ $0.78 = 4.42, indicating that there is a relation between direct manufacturing labor-hours and manufacturing overhead costs.

Regression 2: t-value of coefficient of X_2 = $0.12 ÷ $0.03 = 4.00, indicating that there is a relation between direct materials costs and manufacturing overhead costs.

Regression 3: t-value of coefficient of X_1 = $2.24 ÷ $1.65 = 1.36, indicating that there is no relation between direct manufacturing labor-hours and manufacturing overhead costs given direct materials costs; t-value of coefficient of X_2 = $0.05 ÷ $0.06 = 0.83, indicating that there is no relation between direct materials costs and manufacturing overhead costs given direct manufacturing labor-hours.

2. The t-value indicates that the coefficients in the simple regressions are statistically significant but that the coefficients of the same variables are insignificant in a multiple regression. The likely reason is multicollinearity. Because the two independent variables area correlated, the standard errors of the coefficients increase and make the variables to appear insignificant and difficult to interpret.

10-34 (Cont'd.)

3. Omitting a correlated variable (as the first two regressions do) causes the estimated coefficient of the independent variable to be biased away from its true value. Including both variables induces multicollinearity, which makes interpreting the significance of the coefficients difficult. To make predictions about manufacturing overhead costs, it is probably best to use both direct manufacturing labor-hours and direct materials costs despite the multicollinearity problems.

To understand the separate effects of direct manufacturing labor-hours and direct materials on manufacturing overhead costs, Moore would need to find months of data where either direct manufacturing labor or direct materials were high but not both. Such new data will not suffer from the problems of multicollinearity and will allow Moore to estimate the relationship between each cost driver and manufacturing overhead.

10-36 (30 min.) Evaluating multiple regression models, not for profit.

1. It is economically plausible that the correct form of the model of overhead costs includes both number of academic programs and number of enrolled students as cost drivers. The findings in Problem 10-35 indicate that each of the independent variables affects overhead costs. (Each regression has a significant r^2 and t-value on the independent variable.) Hanks could choose to divide overhead costs into two cost pools, (i) those overhead costs that are more closely related to number of academic program and (ii) those overhead costs more closely related to number of enrolled students, and rerun the simple regression analysis on each overhead cost pool. Alternatively, Hanks could run a multiple regression analysis with total overhead costs as the dependent variable and the number of academic programs and number of enrolled students as the two independent variables.

2. Solution Exhibit 10-36A evaluates the multiple regression model using the format of Exhibit 10-19. Hanks should use the multiple regression model over the two simple regression models of Problem 10-35. The multiple regression model appears economically plausible, and the regression model performs very well when estimating overhead costs. It has an excellent goodness of fit, significant t-values on both independent variables, and meets all the specification assumptions for ordinary least-squares regression.

There is some correlation between the two independent variables but multicollinearity does not appear to be a problem here. The significance of both independent variables (despite some correlation between them) suggests that each variable is a driver of overhead cost. Of course, as the chapter describes, even if the independent variables exhibited multicollinearity, Hanks should still prefer to use the multiple regression model over the simple regression models of Problem 10-35. Omitting any one of the variables will cause the estimated coefficient of the independent variable, included in the model, to be biased away from its true value.

3. Possible uses for the multiple regression results include:

   a. Planning and budgeting at Southwestern University. The regression analysis indicates the variables (number of academic programs and number of enrolled students) that help predict changes in overhead costs.

10-36 (Cont'd.)

    b.   Cost control and performance evaluation. Hanks could compare actual performance with budgeted or expected numbers and seek ways to improve the efficiency of the University operations, and evaluate the performance of managers responsible for controlling overhead costs.

    c.   Cost management. If cost pressures increase, the University might save costs by closing down academic programs that have few students enrolled.

SOLUTION EXHIBIT 10-36A

Evaluation of Cost Function for Overhead Costs Estimated with Multiple Regression for Southwestern University

Criterion	Number of Academic Programs and Number of Enrolled Students as Independent Variables
1. Economic Plausibility	A positive relationship between overhead costs and number of academic programs and number of enrolled students is economically plausible at Southwestern University.
2. Goodness of Fit	$r^2 = 0.81$. Excellent goodness of fit.
3. Significance of Independent Variable(s)	t-values of 3.46 on number of academic programs and 2.03 on number of enrolled students are both significant.
4. Specification Analysis of Estimation Assumptions	The assumptions of linearity, constant variance, and normality of residuals hold, but inferences drawn from only 12 observations are not reliable; the Durbin-Watson statistic = 1.84 indicates that independence of residuals holds.

10-38 (30–40 min.) **Purchasing department cost drivers, multiple regression analysis.** (Continuation of 10-37)

The problem reports the exact *t*-values from the computer runs of the data. Because the coefficients and standard errors given in the problem are rounded to three decimal places, dividing the coefficient by the standard error may yield slightly different *t*-values.

1. Regression 4 is a well-specified regression model:

Economic plausibility: Both independent variables are plausible and are supported by the findings of the Couture Fabrics study.

Goodness of fit: The r^2 of 0.63 indicates an excellent goodness of fit.

Significance of independent variables: The *t*-value on # of POs is 2.14 while the *t*-statistic on # of Ss is 2.00. These *t*-values are either significant or border on significance.

Specification analysis: Results are available to examine the independence of residuals assumption. The Durbin-Watson statistic of 1.90 indicates that the assumption of independence is not rejected.

Regression 4 is consistent with the findings in Problem 10-37 that both the number of purchase orders and the number of suppliers are drivers of purchasing department costs. Regressions 2, 3, and 4 all satisfy the four criteria outlined in the text. Regression 4 has the best goodness of fit (0.63 for Regression 4 compared to 0.42 and 0.39 for Regressions 2 and 3, respectively). Most importantly, it is economically plausible that both the number of purchase orders and the number of suppliers drive purchasing department costs. We would recommend that Lee use Regression 4 over Regressions 2 and 3.

2. Regression 5 adds an additional independent variable (MP$) to the two independent variables in Regression 4. This additional variable (MP$) has a *t*-value of –0.07, implying its slope coefficient is insignificantly different from zero. The r^2 in Regression 5 (0.63) is the same as that in Regression 4 (0.63), implying the addition of this third independent variable adds close to zero explanatory power. In summary, Regression 5 adds very little to Regression 4. We would recommend that Lee use Regression 4 over Regression 5.

3. Budgeted purchasing department costs for the Baltimore store next year are:

$485,384 + ($123.22 \times 3,900) + ($2,952 \times 110) = $1,290,662

4. Multicollinearity is a frequently encountered problem in cost accounting; it does not arise in simple regression because there is only one independent variable in a simple regression. One consequence of multicollinearity is an increase in the standard errors of the coefficients of the individual variables. This frequently shows up in reduced *t*-values in the multiple regression relative to their *t*-values in the simple regression:

10-38 (Cont'd.)

Variables	*t*-value in Multiple Regression	*t*-value from Simple Regressions in Problem 10-37
Regression 4:		
# of POs	2.14	2.43
# of Ss	2.00	2.28
Regression 5:		
# of POs	1.95	2.43
# of Ss	1.84	2.28
MP$	–0.07	0.84

The decline in the *t*-values in the multiple regressions is consistent with some (but not very high) collinearity among the independent variables. Pairwise correlations between the independent variables are:

	Correlation
# of POs / # of Ss	0.29
# of POs / MP$	0.27
# of Ss / MP$	0.34

There is no evidence of difficulties due to multicollinearity in Regressions 4 and 5.

5. Decisions in which the regression results in Problems 10-37 and 10-38 could be used are:

Cost management decisions: Fashion Flair could restructure relationships with the suppliers so that fewer separate purchase orders are made. Alternatively, it may aggressively reduce the number of existing suppliers.

Purchasing policy decisions: Fashion Flair could set up an internal charge system for individual retail departments within each store. Separate charges to each department could be made for each purchase order and each new supplier added to the existing ones. These internal charges would signal to each department ways in which their own decisions affect the total costs of Fashion Flair.

Accounting system design decisions: Fashion Flair may want to discontinue allocating purchasing department costs on the basis of the dollar value of merchandise purchased. Allocation bases better capturing cause-and-effect relations at Fashion Flair are the number of purchase orders and the number of suppliers.

10-40 (40 min.) **High-low method, alternative regression functions, accrual accounting adjustments.**

1.   Solution Exhibit 10-40A presents the two data plots. The plot of engineering support reported costs and machine-hours shows two separate groups of data, each of which may be approximated by a separate cost function. The problem arises because the plant records materials and parts costs on an "as purchased," rather than an "as used," basis. The plot of engineering support restated costs and machine-hours shows a high positive correlation between the two variables (the coefficient of determination is 0.94); a single linear cost function provides a good fit to the data. Better estimates of the cost relation result because Kennedy adjusts the materials and parts costs to an accrual accounting basis.

2.

	Cost Driver Machine-Hours	Reported Engineering Support Costs
Highest observation of cost driver (August)	73	$ 617
Lowest observation of cost driver (September)	19	1,066
Difference	54	$ (449)

$$\text{Slope coefficient, } b \quad = \quad \frac{\text{Difference between costs associated with highest and lowest observations of the cost driver}}{\text{Difference between highest and lowest observations of the cost driver}}$$

$$= \quad \frac{-\$449}{54} = -\$8.31 \text{ per machine-hour}$$

Constant (at highest observation of cost driver)   = $ 617 – (–$8.31 × 73) = $1,224
Constant (at lowest observation of cost driver)   = $1,066 – (–$8.31 × 19) = $1,224

The estimated cost function is $y = \$1,224 – \$8.31X$

	Cost Driver Machine-Hours	Restated Engineering Support Costs
Highest observation of cost driver (August)	73	$966
Lowest observation of cost driver (September)	19	370
Difference	54	$596

$$\text{Slope coefficient, } b \quad = \quad \frac{\text{Difference between costs associated with highest and lowest observations of the cost driver}}{\text{Difference between highest and lowest observations of the cost driver}}$$

$$= \quad \frac{596}{54} = \$11.04 \text{ per machine-hour}$$

10-40 (Cont'd.)

Constant (at highest observation of cost driver)	=	$966 – ($11.04 × 73)	= $160
Constant (at lowest observation of cost driver)	=	$370 – ($11.04 × 19)	= $160

The estimated cost function is $y = \$160 + \$11.04\,X$

3.   The cost function estimated with engineering support restated costs better approximates the regression analysis assumptions. See Solution Exhibit 10-40B for a comparison of the two regressions.

4.   Of all the cost functions estimated in requirements 2 and 3, Kennedy should choose Regression 2 using engineering support restated costs as best representing the relationship between engineering support costs and machine-hours. The cost functions estimated using engineering support reported costs are mis-specified and not-economically plausible because materials and parts costs are reported on an "as-purchased," rather than on an "as-used," basis. With respect to engineering support restated costs, the high-low and regression approaches yield roughly similar estimates. The regression approach is technically superior because it determines the line that best fits all observations. In contrast, the high-low method considers only two points (observations with the highest and lowest cost drivers) when estimating the cost function. Solution Exhibit 10-40B shows that the cost function estimated using the regression approach has excellent goodness of fit ($r^2 = 0.94$) and appears to be well specified.

5.   Using the regression cost function estimated with restated costs, Kennedy should budget $748.38 as engineering support costs for December calculated as follows:
Engineering support costs = $176.38 + ($11.44 per hour × 50 hours) = $748.38

6.   Problems Kennedy might encounter include:
   a.   A perpetual inventory system may not be used in this case; the amounts requisitioned likely will not permit an accurate matching of costs with the independent variable on a month-by-month basis.
   b.   Quality of the source records for usage by engineers may be relatively low; e.g., engineers may requisition materials and parts in batches, but not use them immediately.
   c.   Records may not distinguish materials and parts for maintenance from materials and parts used for repairs and breakdowns; separate cost functions may be appropriate for the two categories of materials and parts.
   d.   Year-end accounting adjustments to inventory may mask errors that gradually accumulate month-by-month.

7.   Picking the correct cost function is important for cost prediction, cost management, and performance evaluation. For example, had United Packaging used Regression 1 (engineering support reported costs) to estimate the cost function, it would erroneously conclude that engineering support costs decrease with machine-hours. In a month with 60 machine-hours, Regression 1 would predict costs of $1,393.20 – ($14.23 × 60) = $539.40. If actual costs turn out to be $800, management would conclude that changes should be made to reduce costs. In fact, on the basis of the preferred Regression 2, support overhead costs are lower than the predicted amount of $176.38 + ($11.44 × 60) = $862.78—a performance that management should seek to replicate, not change.

10-40 (Cont'd.)

On the other hand, if machine-hours worked in a month were low, say 25 hours, Regression 1 would erroneously predict support overhead costs of $1,393.20 – ($14.23 × 25) = $1,037.45. If actual costs are $700, management would conclude that its performance has been very good. In fact, compared to the costs predicted by the preferred Regression 2 of $176.38 + ($11.44 × 25) = $462.38, the actual performance is rather poor. Using Regression 1, management may feel costs are being managed very well when in fact they are much higher than what they should be and need to be managed "down."

SOLUTION EXHIBIT 10-40A
Plots and Regression Lines for Engineering Support
Reported Costs and Engineering Support Restated Costs

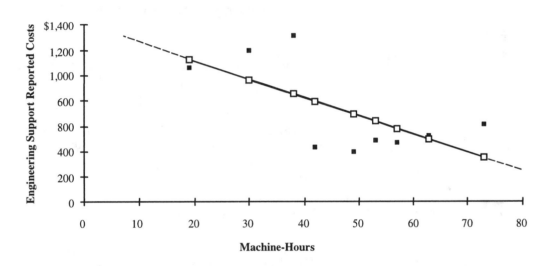

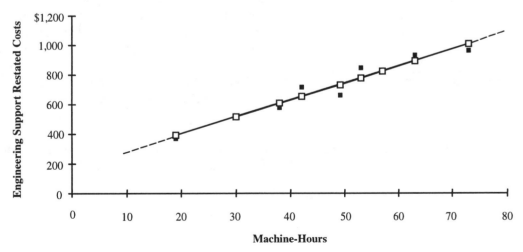

10-40 (Cont'd.)

SOLUTION EXHIBIT 10-40B

Comparison of Alternative Cost Functions for Engineering Support Costs at United Packaging

CRITERION	Regression 1 Dependent Variable: Engineering Support Reported Costs	Regression 2 Dependent Variable: Engineering Support Restated Costs
1. Economic Plausibility	Negative slope relationship is economically implausible over the long run.	Positive slope relationship is economically plausible.
2. Goodness of Fit	$r^2 = 0.43$. Moderate goodness of fit.	$r^2 = 0.94$. Excellent goodness of fit.
3. Significance of Independent Variables	t-statistic on machine-hours is statistically significant ($t = -2.31$), albeit economically implausible.	t-statistic on machine-hours is highly statistically significant ($t=10.59$).
4. Specification Analysis: A. Linearity	Linearity does not describe data very well.	Linearity describes data very well.
B. Constant variance of residuals	Appears questionable, although 12 observations do not facilitate the drawing of reliable inferences.	Appears reasonable, although 12 observations do not facilitate the drawing of reliable inferences.
C. Independence of residuals	Durbin-Watson = 2.26. Residuals serially uncorrelated.	Durbin-Watson = 1.31. Some evidence of serial correlation in the residuals.
D. Normality of residuals	Data base too small to make reliable inferences.	Data base too small to make reliable inferences.

CHAPTER 11
DECISION MAKING AND RELEVANT INFORMATION

11-2 Relevant costs are those expected future costs that differ among alternative courses of action. Historical costs are irrelevant because they are past costs and, therefore, cannot differ among alternative future courses of action.

11-4 Quantitative factors are outcomes that are measured in numerical terms. Some quantitative factors are financial—that is, they can be easily expressed in financial terms. Direct materials is an example of a quantitative financial factor. Qualitative factors are factors that are not measured in numerical terms. An example is employee morale.

11-6 No. Some variable costs may not differ among the alternatives under consideration and, hence, will be irrelevant. Some fixed costs may differ among the alternatives and, hence, will be relevant.

11-8 Opportunity cost is the contribution to income that is forgone (rejected) by not using a limited resource in its next-best alternative use.

11-10 No. Managers should aim to get the highest contribution margin per unit of the constraining (that is, scarce, limiting, or critical) factor. The constraining factor is what restricts or limits the production or sale of a given product (for example, availability of machine-hours).

11-12 Cost written off as depreciation is irrelevant when it pertains to a past cost. But the purchase cost of new equipment to be acquired in the future that will then be written off as depreciation is often relevant.

11-14 The three steps in solving a linear programming problem are:
1. Determine the objective.
2. Specify the constraints.
3. Compute the optimal solution.

11-16 (20 min.) Disposal of assets.

1.   This is an unfortunate situation, yet the $80,000 costs are irrelevant regarding the decision to remachine or scrap. The only relevant factors are the future revenues and future costs. By ignoring the accumulated costs and deciding on the basis of expected future costs, operating income will be maximized (or losses minimized). The difference in favor of remachining is $3,000:

	(a) Remachine	(b) Scrap
Future revenues	$35,000	$2,000
Deduct future costs	30,000	–
Operating income	$ 5,000	$2,000
Difference in favor of remachining	$3,000	

2.   This, too, is an unfortunate situation. But the $100,000 original cost is irrelevant to this decision. The difference in favor of rebuilding is $7,000:

	(a) Replace	(b) Rebuild
New truck	$102,000	–
Deduct current disposal price of existing truck	10,000	–
Rebuild existing truck	–	$85,000
	$ 92,000	$85,000
Difference in favor of rebuilding	$7,000	

Note, here, that the current disposal price of $10,000 is relevant, but the original cost (or book value, if the truck were not brand new) is irrelevant.

11-18 (15 min.) **Multiple choice.**

1. (b)

Special order price per unit	$6.00
Variable manufacturing costs per unit	4.50
Contribution margin per unit	$1.50

Effect on operating income = $1.50 × 20,000 units
= $30,000 increase

2. (b)

Costs of purchases, 20,000 units × $60		$1,200,000
Total relevant costs of making:		
Variable manufacturing costs, $64 – $16	$48	
Fixed costs eliminated	9	
Costs saved by not making	$57	
Multiply by 20,000 units, so total costs saved are $57 × 20,000		1,140,000
Extra costs of purchasing outside		60,000
Minimum savings necessary for Part No. 575		25,000
Necessary relevant costs that would have to be saved in manufacturing Part No. 575		$ 85,000

11-20 (30 min.) **Make versus buy, activity-based costing.**

1. The expected manufacturing cost per unit of CMCBs in 2001 is as follows:

	Total Manufacturing Costs of CMCB (1)	Manufacturing Cost per Unit (2) = (1) ÷ 10,000
Direct materials, $170 × 10,000	$1,700,000	$170
Direct manufacturing labor, $45 × 10,000	450,000	45
Variable batch manufacturing costs, $1,500 × 80	120,000	12
Fixed manufacturing costs		
Avoidable fixed manufacturing costs	320,000	32
Unavoidable fixed manufacturing costs	800,000	80
Total manufacturing costs	$3,390,000	$339

11-20 (Cont'd.)

2. The following table identifies the incremental costs in 2001 if Svenson (a) made CMCBs and (b) purchased CMCBs from Minton.

Incremental Items	Total Incremental Costs Make	Total Incremental Costs Buy	Per-Unit Incremental Costs Make	Per-Unit Incremental Costs Buy
Cost of purchasing CMCBs from Minton		$ 3,000,000		$300
Direct materials	$1,700,000		$170	
Direct manufacturing labor	450,000		45	
Variable batch manufacturing costs	120,000		12	
Avoidable fixed manufacturing costs	320,000		32	
Total incremental costs	$2,590,000	$3,000,000	$259	$300
Difference in favor of making	$410,000		$41	

Note that the opportunity cost of using capacity to make CMCBs is zero since Svenson would keep this capacity idle if it purchases CMCBs from Minton.

Svenson should continue to manufacture the CMCBs internally since the incremental costs to manufacture are $259 per unit compared to the $300 per unit that Minton has quoted. Note that the unavoidable fixed manufacturing costs of $800,000 ($80 per unit) will continue to be incurred whether Svenson makes or buys CMCBs. These are not incremental costs under either the make or the buy alternative and are, hence, irrelevant.

3. Svenson should continue to make CMCBs. The simplest way to analyze this problem is to recognize that Svenson would prefer to keep any excess capacity idle rather than use it to make CB3s. Why? Because expected incremental future revenues from CB3s, $2,000,000 are *less* than expected incremental future costs, $2,150,000. If Svenson keeps its capacity idle, we know from requirement 2 that it should make CMCBs rather than buy them.

An important point to note is that, because Svenson forgoes no contribution by not being able to make and sell CB3s, the opportunity cost of using its facilities to make CMCBs is zero. It is, therefore, not forgoing any profits by using the capacity to manufacture CMCBs. If it does not manufacture CMCBs, rather than lose money on CB3s, Svenson will keep capacity idle.

11-20 (Cont'd.)

A longer and more detailed approach is to use the total alternatives or opportunity cost analyses shown in Exhibit 11-7 of the chapter.

	Choices for Svenson		
Relevant Items	Make CMCBs and Do Not Make CB3s	Buy CMCBs and Do Not Make CB3s	Buy CMCBs and Make CB3s

TOTAL-ALTERNATIVES APPROACH TO MAKE-OR-BUY DECISIONS

Total incremental costs of making/buying CMCBs (from requirement 2)	$2,590,000	$3,000,000	$3,000,000
Excess of future costs over future revenues from CB3s	0	0	150,000
Total relevant costs	$2,590,000	$3,000,000	$3,150,000

Svenson will minimize manufacturing costs by making CMCBs.

OPPORTUNITY-COST APPROACH TO MAKE-OR-BUY DECISIONS

Total incremental costs of making/buying CMCBs (from requirement 2)	$2,590,000	$3,000,000	$3,000,000
Opportunity cost: profit contribution forgone because capacity will not be used to make CB3s	0*	0*	0
Total relevant costs	$2,590,000	$3,000,000	$3,000,000

*Opportunity cost is 0 because Svenson does not give up anything by not making CB3s. Svenson is best off leaving the capacity idle (rather than manufacturing and selling CB3s).

11-22 (10 min.) Inventory decision, opportunity costs.

1.	Unit cost, orders of 20,000	$8.00
	Unit cost, order of 240,000 (0.95 × $8.00)	$7.60

Alternatives under consideration:
(a) Buy 240,000 units at start of year.
(b) Buy 20,000 units at start of each month.

Average investment in inventory:
(a)	(240,000 × $7.60) ÷ 2	$912,000
(b)	(20,000 × $8.00) ÷ 2	80,000
	Difference in average investment	$832,000

11-22 (Cont'd.)

Opportunity cost of interest forgone from 240,000-unit purchase at start of year
= $832,000 × 0.08 = $66,560

2. No. The $66,560 is an opportunity cost rather than an incremental or outlay cost. No actual transaction records the $66,560 as an entry in the accounting system.

3. The following table presents the two alternatives:

	Alternative A: Purchase 240,000 spark plugs at beginning of year (1)	Alternative B: Purchase 20,000 spark plugs at beginning of each month (2)	Difference (3)= (1) – (2)
Annual purchase-order costs			
(1 × $200; 12 × $200)	$ 200	$ 2,400	$ (2,200)
Annual purchase (incremental) costs	1,824,000	1,920,000	(96,000)
(240,000 × $7.60; 240,000 × $8)			
Annual interest income that could be earned			
if investment in inventory were invested			
(opportunity cost)			
(8% × $912,000; 8% × $80,000)	72,960	6,400	66,560
Relevant costs	$1,897,160	$1,928,800	$ (31,640)

Column (3) indicates that purchasing 240,000 spark plugs at the beginning of the year is preferred relative to purchasing 20,000 spark plugs at the beginning of each month because the lower purchase cost exceeds the opportunity cost of holding larger inventory. If other incremental benefits of holding lower inventory such as lower insurance, materials handling, storage, obsolescence, and breakage costs were considered, the costs under Alternative A would have been higher, and Alternative B may have been preferred.

11-24 (10 min.) **Selection of most profitable product.**

Only Model 14 should be produced. The key to this problem is the relationship of manufacturing overhead to product. Note that it takes twice as long to produce Model 9; machine-hours for Model 9 are twice that for Model 14. Management should choose the product mix that maximizes operating income for a given production capacity (the scarce resource in this situation). In this case, Model 14 will yield a $19.00 contribution to fixed costs per unit of machine time, and Model 9 will yield $18.00:

	Model 9	Model 14
Selling price	$100.00	$70.00
Variable costs per unit	82.00	60.50
Contribution margin per unit	$ 18.00	$ 9.50
Relative use of machine-hours per unit of product	× 1	× 2
Contribution margin per unit of machine time	$ 18.00	$19.00

11-26 (20–25 min.) **Customer profitability, choosing customers.**

1. Broadway should not drop the Kelly Corporation business, as the following analysis shows:

Loss in revenues from dropping Kelly	$(80,000)
Savings in costs:	
Variable costs	48,000
Fixed costs 20% × $100,000	20,000
Total savings in costs	68,000
Effect on operating income	$(12,000)

Broadway Printers would be worse off by $12,000 if it drops the Kelly Corporation business.

2.   If Broadway accepts the additional business from Kelly, it would take an additional 500 hours of machine time. If Broadway accepts all of Kelly's and Taylor's business for February, it would require 2,500 hours of machine time (1,500 hours for Taylor and 1,000 hours for Kelly). Broadway has only 2,000 hours of machine capacity. It must, therefore, choose how much of the Taylor or Kelly business to accept. If Broadway accepts any additional business from Kelly, it must forgo some of Taylor's business.

To maximize operating income, Broadway should maximize contribution margin per unit of the constrained resource. (Fixed costs will remain unchanged at $100,000 regardless of the business Broadway chooses to accept in February, and is, therefore, irrelevant.) The contribution margin per unit of the constrained resource for each customer in January is:

	Taylor Corporation	Kelly Corporation
Revenues	$120,000	$80,000
Variable costs	42,000	48,000
Contribution margin	$ 78,000	$32,000

Contribution margin per machine-hour $\qquad \dfrac{\$78,000}{1,500} = \$52 \qquad \dfrac{\$32,000}{500} = \$64$

Since the $80,000 of additional Kelly business in February is identical to jobs done in January, it will also have a contribution margin of $64 per machine-hour, which is greater than the contribution margin of $52 per machine-hour from Taylor. To maximize operating income, Broadway should first allocate all the capacity needed to take the Kelly Corporation business (1,000 machine-hours) and then allocate the remaining 1,000 (2,000 – 1,000) machine-hours to Taylor. Broadway's operating income in February would then be $16,000, which is greater than the $10,000 operating income in January.

	Taylor Corporation	Kelly Corporation	Total
Contribution margin per machine-hour	$52	$64	
Machine-hours to be worked	1,000	1,000	
Contribution margin	$52,000	$64,000	$116,000
Fixed costs			100,000
Operating income			$ 16,000

Alternatively, we could present Broadway's operating income by taking 2/3 (1,000 ÷ 1,500 machine-hours) of Taylor's January revenues and variable costs, and doubling (1,000 ÷ 500 machine-hours) Kelly's January revenues and variable costs.

	Taylor Corporation	Kelly Corporation	Total
Revenues	$80,000	$160,000	$240,000
Variable costs	28,000	96,000	124,000
Contribution margin	52,000	64,000	116,000
Fixed costs			100,000
Operating income			$ 16,000

The problem indicated that Broadway could choose to accept as much of the Taylor and Kelly business for February as it wants. However, some students may raise the question that Broadway should think more strategically before deciding what to do. For example, how would Taylor react to Broadway's inability to satisfy its needs? Will Kelly continue to give Broadway $160,000 of business each month, or is the additional $80,000 of business in February a special order? For example, if Kelly's additional work in February is only a special order and Broadway wants to maintain a long-term relationship with Taylor, it may, in fact, prefer to turn down the additional Kelly business. It may feel that the additional $6,000 in operating income in February is not worth jeopardizing Taylor's long-term relationship. Other students may raise the possibility of Broadway accepting all the Taylor and Kelly business for February if it can subcontract some of it to another reliable, high-quality printer.

11-28 (30 min.) **Equipment upgrade versus replacement.**

1. Solution Exhibit 11-28 presents a cost comparison of the upgrade and replacement alternatives for the three years taken together. It indicates that Pacifica Corporation should replace the production line because it is better off by $180,000 by replacing rather than upgrading.

2a. Suppose the capital expenditure to replace the production line is $X. Using data from Solution Exhibit 11-28, the cost of replacing the production line is equal to $1,620,000 – $90,000 + $X. Using data from Solution Exhibit 11-28, the cost of upgrading the production line is equal to $2,160,000 + $300,000 = $2,460,000. We want to find $X such that

$$\$1,620,000 - \$90,000 + \$X = \$2,460,000$$

that is,
$$\$1,530,000 + \$X = \$2,460,000$$

that is,
$$\$X = \$2,460,000 - \$1,530,000$$

or
$$\$X = \$930,000$$

Pacifica would prefer replacing, rather than upgrading, the existing line if the replacement cost of the new line does not exceed $930,000.

2b. Suppose the units produced and sold each year equal y. Using data from Solution Exhibit 11-28, the cost of replacing the production line is $9y – $90,000 + $750,000, while the cost of upgrading is $12y + $300,000. We solve for the y at which the two costs are the same.

$$\$9y - \$90,000 + \$750,000 = \$12y + \$300,000$$
$$\$9y + \$660,000 = \$12y + \$300,000$$
$$\$3y = \$360,000$$
$$y = 120,000 \text{ units}$$

For expected production and sales of less than 120,000 units over 3 years (40,000 units per year), the upgrade alternative is cheaper. When production and sales are low, the higher operating costs of upgrading are more than offset by the significant savings in capital costs when upgrading relative to replacing. For expected production and sales exceeding 120,000 units over 3 years, the replace alternative is cheaper. For high output, the benefits of the lower operating costs of replacing, relative to upgrading, exceed the higher capital costs.

SOLUTION EXHIBIT 11-28
Comparing Upgrade and Replace Alternatives

	Three Years Together		
	Upgrade (1)	Replace (2)	Difference (3) = (1) – (2)
Cash-operating costs, $12; $9 × 180,000	$2,160,000	$1,620,000	$ 540,000
Current disposal price		(90,000)	90,000
One-time capital costs, written off periodically as depreciation	300,000	750,000	(450,000)
Total relevant costs	$2,460,000	$2,280,000	$ 180,000

11-28 (Cont'd.)

Note that sales and book value of the existing machine are the same under both alternatives and, hence, are irrelevant.

3.   Operating income for the first year under the upgrade and replace alternatives are as follows:

	Upgrade	Replace
Revenues $25 × 60,000	$1,500,000	$1,500,000
Cash-operating costs $12, $9 × 60,000	720,000	540,000
Depreciation	220,000[a]	250,000[b]
Loss on disposal of old production line	—	270,000[c]
Total costs	940,000	1,060,000
Operating income	$ 560,000	$ 440,000

[a]($360,000 + $300,000) ÷ 3 = $220,000   [b]$750,000 ÷ 3 = $250,000
[c]Book value – current disposal price = $360,000 – $90,000 = $270,000

First-year operating income is higher by $120,000 under the upgrade alternative. If first year's operating income is an important component of Azinger's bonus, he would prefer the upgrade over the replace alternative even though the decision model (in requirement 1) prefers the replace to the upgrade alternative. This exercise illustrates the conflict between the decision model and the performance evaluation model.

11-30   (35–40 min.)   Discontinuing a product line, selling more product.

1.   The incremental revenue losses and incremental savings in cost by discontinuing the Tables product line follows:

	Difference: Incremental (Loss in Revenues) and Savings in Costs from Dropping Tables Line
Revenues	$(500,000)
Direct materials and direct manufacturing labor	300,000
Depreciation on equipment	0
Marketing and distribution	70,000
General administration	0
Corporate office costs	0
Total costs	70,000
Operating income (loss)	$(130,000)

Dropping the Tables product line results in revenue losses of $500,000 and cost savings of $370,000. Hence, Grossman Corporation's operating income will be $130,000 higher if it does not drop the Tables line.

Note that, by dropping the Tables product line, Home Furnishings will save none of the depreciation on equipment, general administration and facilities costs, and corporate office costs, but it will save all variable manufacturing costs and marketing and distribution costs on the Tables product line.

11-30 (Cont'd.)

2. Grossman's will generate incremental operating income of $128,000 from selling 4,000 additional tables and, hence, should try to increase table sales. The calculations follow:

	Incremental Revenues (Costs) and Operating Income
Sales	$500,000
Direct materials and direct manufacturing labor	(300,000)
Cost of equipment written off as depreciation	(42,000)*
Marketing and distribution costs	(30,000)†
General administration costs	0**
Corporate office costs	0**
Operating income	$128,000

*Note that the additional costs of equipment are relevant future costs for the "selling more tables decision" because they represent incremental future costs that differ between the alternatives of selling and not selling additional tables.

†Current marketing and distribution costs which varies with number of shipments = $70,000 – $40,000 = $30,000. As the sales of tables double, the number of shipments will double, resulting in incremental marketing and distribution costs of (2 × $30,000) – $30,000 = $30,000.

**General administration and corporate office costs will be unaffected if Grossman decides to sell more tables. Hence, these costs are irrelevant for the decision.

11-32 (30–40 min.) Relevant costs, opportunity costs

1. Easyspread 2.0 has a higher relevant operating income than Easyspread 1.0. Based on this analysis, Easyspread 2.0 should be introduced immediately:

	Easyspread 1.0		Easyspread 2.0	
Relevant revenues		$150		$185
Relevant costs:				
Manuals, diskettes	$ 0		$25	
Total relevant costs		0		25
Relevant operating income		$150		$160

Reasons for other cost items being irrelevant are:
Easyspread 1.0
- Manuals, diskettes—already incurred
- Development costs—already incurred
- Marketing and administration—fixed costs of period

Easyspread 2.0
- Development costs—already incurred
- Marketing and administration—fixed costs of period

Note that total marketing and administration costs will not change whether Easyspread 2.0 is introduced on July 1, 2000 or on October 1, 2000.

11-32 (Cont'd.)

An alternative way to show that Easyspread 2.0 should be introduced immediately is:

	Total (1)	Per Unit (2) = (1) ÷ 60,000
Incremental revenues from July–September 2000 by introducing Easyspread 2.0 immediately on July 1, 2000	$11,100,000[a]	$185
Incremental costs of manuals and diskettes in July–September 2000 if Easyspread 2.0 is introduced on July 1, 2000	1,500,000[b]	25
Incremental increase in operating income	9,600,000	160
Opportunity cost of selling Easyspread 2.0 is the lost revenue from not selling the existing stock of 60,000 units of Easyspread 1.0 (recall that there are no further costs to be incurred to sell Easyspread 1.0)	9,000,000[c]	150
Net relevant benefit	$ 600,000	$ 10

[a] $11,100,000 = $185 × 60,000   [b] $1,500,000 = $25 × 60,000   [c] $9,000,000 = $150 × 60,000

2. Other factors to be considered:
   a. Customer satisfaction. If 2.0 is significantly better than 1.0 for its customers, a customer-driven organization would immediately introduce it unless other factors offset this bias towards "do what is best for the customer."
   b. Quality level of Easyspread 2.0. It is critical for new software products to be fully debugged. Easyspread 2.0 must be error-free. Consider an immediate release only if 2.0 passes all quality tests and can be fully supported by the salesforce.
   c. Importance of being perceived to be a market leader. Being first in the market with a new product can give Basil Software a "first-mover advantage," e.g., capturing an initial large share of the market that, in itself, causes future potential customers to lean towards purchasing Easyspread 2.0. Moreover, by introducing 2.0 earlier, Basil can get quick feedback from users about ways to further refine the software while its competitors are still working on their own first versions. Moreover, by locking in early customers, Basil may increase the likelihood of these customers also buying future upgrades of Easyspread 2.0.
   d. Morale of developers. These are key people at Basil Software. Delaying introduction of a new product can hurt their morale, especially if a competitor then preempts Basil from being viewed as a market leader.
   e. Development of business relationships with distributors. There are pros and cons here. The pro is that, with 2.0, they will have a new product that will generate more sales at a higher selling price. Moreover, if rumors arise about 2.0 being planned, sales of 1.0 may plummet as people hold off buying until the new product is introduced. A possible con is that distributors may be stuck with unsold versions of 1.0. Will Basil be willing to take these units back as a credit against supplying 2.0?

11-32 (Cont'd.)

    f.   Alternative ways of disposing of Easyspread 1.0. Basil can donate all 60,000 Easyspread 1.0 packages to public schools and claim a tax deduction. Basil must also consider the costs of disposing of Easyspread 1.0 (e.g., shredding the packages).

    g.   Incentive compensation scheme at Basil Software. How will the write off (if any) on Easyspread 1.0 packages affect the compensation plan? Management at Basil may not view the costs of Easyspread 1.0 as a sunk cost if their bonus will be affected by a write off on Easyspread 1.0. That is, the performance evaluation model may conflict with the decision model.

11-34 (30 min.) Contribution approach, relevant costs.

1.

Average one-way fare per passenger		$ 500
Commission at 8% of $500		40
Net cash to Air Frisco per ticket		$ 460
Average number of passengers per flight		× 200
Revenues per flight ($460 × 200)		$ 92,000
Food and beverage cost per flight ($20 × 200)		4,000
Total contribution from passengers		88,000
Fuel costs per flight		14,000
Contribution per flight		74,000
Fixed costs allocated to each flight:		
Lease costs	$53,000	
Ground services	7,000	
Flight crew	4,000	64,000
Operating income per flight		$10,000

2.

If fare is	$480.00
Commission at 8% of $480	38.40
Net cash per ticket	441.60
Food and beverage cost per ticket	20.00
Contribution per passenger	$421.60
Total contribution margin from passengers	
($421.60 × 212)	$89,379.20

All other costs are irrelevant.

On the basis of quantitative factors alone, Air Frisco should decrease its fare to $480 because reducing the fare gives Air Frisco a higher contribution margin from passengers ($89,379.20 versus $88,000).

3.   In evaluating whether Air Frisco should charter its plane to Travel International, we compare the charter alternative to the solution in requirement 2 because requirement 2 is preferred to requirement 1.

Under requirement 2, Air Frisco gets	$89,379.20
Deduct fuel costs	14,000.00
Total contribution per flight	$75,379.20

11-34 (Cont'd.)

Air Frisco gets $75,000 per flight from chartering the plane to Travel International. On the basis of quantitative financial factors, Air Frisco is better off not chartering the plane and, instead, lowering its own fares.

Students who compare the $75,000 that Air Frisco earns from chartering its plane to the contribution from passengers in requirement 1 ($74,000) will conclude that Air Frisco should charter the plane to Travel International. Strictly speaking, though, the correct answer must compare the charter fee of $75,000 to the $75,379.20 passenger contribution in requirement 2, since lowering the fare is certainly an alternative available to Air Frisco.

Other qualitative factors that Air Frisco should consider in coming to a decision are:
a. The lower risk from chartering its plane relative to the uncertainties regarding the number of passengers it might get on its scheduled flights.
b. Chartering to Travel International means that Air Frisco would not have a regular schedule of flights each week. This arrangement could cause inconvenience to some of its passengers.
c. The stability of the relationship between Air Frisco and Travel International. If this is not a long-term arrangement, Air Frisco may lose current market share and not benefit from sustained charter revenues.

11-36 (30 min.) Make versus buy, activity-based costing, opportunity costs.

1. Relevant costs under buy alternative:

Purchases, 10,000 × $8.20	<u>$82,000</u>

Relevant costs under make alternative:

Direct materials	$40,000
Direct manufacturing labor	20,000
Variable manufacturing overhead	15,000
Inspection, setup, materials handling	2,000
Machine rent	3,000
Total relevant costs under make alternative	<u>$80,000</u>

The allocated fixed plant administration, taxes, and insurance will not change if Ace makes or buys the chains. Hence, these costs are irrelevant to the make-or-buy decision. The analysis indicates that Ace should not buy the chains from the outside supplier.

2. Relevant costs under the make alternative:

Relevant costs (as computed in requirement 1)	<u>$80,000</u>

Relevant costs under the buy alternative:

Costs of purchases (10,000 × $8.20)	$82,000
Additional fixed costs	16,000
Additional contribution margin from using the space where the chains were made to upgrade the bicycles by adding mud flaps and reflector bars, 10,000 × ($20 − $18)	(20,000)
Total relevant costs under the buy alternative	<u>$78,000</u>

11-36 (Cont'd.)

Ace should now buy the chains from an outside vendor and use its own capacity to upgrade its own bicycles.

3. In this requirement, the decision on mud flaps and reflectors is irrelevant to the analysis.

Cost of manufacturing chains:	
Variable costs, ($4 + $2 + $1.50 = $7.50) × 6,200	$46,500
Batch costs, $200/batch[a] × 8 batches	1,600
Machine rent	3,000
	$51,100
Cost of buying chains, $8.20 × 6,200	$50,840

[a]$2,000 ÷ 10 batches

In this case, Ace should buy the chains from the outside vendor.

11-38 (15 min.) Make or buy. (Continuation of 11-37)

The maximum price Class Company should be willing to pay is $3.9417 per unit.

Expected unit production and sales of new product must be half of the old product (1/2 × 240,000 = 120,000) because the fixed manufacturing overhead rate for the new product is twice that of the fixed manufacturing overhead rate for the old product.

		Proposed		
		Make New	**Old**	
	Present	**Product**	**Product**	**Total**
Revenues	$1,440,000	$1,080,000	$1,440,000	$2,520,000
Variable (or purchase) costs:				
Manufacturing	720,000	600,000	946,000*	1,546,000
Marketing and other	360,000	240,000	288,000	528,000
Total variable costs	1,080,000	840,000	1,234,000	2,074,000
Contribution margin	360,000	240,000	206,000	446,000
Fixed costs:				
Manufacturing	120,000	120,000		120,000
Marketing and other	216,000	60,000	216,000	276,000
Total fixed costs	336,000	180,000	216,000	396,000
Operating income	$ 24,000	$ 60,000	$ (10,000)	$ 50,000

*This is an example of opportunity costs, whereby subcontracting at a price well above the $3.50 current manufacturing (absorption) cost is still desirable because the old product will be displaced in manufacturing by a new product that is more profitable.

11-38 (Cont'd.)

Because the new product promises an operating income of $60,000 (ignoring the irrelevant problems of how fixed marketing costs may be newly reallocated between products), the old product can sustain up to a $10,000 loss and still help accomplish management's overall objectives. Maximum costs that can be incurred on the old product are $1,440,000 plus the $10,000 loss, or $1,450,000. Maximum purchase cost: $1,450,000 – ($288,000 + $216,000) = $946,000. Maximum purchase cost per unit: $946,000 ÷ 240,000 units = $3.9417 per unit.

Alternative Computation

Operating income is $9.00 – $8.50 = $0.50 per unit		
for 120,000 new units		$60,000
Target operating income		50,000
Maximum loss allowed on old product		$10,000
Maximum loss per unit allowed on old product,		
$10,000 ÷ 240,000 =		$0.0417
Selling price of old product		$6.0000
Allowance for loss		0.0417
Total costs allowed per unit		6.0417
Continuing costs for old product other than purchase cost:		
Fixed manufacturing costs—all transferred to new product	$ –	
Variable marketing costs	1.20	
Fixed marketing costs	0.90	2.1000
Maximum purchase cost per unit		$3.9417

11-40 (30–40 min.) Optimal production mix.

1. Let D represent the batches of Della's Delight made and sold.
    Let C represent the batches of Cathy's Chocolate Chips made and sold.
The contribution margin per batch for Della's Delight is $525 – $175 = $350.
The contribution margin per batch for Cathy's Chocolate Chip is $335 – $85 = $250.

The LP formulation for the decision is:

        Maximize $350D + $250 C
        Subject to 30D + 15C ≤ 600 (Mixing Department constraint)
                    10D + 15C ≤ 300 (Baking Department constraint)
                    20D   ≤ 320 (Dipping Department constraint)

2. Solution Exhibit 11-40 presents a graphical summary of the relationships. The optimal corner is the point (15,10), 15 Della's Delights and 10 Cathy's Chocolate Chips.

11-40 (Cont'd.)

SOLUTION EXHIBIT 11-40
Graphic Solution to Find Optimal Mix, Della Simpson, Inc.

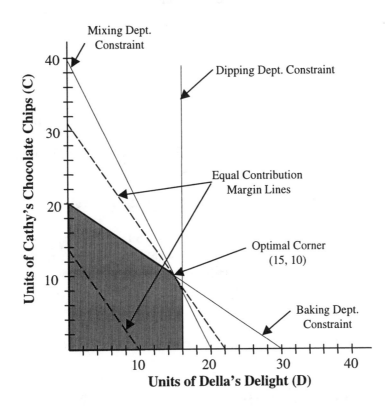

We next calculate the optimal production mix using the trial-and-error method.

The corner point where the Mixing Dept. and Baking Dept. constraints meet can be calculated by solving:

$$30D + 15C = 600 \text{ (1) Mixing Dept. constraint}$$
$$10D + 15C = 300 \text{ (2) Baking Dept. constraint}$$

Substracting (2) from (1), we have
$$20D = 300$$
$$\text{or } D = 15$$

Substituting in (2)
$$10 \times 15 + 15C = 300$$
that is, $$15C = 300 - 150 = 150$$
or $$C = 10$$

11-40 (Cont'd.)

The corner point where the Mixing Dept. and Dipping Dept. constraints meet can be calculated by solving

$$30D + 15C = 600 \ (1) \text{ Mixing Dept. constraint}$$
$$20D = 320 \ (3) \text{ Dipping Dept. constraint}$$

From equation (3), $D = 320 \div 20 = 16$
Substituting in (1),

$$(30 \times 16) + 15C = 600$$
$$15C = 600 - 480 = 120$$
$$C = 8$$

We next use the trial-and-error method to check the contribution margins at each of the five corner points of the area of feasible solutions.

Trial	Corner (D, C)	Total Contribution Margin
1	(0, 0)	($350 × 0) + ($250 × 0) = $0
2	(16, 0)	($350 × 16) + ($250 × 0) = $5,600
3	(16, 8)	($350 × 16) + ($250 × 8) = $7,600
4	(15, 10)	($350 × 15) + ($250 × 10) = $7,750
5	(0, 20)	($350 × 0) + ($250 × 20) = $5,000

The optimal solution that maximizes operating income is 15 Della's Delights and 10 Cathy's Chocolate Chips.

11-42 (40 min.) Optimal product mix.

In order to maximize OmniSport Inc.'s profitability, OmniSport should manufacture 12,000 snowboard bindings, manufacture 1,000 pairs of skates, and purchase 6,000 pairs of skates from Colcott Inc. This combination of manufactured and purchased goods maximizes the contribution per available machine-hour, which is the limiting resource, as shown below.

Because snowboards have a higher contribution per machine-hour than in-line skates, OmniSport should manufacture the maximum number of snowboards. Because the contribution per manufactured pair of in-line skates is higher than the contribution from a purchased pair of in-line skates, total contribution will be maximized by using the remaining manufacturing capacity to produce in-line skates and then purchasing the remaining required skates. The calculations for the optimal combination follow:

11-42 (Cont'd.)

	Purchased In-line Skates 6,000		Manufactured In-line Skates 1,000		Manufactured Snowboard Bindings 12,000		Total
	Per Unit	Total	Per Unit	Total	Per Unit	Total	
Selling price	$98	$588,000	$98	$98,000	$60	$720,000	$1,406,000
Variable costs							
Direct & other materials	75	450,000	20	20,000	20	240,000	710,000
Machine operating costs	–	–	24	24,000	8	96,000	120,000
Manufacturing overhead costs (1)	–	–	12	12,000	4	48,000	60,000
Selling & administrative costs	4	24,000	9	9,000	8	96,000	129,000
Variable costs	79	474,000	65	65,000	40	480,000	1,019,000
Contribution margin	19	114,000	33	33,000	20	240,000	387,000
Fixed costs							
Manufacturing overhead							30,000
Marketing & administrative costs							60,000
Fixed costs							90,000
Operating income							$ 297,000
Machine-hours per unit	–		1.5		0.5		
Contribution per machine-hour ($33 ÷ 1.5; $20 ÷ 0.5)	–		$22.0		$40.0		

Supporting calculations

(1) Manufacturing overhead

Manufactured in-line skates
Machine-hours	=	$24.00 per pair/$16.00 per hour = 1.5 hours per pair
Manufacturing capacity	=	5,000 pairs × 1.5 hours per pair = 7,500 hours
Overhead per machine-hour	=	$18.00 per pair/1.5 hours per pair = $12.00 per hour
Total overhead	=	7,500 hours × $12.00 per hour = $90,000
Total variable overhead	=	$90,000 (total) – $30,000 (fixed) = $60,000 (variable)
Variable overhead per machine-hour	=	$60,000/7,500 hours = $8.00 per hour
Fixed overhead per machine-hour	=	$30,000 fixed overhead/7,500 hours = $4.00 per hour
Variable overhead per pair of skates	=	1.5 hours × $8.00 per hour = $12.00 per pair
Fixed overhead per pair of skates	=	1.5 hours × $4.00 per hour = $6.00 per pair

Snowboard bindings
Machine-hours	=	$8 per board/$16.00 per hour = 0.5 hour per board
Variable overhead per snowboard	=	$8.00 per hour × 0.5 hour per board = $4.00 per board
Fixed overhead per snowboard	=	$4.00 per hour × 0.5 hour per board = $2.00 per board

OmniSport Inc. Contribution Analysis

	Quantity (1)	Machine Hours per Unit (2)	Total Machine Hours Used (3)= (1) × (2)	Machine Hour Balance (4)	Unit Contribution (5)	Total Product Contribution (6) = (1) × (5)
Machine-hours available				7,500		
Snowboard bindings	12,000	0.5	6,000	1,500	$20	$240,000
In-line skates—manufacture	1,000	1.5	1,500	–	33	33,000
In-line skates—purchase	6,000	–	–	–	19	114,000
Total contribution						387,000
Less original contribution (5,000 pairs of skates × $33.00 per pair)						(165,000)
Improvement in contribution						$222,000

CHAPTER 12
PRICING DECISIONS AND COST MANAGEMENT

12-2 Not necessarily. For a one-time-only special order, the relevant costs are only those costs that will change as a result of accepting the order. In this case, full product costs will rarely be relevant. It is more likely that full product costs will be relevant costs for long-run pricing decisions.

12-4 Activity-based costing helps managers in pricing decisions in two ways.
1. It gives managers more accurate product-cost information for making pricing decisions.
2. It helps managers to manage costs during value engineering by identifying the cost impact of eliminating, reducing, or changing various activities.

12-6 A target cost per unit is the estimated long-run cost per unit of a product (or service) that, when sold at the target price, enables the company to achieve the targeted operating income per unit.

12-8 A value-added cost is a cost that customers perceive as adding value, or utility, to a product or service. Examples are costs of materials, direct labor, tools, and machinery. A nonvalue-added cost is a cost that customers do not perceive as adding value, or utility, to a product or service. Examples of nonvalue-added costs are costs of rework, scrap, expediting, and breakdown maintenance.

12-10 Cost-plus pricing is a pricing approach in which managers add a markup to cost in order to determine price.

12-12 Two examples where the difference in the incremental costs of two products or services are much smaller than the differences in their prices follow:
1. The difference in prices charged for a telephone call, hotel room, or car rental during busy versus slack periods is often much greater than the difference in costs to provide these services.
2. The difference in incremental costs for an airplane seat sold to a passenger traveling on business or a passenger traveling for pleasure is roughly the same. However, airline companies routinely charge business travelers—those who are likely to start and complete their travel during the same week excluding the weekend—a much higher price than pleasure travelers who generally stay at their destinations over at least one weekend.

12-14 Three benefits of using a product life-cycle reporting format are:
1. The full set of revenues and costs associated with each product becomes more visible.
2. Differences among products in the percentage of total costs committed at early stages in the life cycle are highlighted.
3. Interrelationships among business function cost categories are highlighted.

12-16 (20–30 min.) **Relevant-cost approach to pricing decisions, special order.**

1.

Relevant revenues, $3.80 × 1,000		$3,800
Relevant costs		
Direct materials, $1.50 × 1,000	$1,500	
Direct manufacturing labor, $0.80 × 1,000	800	
Variable manufacturing overhead, $0.70 × 1,000	700	
Variable selling costs, 0.05 × $3,800	190	
Total relevant costs		3,190
Increase in operating income		$ 610

This calculation assumes that:
- a. The monthly fixed manufacturing overhead of $150,000 and $65,000 of monthly fixed marketing costs will be unchanged by acceptance of the 1,000 unit order.
- b. The price charged and the volumes sold to other customers are not affected by the special order.

Chapter 12 uses the phrase "one-time-only special order" to describe this special case.

2. The president's reasoning is defective on at least two counts:
- a. The inclusion of irrelevant costs—assuming the monthly fixed manufacturing overhead of $150,000 will be unchanged; it is irrelevant to the decision.
- b. The exclusion of relevant costs—variable selling costs (5% of the selling price) are excluded.

3. Key issues are:
- a. Will the existing customer base demand price reductions? If this 1,000-tape order is not independent of other sales, cutting the price from $5.00 to $3.80 can have a large negative effect on total revenues.
- b. Is the 1,000-tape order a one-time-only order, or is there the possibility of sales in subsequent months? The fact that the customer is not in Dill Company's "normal marketing channels" does not necessarily mean it is a one-time-only order. Indeed, the sale could well open a new marketing channel. Dill Company should be reluctant to consider only short-run variable costs for pricing long-run business.

12-18 (25 min.) **Short-run pricing, capacity constraints.**

1. With no constraints on availability of Pyrone or on plant capacity, Boutique would want to charge a minimum price for Seltium that would cover its incremental costs to manufacture Seltium. (Because there is excess capacity, there is no opportunity cost.) In this case, the incremental costs are the variable costs to manufacture a kilogram of Seltium:

Pyrone (2 kilograms × $4 per kilogram)	$ 8
Direct manufacturing labor	4
Variable manufacturing overhead costs	3
Total variable manufacturing costs	$15

Hence, the minimum price that Boutique should charge to manufacture Seltium is $15 per kilogram. For 3,000 kilograms of Seltium, it should charge a minimum of $45,000 ($15 × 3,000).

2. Now Pyrone is in short supply. Using it to make Seltium reduces the Bolzene that Boutique can make and sell. There is, therefore, an opportunity cost of manufacturing Seltium, the lost contribution from using the Pyrone to manufacture Bolzene. To make 3,000 kilograms of Seltium requires 6,000 (2 × 3,000) kilograms of Pyrone.

The 6,000 kilograms of Pyrone can be used to manufacture 4,000 (6,000 ÷ 1.5) kilograms of Bolzene, since each kilogram of Bolzene requires 1.5 kilograms of Pyrone.

The contribution margin from 4,000 kilograms of Bolzene is $24,000 ($6 per kilogram × 4,000 kilograms). This is the opportunity cost of using Pyrone to manufacture Seltium. The minimum price that Boutique should charge to manufacture Seltium should cover not only the incremental (variable) costs of manufacturing Seltium but also the opportunity cost:

	Costs of Manufacturing Seltium	
	Total for 3,000 Kilograms	**Per Kilogram**
Relevant Costs	**(1)**	**(2) = (1) ÷ 3,000**
Incremental (variable) costs of manufacturing Seltium	$45,000	$15
Opportunity cost of forgoing manufacture and sale of Bolzene	24,000	8
Minimum cost of order	$69,000	$23

The minimum price per kilogram that Boutique should charge for Seltium is $23 per kilogram. For 3,000 kilograms of Seltium, Boutique should charge a minimum of $69,000 ($23 × 3,000 kgs).

12-20 (25–30 min.) **Target operating income, value-added costs, service company.**

1.   The classification of total costs in 2001 into value-added, nonvalue added, or in the gray area in between follows.

	Value Added (1)	Gray Area (2)	Nonvalue added (3)	Total (4)= (1)+(2)+(3)
Doing calculations and preparing drawings				
75% × $400,000	$300,000			$300,000
Checking calculations and drawings				
4% × $400,000		$16,000		16,000
Correcting errors found in drawings				
7% × $400,000			$28,000	28,000
Making changes in response to client requests				
6% × $400,000	24,000			24,000
Correcting errors to meet government				
building code, 8% × $400,000			32,000	32,000
Total professional labor costs	324,000	16,000	60,000	400,000
Administration and support costs at 40%				
($160,000 ÷ $400,000) of professional				
labor costs	129,600	6,400	24,000	160,000
Travel	18,000		–	18,000
Total	$471,600	$22,400	$84,000	$578,000

Doing calculations and responding to client requests for changes are value-added costs because customers perceive these costs as necessary for the service of preparing architectural drawings. Costs incurred on correcting errors in drawings and making changes because they were inconsistent with building codes are nonvalue-added costs. Customers do not perceive these costs as necessary and would be unwilling to pay for them. Carasco should seek to eliminate these costs. Checking calculations and drawings is in the gray area (some, but not all, checking may be needed). There is room for disagreement on these classifications. For example, checking calculations may be regarded as value added, and making changes to conform to the building code might be regarded as in the gray area.

Carasco's staff can reduce nonvalue-added costs by checking government building code requirements before drawing up the plans and taking more care when doing the actual work. To reduce value-added costs, Carasco's staff must work faster and more efficiently while at the same time maintaining quality. To achieve these goals, Carasco may want to consider investing in computer-aided drawing programs and training its professional staff to work with these tools.

12-20 (Cont'd.)

2. Reduction in professional labor-hours by

a.	Correcting errors in drawings ($7\% \times 8,000$)	560 hours
b.	Correcting errors to conform to building code ($8\% \times 8,000$)	640 hours
	Total	1,200 hours
	Cost savings in professional labor costs (1,200 hours × $50)	$ 60,000
	Cost savings in variable administration and support costs (40% × $60,000)	24,000
	Total cost savings	$ 84,000

Current operating income in 2001	$102,000
Add cost savings from eliminating errors	84,000
Operating income in 2001 if errors eliminated	$186,000

3. Currently 85% × 8,000 hours = 6,800 hours are billed to clients generating revenues of $680,000. The remaining 15% of professional labor-hours (15% × 8,000 = 1,200 hours) is lost in making corrections. Carasco bills clients at the rate of $\dfrac{\$680,000}{6,800} = \$100$ per professional labor-hour. If the 1,200 professional labor-hours currently not being billed to clients were billed to clients, Carasco's revenues would increase by 1,200 hours × $100 = $120,000 from $680,000 to $800,000.

Costs remain unchanged

Professional labor costs	$400,000
Administration and support (40% × $400,000)	160,000
Travel	18,000
Total costs	$578,000

Carasco's operating income would be

Revenues	$800,000
Total costs	578,000
Operating income	$222,000

12-22 (20 min.)   **Cost-plus target return on investment pricing.**

1. Target operating income = target return on investment × invested capital

Target operating income (25% of $960,000)	$240,000
Total fixed costs	352,000
Target contribution margin	$592,000

Target contribution per room, ($592,000 ÷ 16,000)	$37
Add variable costs per room	3
Price to be charged per room	$40

    Proof

Total room revenues ($40 × 16,000 rooms)		$640,000
Total costs:		
Variable costs ($3 × 16,000)	$ 48,000	
Fixed costs	352,000	
Total costs		400,000
Operating income		$240,000

    The full cost of a room = variable cost per room + fixed cost per room
    The full cost of a room = $3 + ($352,000 ÷ 16,000) = $3 + $22 = $25

Markup per room	=	Rental price per room – Full cost of a room
	=	$40 – $25 = $15

    Markup percentage as a fraction of full cost = $15 ÷ $25 = 60%

2. If price is reduced by 10%, the number of rooms Beck could rent would increase by 10%.

The new price per room would be 90% of $40	$36
The number of rooms Beck expects to rent is 110% of 16,000	17,600
The contribution margin per room would be $36 – $3	$33
Contribution margin ($33 ×17,600)	$580,800

    Because the contribution margin of $580,800 at the reduced price of $36 is less than the contribution margin of $592,000 at a price of $40, Beck should not reduce the price of the rooms. Note that the fixed costs of $352,000 will be the same under the $40 and the $36 price alternatives and are, hence, irrelevant to the analysis.

12-24 (25 min.) **Target costs, effect of product-design changes on product costs.**

1. & 2. Indirect cost-allocation rates for 2000 and 2001 are as follows:

	2000			2001		
Indirect cost category	**Total Costs** (1)	**Quantity of Cost-Allocation Base** (2)	**Cost Allocation Rate** (3)= (1) ÷ (2)	**Total Costs** (4)	**Quantity of Cost-Allocation Base** (5)	**Cost-Allocation Rate** (6)= (4) ÷ (5)
Batch-level costs	$ 7,200,000	900	$ 8,000	$ 7,500,000	1,000	$ 7,500
Manuf. operations costs	12,100,000	220,000	55	12,500,000	250,000	50
Engineering change costs	2,640,000	220	12,000	2,000,000	200	10,000

Manufacturing costs of HJ6 in 2000 and 2001 are as follows:

	2000		2001	
	Total (1)	**Per Unit** (2)= (1) ÷ 3,500	**Total** (3)	**Per Unit** (4)= (3) ÷ 4,000
Direct materials, $1,200 × 3,500; $1,100 × 4,000	$4,200,000	$1,200	$4,400,000	$1,100
Batch-level costs, $8,000 × 70; $7,500 × 80	560,000	160	600,000	150
Manuf. operations costs, $55 × 21,000; $50 × 22,000	1,155,000	330	1,100,000	275
Engineering change costs, $12,000 × 14; $10,000 × 10	168,000	48	100,000	25
Total	$6,083,000	$1,738	$6,200,000	$1,550

3.
$$\frac{\text{Target manufacturing cost}}{\text{per unit of HJ6 in 2001}} = \frac{\text{Manufacturing cost}}{\text{per unit in 2000}} \times 88\%$$
$$= \$1,738 \times 0.88 = \$1,529.44$$

Actual manufacturing cost per unit of HJ6 in 2001 was $1,550. Hence, Medical Instruments did not achieve its target manufacturing cost per unit of $1,529.44.

4.   To reduce the manufacturing cost per unit in 2001, Medical Instruments reduces the cost per unit in each of the four cost categories—direct materials costs, batch-level costs, manufacturing operations costs, and engineering change costs. It achieves this by reducing setup, production order, and materials handling costs per batch, the cost per machine hour, and cost per engineering change, perhaps by becoming more efficient in performing these activities. Efficiency improvements also helped Medical Instruments reduce the quantities of the cost allocation bases used to manufacture HJ6. For example, although production of HJ6 increased by 14.3% [(4,000 − 3,500) ÷ 3,500] between 2000 and 2001, machine-hours worked increased by only 4.8% [(22,000 ÷ 21,000) ÷ 21,000]. Medical Instruments achieved these gains through value engineering activities that retained only those product features that customers wanted while eliminating nonvalue-added activities and costs.

12-26 (25 min.) **Life-cycle product costing, activity-based costing.**

1.   The budgeted life-cycle operating income for the new watch MX3 is $2,420,000, as shown below.

	Life-Cycle Revenues And Costs
Revenues, $40 × 400,000	$16,000,000
R&D and design costs	1,000,000
Manufacturing costs:	
Variable, $15 × 400,000	6,000,000
Batch, $600 × 800[1] batches	480,000
Fixed	1,800,000
Marketing costs:	
Variable, $3.20 × 400,000	1,280,000
Fixed	1,000,000
Distribution costs:	
Batch, $280 × 2,500[2] batches	700,000
Fixed	720,000
Customer-service costs:	
Variable, $1.50 × 400,000	600,000
Total costs	13,580,000
Operating income	$ 2,420,000

[1]400,000 watches ÷ 500 watches per batch = 800 batches
[2]400,000 watches ÷ 160 watches per batch = 2,500 batches

2.   Budgeted product life-cycle costs for R&D and design $1,000,000
Total budgeted product life-cycle costs $13,580,000

$$\text{Percentage of budgeted product life - cycle costs incurred till the R \& D and design stages} = \frac{\$1,000,000}{\$13,580,000} = 7.36\%$$

3.   An analysis reveals that 80% of the total product life-cycle costs of the new watch will be locked in at the end of the R&D and design stages when only 7.36% of the costs are incurred (requirement 2). The implication is that it will be difficult to alter or reduce the costs of MX3 once Destin finalizes the design of MX3. To reduce and manage total costs, Destin must act to modify the design before costs get locked in.

4.   The budgeted life-cycle operating income for MX3 if Destin reduces its price by $3 is $1,912,000, as shown next. This is less than the operating income of $2,420,000 calculated in requirement 1. Therefore, Destin should not reduce MX3's price by $3.

12-26 (Cont'd.)

	Life-Cycle Revenues And Costs
Revenues, $37 × 440,000	$16,280,000
R&D and design costs	1,000,000
Manufacturing costs:	
Variable, $15 × 440,000	6,600,000
Batch, $600 × 800[3] batches	480,000
Fixed	1,800,000
Marketing costs:	
Variable, $3.20 × 440,000	1,408,000
Fixed	1,000,000
Distribution costs:	
Batch, $280 × 2,500[4] batches	700,000
Fixed	720,000
Customer-service costs:	
Variable, $1.50 × 440,000	660,000
Total costs	14,368,000
Operating income	$ 1,912,000

[3]440,000 watches ÷ 550 watches per batch = 800 batches
[4]440,000 watches ÷ 176 watches per batch = 2,500 batches

12-28 (30 min.) Relevant-cost approach to pricing decisions.

1. Revenues (1,000 crates at $100 per crate)		$100,000
Variable costs:		
Manufacturing	$40,000	
Marketing	14,000	
Total variable costs		54,000
Contribution margin		46,000
Fixed costs:		
Manufacturing	$20,000	
Marketing	16,000	
Total fixed costs		36,000
Operating income		$ 10,000

Normal markup percentage: $46,000 ÷ $54,000 = 85.19% of total variable costs.

12-28 (Cont'd.)

2. Only the manufacturing-cost category is relevant to considering this special order; no additional marketing costs will be incurred. The relevant manufacturing costs for the 200-crate special order are:

Variable manufacturing cost per unit	
$40 × 200 crates	$ 8,000
Special packaging	2,000
	$10,000

Any price above $50 per crate ($10,000 ÷ 200) will make a positive contribution to operating income. Hence, based on financial considerations, Stardom should accept the 200-crate special order.

The reasoning based on a comparison of $55 per crate price with the $60 per crate absorption cost ignores monthly cost-volume-profit relationships. The $60 per crate absorption cost includes a $20 per crate cost component that is irrelevant to the special order. The relevant range for the fixed manufacturing costs is from 500 to 1,500 crates per month; the special order will increase production from 1,000 to 1,200 crates per month. Furthermore, the special order requires no incremental marketing costs.

3. If the new customer is likely to remain in business, Stardom should consider whether a strictly short-run focus is appropriate. For example, what is the likelihood of demand from other customers increasing over time? If Stardom accepts the 200-crate special offer for more than one month, it may preclude accepting other customers at prices exceeding $55 per crate. Moreover, the existing customers may learn about Stardom's willingness to set a price based on variable cost plus a small contribution margin. The longer time frame over which Stardom keeps selling 200 crates of canned peaches at $55 a crate, the more likely that the existing customers will approach Stardom for their own special price reductions. If the new customer wants the contract to extend over a longer time period, Stardom should negotiate a higher price.

12-30 (25 min.)   **Cost-plus and market-based pricing.**

1.   California Temps's full cost per hour of supplying contract labor is:

Variable costs	$12
Fixed costs ($240,000 ÷ 80,000 hours)	3
Full cost per hour	$15

Price per hour at full cost plus 20% = $15 × 1.20 = $18 per hour.

2.   Contribution margins for different prices and demand realizations are as follows:

Price per Hour (1)	Variable Cost per Hour (2)	Contribution Margin per Hour (3)=(1)–(2)	Demand in Hours (4)	Total Contribution (5)=(3)• (4)
$16	$12	$4	120,000	$480,000
17	12	5	100,000	500,000
18	12	6	80,000	480,000
19	12	7	70,000	490,000
20	12	8	60,000	480,000

Fixed costs will remain the same regardless of the demand realizations. Fixed costs are, therefore, irrelevant since they do not differ among the alternatives.

The table above indicates that California Temps can maximize contribution margin and, hence, operating income by charging a price of $17 per hour.

3.   The cost-plus approach to pricing in requirement 1 does not explicitly consider the effect of prices on demand. The approach in requirement 2 models the interaction between price and demand and determines the optimal level of profitability using concepts of relevant costs. The two different approaches lead to two different prices in requirements 1 and 2. As the chapter describes, pricing decisions should consider both demand or market considerations and supply or cost factors. The approach in requirement 2 is the more balanced approach. In most cases, of course, managers use the cost-plus method of requirement 1 as only a starting point. They then modify the cost-plus price on the basis of market considerations—anticipated customer reaction to alternative price levels and the prices charged by competitors for similar products.

12-32 (40–45 min.) **Target prices, target costs, value engineering, cost incurrence, locked-in cost, activity-based costing.**

1.

	Old CE100	Cost Change	New CE100
Direct materials costs	$182,000	$2.20 × 7,000 = $15,400 less	$166,600
Direct manufacturing labor costs	28,000	$0.50 × 7,000 = $3,500 less	24,500
Machining costs	31,500	Unchanged because capacity same	31,500
Testing costs	35,000	(20% × 2.5 × 7,000) × $2 = $7,000 less	28,000
Rework costs	14,000	(See Note 1)	5,600
Ordering costs	3,360	(See Note 2)	2,100
Engineering costs	21,140	Unchanged because capacity same	21,140
Total manufacturing costs	$315,000		$279,440

Note 1:
10% of old CE100s are reworked. That is, 700 (10% of 7,000) CE100s made are reworked. Rework costs = $20 per unit reworked × 700 = $14,000. If rework falls to 4% of New CE100s manufactured, 280 (4% of 7,000) New CE100s manufactured will require rework. Rework costs = $20 per unit × 280 = $5,600.

Note 2 :
Ordering costs for New CE100 = 2 orders/month × 50 components × $21/order
$$= \$2,100$$

Unit manufacturing costs of New CE100 = $279,440 ÷ 7,000 = $39.92

2. Total manufacturing cost reductions based on new design
= $315,000 – $279,440
= $35,560

Reduction in unit manufacturing costs based on new design
= $35,560 ÷ 7,000
= $5.08 per unit.

The reduction in unit manufacturing costs based on the new design can also be calculated as :
Unit cost of old design, $45 ($315,000 ÷ 7,000 units) – Unit cost of new design, $39.92 = $5.08

Hence, the target cost reduction of $6 per unit is not achieved by the redesign.

3. Changes in design have a considerably larger impact on costs per unit relative to improvements in manufacturing efficiency ($5.08 versus $1.50). One explanation is that many costs are locked in once the design of the radio-cassette is completed. Improvements in manufacturing efficiency cannot reduce many of these costs. Design choices can influence many direct and overhead cost categories, for example, by reducing direct materials requirements, by reducing defects requiring rework, and by designing in fewer components that translate into fewer orders placed and lower ordering costs.

12-34 (50–60 min.) **Target cost, activity-based costing systems.**
(Continuation of 12-33)

1.   A target cost per unit is the estimated long-run cost per unit of a product (or service) that, when sold at the target price, enables the company to achieve the target operating income per unit. A target cost per unit is the estimated unit long-run cost of a product that will enable a company to enter or to remain in the market and compete profitably against its competitors.

2.   The following table presents the manufacturing cost per unit for different cost categories for P-41REV and P-63 REV.

Cost Categories	P-41 REV	P-63 REV
Direct manufacturing product costs:		
Direct materials	$381.20	$263.10
Indirect manufacturing product costs:		
Materials handling (71 × $1.20; 39 × $1.20)	85.20	46.80
Assembly management (2.1 × $40; 1.6 × $40)	84.00	64.00
Machine insertion of parts (59 × $0.70; 29 × $0.70)	41.30	20.30
Manual insertion of parts (12 × $2.10; 10 × $2.10)	25.20	21.00
Quality testing (1.2 × $25; 0.9 × $25)	30.00	22.50
Total indirect manufacturing costs	265.70	174.60
Total manufacturing costs	$646.90	$437.70
Target cost	$680.00	$390.00

P-41 REV is $33.10 below its target cost. However, P-63 REV is $47.70 above its target cost. It appears Executive Power will have major problems competing with the foreign printer costing $390.

3.

P-41	=	$782.40	P-63	=	$504.00
P-41 REV	=	646.90	P-63 REV	=	437.70
Difference	=	$135.50	Difference	=	$ 66.30

12-34 (Cont'd.)

The sources of the cost reductions in the redesigned products are:

		P-41	P-63
(a)	Reduction in direct materials costs	$ 26.30	$29.00
(b)	Changes in design:		
	Reduced materials handling costs due to fewer parts		
	$(85 – 71); (46 – 39) \times \$1.20$	16.80	8.40
	Reduced assembly time		
	$(3.2 – 2.1); (1.9 – 1.6) \times \$40$	44.00	12.00
	Reduced insertion of parts[1]		
	$(49 – 59) \times \$0.70 + (36 – 12) \times \$2.10$	43.40	
	$(31 – 29) \times \$0.70 + (15 – 10) \times \$2.10$		11.90
	Reduced quality testing		
	$(1.4 – 1.2); (1.1 – 0.9) \times \$25$	5.00	5.00
		$135.50	$66.30

[1] Note that the reduced costs for insertion of parts comes from two sources: (a) a reduction in total number of parts to be inserted, and (b) an increase in the percentage of parts inserted by the lower-cost machine method.

4.   The $12 reduction in cost per hour of assembly time (from $40 to $28) reduces product costs as follows:

P-41 REV: 12×2.1 hours = $25.20.   The new total manufacturing product cost is $621.70 ($646.90 – $25.20)

P-63 REV: 12×1.6 hours = $19.20.   The new total manufacturing product cost is $418.50 ($437.70 – $19.20)

The reduction in the assembly management activity rate further reduces the cost of P-41 REV below the target cost. It also makes it more likely that P-63 REV will achieve its target cost.

12-36   (25 min.)   Ethics and pricing.

1.   Full product costs for the new ball-bearings order are as follows:

Direct materials		$40,000
Direct manufacturing labor		10,000
Overhead costs		
Design and parts administration overhead	$4,000	
Production-order overhead	5,000	
Setup overhead	5,500	
Materials handling overhead	6,500	
General and administration overhead	9,000	
Total overhead costs		30,000
Full product costs		$80,000

Baker prices at full product costs plus a mark-up of 10% = $80,000 + 10% of $80,000 = $80,000 + $8,000 = $88,000.

12-36 (Cont'd.)

2. The incremental costs of the order are as follows:

Direct materials	$40,000
Direct manufacturing labor	10,000
30% of overhead costs 30% × $30,000	9,000
Incremental costs	$59,000

Any bid above $59,000 will generate a positive contribution margin for Baker. Baker may prefer to use full product costs because it regards the new ball-bearings order as a long-term business relationship rather than a special order. For long-run pricing decisions, managers prefer to use full product costs because it indicates the bare minimum costs they need to recover to continue in business rather than shut down. For a business to be profitable in the long run, it needs to recover *both* its variable and its fixed product costs. Using only variable costs may tempt the manager to engage in excessive long-run price cutting as long as prices give a positive contribution margin. Using full product costs for pricing thereby prompts price stability.

If Baker had regarded the ball-bearings order as a one-time-only special order and if Baker had excess capacity, it may have bid on the basis of its incremental costs with the goal of earning some contribution margin. On the other hand, if this were a special order and Baker was already operating at capacity, it would need to consider *both* the incremental costs and the opportunity costs of using limited capacity to satisfy the ball-bearings order, once again driving the price up toward its full product costs.

3. Not using full product costs (including an allocation of fixed overhead) to price the order, particularly if it is in direct contradiction of company policy, may be unethical. In assessing the situation, the specific "Standards of Ethical Conduct for Management Accountants," described in Chapter 1 (p. 10), that the management accountant should consider are listed below.

Competence
Clear reports using relevant and reliable information should be prepared. Reports prepared on the basis of excluding certain fixed costs that should be included would violate the management accountant's responsibility for competence. It is unethical for Lazarus to suggest that Decker change the cost numbers that were prepared for the bearings order and for Decker to change the numbers in order to make Lazarus's performance look good.

Integrity
The management accountant has a responsibility to avoid actual or apparent conflicts of interest and advise all appropriate parties of any potential conflict. Lazarus's motivation for wanting Decker to reduce costs was precisely to earn a larger bonus. This action could be viewed as violating the responsibility for integrity. The Standards of Ethical Conduct require the management accountant to communicate favorable as well as unfavorable information. In this regard, both Lazarus's and Decker's behavior (if Decker agrees to reduce the cost of the order) could be viewed as unethical.

12-36 (Cont'd.)

Objectivity
The Standards of Ethical Conduct for Management Accountants require that information should be fairly and objectively communicated and that all relevant information should be disclosed. From a management accountant's standpoint, reducing fixed overhead costs in deciding on the price to bid are clearly violating both of these precepts. For the various reasons cited above, we should take the position that the behavior described by Lazarus and Decker (if he goes along with Lazarus's wishes) is unethical.

Decker should indicate to Lazarus that the costs were correctly computed given the long-term nature of the ball-bearings contract, and that determining prices on the basis of full product costs plus a mark-up of 10% are also required by company policy. If Lazarus still insists on making the changes and reducing the costs of the order, Decker should raise the matter with Lazarus's superior. If, after taking all these steps, there is continued pressure to understate the costs, Decker should consider resigning from the company, rather than engaging in unethical behavior.

CHAPTER 13
STRATEGY, BALANCED SCORECARD AND STRATEGIC PROFITABILITY ANALYSIS

13-2 The five key forces to consider in industry analysis are: (a) competitors, (b) potential entrants into the market, (c) equivalent products, (d) bargaining power of customers, and (e) bargaining power of input suppliers.

13-4 The four key perspectives in the balanced scorecard are: (1) Financial perspective—this perspective evaluates the profitability of the strategy, (2) Customer perspective—this perspective identifies the targeted market segments and measures the company's success in these segments, (3) Internal business process perspective—this perspective focuses on internal operations that further both the customer perspective by creating value for customers and the financial perspective by increasing shareholder wealth, and (4) Learning and growth perspective—this perspective identifies the capabilities in which the organization must excel in order to achieve superior internal processes that create value for customers and shareholders.

13-6 A good balanced scorecard design has several features:
1. It tells the story of a company's strategy by articulating a sequence of cause-and-effect relationships.
2. It helps to communicate the strategy to all members of the organization by translating the strategy into a coherent and linked set of understandable and measurable operational targets.
3. It places strong emphasis on financial objectives and measures in for-profit companies. Nonfinancial measures are regarded as part of a program to achieve future financial performance.
4. It limits the number of measures to only those that are critical to the implementation of strategy.
5. It highlights suboptimal tradeoffs that managers may make when they fail to consider operational and financial measures together.

13-8 Three key components in doing a strategic analysis of operating income are:
1. The growth component which measures the change in operating income attributable solely to an increase in the quantity of output sold from one year to the next.
2. The price-recovery component which measures the change in operating income attributable solely to changes in the prices of inputs and outputs from one year to the next.
3. The productivity component which measures the change in costs attributable to a change in the quantity of inputs used in the current year relative to the quantity of inputs that would have been used in the previous year to produce current year output.

13-10 Engineered costs result from a cause-and-effect relationship between the cost driver, output, and the (direct or indirect) resources used to produce that output. Discretionary costs arise from periodic (usually) annual decisions regarding the maximum amount to be incurred. There is no measurable cause-and-effect relationship between output and resources used.

13-12 Downsizing (also called rightsizing) is an integrated approach configuring processes, products, and people in order to match costs to the activities that need to be performed for operating effectively and efficiently in the present and future.

13-14 Total factor productivity is the quantity of output produced divided by the costs of all inputs used, where the inputs are costed on the basis of current period prices.

13-16 (15 min.) **Balanced scorecard.**

1. La Quinta's 2001 strategy is a cost leadership strategy. La Quinta plans to grow by producing high-quality boxes at a low cost delivered to customers in a timely manner. La Quinta's boxes are not differentiated, and there are many other manufacturers who produce similar boxes. To succeed, La Quinta must achieve lower costs relative to competitors through productivity and efficiency improvements.

2. Measures that we would expect to see on a La Quinta's balanced scorecard for 2001 are

Financial Perspective
(1) Operating income from productivity gain, (2) operating income from growth, (3) cost reductions in key areas.
　　These measures evaluate whether La Quinta has successfully reduced costs and generated growth through cost leadership.

Customer Perspective
(1) Market share, (2) new customers, (3) customer satisfaction index, (4) customer retention, (5) time taken to fulfill customer orders.
　　The logic is that improvements in these customer measures are leading indicators of superior financial performance.

Internal Business Process Perspective
(1) Yield, (2) productivity, (3) order delivery time, (4) on-time delivery.
　　Improvements in these measures are expected to lead to more satisfied customers and in turn to superior financial performance

Learning and Growth Perspective
(1) Percentage of employees trained in process and quality management, (2) employee satisfaction, (3) number of major process improvements.
　　Improvements in these measures have a cause-and-effect relationship with improvements in internal business processes, which in turn lead to customer satisfaction and financial performance.

13-18 (15 min.) Strategy, balanced scorecard.

1.   Meredith Corporation follows a product differentiation strategy in 2000. Meredith's D4H machine is distinct from its competitors and generally regarded as superior to competitors' products.   To succeed, Meredith must continue to differentiate its product and charge a premium price.

2.   Balanced Scorecard measures for 2000 follow:

Financial Perspective

(1) Increase in operating income from charging higher margins, (2) Price premium earned on products.

These measures indicate whether Meredith has been able to charge premium prices and achieve operating income increases through product differentiation.

Customer Perspective

(1) Market share in high-end special-purpose textile machines, (2) customer satisfaction, (3) new customers.

Improvements in these customer measures are leading indicators of superior financial performance.

Internal Business Process Perspective

(1) Manufacturing quality, (2) new product features added, (3) order delivery time.

Improvements in these measures are expected to result in more satisfied customers and in turn superior financial performance.

Learning and Growth Perspective

(1) Development time for designing new machines, (2) improvements in manufacturing processes, (3) employee education and skill levels, (4) employee satisfaction.

Improvements in these measures have a cause-and-effect relationship with improvements in internal business processes, which in turn lead to customer satisfaction and financial performance.

13-20 (20 min.) **Analysis of growth, price-recovery, and productivity components.** (Continuation of 13-19)

Effect of the industry-market-size factor

If the 10-unit increase in sales from 200 to 210 units, 3% or 6 (3% × 200) units is due to growth in market size, and 4 (10 − 6) units is due to an increase in market share.

The change in Meredith's operating income from the industry-market size factor rather than from specific strategic actions is:

$280,000 (the growth component in Exercise 13-19) × $\dfrac{6}{10}$ $168,000 F

Effect of product differentiation

The change in operating income due to:

Increase in the selling price of D4H (revenue effect of price recovery)	$420,000 F
Increase in price of inputs (cost effect of price recovery)	184,500 U
Growth in market share due to product differentiation	

$280,000 (the growth component in Exercise 13-19) × $\dfrac{4}{10}$ 112,000 F

Change in operating income due to product differentiation $347,500 F

Effect of cost leadership

The change in operating income from cost leadership is:

Productivity component $92,000 F

The change in operating income between 1999 and 2000 can be summarized as follows:

Change due to industry-market-size	$168,000 F
Change due to product differentiation	347,500 F
Change due to cost leadership	92,000 F
Change in operating income	$607,500 F

Meredith has been successful in implementing its product differentiation strategy. Nearly 57% ($347,500 ÷ $607,500) of the increase in operating income during 2000 was due to product differentiation. Meredith's operating income increase in 2000 was also helped by a growth in the overall market and some productivity improvements.

13-22 (15 min.) **Strategy, balanced scorecard, service company.**

1. Snyder Corporation's strategy in 2000 is cost leadership. Snyder's consulting services for implementing sales management software is not distinct from its competitors. The market for these services is very competitive. To succeed, Snyder must deliver quality service at low cost. Improving productivity while maintaining quality is key.

2. Balanced Scorecard measures for 2000 follow:

Financial Perspective
(1) Increase operating income from productivity gains and growth, (2) revenues per employee, (3) cost reductions in key areas, for example, software implementation and overhead costs.

These measures indicate whether Snyder has been able to reduce costs and achieve operating income increases through cost leadership.

Customer Perspective
(1) Market share, (2) new customers, (3) customer responsiveness, (4) customer satisfaction.

Improvements in these customer measures are regarded as leading indicators of superior financial performance.

Internal Business Process Perspective
(1) Time to complete customer jobs, (2) time lost due to errors, (3) quality of job (Is system running smoothly after job is completed?)

Improvements in these measures are expected to lead to more satisfied customers, lower costs, and superior financial performance.

Learning and Growth Perspective
(1) Time required to analyze and design implementation steps, (2) time taken to perform key steps implementing the software, (3) skill levels of employees, (4) hours of employee training, (5) employee satisfaction and motivation.

Improvements in these measures have a cause-and-effect relationship with improvements in internal business processes, customer satisfaction, and financial performance.

13-24 (25 min.) **Analysis of growth, price-recovery and productivity components.** (Continuation of 13-23)

Effect of industry-market-size factors

Of the 10-unit increase in sales from 60 to 70 units, 5% or 3 units (5% × 60) is due to growth in market size, and 7 (10 − 3) units is due to an increase in market share.

The change in Snyder's operating income from the industry market-size factor rather than from specific strategic actions is:

$200,000 (the growth component in Exercise 13-23) × $\frac{3}{10}$ $60,000 F

Effect of product differentiation

Of the $2,000 decrease in selling price, 1% or $500 (1% × $50,000) is due to a general decline in prices, and the remaining decrease of $1,500 ($2,000 − $500) is due to a strategic decision by Snyder's management to implement its cost leadership strategy of lowering prices to stimulate demand.

The change in operating income due to a decline in selling price	
(other than the strategic reduction in price included in	
the cost leadership component) $500 × 70 units	$ 35,000 U
Increase in prices of inputs (cost effect of price recovery)	129,000 U
Change in operating income due to product differentiation	$164,000 U

Effect of cost leadership

Productivity component	$189,000 F
Effect of strategic decision to reduce selling price, $1,500 × 70	105,000 U

Growth in market share due to productivity improvement	
and strategic decision to reduce selling price	
$200,000 (the growth component in Exercise 13-23) × $\frac{7}{10}$	140,000 F
Change in operating income due to cost leadership	$224,000 F

The change in operating income between 1999 and 2000 can then be summarized as

Change due to industry-market-size	$ 60,000 F
Change due to product differentiation	164,000 U
Change due to cost leadership	224,000 F
Change in operating income	$120,000 F

Snyder has been very successful in implementing its cost leadership strategy. Due to a lack of product differentiation, Snyder was unable to pass along increases in labor costs by increasing the selling price—in fact selling price declined by $2,000 per work unit. However, Snyder was able to take advantage of its productivity gains to reduce price, gain market share, and increase operating income.

13-26 (20 min.) Balanced scorecard.

1. Caltex's strategy is to focus on "service-oriented customers" who are willing to pay a higher price for services. Even though its product is largely a commodity product, gasoline, Caltex wants to differentiate itself through the service it provides at its retailing stations.

Does the scorecard represent Caltex's strategy? By and large it does. The focus of the scorecard is on measures of process improvement, quality, market share, and financial success from product differentiation. There are some deficiencies that the subsequent assignment questions raise but, abstracting from these concerns for the moment, the scorecard does focus on implementing a product differentiation strategy.

Having concluded that the scorecard has been reasonably well designed, how has Caltex performed relative to its strategy in 2001? It appears from the scorecard that Caltex was successful in implementing its strategy in 2001. It achieved all targets in the financial, internal business, and learning and growth perspectives. The only target it missed was the market share target in the customer perspective. At this stage, students may raise some questions about whether this is a good scorecard measure. Requirement 3 gets at this issue in more detail. The bottom line is that measuring "market share in the overall gasoline market" rather than in the "service-oriented customer" market segment is not a good scorecard measure, so not achieving this target may not be as big an issue as it may seem at first.

2. Yes, Caltex should include some measure of employee satisfaction and employee training in the learning and growth perspective. Caltex's differentiation strategy and ability to charge a premium price is based on customer service. The key to good, fast, and friendly customer service is well-trained and satisfied employees. Untrained and dissatisfied employees will have poor interactions with customers and cause the strategy to fail. Hence, training and employee satisfaction are very important to Caltex for implementing its strategy. These measures are leading indicators of whether Caltex will be able to successfully implement its strategy and, hence, should be measured on the balanced scorecard.

3. Caltex's strategy is to focus on the 60% of gasoline consumers who are service-oriented not on the 40% price-shopper segment. To evaluate if it has been successful in implementing its strategy, Caltex needs to measure its market share in its targeted market segment, "service-oriented customer," not its market share in the overall market. Given Caltex's strategy, it should not be concerned if its market share in the price-shopper segment declines. In fact, charging premium prices will probably cause its market share in this segment to decline. Caltex should replace "market share in overall gasoline market" with "market share in the service-oriented customer segment" in its balanced scorecard customer measure. Caltex may also want to consider putting a customer satisfaction measure on the scorecard. This measure should capture an overall evaluation of customer reactions to the facility, the convenience store, employee interactions, and quick turnaround. The customer satisfaction measure would serve as a leading indicator of market share in the service-oriented customer segment.

4. Although there is a cause-and-effect link between internal business process measures and customer measures on the current scorecard, Caltex should add more measures to tighten this linkage. In particular, the current scorecard measures focus exclusively on refinery operations and not on gas station operations. Caltex should add measures of gas station performance such as cleanliness of the facility, turnaround time at the gas pumps, the shopping experience at the convenience store, and the service provided by employees. Many companies do random audits of their facilities to evaluate how well their branches and retail outlets are performing. These measures would serve as leading indicators of customer satisfaction and market share in Caltex's targeted segments.

5. Caltex is correct in not measuring changes in operating income from productivity improvements on its scorecard under the financial perspective. Caltex's strategy is to grow by charging premium prices for customer service. The scorecard measures focus on Caltex's success in implementing this strategy. Productivity gains per se are not critical to Caltex's strategy and, hence, should not be measured on the scorecard.

13-28 (35 min.) Strategic analysis of operating income.

1. Halsey is following a product differentiation strategy. Halsey offers a wide selection of clothes and excellent customer service. Halsey's strategy is to distinguish itself from its competitors and to charge a premium price.

2. Operating income for each year is as follows:

	2001	2002
Revenues ($60 × 40,000; $59 × 40,000)	$2,400,000	$2,360,000
Costs		
Materials costs ($40 × 40,000; $41 × 40,000)	1,600,000	1,640,000
Selling & customer service costs ($7 × 51,000); $6.90 × 43,000)	357,000	296,700
Purchasing & admin. costs ($250 × 980; $240 × 850)	245,000	204,000
Total costs	2,202,000	2,140,700
Operating income	$ 198,000	$ 219,300
Change in operating income	$21,300 F	

3. **The Growth Component**

$$
\begin{array}{l}
\text{Revenue effect} \\
\text{of growth} \\
\text{component}
\end{array}
=
\left(
\begin{array}{l}
\text{Actual units of} \\
\text{output sold} \\
\text{in 2002}
\end{array}
-
\begin{array}{l}
\text{Actual units of} \\
\text{output sold} \\
\text{in 2001}
\end{array}
\right)
\times
\begin{array}{l}
\text{Output} \\
\text{price} \\
\text{in 2001}
\end{array}
$$

$$= (40{,}000 - 40{,}000) \times \$60 = \$0$$

13-28 (Cont'd.)

$$\begin{matrix}\text{Cost effect} \\ \text{of growth} \\ \text{component}\end{matrix} = \left(\begin{matrix}\text{Actual units of input or} \\ \text{capacity that would} \\ \text{have been used to produce} \\ \text{year 2002 output assuming} \\ \text{the same input - output} \\ \text{relationship that existed in 2001}\end{matrix} - \begin{matrix}\text{Actual units of} \\ \text{inputs or capacity} \\ \text{to produce} \\ \text{2001 output}\end{matrix}\right) \times \begin{matrix}\text{Input} \\ \text{prices} \\ \text{in 2001}\end{matrix}$$

Materials costs that would be required in 2002 would be the same as that required in 2001 because output is the same between 2001 and 2002. Manufacturing conversion costs and selling and customer-service costs will not change since adequate capacity exists in 2001 to support year 2002 output and customers.

The cost effects of growth component are:

Materials costs	$(40,000 - 40,000)$	×	$60	=	$0
Selling & cust.-serv. costs	$(51,000 - 51,000)$	×	$7	=	0
Purch. & admin. costs	$(980 - 980)$	×	$250	=	0
Cost effect of growth component					$0

In summary, the net effect on operating income as a result of the growth component equals:

Revenue effect of growth component	$0
Cost effect of growth component	0
Change in operating income due to growth component	$0

The Price-Recovery Component

$$\begin{matrix}\text{Revenue effect of} \\ \text{price - recovery} \\ \text{component}\end{matrix} = \left(\begin{matrix}\text{Output price} \\ \text{in 2002}\end{matrix} - \begin{matrix}\text{Output price} \\ \text{in 2001}\end{matrix}\right) \times \begin{matrix}\text{Actual units} \\ \text{of output} \\ \text{sold in 2002}\end{matrix}$$

$$= (\$59 - \$60) \times 40,000 = \$40,000 \text{ U}$$

$$\begin{matrix}\text{Cost effect of} \\ \text{price - recovery} \\ \text{component}\end{matrix} = \left(\begin{matrix}\text{Input} \\ \text{prices in} \\ \text{year} \\ 2002\end{matrix} - \begin{matrix}\text{Input} \\ \text{prices in} \\ \text{year} \\ 2001\end{matrix}\right) \times \begin{matrix}\text{Actual units of inputs or capacity} \\ \text{that would have been used} \\ \text{to produce year 2002 output} \\ \text{assuming the same input - output} \\ \text{relationship that} \\ \text{existed in 2001}\end{matrix}$$

Materials costs	$(\$41 - \$40)$	×	40,000	=	$40,000 U
Selling & cust.-serv. costs	$(\$6.90 - \$7)$	×	51,000	=	5,100 F
Purchas. & admin. costs	$(\$240 - \$250)$	×	980	=	9,800 F
Total cost effect of price-recovery component					$25,100 U

13-28 (Cont'd.)

In summary, the net decrease in operating income as a result of the price-recovery component equals:

Revenue effect of price-recovery component	$40,000 U
Cost effect of price-recovery component	25,100 U
Change in operating income due to price-recovery component	$65,100 U

The Productivity Component

$$\text{Productivity component} = \left(\begin{array}{c} \text{Actual units of} \\ \text{inputs or capacity} \\ \text{used to produce} \\ \text{year 2002 output} \end{array} - \begin{array}{c} \text{Actual units of} \\ \text{inputs or capacity that} \\ \text{would have been used} \\ \text{to produce year 2002} \\ \text{output assuming the same} \\ \text{input - output relationship} \\ \text{that existed in 2001} \end{array} \right) \times \begin{array}{c} \text{Input} \\ \text{prices in} \\ \text{2002} \end{array}$$

The productivity component of cost changes are:

Materials costs	$(40,000 - 40,000) \times \$41$	=	0
Selling & cust.-serv. costs	$(43,000 - 51,000) \times \$6.90$	=	$55,200 F
Purchasing & admin. costs	$(850 - 980) \times \$240$	=	31,200 F
Change in operating income due to productivity component			$86,400 F

The change in operating income between 2001 and 2002 can be analyzed as follows:

	Income Statement Amounts in 1999 (1)	Revenue and Cost Effects of Growth Component in 2000 (2)	Revenue and Cost Effects of Price-Recovery Component in 2000 (3)	Cost Effect of Productivity Component in 2000 (4)	Income Statement Amounts in 2000 (5) = (1) + (2) + (3) + (4)
Revenues	$2,400,000	$0	$40,000 U	—	$2,360,000
Costs	2,202,000	0	25,100 U	$ 86,400 F	2,140,700
Operating income	$ 198,000	$0	$65,100 U	$ 86,400 F	$ 219,300

$21,300 F
Change in operating income

13-28 (Cont'd.)

4.   The analysis of operating income indicates that a significant amount of the increase in operating income resulted from productivity gains rather than product differentiation. The company was unable to charge a premium price for its clothes. Thus, the strategic analysis of operating income indicates that Halsey has not been successful at implementing its premium price, product differentiation strategy, despite the fact that operating income increased by more than 10% between 2001 and 2002. Halsey could not pass on increases in purchase costs to its customers via higher prices. Halsey must either reconsider its strategy or focus managers on increasing margins and growing market share by offering better product variety and superb customer service.

13-30   (20 min.)   Engineered and discretionary overhead costs, unused capacity, repairs and maintenance.

1.   Rowland's repair and maintenance costs are indirect, engineered costs. The amount of repair and maintenance costs each year may not correlate directly to the quantity of gears produced. Over time, however, there is a clear cause-and-effect relationship between the output (quantity of gears produced) and repair and maintenance costs—the more gears that are produced, the greater the number of hours the machines will be run, and the greater the repairs and maintenance the machines will need.

2.   (1)   Available repair and maintenance capacity
            8 hours per day × 250 days × 4 workers   8,000 hours
       (2)   Repair and maintenance work actually done   6,000 hours
       (3) = (1) − (2) Hours of unused repair and maintenance capacity   2,000 hours
       (4)   Repair and maintenance cost per hour, $40,000 ÷ 2,000 $20 per hour
       (5) = (3) × (4) Cost of unused repair and maintenance capacity $40,000

Reasons why Rowland might want to downsize its repair and maintenance capacity are:
       a.   to reduce costs of carrying unused capacity
       b.   to create a culture of streamlining processes and operating efficiently

Reasons why Rowland might not want to downsize its repair and maintenance capacity are:
       a.   it projects greater demand for repairs and maintenance activity in the near future
       b.   it would negatively affect employee morale
       c.   it may want to use the expertise of the repairs and maintenance staff in other areas such as process improvements
       d.   it does not regard the unused capacity as particularly excessive

3.   If repair and maintenance costs are discretionary costs, calculating unused capacity is much more difficult. Repair and maintenance costs would be discretionary if repair and maintenance are mostly of a preventive type that management can choose when to do. In this case, the lack of a cause-and-effect relationship between output and repair and maintenance activity means that Rowland cannot determine the repair and maintenance resources used and, hence, the amount of unused capacity.

13-32 (20 min.) Partial productivity measurement.

1. Berkshire Corporations partial productivity ratios in 2002 are as follows:

$$\text{Direct materials partial productivity} = \frac{\text{Quantity of output produced in 2002}}{\text{Kilograms of direct materials used in 2002}} = \frac{525{,}000}{610{,}000} = 0.86 \text{ units per kg.}$$

$$\text{Direct manuf. labor partial productivity} = \frac{\text{Quantity of output produced in 2002}}{\text{Direct manuf. labor - hours used in 2002}} = \frac{525{,}000}{9{,}500} = 55.26 \text{ units per labor - hour}$$

$$\text{Manufacturing overhead partial productivity} = \frac{\text{Quantity of output produced in 2002}}{\text{Units of manuf. capacity in 2002}} = \frac{525{,}000}{582{,}000} = 0.90 \text{ units per unit of capacity}$$

To compare partial productivities in 2002 with partial productivities in 2001, we first calculate the inputs that would have been used in 2001 to produce year 2002's 525,000 units of output assuming the year 2001 relationship between inputs and outputs.

Direct materials $= 450{,}000 \text{ kg (2001)} \times \dfrac{525{,}000 \text{ output units in 2002}}{375{,}000 \text{ output units in 2001}}$

$\qquad\qquad\quad = 450{,}000 \times 1.4 = 630{,}000 \text{ kg.}$

Direct manuf. labor $= 7{,}500 \text{ hours (2001)} \times \dfrac{525{,}000 \text{ output units in 2002}}{375{,}000 \text{ output units in 2001}}$

$\qquad\qquad\quad = 7{,}500 \times 1.4 = 10{,}500 \text{ labor-hours}$

Manufacturing capacity $=$ 600,000 units of capacity, because manufacturing capacity is fixed, and adequate capacity existed in 2001 to produce year 2002 output.

Partial productivity calculations for 2001 based on year 2002 output (to make the partial productivities comparable across the two years)

$$\text{Direct materials partial productivity} = \frac{\text{Quantity of output produced in 2002}}{\substack{\text{Kilograms of direct materials that would} \\ \text{have been used in 2001 to produce} \\ \text{year 2002 output}}} = \frac{525{,}000}{630{,}000} = 0.83 \text{ units per kg}$$

$$\text{Direct manufac. labor partial productivity} = \frac{\text{Quantity of output produced in 2002}}{\substack{\text{Direct manuf. labor - hours that would} \\ \text{have been used in 2001 to produce} \\ \text{year 2002 output}}} = \frac{525{,}000}{10{,}500} = 50 \text{ units per labor - hour}$$

$$\text{Manufacturing overhead partial productivity} = \frac{\text{Quantity of output produced in 2002}}{\substack{\text{Units of manuf. capacity that would} \\ \text{have been used in 2001 to produce} \\ \text{year 2002 output}}} = \frac{525{,}000}{600{,}000} = 0.875 \text{ units per unit of capacity}$$

13-32 (Cont'd.)

The calculations indicate that Berkshire improved the partial productivity of all its inputs between 2001 and 2002 via improvements in efficiency of direct materials and direct manufacturing labor and by reducing unused manufacturing capacity.

2.   All partial productivity ratios increase from 2001 to 2002. We can therefore, conclude that total factor productivity definitely increased from 2001 to 2002. Partial productivities cannot, however, tell us how much total factor productivity changed, because partial productivity measures cannot be aggregated over different inputs.

3.   Berkshire Corporation management can use the partial productivity measures to set targets for the next year. Partial productivity measures can easily be compared over multiple periods. For example, they may specify bonus payments if partial productivity of direct manufacturing labor increases to 60 units of output per direct manufacturing labor-hour and if partial productivity of direct materials improves to 0.90 units of output per kilogram of direct materials. A major advantage of partial productivity measures is that they focus on a single input; hence, they are simple to calculate and easy to understand at the operations level. Managers and operators can also examine these numbers to understand the reasons underlying productivity changes from one period to the next—better training of workers, lower absenteeism, lower labor turnover, better incentives, or improved methods. Management can then implement and sustain these factors in the future.

13-34   (25 min.)   Balanced scorecard, ethics.

1.   Yes, the Household Products Division (HPD) should include measures of employee satisfaction and customer satisfaction even if these measures are subjective. For a maker of kitchen dishwashers, employee and customer satisfaction are leading indicators of future financial performance. There is a cause-and-effect linkage between these measures and future financial performance. If HPD's strategy is correct and if the scorecard has been properly designed, employee and customer satisfaction information is very important in evaluating the implementation of HPD's strategy.

HPD should use employee and customer satisfaction measures even though these measures are subjective. One of the pitfalls to avoid when implementing a balanced scorecard is not to use only objective measures in the scorecard. Of course, HPD should guard against imprecision and potential for manipulation. Patricia Conley appears to be aware of this. She has tried to understand the reasons for the poor scores and has been able to relate these scores to other objective evidence such as employee dissatisfaction with the new work rules and customer unhappiness with missed delivery dates.

2.   Incorrect reporting of employee and customer satisfaction ratings to make divisions performance look good is unethical. In assessing the situation, the specific "Standards of Ethical Conduct for Management Accounts" (described in Exhibit 1-7) that the management account should consider are listed below.

Competence
Clear reports using relevant and reliable information should be prepared. Preparing reports on the basis of incorrect employee and customer satisfaction ratings in order to make the division's performance look better than it is violates competence standards. It is unethical for Conley to change the employee and customer satisfaction ratings in order to make the division's performance look good.

Integrity
The management accountant has a responsibility to avoid actual or apparent conflicts of interest and advise all appropriate parties of any potential conflict. Conley may be tempted to report better employee and customer satisfaction ratings to please Emburey. This action, however, violates the responsibility for integrity. The Standards of Ethical Conduct require the management accountant to communicate favorable as well as unfavorable information.

Objectivity
The management accountant's standards of ethical conduct require that information should be fairly and objectively communicated and that all relevant information should be disclosed. From a management accountant's standpoint, modifying employee and customer satisfaction ratings to make division performance look good would violate the standard of objectivity.

Conley should indicate to Emburey that the employee and customer satisfaction ratings are, indeed, appropriate. If Emburey still insists on reporting better employee and customer satisfaction numbers, Conley should raise the matter with one of Emburey's superiors. If, after taking all these steps, there is continued pressure to overstate employee and customer satisfaction ratings, Conley should consider resigning from the company and not engage in unethical behavior.

CHAPTER 14
COST ALLOCATION

14-2   The salary of a plant security guard would be a direct cost when the cost object is the security department of the plant. It would be an indirect cost when the cost object is a product.

14-4   Exhibit 14-2 lists four criteria used to guide cost allocation decisions:
1.   Cause and effect.
2.   Benefits received.
3.   Fairness or equity.
4.   Ability to bear.

Either the cause-and-effect criterion or the benefits-received criterion is the dominant one when the purpose of the allocation is related to the economic decision purpose or the motivation purpose.

14-6   A cost-hierarchy approach results in a better understanding of the causes of costs being incurred. A cost-hierarchy also facilitates implementing a performance evaluation approach based on controllability.

14-8   The chapter gives the following examples of bases used to allocate corporate cost pools to the operating divisions of an organization:

> Treasury costs—allocated using cost of new assembly equipment.
> Corporate human resource management costs—allocated using salary and labor costs of
>   divisions.
> Corporate administration costs—allocated using division administration costs.

14-10   Disagree. Allocating costs on "the basis of estimated long-run use by user department managers" means department managers can lower their cost allocations by deliberately underestimating their long-run use.

14-12   The *reciprocal method* is theoretically the most defensible method because it explicitly recognizes the mutual services provided among all departments, irrespective of whether those departments are operating or support departments.

14-14   All contracts with U.S. government agencies must comply with cost accounting standards issued by the Cost Accounting Standards Board (CASB).

14-16 (15-20 min.) **Cost allocation in hospitals, alternative allocation criteria.**

1. Direct costs   = $2.40
    Indirect costs   = $11.52 – $2.40 = $9.12
    Overhead rate   = $\dfrac{\$9.12}{\$2.40}$ = 380%

2. The answers here are less than clear-cut in some cases.

Overhead Cost Item	Allocation Criteria
Processing of paperwork for purchase	Cause and effect
Supplies room management fee	Benefits received
Operating-room and patient-room handling charge	Cause and effect
Administrative hospital costs	Benefits received
University teaching-related costs	Ability to bear
Malpractice insurance costs	Ability to bear or benefits received
Costing of treating uninsured patients	Ability to bear
Profit component	None. This is not a cost.

3. Assuming that Meltzer's insurance company is responsible for paying the $4,800 bill, Meltzer probably can only express outrage at the amount of the bill. The point of this question is to note that even if Meltzer objects strongly to one or more overhead items, it is his insurance company that likely has the greater incentive to challenge the bill. Individual patients have very little power in the medical arena. In contrast, insurance companies have considerable power and may decide that certain costs are not reimbursable–for example, the costs of treating uninsured patients.

One student commented that Meltzer is best advised to avoid subsequent visits to Sierra University Hospital by becoming a better skier.

14-18 (20 min.) **Single-rate versus dual-rate allocation methods, support department.**

Bases available (kilowatt hours):

	Rockford	Peoria	Hammond	Kankakee	Total
Practical capacity	10,000	20,000	12,000	8,000	50,000
Expected monthly usage	8,000	9,000	7,000	6,000	30,000

1. a. Single-rate method based on practical capacity:

Total costs in pool	=	$6,000 + $9,000	= $15,000
Practical capacity	=	50,000 kilowatt hours	
Allocation rate	=	$15,000 ÷ 50,000	= $0.30 per hour of capacity

	Rockford	Peoria	Hammond	Kankakee	Total
Practical capacity in hours	10,000	20,000	12,000	8,000	50,000
Costs allocated at $0.30 per hour	$3,000	$6,000	$3,600	$2,400	$15,000

   b. Single-rate method based on expected monthly usage:

Total costs in pool	= $6,000 + $9,000 = $15,000
Expected usage	= 30,000 kilowatt hours
Allocation rate	= $15,000 ÷ 30,000 = $0.50 per hour of expected usage

	Rockford	Peoria	Hammond	Kankakee	Total
Expected monthly usage in hours	8,000	9,000	7,000	6,000	30,000
Costs allocated at $0.50 per hour	$4,000	$4,500	$3,500	$3,000	$15,000

2. Variable-Cost Pool:

Total costs in pool	=	$6,000
Expected usage	=	30,000 kilowatt hours
Allocation rate	=	$0.20 per hour of expected usage

   Fixed-Cost Pool:

Total costs in pool	=	$9,000
Practical capacity	=	50,000 kilowatt hours
Allocation rate	=	$0.18 per hour of capacity

14-18 (Cont'd.)

	Rockford	Peoria	Hammond	Kankakee	Total
Variable-cost pool	$1,600	$1,800	$1,400	$1,200	$ 6,000
Fixed-cost pool	1,800	3,600	2,160	1,440	9,000
Total	$3,400	$5,400	$3,560	$2,640	$15,000

The dual-rate method permits a more refined allocation of the power department costs; it permits the use of different allocation bases for different cost pools. The fixed costs result from decisions most likely associated with the practical capacity level. The variable costs result from decisions most likely associated with monthly usage.

14-20 (10–15 min.) **Single-rate cost allocation method, budgeted versus actual costs and quantities.**

1. a. $\dfrac{\text{Budgeted indirect costs}}{\text{Budgeted trips}} = \dfrac{\$575,000}{250 \text{ trips}}$

   $= \$2,300 \text{ per round trip}$

   b. $\dfrac{\text{Actual indirect costs}}{\text{Actual trips}} = \dfrac{\$645,000}{300 \text{ trips}}$

   $= \$2,150 \text{ per round trip}$

Charges With Single-Rate Method:

   a. Budgeted indirect costs/Budgeted quantities using actual trips

   Orange Juice: $2,300 × 200   = $460,000
   Grapefruit Juice: $2,300 × 100   = $230,000

   b. Actual indirect costs/Actual quantities using actual trips

   Orange Juice: $2,150 x 200   = $430,000
   Grapefruit Juice: $2,150 x 100   = $215,000

2. When budgeted costs/budgeted quantities are used, the Orange Juice Division knows at the start of 2001 that it will be charged a rate of $2,300 per trip. This enables it to make operating decisions knowing the rate it will have to pay for transportation. In contrast, when actual costs/actual quantities are used, the Orange Juice Division must wait until year-end to know its transportation charges.

The use of actual costs/actual quantities makes the costs allocated to one user a function of the actual demand of other users. In 2001, the actual usage was 300 trips, which is 50 trips above the 250 trips budgeted. These extra trips are one explanation for the actual cost rate being less than the budgeted rate. In 2001, the Orange Juice Division would have had lower costs had the actual rate been used. However, the reverse also will occur when there is lower use than budgeted by other plants.

14-22 (30 min.)   **Contracting, cost allocation.**

1.

Revenues: 450,000 × $5.60	$ 2,520,000
Variable costs: 450,000 × $2.80	1,260,000
Contribution margin	1,260,000
Fixed costs	1,350,000
Operating income	$ (90,000)

2.

Fixed costs per baseball in 2000 $= \dfrac{\$1,350,000}{450,000}$

= $3.00 per baseball

Total costs per baseball:

Variable costs	$2.80
Fixed costs	3.00
Total costs	$5.80

3.

Unit sales for 2001: 450,000 × 1.12 = 504,000
Variable costs per unit: $2.80 × 0.90 = $2.52
Fixed costs = $1,350,000 × 0.75 = $1,012,500
Unit fixed costs = $1,012,500 ÷ 504,000 = $2.01
Total unit costs per baseball = $2.52 + $2.01 = $4.53

Revenues: 504,000 × $5.60	$2,822,400
Variable costs: 504,000 × $2.52	1,270,080
Contribution margin	1,552,320
Fixed costs	1,012,500
Operating income[a]	$ 539,820

[a.] Before payment to Sprout.

4. Remuneration is:

a. Fixed fee	$ 50,000
b. 10% of cost savings	
0.10 × ($5.80 − $4.53) × 450,000	57,150
c. 0.10 on sales > 450,000	
$0.10 × (504,000 − 450,000)	5,400
	$112,550

Operating income after full payment to Sprout is: $539,820 − $112,550 = $427,270

14-24 (20 min.)   **Allocation of travel costs.**

1.   Allocation of the $1,800 airfare: Alternative approaches include:

a.   The stand-alone cost allocation method. This method would allocate the air fare on the basis of each user's percentage of the total of the individual stand-alone costs:

New York employer $\qquad \dfrac{\$1,400}{(\$1,400 + \$1,100)} \times \$1,800 = \quad \$1,008$

Chicago employer $\qquad \dfrac{\$1,100}{(\$1,400 + \$1,100)} \times \$1,800 = \quad \underline{\quad 792\quad}$

$\hphantom{Chicago employer \qquad \dfrac{\$1,100}{(\$1,400 + \$1,100)} \times \$1,800 = \quad} \underline{\$1,800}$

Advocates of this method often emphasize an equity or fairness rationale.

b.   The incremental cost allocation method. This requires the choice of a primary party and an incremental party.

If the New York employer is the primary party, the allocation would be:

New York employer	$1,400
Chicago employer	400
	$1,800

One rationale is Ernst was planning to make the New York trip, and the Chicago stop was added subsequently. Some students have suggested allocating as much as possible to the New York employer since Ernst was not joining them.

If the Chicago employer is the primary party, the allocation would be:

Chicago employer	$1,100
New York employer	700
	$1,800

One rationale is that the Chicago employer is the successful recruiter and presumably receives more benefits from the recruiting expenditures.

2.   A simple approach is to split the $60 equally between the two employers. The limousine costs at the San Francisco end are not a function of distance traveled on the plane.

14-24 (Cont'd.)

An alternative approach is to add the $60 to the $1,800 and repeat requirement 1:

a. Stand-alone cost allocation method:

New York employer
$$\frac{\$1,460}{(\$1,460 + \$1,160)} \times \$1,860 = \$1,036$$

Chicago employer
$$\frac{\$1,160}{(\$1,460 + \$1,160)} \times \$1,860 = \$824$$

b. Incremental cost allocation method. With New York employer as the primary party:

New York employer	$1,460
Chicago employer	400
	$1,860

With Chicago employer as the primary party:

Chicago employer	$1,160
New York employer	700
	$1,860

Note: Ask any students in the class how they handled this situation if they have faced it.

14-26 (30 min.) **Support department cost allocation, reciprocal method (continuation of 14-25).**

1.

	A/HR	IS	Govt.	Corp.
Costs	$600,000	$2,400,000		
Alloc. of A/HR (0.25, 0.40, 0.35))	(861,538)	215,385	$ 344,615	$ 301,538
Alloc. of I.S. (0.10, 0.30, 0.60)	261,538	(2,615,385)	784,615	1,569,231
			$1,129,230	$1,870,769

Reciprocal Method Computation

$$A = \$600,000 + 0.10IS$$
$$IS = \$2,400,000 + 0.25A$$

$$IS = \$2,400,000 + 0.25 (\$600,000 + 0.10IS)$$
$$= \$2,400,000 + \$150,000 + 0.025IS$$
$$0.975IS = \$2,550,000$$
$$IS = \$2,550,000 \div 0.975$$
$$= \$2,615,385$$

$$A = \$600,000 + 0.10 (\$2,615,385)$$
$$= \$600,000 + \$261,538$$
$$= \$861,538$$

2.

		Govt. Consulting	Corp. Consulting
a.	Direct	$1,120,000	$1,880,000
b.	Step-Down (Ad/HR first)	1,090,000	1,910,000
c.	Step-Down (IS first)	1,168,000	1,832,080
d.	Reciprocal	1,129,230	1,870,769

The four methods differ in the level of service department cost allocation across service departments. The level of reciprocal service department is material. Administrative/HR supplies 25% of its services to Information Systems. Information Systems supplies 10% of its services to Administrative/HR. The Information Department has a budget of $2,400,000 which is 400% higher than Administrative/HR.

The reciprocal method recognizes all the interactions and is thus the most accurate.

14-28 (30 min.)   **Reciprocal cost allocation.**

1. The reciprocal allocation method explicitly includes the mutual services provided among all support departments. Interdepartmental relationships are fully incoporated into the support department cost allocations.

2.   AD $= \$72,700 + .0833\text{IS}$

 IS $= \$234,400 + .2308\text{AD}$

 AD $= \$72,700 + [.0833(\$234,400 + .2308\text{AD})]$

  $= \$72,700 + [\$19,525.52 + 0.019226\text{AD}]$

$0.980774\text{AD} = \$92,225.52$

 AD $= \$92,225.52 \div 0.980774$

  $= \$94,033$

 IS $= \$234,400 + (0.2308 \times \$94,033)$

  $= \$256,103$

	Support Depts		Operating Depts		
	Administ.	Info. Systems	Corporate	Consumer	Total
Costs Incurred	$72,700	$234,400	$ 998,270	$489,860	$1,795,230
Alloc. of Admin.					
(21/91, 42/91, 28/91)	(94,033)	21,700	43,400	28,933	
Alloc. of Info. Syst.					
(320/3,840, 1,920/3,840,					
1,600/3,840)	21,342	(256,103)	128,051	106,710	
	$ 9*	$ (3)*	$1,169,721	$625,503	$1,795,230

 * Rounding causes not to be exactly $0.

3. The reciprocal method is more accurate than the direct and step-down methods when there is reciprocal relationships among support departments.
A summary of the alternatives is:

	Corporate Sales	Consumer Sales
Direct method	$1,169,745	$625,485
Step-down method		
(Admin. first)	1,168,830	626,400
Reciprocal method	1,169,721	625,503

The reciprocal method is the preferred method, although for September 2001 the numbers do not appear materially different across the alternatives.

14-30 (30 min.)   **Cost allocation, monthly reports.**

1. Problems with the monthly allocation report include:

   a. The single-rate method used does not distinguish between fixed vs. variable costs.
   b. Actual costs and actual quantities are used. This results in managers not knowing cost rates until year-end.
   c. Monthly time periods are used to determine cost rates. The use of a monthly time period can result in highly variable cost rates depending on seasonality, days in a month, demand surges and so on.

Budgeted variable cost (based on normal usage):

$$\frac{\$7,500,000}{100,000,000} = \$0.075 \text{ per kwh}$$

Monthly Allocation Report
November 2000

Allocations of Variable Costs (based on budgeted rate × actual usage)*

To Department A: 60,000,000 x $0.075 $4,500,000
To Department B: 20,000,000 x $0.075   1,500,000
                                                $6,000,000

*There will be $1,500,000 of unallocated variable costs for November 2000.

Allocation of Fixed Costs (Based on budgeted usage × budgeted amount)

To Department A: 60% × $30,000,000 $18,000,000
To Department B: 40% × $30,000,000   12,000,000
                                            $30,000,000

Department A
   Variable costs $ 4,500,000
   Fixed costs   18,000,000
                       $22,500,000

Department B
   Variable costs $ 1,500,000
   Fixed costs   12,000,000
                       $13,500,000

3. Under Lamb's allocation report, the production manager has both risk-exposure and uncertainty concerns:

- *Risk-exposure*—Changes in the demand for energy by Department A affect the costs Lamb will report for Department B. Increases in demand by A will reduce B's cost per kwh and vice versa. Department B's production manager may seek to curtail production in periods when Departments A's production declines. This could create an ever-diminishing cycle of production. Alternatively, Department B may subcontract outside to avoid a higher energy rate, even if it is not in Bulldog's best interest to subcontract.
- *Uncertainty*—When actual costs are used, managers cannot plan costs with certainty. Managers typically have less ability to bear uncertainty than do companies. The result is that managers may reject alternatives that are good risks from Bulldog's perspectives but not attractive risks for themselves.

14-32 (40-60 min.) **Support department cost allocations; single-department cost pools; direct, step-down, and reciprocal methods.**

All the following computations are in dollars.

1.

Direct method:

	To X	To Y
A	250/400 × $100,000 = $62,500	150/400 × $100,000 = $37,500
B	100/500 × $40,000 = 8,000	400/500 × $40,000 = 32,000
Total	$70,500	$69,500

Step-down method, allocating A first:

	A	B	X	Y
Costs to be allocated	$100,000	$40,000	—	—
Allocate A: (0.2, 0.5, 0.3)	(100,000)	20,000	$50,000	$30,000
Allocate B: (0.2, 0.8)	—	(60,000)	12,000	48,000
Total	$ 0	$ 0	$62,000	$78,000

Step-down method, allocating B first:

	A	B	X	Y
Costs to be allocated	$100,000	$40,000	—	—
Allocate B: (0.5, 0.1, 0.4)	20,000	(40,000)	$ 4,000	$16,000
Allocate A: (250/400, 150/400)	(120,000)	—	75,000	45,000
Total	$ 0	$ 0	$79,000	$61,000

Note that these methods produce significantly different results, so the choice of method may frequently make a difference in the budgeted department overhead rates.

Reciprocal method:

Stage 1: Let A = total costs of materials-handling department
B = total costs of power-generating department

(1) A = $100,000 + 0.5B
(2) B = $ 40,000 + 0.2A

Stage 2: Substituting in (1):
A = $100,000 + 0.5($40,000 + 0.2A)
A = $100,000 + $20,000 + 0.1A
0.9A = $120,000
A = $133,333

Substituting in (2):
B = $40,000 + 0.2($133,333)
B = $66,666

14-32 (Cont'd.)

Stage 3:

	A	B	X	Y
Original amounts	100,000	40,000	—	—
Allocation of A	(133,333)	26,666(20%)	66,667(50%)	
	40,000(30%)			
Allocation of B	33,333(50%)	(66,666)	6,667(10%)	
26,666(40%)				
Totals accounted for	—	—	73,334	66,666

Comparison of methods:

Method of Allocation	X	Y
Direct method	$70,500	$69,500
Step-down: A first	62,000	78,000
Step-down: B first	79,000	61,000
Reciprocal method	73,334	66,666

Note that *in this case* the direct method produces answers that are the closest to the "correct" answers (that is, those from the reciprocal method), step-down allocating B first is next, and step-down allocating A first is least accurate.

2.   At first glance, it appears that the cost of power is $40 per unit plus the material handling costs. If so, Manes would be better off by purchasing from the power company. However, the decision should be influenced by the effects of the interdependencies and the fixed costs. Note that the power needs would be less (students miss this) if they were purchased from the outside:

	Outside Power Units Needed
X	100
Y	400
A (500 units minus 20% of 500 units, because there is no need to service the nonexistent power department)	400
Total units	900

Total costs, 900 x $40 = $36,000

14-32 (Cont'd.)

In contrast, the total costs that would be saved by not producing the power inside would depend on the effects of the decision on various costs:

	Avoidable Costs of 100 Units of Power Produced Inside
Variable indirect labor and indirect material costs	$10,000
Supervision in power department	10,000
Materials handling, 20% of $70,000*	14,000
Probable minimum cost savings	$34,000
Possible additional savings:	
a. Can any supervision in materials handling be saved because of overseeing less volume? Minimum savings is probably zero; the maximum is probably 20% of $10,000 or $2,000.	?
b. Is any depreciation a truly variable, wear-and-tear type of cost?	?
Total savings by not producing 100 units of power	$34,000 + ?
* Materials handling costs are higher because the power department uses 20% of materials handling. Therefore, materials-handling costs will decrease by 20%.	

In the short run (at least until a capital investment in equipment is necessary), the data suggest continuing to produce internally because the costs eliminated would probably be less than the comparable purchase costs.

14-34 (30–40 min.) **Overhead disputes.**

1. This problem, which is based on an actual case, shows how overhead cost allocation can affect contract pricing. The Navy would claim a refund of $689,658.

The overhead cost would be allocated differently:

Previous overhead allocation rate $\quad = \dfrac{\$30}{\$50 + \$100} = 20\% \times DL\$$

Revised overhead allocation rate $\quad = \dfrac{\$30}{\$45 + \$100} = 20.68965\%$

	Navy Costs	Commercial Costs
Original cost assignment:		
Direct materials	$ –	$ –
Direct labor	45,000,000	100,000,000
SE group	5,000,000	–
Allocated overhead (20% x DL$)	10,000,000[a.]	20,000,000[b.]
Total	$60,000,000	$120,000,000
Revised cost assignment:		
Direct materials	$ —	$ –
Direct labor	45,000,000	100,000,000
SE group	5,000,000	–
Allocated overhead (20.68965% x DL$)	9,310,342[c.]	20,689,650[d.]
Total	$59,310,342	$120,689,650

a. 20% × ($45,000,000 direct labor + $5,000,000 SE group classified as direct labor) = $10,000,000

b. 20% × $100,000,000 = $20,000,000

c. 20.68965% × $45,000,000 = $9,310,342

d. 20.68965% × $100,000,000 = $20,689,650

14-34 (Cont'd.)

The Navy claim would be:

Remove the original overhead allocation of $50 million x 0.20	$10,000,000

This means that the overhead pool, which has been totally
    allocated to products, is now underallocated by $10 million. This
    overhead must be reallocated in proportion to the "corrected"
    direct labor in nuclear work and commercial work. In short,
    if the overhead allocation base shrinks from $150 to $145
    million, the overhead rate increases from 20% to 20.68965%.

The revised allocation is $45 million $\times$ .2068965.	9,310,342
	$ 689,658

2.   Revised overhead allocation rate $= \dfrac{\$26}{\$45 + \$100} = 17.93103\%$

	Navy Costs	Commercial Costs
Revised cost assignment:		
Direct materials	$ –	$ –
Direct labor	45,000,000	100,000,000
SE group	5,000,000	–
Commercial purchasing	–	4,000,000
Allocated overhead (17.93103% x DL$)	8,068,964	17,931,030
	$58,068,964	$ 121,931,030

       Given that the original Navy cost is $60,000,000, and the revised cost is
$58,068,964, the Navy would claim a total refund of $1,931,036.

CHAPTER 15
COST ALLOCATION: JOINT PRODUCTS AND BYPRODUCTS

15-2 A *joint cost* is a cost of a single production process that yields multiple products simultaneously. *Separable costs* are costs incurred beyond the splitoff point that are assignable to one or more individual products.

15-4 A *product* is any output that has a positive sales value (or an output that enables an organization to avoid incurring costs). In some joint-cost settings, outputs can occur that do not have a positive sales value. The offshore processing of hydrocarbons yields water that is recycled back into the ocean as well as yielding oil and gas. The processing of mineral ore to yield gold and silver also yields dirt as an output, which is recycled back into the ground.

15-6 The joint production process yields individual products that are either sold this period or held as inventory to be sold in subsequent periods. Hence, the joint costs need to be allocated between total production rather than just those sold this period.

15-8 Both methods use market selling-price data in allocating joint costs, but they differ in which sales-price data they use. The *sales value at splitoff method* allocates joint costs on the basis of each product's relative sales value at the splitoff point. The *estimated net realizable value method* allocates joint costs on the basis of the relative estimated net realizable value (expected final sales value in the ordinary course of business minus the expected separable costs of production and marketing).

15-10 The estimated NRV method can be simplified by assuming (a) a standard set of post-splitoff point processing steps, and (b) a standard set of selling prices. The use of (a) and (b) achieves the same benefits that the use of standard costs does in costing systems.

15-12 No. Any method used to allocate joint costs to individual products that is applicable to the problem of joint product-cost allocation should not be used for management decisions regarding whether a product should be sold or processed further. When a product is an inherent result of a joint process, the decision to process further should not be influenced by either the size of the total joint costs or by the portion of the joint costs assigned to particular products. Joint costs are irrelevant for these decisions. The only relevant items for these decisions are the incremental revenue and the incremental costs beyond the splitoff point.

15-14 Two methods to account for byproducts are:
a. Production method - recognizes byproducts in the financial statements at the time production is completed.
b. Sales method - delays recognition of byproducts until the time of sale.

15-16 (20-30 min.) **Joint cost allocation, insurance settlement.**

1.   (a)   Sales value at splitoff-point method.

	Pounds of Product	Wholesale Selling Price per Pound	Sales Value at Splitoff	Weighting: Sales Value at Splitoff	Joint Costs Allocated	Allocated Costs per Pound
Breasts	100	$1.10	$110	0.675	$67.50	0.6750
Wings	20	0.40	8	0.049	4.90	0.2450
Thighs	40	0.70	28	0.172	17.20	0.4300
Bones	80	0.20	16	0.098	9.80	0.1225
Feathers	10	0.10	1	0.006	0.60	0.0600
	250		163	1.000	$100.00	

Costs of Destroyed Product

Breasts: $0.6750 × 20	=	$13.50
Wings: $0.2450 × 10	=	2.45
		$15.95

b.   Physical measures method

	Pounds of Product	Weighting: Physical Measures	Joint Costs Allocated	Allocated Costs per Pound
Breasts	100	0.400	$ 40.00	$0.400
Wings	20	0.080	8.00	0.400
Thighs	40	0.160	16.00	0.400
Bones	80	0.320	32.00	0.400
Feathers	10	0.040	4.00	0.400
	250	1.000	$100.00	

Costs of Destroyed Product

Breast: $0.40 × 20	=	$8
Wings: $0.40 × 10	=	4
		$12

Note: Although not required, it is useful to highlight the individual product profitability figures:

Product	Sales Value	Sales Value at Splitoff Method		Physical Measures Method	
		Joint Costs Allocated	Gross Income	Joint Costs Allocated	Gross Income
Breasts	$110	$67.50	$42.50	$40.00	$70.00
Wings	8	4.90	3.10	8.00	0.00
Thighs	28	17.20	10.80	16.00	12.00
Bones	16	9.80	6.20	32.00	(16.00)
Feathers	1	0.60	0.40	4.00	(3.00)

2.   The sales-value at splitoff method captures the benefits-received criterion of cost allocation. The costs of processing a chicken are allocated to products in proportion to the ability to contribute revenue. Chicken Little's decision to process chicken is heavily influenced by the revenues from breasts and thighs. The bones provide relatively few benefits to Chicken Little despite their high physical volume.

     The physical measures method shows profits on breasts and thighs and losses on bones and feathers. Given that Chicken Little has to jointly process all the chicken products, it is non-intuitive to single out individual products that are being processed simultaneously as making losses while the overall operations make a profit.

15-18 (10 min.) Estimated net realizable value method.

A diagram of the situation is in Solution Exhibit 15-18 (all numbers are in thousands).

	Cooking Oil	Soap Oil	Total
Expected final sales value of production, CO, 1,000 × $50; SO, 500 × $25	$50,000	$12,500	$62,500
Deduct expected separable costs to complete and sell	30,000	7,500	37,500
Estimated net realizable value at splitoff point	$20,000	$ 5,000	$25,000
Weighting	$\frac{\$20,000}{\$25,000} = 0.8$	$\frac{\$5,000}{\$25,000} = 0.2$	
Joint costs allocated, CO, 0.8 × $24,000; SO, 0.2 × $24,000	$19,200	$ 4,800	$24,000

15–18 (Cont'd.)

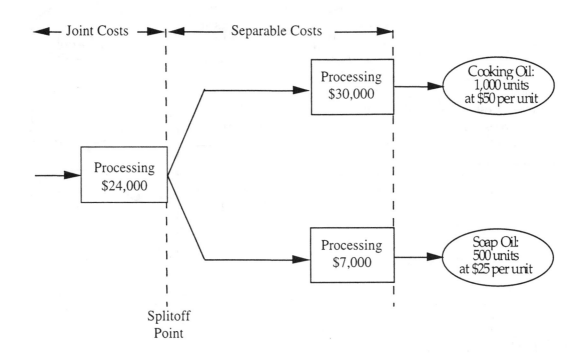

15-20 (30 min.) **Joint-cost allocation, process further.**

1.

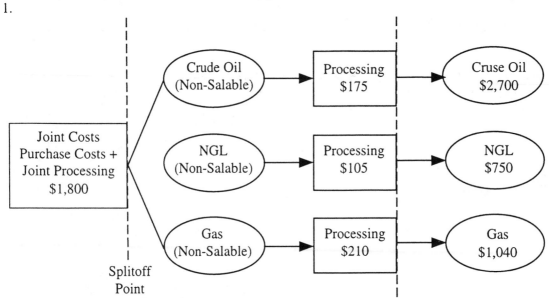

Splitoff
Point

2. a. Physical Measure Method

		Crude Oil	NGL	Gas	Total
1.	Physical measures	150	50	800	1,000
2.	Weighting	0.15	0.05	0.80	1.00
3.	Joint costs allocated				
	(Weights × $1,800)	$270	$90	$1,440	$1,800

b. Estimated NRV Method

		Crude Oil	NGL	Gas	Total
1.	Expected final sales value of production	$2,700	$750	$1,040	$4,490
2.	Deduct expected separable costs	175	105	210	490
3.	Estimated NRV at splitoff	$2,525	$645	$ 830	$4,000
4.	Weighting	0.63125	0.16125	0.20750	1.000
5.	Joint costs allocated (Weights × $1,800)	$1,136.25	$290.25	$373.50	$1,800

15-20 (Cont'd.)

3.　　The operating-income amounts for each product using each method is:

(a)　　Physical Measures Method

	Crude Oil	NGL	Gas	Total
Sales	$2,700	$750	$1,040	$4,490
Operating Costs				
Joint costs	270	90	1,440	1,800
Separable costs	175	105	210	490
Total operating costs	445	195	1,650	2,290
Operating margin	$2,255	$555	$ (610)	$2,200

(b)　　Estimated NRV Method

	Crude Oil	NGL	Gas	Total
Sales	$2,700.00	$750.00	$1,040.00	$4,490.00
Operating Costs				
Joint costs	1,136.25	290.25	373.50	1,800.00
Separable costs	175.00	105.00	210.00	490.00
Total operating costs	1,311.25	395.25	583.50	2,290.00
Operating margin	$1,388.75	$354.75	$ 456.50	$2,200.00

4. Neither method should be used for product emphasis decisions. It is inappropriate to use joint-cost-allocated data to decide dropping individual products, or pushing individual products, as they are joint by definition. Product-emphasis decisions should be made based on relevant revenues and relevant costs. The con of each method is that either can lead to product emphasis decisions not leading to maximization of operating income.

5. A letter to the taxation authorities would stress the conceptual superiority of the estimated NRV method. Chapter 15 argues that, using a benefits-received cost allocation criterion, market-based joint cost allocation methods are preferable to physical-measure methods. A meaningful common denominator (revenues) is available when the sales value at splitoff point method is used. The physical-measures method requires non-homogeneous products (liquids and gases) to be converted to a common denominator.

15-22 (40 min.) Alternative methods of joint-cost allocation, ending inventories.

Total production for the year was:

	Sold	Ending Inventories	Total Production
X	120	180	300
Y	340	60	400
Z	475	25	500

A diagram of the situation is in Solution Exhibit 15-22.

1. a. Estimated net realizable value (NRV) method:

	X	Y	Z	Total
Expected final sales value of production, X, 300 × $1,500; Y, 400 × $1,000; Z, 500 × $700	$450,000	$400,000	$350,000	$1,200,000
Deduct separable costs	-	-	200,000	200,000
Estimated net realizable value at splitoff point	$450,000	$400,000	$150,000	$1,000,000

Weighting: $\dfrac{\$450}{\$1,000} = 0.45$ $\dfrac{\$400}{\$1,000} = 0.40$ $\dfrac{\$150}{\$1,000} = 0.15$ 1.0

	X	Y	Z	Total
Joint costs allocated, 0.45, 0.40, 0.15 × $400,000	$180,000	$160,000	$ 60,000	$ 400,000

Ending Inventory Percentages:

	X	Y	Z
Ending inventory	180	60	25
Total production	300	400	500
Ending inventory percentage	60%	15%	5%

15-22 (Cont'd.)

Income Statement

	X	Y	Z	Total
Sales, X, 120 × $1,500; Y, 340 × $1,000; Z, 475 × $700	$180,000	$340,000	$332,500	$852,500
Cost of goods sold:				
Joint costs allocated	180,000	160,000	60,000	400,000
Separable costs	-	-	200,000	200,000
Cost of goods available for sale	180,000	160,000	260,000	600,000
Deduct ending inventory, X, 60%; Y, 15%; Z, 5%	108,000	24,000	13,000	145,000
Cost of goods sold	72,000	136,000	247,000	455,000
Gross margin	$108,000	$204,000	$ 85,500	$397,500
Gross-margin percentage	60%	60%	25.71%	

b. Constant gross-margin percentage NRV method:

Step 1:

Total final sales value, (300 × $1,500) + (400 × $1,000) + (500 × $700) =	$1,200,000
Deduct joint and separable costs, $400,000 + $200,000	600,000
Gross margin	$ 600,000
Gross-margin percentage, $600,000 ÷ $1,200,000 =	50%

	X	Y	Z	Total
Expected final sales value of production, X, 300 × $1,500; Y, 400 × $1,000; Z, 500 × $700	$450,000	$400,000	$350,000	$1,200,000
Step 2: Deduct gross margin, using overall gross-margin percentage of sales, 50%	225,000	200,000	175,000	600,000
Step 3: Deduct separable costs	-	-	200,000	200,000
Joint costs allocated	$225,000	$200,000	$(25,000)	$ 400,000

15-8

The negative joint-cost allocation to Product Z illustrates one "unusual" feature of the constant gross-margin percentage NRV method. Some products may receive negative cost allocations in order that all individual products have the same gross-margin percentage.

Income Statement

	X	Y	Z	Total
Sales X, 120 × $1,500; Y, 340 × $1,000; Z, 475 × $700	$180,000	$340,000	$332,500	$852,500
Cost of goods sold:				
Joint costs allocated	225,000	200,000	(25,000)	400,000
Separable costs	-	-	200,000	200,000
Cost of goods available for sale	225,000	200,000	175,000	600,000
Deduct ending inventory, X, 60%; Y, 15%; Z, 5%	135,000	30,000	8,750	173,750
Cost of goods sold	90,000	170,000	166,250	426,250
Gross margin	$ 90,000	$170,000	$166,250	$426,250
Gross-margin percentage	50%	50%	50%	50%

Summary

	X	Y	Z	Total
a. Estimated NRV method:				
Inventories on balance sheet	$108,000	$ 24,000	$ 13,000	$145,000
Cost of goods sold on income statement	72,000	136,000	247,000	455,000
				$600,000
b. Constant gross-margin percentage NRV method				
Inventories on balance sheet	$135,000	$ 30,000	$ 8,750	$173,750
Cost of goods sold on income statement	90,000	170,000	166,250	426,250
				$600,000

2.   Gross-margin percentages:

	X	Y	Z
Estimated NRV method	60%	60%	25.71%
Constant gross-margin percentage NRV	50%	50%	50.00%

15-22 (Cont'd.)

SOLUTION EXHIBIT 15-22

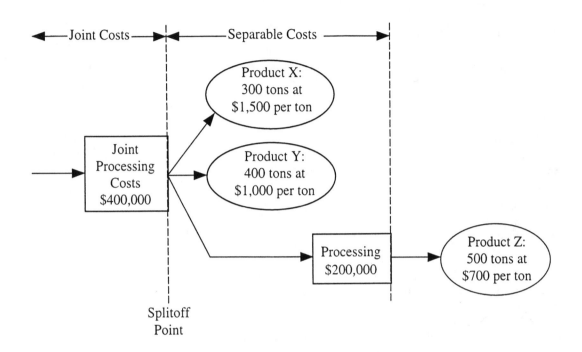

15-24 (40 min.)   **Process further or sell, byproduct.**

1.   The analysis shown below indicates that it would be more profitable for Newcastle Mining Company to continue to sell raw bulk coal without further processing. (This analysis ignores any value related to coal fines.)

Incremental sales revenues:
Sales revenue after further processing (9,500,000 tons × $36)	$342,000,000
Sales revenue from bulk raw coal (10,000,000 tons × $27)	270,000,000
Incremental sales revenue	72,000,000

Incremental costs:
Direct labor	600,000
Supervisory personnel	100,000
Heavy equipment costs ($25,000 × 12 months)	300,000
Sizing and cleaning (10,000,000 tons × $3.50)	35,000,000
Outbound rail freight (9,500,000 tons ÷ 60 tons) × $240 per car	38,000,000
Incremental costs	74,000,000
Incremental gain (loss)	$(2,000,000)

2.   The analysis shown below indicates that the potential revenue from the coal fines byproduct would result in additional revenue, ranging between $5,250,000 and $9,000,000, depending on the market price of the fines.

1.   Coal fines   =   75% of 5% of raw bulk tonnage
                      =   .75 × (10,000,000 × .05)
                      =   375,000 tons

Potential additional revenue:

	Market price	
	Minimum	Maximum
	$14 per ton	$24 per ton
Additional revenue	$5,250,000	$9,000,000

      Since the incremental loss is $2 million, as calculated in requirement 1, including the coal fines in the analysis indicates that further processing provides a positive result and is, therefore, favorable.

15–24 (Cont'd.)

3. Other factors that should be considered in evaluating a sell-or-process-further decision include:

- Stability of the current customer market and how it compares to the market for sized and cleaned coal.
- Storage space needed for the coal fines until they are sold and the handling costs of coal fines.
- Reliability of cost (e.g., rail freight rates) and revenue estimates, and the risk of depending of these estimates.
- Timing of the revenue stream from coal fines and impact on the need for liquidity.
- Possible environmental problems, i.e., dumping of waste and smoke from unprocessed coal.

15-26 (35-45 min.)   **Joint costs and byproducts.**

A diagram of the situation is in Solution Exhibit 15-26.

1.   Computing byproduct deduction to joint costs:

Marketing price of X, 100,000 × $3	$300,000
Deduct: Gross margin, 10% of sales	30,000
Marketing costs, 25% of sales	75,000
Department 3 separable costs	50,000
Estimated net realizable value of X	$145,000

Joint costs	$800,000
Deduct byproduct contribution	145,000
Net joint costs to be allocated	$655,000

	Quantity	Unit Sales Price	Final Sales Value	Deduct Separable Processing Cost	Est. Net Realizable Value at Splitoff	Weighting	Allocation of $655,000 Joint Costs
L	50,000	$10	$ 500,000	$100,000	$ 400,000	40%	$262,000
W	300,000	2	600,000	-	600,000	60%	393,000
Totals			$1,100,000	$100,000	$1,000,000		$655,000

	Joint Costs Allocation	Add Separable Processing Costs	Total Costs	Units	Unit Cost
L	$262,000	$100,000	$362,000	50,000	$7.24
W	393,000	-	393,000	300,000	1.31
Totals	$655,000	$100,000	$755,000	350,000	

Unit cost for X: $1.45 + $0.50   = $1.95,
or $3.00 − $0.30 − $0.75 = $1.95.

15-26 (Cont'd.)

2. If all three products are treated as joint products:

	Quantity	Unit Sales Price	Final Sales Value	Deduct Separable Processing Cost	Est. Net Realizable Value at Splitoff	Weighting	Allocation of $800,000 Joint Costs
L	50,000	$10	$ 500,000	$100,000	$ 400,000	40/125	$256,000
W	300,000	2	600,000	-	600,000	60/125	384,000
X	100,000	3	300,000	50,000	250,000	25/125	160,000
Totals			$1,400,000	$150,000	$1,250,000		$800,000

	Joint Costs Allocation	Add Separable Processing Costs	Total Costs	Units	Unit Cost
L	$256,000	$100,000	$356,000	50,000	$7.12
W	384,000	-	384,000	300,000	1.28
X	160,000	50,000	210,000	100,000	2.10
Totals	$800,000	$150,000	$950,000	450,000	

Call the attention of students to the differing unit "costs" between the two assumptions regarding the relative importance of Product X. The point is that costs of individual products depend heavily on which assumptions are made and which accounting methods and techniques are used.

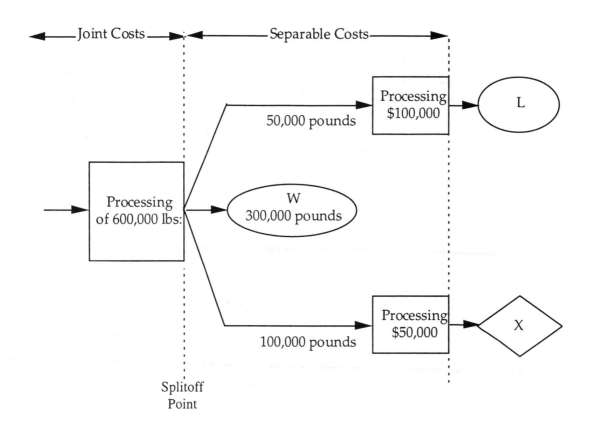

15-28 (40 min.)   **Alternative methods of joint-cost allocation, product-mix decisions.**

A diagram of the situation is in Solution Exhibit 15-28.

1.   Computation of joint-cost allocation proportions:

a.

	Sales Value at Splitoff	Proportions	Allocation of $100,000 Joint Costs
A	$ 50,000	50/200 = 0.25	$ 25,000
B	30,000	30/200 = 0.15	15,000
C	50,000	50/200 = 0.25	25,000
D	70,000	70/200 = 0.35	35,000
	$200,000	1.00	$100,000

b.

	Physical Measure	Proportions	Allocation of $100,000 Joint Costs
A	300,000 gallons	300/500 = 0.60	$ 60,000
B	100,000 gallons	100/500 = 0.20	20,000
C	50,000 gallons	50/500 = 0.10	10,000
D	50,000 gallons	50/500 = 0.10	10,000
	500,000 gallons	1.00	$100,000

c.

	Final Sales Value	Separable Costs	Estimated Net Realizable Value	Proportions	Allocation of $100,000 Joint Costs
A	$300,000	$200,000	$100,000	100/200 =0.50	$ 50,000
B	100,000	80,000	20,000	20/200 = 0.10	10,000
C	50,000	–	50,000	50/200 = 0.25	25,000
D	120,000	90,000	30,000	30/200 = 0.15	15,000
			$200,000	1.00	$100,000

Computation of gross-margin percentages:

a.   Sales value at splitoff method:

	Super A	Super B	C	Super D	Total
Sales	$300,000	$100,000	$50,000	$120,000	$570,000
Joint costs	25,000	15,000	25,000	35,000	100,000
Separable costs	200,000	80,000	0	90,000	370,000
Total costs	225,000	95,000	25,000	125,000	470,000
Gross margin	$ 75,000	$ 5,000	$25,000	$ (5,000)	$100,000
Gross-margin percentage	25%	5%	50%	(4.17%)	17.54%

15-28 (Cont'd)

b.   Physical-measure method:

	Super A	Super B	C	Super D	Total
Sales	$300,000	$100,000	$50,000	$120,000	$570,000
Joint costs	60,000	20,000	10,000	10,000	100,000
Separable costs	200,000	80,000	0	90,000	370,000
Total costs	260,000	100,000	10,000	100,000	470,000
Gross margin	$ 40,000	$ 0	$40,000	$ 20,000	$100,000
Gross-margin percentage	13.33%	0%	80%	16.67%	17.54%

c.   Estimated net realizable value method:

	Super A	Super B	C	Super D	Total
Sales	$300,000	$100,000	$50,000	$120,000	$570,000
Joint costs	50,000	10,000	25,000	15,000	100,000
Separable costs	200,000	80,000	0	90,000	370,000
Total costs	250,000	90,000	25,000	105,000	470,000
Gross margin	$ 50,000	$ 10,000	$25,000	$ 15,000	$100,000
Gross-margin percentage	16.67%	10%	50%	12.5%	17.54%

Summary of gross-margin percentages:

Joint-Cost Allocation Method	Super A	Super B	C	Super D
Sales value at splitoff	25.00%	5%	50%	(4.17%)
Physical measure	13.33%	0%	80%	16.67%
Estimated net realizable value	16.67%	10%	50%	12.50%

15-28 (Cont'd.)

2. Further Processing of A into Super A:

Incremental revenue, $300,000 – $50,000	$250,000
Incremental costs	200,000
Incremental operating income from further processing	$ 50,000

Further processing of B into Super B:

Incremental revenue, $100,000 – $30,000	$ 70,000
Incremental costs	80,000
Incremental operating income from further processing	($ 10,000)

Further Processing of D into Super D:

Incremental revenue, $120,000 – $70,000	$ 50,000
Incremental costs	90,000
Incremental operating income from further processing	$ (40,000)

Operating income can be increased by $50,000 if both B and D are sold at their splitoff point.

SOLUTION EXHIBIT 15-28

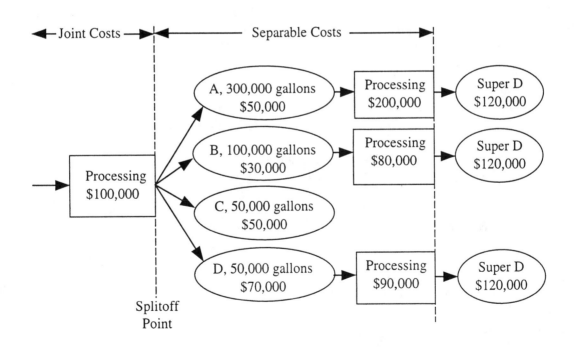

15-30 (30 min.)   **Joint-cost allocation, process further or sell.**

1.

a. Relative sales value method at splitoff.

	Monthly Unit Output	Selling Price Per Unit	Relative Sales Value at Splitoff	% of Sales	Allocated Joint Costs
Studs (Building)	75,000	$8	$600,000	46.15%	$461,539
Decorative Pieces	5,000	60	300,000	23.08	230,769
Posts	20,000	20		30.77	307,692
			400,000		
Totals			$1,300,000	100.00%	$1,000,000

b. Physical output (volume) method at splitoff.

	Physical Unit Volume	% of Total Unit Volume	Allocated Joint Costs
Studs (Building)	75,000	75.00%	$750,000
Decorative Pieces	5,000	5.00	50,000
Posts	20,000	20.00	200,000
Totals	100,000	100.00%	$1,000,000

c. Estimated net realizable value method.

	Monthly Unit Output	Fully Processed Selling Price per Unit	Estimated Net Realizable Value	% of Sales	Allocated Joint Costs
Studs (Building)	75,000	$8	$600,000	44.44%	$444,445
Decorative Pieces	4,500[a]	100	350,000[b]	25.93	259,259
Posts	20,000	20	400,000	29.63	296,296
Totals			$1,350,000	100.00%	$1,000,000

Notes:

a. 5,000 monthly units of output - 10% normal spoilage = 4,500 good units.

b. 4,500 good units X $100 = $450,000 - Further processing costs of $100,000 = $350,000

2.   Presented below is an analysis for Sonimad Sawmill Inc. comparing the processing of decorative pieces further versus selling the rough-cut product immediately at split-off.

	Units	Dollars
Monthly unit output	5,000	
Less: Normal further processing shrinkage	500	
Units available for sale	4,500	
Final sales value (4,500 units @ $100 per unit)		$450,000
Less: Sales value at splitoff		300,000
Differential revenue		150,000
Less: Further processing costs		100,000
Additional contribution from further processing		$50,000

15–30 (Cont'd.)

3. Assuming Sonimad Sawmill Inc. announces that in six months it will sell the rough-cut product at split-off, due to increasing competitive pressure, at least three types of likely behavior that will be demonstrated by the skilled labor in the planing and sizing process include the following.

- Poorer quality.
- Reduced motivation and morale.
- Job insecurity, leading to nonproductive employee time looking for jobs elsewhere.

Management actions that could improve this behavior include the following.

- Improve communication by giving the workers a more comprehensive explanation as to the reason for the change in order to better understand the situation and bring out a plan for future operation of the rest of the plant.
- The company can offer incentive bonuses to maintain quality and production and align rewards with goals.
- The company could provide job relocation and internal job transfers.

SOLUTION EXHIBIT 15-30

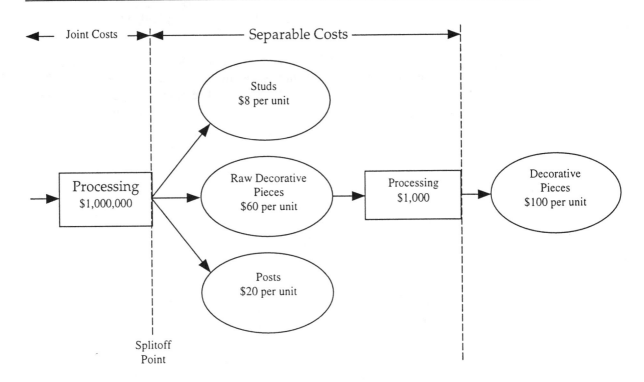

15-32 (30 min.) **Joint-cost allocation, relevant costs.**

1. The "six-day progressive product trimming" ignores the fundamental point that the $300 cost to buy the pig is a joint cost. A pig is purchased as a whole. The butcher's challenge is to maximize the total revenues minus incremental costs (assumed zero) from the sale of all products.

At each stage, the decision taken ignores the general rule that product emphasis decisions should consider relevant relevants and relevant costs. Allocated joint costs are not part of the relevant cost numbers. For example, the Day I decision to drop pig's feet ignores the fact that the $300 point cost has been paid to acquire the who pig. The $15 of revenues are relevant inflows. This same position also holds for the Day 2 to Day 6 decisions.

2. The revenue amounts are the figures to use in the sales value at splitoff method:

	Revenue	Weighting	Joint Costs Allocated
Pork chops	$120	0.2425	$72.75
Ham	150	0.3030	90.90
Bacon	160	0.3232	96.96
Pig's feet	15	0.0303	9.09
Hide	50	0.1010	30.30
	$495	1.0000	$300.00

3. No. The decision to sell or not sell individual products should consider relevant revenues and relevant costs. In the butcher's context, the relevant costs would be the additional time and other incidentals to take each pig part and make it a salable product. The relevant revenues would be the difference between selling price at the consumer level and what the butcher may receive for pig parts in unprocessed form.

15-34 (20–30 min.) **Joint product/byproduct distinctions, ethics. (continuation of 15-33)**

1.   The 2000 method gives Princess managers relatively little discretion vis-a-vis the pre-2000 method. The 2000 method recognizes all four products in the accounting system at the time of production.

The pre-2000 method recognizes only two products (apple slices and applesauce) at the time of production. Consider the data in the question. The $60,000 of joint costs would be allocated as follows (using the $60,000 and $36,000 estimated NRV amounts):

Apple Slices: $\dfrac{\$60,000}{\$96,000} \times \$60,000$ = $37,500

Applesauce: $\dfrac{\$36,000}{\$96,000} \times \$60,000$ = $22,500

The gross margin on each product is:

Apple Slices   = $\dfrac{(\$71,280 - \$37,500 - \$11,280)}{\$71,280}$ =   31.57%

Applesauce   = $\dfrac{(\$44,550 - \$22,500 - \$8,550)}{\$44,550}$ =   30.30%

The gross margins on the two "byproducts" are:

Apple juice   = $\dfrac{\$27,000 - \$3,000}{\$27,000}$ =   88.89%

Animal feed   = $\dfrac{\$2,700 - \$700}{\$2,700}$ =   74.07%

With the pre-2000 method, managers have flexibility as to when to sell the apple juice and the animal feed. Both are frozen and can be kept in cold storage until needed. If there is a need for a large "dose" of gross margin at year-end to meet the target ratio, high gross margins from apple juice or animal feed can be drawn on to help achieve the target.

2.   The controller could examine the sales patterns of apple juice and animal feed at year-end. Do managers who have ratios from existing sales below the target sell apple juice and animal feed inventories to achieve the target ratio? Do managers who have ratios above the target put apple juice and animal feed production into inventory so as to provide a "cushion" for subsequent years?

One piece of evidence here would be physical inventory-holding patterns on a monthly basis. If there were a different pattern of inventory holding for the two byproducts than the two joint products, there would be grounds for further investigating whether managers are abusing the bonus system.

CHAPTER 16
REVENUES, SALES VARIANCES, AND
CUSTOMER-PROFITABILITY ANALYSIS

16-2 The *stand-alone revenue-allocation method* uses product-specific information on the products in the bundle as weights for allocating the bundled revenues to the individual products.

The *incremental revenue allocation method* ranks the individual products in a bundle according to criteria determined by management, and then uses this ranking to allocate the bundled revenues to the individual products.

16-4 A dispute over allocation of revenues of a bundled product could be resolved by (a) having an agreement that outlines the preferred method in the case of a dispute, or (b) having a third party (such as the company president or an independent arbitrator) make a decision.

16-6 The total sales-mix variance for contribution margin arises from shifts in the contribution margin of individual products. The composite product unit concept enables the effect of individual product changes to be summarized in a single intuitive number.

16-8 The sales-quantity variance can be decomposed into (a) a market-size variance (the actual total market-size change from that budgeted), and (b) a market-share variance (the actual market-share change from that budgeted). Both variances use the budgeted average selling price per unit, when the focus is on revenues.

16-10 Customer profitability analysis highlights to managers how individual customers differentially contribute to total profitability. It helps managers to see whether customers who contribute sizably to total profitability are receiving a comparable level of attention from the organization.

16-12 No. A customer-profitability profile highlights differences in current period's profitability across customers. Dropping customers should be the last resort. An unprofitable customer in one period may be highly profitable in subsequent future periods. Moreover, costs assigned to individual customers need not be purely variable with respect to short-run elimination of sales to those customers. Thus, when customers are dropped, costs assigned to those customers may not disappear in the short run.

16-14 A process where the inputs are nonsubstitutable leaves workers no discretion as to the components to use. A process where the inputs are substitutable means there is discretion about the exact number and type of inputs or about the weighting of inputs where the number and type is mandated.

16-16 (30 min.) Revenue allocation, speaking fees.

1. The total revenues from the seminar are:
   500 x $200 = $100,000.
   Revenues to be shared by speakers
   0.30 x $100,000 = $30,000.

The stand-alone revenue allocation method could guide the allocations. Possible weights are individual speaking fees, number of speeches, and speaking fee revenues:

	Individual Speaking Fee (1)	Relative Speaking Fee% (2)=(1)÷16,000	# of Speeches (3)	Relative Number of Speeches (4)=(3)÷96	Speaking Fee Revenues (5)=(1)x(3)	Relative Speaking Fee Revenues (6)=(5)÷34,0108
Linda Young	$10,000	0.625	6	0.0625	$ 60,000	0.1765
Vince Rock	4,000	0.250	50	0.5208	200,000	0.5882
Juan Malvido	2,000	0.125	40	0.4167	80,000	0.2353
	$16,000	1.000	96	1.0000	$340,000	1.0000

These three weightings give the following allocation of $30,000:

	Relative Speaking Fee Weights (1)	Allocation of $30,000 (2)	Relative Number of Speeches Weights (3)	Allocation of $30,000 (4)	Relative Speaking Fee Revenues (5)	Allocation of $30,000 (6)
Linda Young	0.625	$18,750	0.0625	$ 1,875	0.1765	$ 5,295
Vince Rock	0.250	7,500	0.5208	15,624	0.5882	17,646
Juan Malvido	0.125	3,750	0.4167	12,501	0.2353	7,059
	1.000	$30,000	1.0000	$30,000	1.0000	$30,000

The incremental revenue-allocation method is not straightforward, as the sum of the individual speaking fees ($10,000 + $4,000 + $2,000 = $16,000) is less than the total $30,000 to be allocated.

2. Young could argue that she has the highest individual speaking fee and is high in demand. In contrast, the other two speakers have given numerous talks and likely will attract fewer people to the seminar. She could argue that Malvido should pay to be on the program, as he is marketing for the television network. The net of these arguments is that Young wants more than $10,000.

Rock could argue that he is in huge demand as a speaker, as is evidenced by his 50 speeches at $4,000. People pay this amount because he is both entertaining and dynamic. He could also claim his Olympic gold medal brings an aura of accomplishment to the seminar. The net of these arguments is that Rock wants more than $10,000.

Malvido could argue that he is the "television personality" everyone wants to meet and hear. He could also argue he could give the seminar invaluable publicity by promoting it on his television show. The net of these arguments is that Malvido wants more than $10,000.

16-18 (10–15 min.)   **Revenue allocation, bundled products, additional complexities (continuation of 16-17).**

Alternatives include:

a.   Use information about how each individual package is used to make the revenue allocations. Thus, if one party uses only lodging and food, the $700 is allocated among those two groups. This would be the most accurate approach, as it captures actual usage and non-usage of the facilities.

b.   Use the average non-usage information to compute an "adjusted unit selling price:"

Lodging: $640 × 1.00	$ 640
Food: $160 × 0.95	152
Recreation: $300 × 0.90	270
	$1,062

These adjusted revenues can be used in either the stand-alone or incremental methods. For example, the stand-alone allocations are:

Lodging: $\dfrac{\$640}{\$1,062} \times \$700 \quad = \quad \$422$

Food: $\dfrac{\$152}{\$1,062} \times \$700 \quad = \quad \$100$

Recreation: $\dfrac{\$270}{\$1,062} \times \$700 \quad = \quad \underline{\$178}$

$$\underline{\$700}$$

16-20 (20 min.)   **7-Up using variances to read the market.**

1. 7-Up should have conducted a Level 1 to 4 variance analysis (as in Exhibit 16-3) that is focused on the U.S. soft-drink market. If information is available, individual 7-Up products (7-Up and Diet 7-Up) could be included to compute a sales mix-variance. The sales-quantity variance could be divided into a market-share variance and a market-size variance. 7-Up's market share has steadily declined from 3.2% to 2.4% over a 10-year period. This is a large decline.

7-Up could also conduct more detailed analyses, including:
1) Changes in the market share and the market size of the citrus-flavored category.
2) Changes in its market share and market size share by demographic segment (0-11 years, 12-24 years, and so on).

2. The brand objectives are critical to consider when evaluating 7-Up's strategy. The *Fortune* article has a negative tone. Much depends on whether 7-Up's management has attempted to make the brand investments required to compete in the soft drink market. If 7-Up's management has invested heavily in marketing, sales promotions, product extension, and so on, its decline in market share is a negative indicator. Suppose, however, 7-Up management has decided that they do not have the resources to compete with Coca-Cola or Pepsi-Cola. Their strategy is to budget for market declines, but extract higher profitability from the brand in the short run. This is a classic "milk-the-brand" strategy. Here, the issue is what is the optimal "milk-the-brand" strategy, which would consider the time period over which a market-share decline is predicted and the rate of decrease with alternative cutbacks in marketing outlays.

16-22 (30–40 min.) Variance analysis, multiple countries.

1.   All amounts are in thousands. Solution Exhibit 16-22 provides a summary of the variances.

Budget for 2000

	Selling Price per Unit (1)	Variable Cost per Unit (2)	Contrib. Margin per Unit (3) = (1) – (2)	Units Sold (4)	Sales Mix (5)	Contribution Margin (6) = (3) × (4)
Canada	$6.00	$4.00	$2.00	400,000	16%	$ 800,000
Mexico	4.00	2.80	1.20	600,000	24	720,000
United States	7.00	4.50	2.50	1,500,000	60	3,750,000
Total				2,500,000	100%	$5,270,000

Actual for 2000

	Selling Price per Unit (1)	Variable Cost per Unit (2)	Contrib. Margin per Unit (3) = (1) – (2)	Units Sold (4)	Sales Mix (5)	Contribution Margin (6) = (3) × (4)
Canada	$6.20	$4.50	$1.70	480,000	16%	$ 816,000
Mexico	4.25	2.75	1.50	900,000	30	1,350,000
United States	6.80	4.60	2.20	1,620,000	54	3,564,000
Total				3,000,000	100%	$5,730,000

$$\text{Static-budget variance of contribution margin} = \text{Actual results} - \text{Static-budget amount}$$

Canada	=	$ 816,000	– $ 800,000	=	$ 16,000 F
Mexico	=	$1,350,000	– $ 720,000	=	630,000 F
United States	=	$3,564,000	– $3,750,000	=	186,000 U
Total					$460,000 F

$$\text{Flexible-budget variance of contribution margin} = \text{Actual results} - \text{Flexible-budget amount}$$

Canada	=	$ 816,000 – ($2.00 × 480,000)	=	$144,000 U
Mexico	=	$1,350,000 – ($1.20 × 900,000)	=	270,000 F
United States	=	$3,564,000 – ($2.50 × 1,620,000)	=	486,000 U
Total				$360,000 U

16-22 (Cont'd.)

$$\text{Sales - volume variance of contribution margin} = \begin{pmatrix} \text{Actual Sales} \\ \text{quantity} \\ \text{in units} \end{pmatrix} - \begin{pmatrix} \text{Budgeted sales} \\ \text{quantity} \\ \text{in units} \end{pmatrix} \times \begin{array}{c} \text{Budgeted} \\ \text{contrib. margin} \\ \text{per unit} \end{array}$$

Canada	= (	480,000 –	400,000) × \$2.00	= \$ 160,000 F
Mexico	= (	900,000 –	600,000) × \$1.20	= 360,000 F
United States	= (1,620,000 –	1,500,000) × \$2.50	= 300,000 F
Total				\$820,000 F

$$\text{Sales-quantity variance of contribution margin} = \begin{pmatrix} \text{Actual units} \\ \text{of all products} \\ \text{sold} \end{pmatrix} - \begin{pmatrix} \text{Budgeted units} \\ \text{of all products} \\ \text{sold} \end{pmatrix} \times \begin{array}{c} \text{Budgeted} \\ \text{sales-mix} \\ \text{percentage} \end{array} \times \begin{array}{c} \text{Budgeted} \\ \text{contrib. margin} \\ \text{per unit} \end{array}$$

Canada	= (3,000,000 – 2,500,000) × 0.16 × \$2.00	=	\$ 160,000 F
Mexico	= (3,000,000 – 2,500,000) × 0.24 × \$1.20	=	144,000 F
United States	= (3,000,000 – 2,500,000) × 0.60 × \$2.50	=	750,000 F
Total			\$1,054,000 F

$$\text{Sales-mix variance of contribution margin} = \begin{array}{c} \text{Actual units} \\ \text{of all} \\ \text{products sold} \end{array} \times \begin{bmatrix} \text{Actual} \\ \text{sales - mix} \\ \text{percentage} \end{bmatrix} - \begin{array}{c} \text{Budgeted} \\ \text{sales - mix} \\ \text{percentage} \end{array} \times \begin{array}{c} \text{Budgeted} \\ \text{contrib. margin} \\ \text{per unit} \end{array}$$

Canada	= 3,000,000 × (0.16 – 0.16) × \$2.00	=	\$ 0
Mexico	= 3,000,000 × (0.30 – 0.24) × \$1.20	=	216,000 F
United States	= 3,000,000 × (0.54 – 0.60) × \$2.50	=	450,000 U
Total			\$ 234,000 U

2.   There is a favorable static-budget variance (Level 1) of contribution margin of \$460,000. This is the result of two offsetting variances—an unfavorable flexible-budget variance of \$360,000 (due to the average actual contribution margin being below the budgeted margin), and a favorable sales-volume variance of \$820,000 (due to actual sales being 500,000 units above that budgeted).

The Level 3 breakdown of the favorable sales-volume variance of \$820,000 shows that the biggest contributor is the 500,000 unit increase in sales. There is a partially offsetting unfavorable sales-mix variance of \$234,000 in contribution margin.

SOLUTION EXHIBIT 16-22

Contribution-Margin Variance Analysis for Cola-King

Static-Budget Variance of C.M.

Canada	$ 16,000 F
Mexico	630,000 F
United States	186,000 U
Total	$460,000 F

Flexible-Budget Variance of C.M.		**Sales-Volume Variance of Revenues**	
Canada	$144,000 U	Canada	$160,000 F
Mexico	270,000 F	Mexico	360,000 F
United States	486,000 U	United States	300,000 F
Total	$360,000 U	Total	$820,000 F

Sales-Mix Variance of C.M.		**Sales-Quantity Variance of C.M.**	
Canada	$ 0	Canada	$ 160,000 F
Mexico	216,000 F	Mexico	144,000 F
United States	450,000 U	United States	750,000 F
Total	$234,000 U	Total	$1,054,000 F

16-24 (20–25 min.) Customer profitability, distribution.

1.   The activity-based costing for each customer is:

		Charleston Pharmacy	Chapel Hill Pharmacy
1.	Order processing,		
	$40 × 12; 10	$ 480	$ 400
2.	Line-item ordering,		
	$3 × (12 × 10; 10 × 18)	360	540
3.	Store deliveries,		
	$50 × 6; 10	300	500
4.	Carton deliveries,		
	$1 × (6 × 24; 10 × 20)	144	200
5.	Shelf-stocking,		
	$16 × (6 × 0; 10 × 0.5)	0	80
	Operating costs	$1,284	$1,720

The operating income of each customer is:

	Charleston Pharmacy	Chapel Hill Pharmacy
Revenues,		
$2,400 × 6; 1,800 × 10	$14,400	$18,000
Cost of goods sold,		
$2,100 × 6; $1,650 × 10	12,600	16,500
Gross margin	1,800	1,500
Operating costs	1,284	1,720
Operating income	$ 516	$ (220)

Chapel Hill Pharmacy has a lower gross margin percentage than Charleston (8.33% vs. 12.50%) and consumes more resources to obtain this lower margin.

16-24 (Cont'd.)

2. Ways Figure Four could use this information include:

a. Pay increased attention to the top 20% of the customers. This could entail asking them for ways to improve service. Alternatively, you may want to highlight to your own personnel the importance of these customers; e.g., it could entail stressing to delivery people the importance of never missing delivery dates for these customers.

b. Work out ways internally at Figure Four to reduce the rate per cost driver; e.g., reduce the cost per order by having better order placement linkages with customers. This cost reduction by Figure Four will improve the profitability of all customers.

c. Work with customers so that their behavior reduces the total "system-wide" costs. At a minimum, this approach could entail having customers make fewer orders and fewer line items. This latter point is controversial with students; the rationale is that a reduction in the number of line items (diversity of products) carried by Ma and Pa stores may reduce the diversity of products Figure Four carries.

   There are several options here:
   - Simple verbal persuasion by showing customers cost drivers at Figure Four
   - Explicitly pricing out activities like cartons delivered and shelf-stocking so that customers pay for the costs they cause.
   - Restricting options available to certain customers, e.g., customers with low revenues could be restricted to one free delivery per week.

An even more extreme example is working with customers so that deliveries are easier to make and shelf-stocking can be done faster.

d. Offer salespeople bonuses based on the operating income of each customer rather than the gross margin of each customer.

   Some students will argue that the bottom 40% of the customers should be dropped. This action should be only a last resort after all other avenues have been explored. Moreover, an unprofitable customer today may well be a profitable customer tomorrow, and it is myopic to focus on only a 1-month customer-profitability analysis to classify a customer as unprofitable.

16-26 (35 min.) Direct materials price, efficiency, mix and yield variances.

1. Solution Exhibit 16-26A presents the total price variance ($3,100F), the total efficiency variance ($2,560U) and the total flexible-budget variance ($540F).

Total direct materials price variance can also be computed as:

$$\begin{pmatrix} \text{Direct materials} \\ \text{price variance} \\ \text{for each input} \end{pmatrix} = \begin{pmatrix} \text{Actual} \\ \text{Price} \end{pmatrix} - \begin{pmatrix} \text{Budgeted} \\ \text{Price} \end{pmatrix} \times \begin{matrix} \text{Actual} \\ \text{Inputs} \end{matrix}$$

Tolman	= ($0.28 – $0.30) × 62,000	=	$1,240 F
Golden Delicious	= ($0.26 – $0.26) × 155,000	=	0
Ribston	= ($0.20 – $0.22) × 93,000	=	1,860 F
Total direct materials price variance			$3,100 F

Total direct materials efficiency variance can also be computed as:

$$\begin{pmatrix} \text{Direct materials} \\ \text{efficiency variance} \\ \text{for each input} \end{pmatrix} = \begin{pmatrix} \text{Actual} \\ \text{inputs} \end{pmatrix} - \begin{pmatrix} \text{Budgeted inputs allowed} \\ \text{for actual outputs achieved} \end{pmatrix} \times \begin{matrix} \text{Budgeted} \\ \text{prices} \end{matrix}$$

Tolman	= (62,000 – 45,000) × $0.30	=	$5,100 U
Golden Delicious	= (155,000 – 180,000) × $0.26	=	6,500 F
Ribston	= (93,000 – 75,000) × $0.22	=	3,960 U
Total direct materials efficiency variance			$2,560 U

SOLUTION EXHIBIT 16-26A
Columnar Presentation of Direct Materials Price and Efficiency Variances for Greenwood Inc.
for November 2000

	Actual Costs Incurred (Actual Inputs × Actual Prices) (1)		Actual Input × Budgeted Prices (2)		Flexible Budget (Budgeted Inputs Allowed for Actual Outputs Achieved × Budgeted Prices) (3)	
Tolman	62,000 × $0.28 =	$17,360	62,000 × $0.30 =	$18,600	45,000 × $0.30 =	$13,500
Golden Delicious	155,000 × $0.26 =	40,300	155,000 × $0.26 =	40,300	180,000 × $0.26 =	46,800
Ribston	93,000 × $0.20 =	18,600	93,000 × $0.22 =	20,460	75,000 × $0.22 =	16,500
		$76,260		$79,360		$76,800

$3,100 F
Total price variance

$2,560 U
Total efficiency variance

$540 F
Total flexible-budget variance

F = favorable effect on operating income; U = unfavorable effect on operating income

16-26 (Cont'd.)

2. Solution Exhibit 16-26B presents the total direct materials yield and mix variances for Greenwood Inc. for November 2000.

The total direct materials yield variance can also be computed as the sum of the direct materials yield variances for each input:

$$\begin{pmatrix} \text{Direct} \\ \text{materials} \\ \text{yield variance} \\ \text{for each input} \end{pmatrix} = \begin{pmatrix} \text{Actual total} \\ \text{quantity of all} \\ \text{direct materials} \\ \text{inputs used} \end{pmatrix} - \begin{pmatrix} \text{Budgeted total quantity} \\ \text{of all direct materials} \\ \text{inputs allowed for} \\ \text{actual output achieved} \end{pmatrix} \times \begin{pmatrix} \text{Budgeted} \\ \text{direct materials} \\ \text{input mix} \\ \text{percentage} \end{pmatrix} \times \begin{pmatrix} \text{Budgeted} \\ \text{price of} \\ \text{direct materials} \\ \text{inputs} \end{pmatrix}$$

Tolman	$= (310,000 - 300,000) \times 0.15 \times \$0.30 = 10,000 \times 0.15 \times \$0.30 =$	$ 450 U
Golden Delicious	$= (310,000 - 300,000) \times 0.60 \times \$0.26 = 10,000 \times 0.60 \times \$0.26 =$	1,560 U
Ribston	$= (310,000 - 300,000) \times 0.25 \times \$0.22 = 10,000 \times 0.25 \times \$0.22 =$	550 U

Total direct materials yield variance $2,560 U

The total direct materials mix variance can also be computed as the sum of the direct materials mix variances for each input:

$$\begin{pmatrix} \text{Direct} \\ \text{materials} \\ \text{mix variance} \\ \text{for each input} \end{pmatrix} = \begin{pmatrix} \text{Actual} \\ \text{direct materials} \\ \text{input mix} \\ \text{percentage} \end{pmatrix} - \begin{pmatrix} \text{Budgeted} \\ \text{direct materials} \\ \text{input mix} \\ \text{percentage} \end{pmatrix} \times \begin{pmatrix} \text{Actual total} \\ \text{quantity of all} \\ \text{direct materials} \\ \text{inputs used} \end{pmatrix} \times \begin{pmatrix} \text{Budgeted} \\ \text{price of} \\ \text{direct materials} \\ \text{inputs} \end{pmatrix}$$

Tolman	$= (0.20 - 0.15) \times 310,000 \times \$0.30 = 0.05 \times 310,000 \times \$0.30 =$	$4,650 U
Golden Delicious	$= (0.50 - 0.60) \times 310,000 \times \$0.26 = -0.10 \times 310,000 \times \$0.26 =$	8,060 F
Ribston	$= (0.30 - 0.25) \times 310,000 \times \$0.22 = 0.05 \times 310,000 \times \$0.22 =$	3,410 U

Total direct materials mix variance $ 0 U

3. Greenwood paid less for Tolman and Ribston apples and, so, had a favorable direct materials price variance of $3,100. It also had an unfavorable efficiency variance of $2,560. Greenwood would need to evaluate if these were unrelated events or if the lower price resulted from the purchase of apples of poorer quality that affected efficiency. The net effect in this case from a cost standpoint was favorable—the savings in price being greater than the loss in efficiency. Of course, if the applesauce is of poorer quality, Greenwood must also evaluate the potential effects on current and future revenues that have not been considered in the variances described in requirements 1 and 2.

The unfavorable efficiency variance is entirely attributable to an unfavorable yield. The actual mix does deviate from the budgeted mix but at the budgeted prices, the greater quantity of Tolman and Ribston apples used in the actual mix exactly offsets the fewer Golden Delicious apples used. Again, management should evaluate the reasons for the unfavorable yield variance. Is it due to poor quality Tolman and Ribston apples (recall from requirement 1 that these apples were acquired at a price lower than the standard price)? Is it due to the change in mix (recall that the mix used is different from the budgeted mix, even though the mix variance is $0)? Isolating the reasons can lead management to take the necessary corrective actions.

16-26 (Cont'd.)

SOLUTION EXHIBIT 16-26B
Columnar Presentation of Direct Materials Yield and Mix Variances
for Greenwood Inc. for November 2000

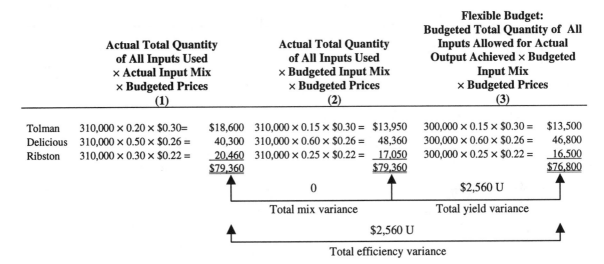

F = favorable effect on operating income; U = unfavorable effect on operating income

16-28 (60 min.) Variance analysis, sales-mix, and sales-quantity variances.

1. Actual Contribution Margins

Product	Actual Selling Price	Actual Variable Costs per Unit	Actual Contribution Margin per Unit	Actual Sales Volume in Units	Actual Contribution Dollars	Actual Contribution Percent
PalmPro	$349	$178	$171	11,000	$ 1,881,000	16%
PalmCE	285	92	193	44,000	8,492,000	71%
PalmKid	102	73	29	55,000	1,595,000	13%
				110,000	$11,968,000	100%

The actual average contribution margin per unit is $108.80 ($11,968,000 ÷ 110,000 units).

Budgeted Contribution Margins

Product	Budgeted Selling Price	Budgeted Variable Costs per Unit	Budgeted Contribution Margin per Unit	Budgeted Sales Volume in Units	Budgeted Contribution Dollars	Budgeted Contribution Percent
PalmPro	$379	$182	$197	12,500	$ 2,462,500	19%
PalmCE	269	98	171	37,500	6,412,500	49%
PalmKid	149	65	84	50,000	4,200,000	32%
				100,000	$13,075,000	100%

The budgeted average contribution margin per unit is $130.75 ($13,075,000 ÷ 100,000 units).

16-28 (Cont'd.)

2. Actual Sales Mix

Product	Actual Selling Price	Actual Variable Costs per Unit	Actual Contribution Margin per Unit	Actual Sales Volume in Units	Actual Sales Mix
PalmPro	$349	$178	$171	11,000	10.0%
PalmCE	285	92	193	44,000	40.0%
PalmKid	102	73	29	55,000	50.0%
				110,000	100%

Budgeted Sales Mix

Product	Budgeted Selling Price	Budgeted Variable Costs per Unit	Budgeted Contribution Margin per Unit	Budgeted Sales Volume in Units	Budgeted Sales Mix
PalmPro	$379	$182	$197	12,500	12.5%
PalmCE	269	98	171	37,500	37.5%
PalmKid	149	65	84	50,000	50.0%
				100,000	100%

3. Flexible-budget variance of contribution margin:

$$= \frac{\text{Actual}}{\text{Results}} - \frac{\text{Flexible-budget}}{\text{amount}}$$

PalmPro $= (\$171 \times 11{,}000) - (\$197 \times 11{,}000)$

$\qquad = \$1{,}881{,}000 - \$2{,}167{,}000 \qquad = \$\ \ 286{,}000$ U

PalmCE $= (193 \times 44{,}000) - (\$171 \times 44{,}000)$

$\qquad = \$8{,}492{,}000 - \$7{,}524{,}000 \qquad = \ \ 968{,}000$ F

PalmKid $= (\$29 \times 55{,}000) - (\$84 \times 55{,}000)$

$\qquad = \$1{,}595{,}000 - \$4{,}620{,}000 \qquad = \underline{\ 3{,}025{,}000}$ U

Total flexible-budget variance $\qquad\qquad = \underline{\$2{,}343{,}000}$ U

Sales-volume variance of contribution margin:

$$= \left(\begin{array}{c} \text{Actual sales} \\ \text{quantity} \\ \text{in units} \end{array} - \begin{array}{c} \text{Budgeted sales} \\ \text{quantity} \\ \text{in units} \end{array} \right) \times \begin{array}{c} \text{Budgeted} \\ \text{contrib. margin} \\ \text{per unit} \end{array}$$

PalmPro $= (11{,}000 - 12{,}500) \times \$197$

$\qquad = -1{,}500 \times \$197 \qquad = \$\ \ 295{,}500$ U

PalmCE $= (44{,}000 - 37{,}500) \times \$171$

$\qquad = 6{,}500 \times \$171 \qquad = \ \ 1{,}111{,}500$ F

16-28 (Cont'd.)

PalmKid $=$ $(55{,}000 - 50{,}000) \times \$84$

$\quad\quad\quad = 5{,}000 \times \$84$ $\quad\quad\quad\quad\quad = \underline{\quad420{,}000\quad}$ F

Total sales-volume variance $\quad\quad\quad\quad = \underline{\$1{,}236{,}000}$ F

Sales-mix variance of contribution-margin:

$$= \begin{pmatrix} \text{Actual units} \\ \text{of all} \\ \text{products sold} \end{pmatrix} \times \begin{pmatrix} \text{Actual} & & \text{Budgeted} \\ \text{sales mix} & - & \text{sales mix} \\ \text{percentage} & & \text{percentage} \end{pmatrix} \times \begin{pmatrix} \text{Budgeted} \\ \text{contrib. margin} \\ \text{per unit} \end{pmatrix}$$

PalmPro $=$ $110{,}000 \times (0.10 - 0.125) \times \$197$

$\quad\quad\quad = 110{,}00 \times -0.025 \times \$197$ $\quad\quad = \$541{,}750$ U

PalmCE $=$ $110{,}000 \times (0.40 - 0.375) \times \$171$

$\quad\quad\quad = 110{,}000 \times 0.025 \times \$171$ $\quad\quad = 470{,}250$ F

PalmKid $=$ $110{,}000 \times (0.50 - 0.50) \times \$84$

$\quad\quad\quad = 110{,}000 \times 0.00 \times \$84$ $\quad\quad\quad = \quad\quad 0$ F

Total sales-mix variance $\quad\quad\quad\quad = \underline{\$\ \ 71{,}500}$ U

Sales-quantity variance of contribution margin:

$$= \begin{pmatrix} \text{Actual units} & \text{Budgeted units} \\ \text{of all} & - & \text{of all} \\ \text{products sold} & \text{products sold} \end{pmatrix} \times \begin{pmatrix} \text{Budgeted} \\ \text{sales mix} \\ \text{percentage} \end{pmatrix} \times \begin{pmatrix} \text{Budgeted} \\ \text{contrib. margin} \\ \text{per unit} \end{pmatrix}$$

PalmPro $=$ $(110{,}000 - 100{,}000) \times 0.125) \times \$197$

$\quad\quad\quad = 10{,}000 \times 0.125 \times \$197$ $\quad\quad = \$\ 246{,}250$ F

PalmCE $=$ $(110{,}000 - 100{,}000) \times 0.375 \times \$171$

$\quad\quad\quad = 10{,}000 \times 0.375 \times \$171$ $\quad\quad = 641{,}250$ F

PalmKid $=$ $(110{,}000 - 100{,}000) \times 0.50 \times \$84$

$\quad\quad\quad = 10{,}000 \times 0.50 \times \$84$ $\quad\quad = 420{,}000$ F

Total sales-quantity variance $\quad\quad\quad = \underline{\$1{,}307{,}500}$ F

16-14

16-28 (Cont'd.)

4.

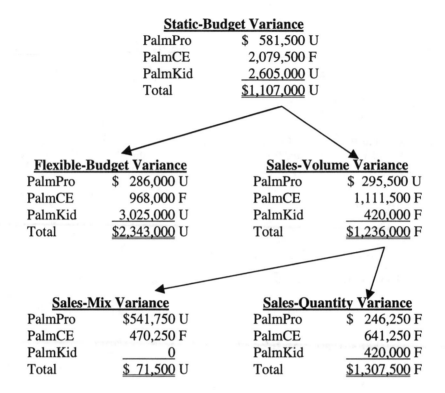

Static-Budget Variance

PalmPro	$ 581,500 U
PalmCE	2,079,500 F
PalmKid	2,605,000 U
Total	$1,107,000 U

Flexible-Budget Variance

PalmPro	$ 286,000 U
PalmCE	968,000 F
PalmKid	3,025,000 U
Total	$2,343,000 U

Sales-Volume Variance

PalmPro	$ 295,500 U
PalmCE	1,111,500 F
PalmKid	420,000 F
Total	$1,236,000 F

Sales-Mix Variance

PalmPro	$541,750 U
PalmCE	470,250 F
PalmKid	0
Total	$ 71,500 U

Sales-Quantity Variance

PalmPro	$ 246,250 F
PalmCE	641,250 F
PalmKid	420,000 F
Total	$1,307,500 F

5. Some factors to consider are:
   - The difference in actual vs. budgeted contribution was $1,107,000. However, the contribution from the PalmCE exceeded budget by $2,079,500 while the contributions from the PalmPro and the PalmKid were lower than expected to an offsetting degree.
   - In percentage terms, the PalmCE accounted for 71% of total contribution vs. a planned 49% contribution. However, the PalmPro accounted for 16% vs. planned 19% and the PalmKid accounted for only 13% vs. a planned 32%.
   - In unit terms (rather than in contribution terms), the PalmKid accounted for 50% of the sales mix as planned. However, the PalmPro accounted for only 10% vs. a budgeted 12.5% and the PalmCE accounted for 40% vs. a planned 37.5%.
   - Variance analysis for the PalmPro shows an unfavorable sales-mix variance outweighing a favorable sales-quantity variance and producing an unfavorable sales-volume variance of $295,500. The drop in sales-mix share was far larger than the gain from an overall greater quantity sold.
   - The PalmCE gained both from an increase in share of the sales mix as well as from the increase in the overall number of units sold. These factors combined to a $1,111,500 favorable sales-volume variance.
   - The PalmKid maintained sales-mix share – as a result, the sales-mix variance is zero. However, PalmKid sales did gain from the overall increase in units sold.

16-28 (Cont'd.)

- Overall, there was a favorable total sales-volume variance. However, the large drop in PalmKid's contribution margin per unit combined with a decrease in the number of PalmPro units purchased vs. budget, led to the total contribution margin being much lower than budgeted.

Other factors could be discussed here – for example, it seems that the PalmKid did not achieve much success with a three digit price point – selling price was budgeted at $149 but dropped to $102. At the same time, variable costs increased. This could have been due to a marketing push aimed at announcing the lower price in some markets.

16-30 (40 min.) **Variance analysis, multiple products.**

1, 2, and 3.   Solution Exhibit 16-30 presents the sales-volume, sales-quantity, and sales-mix variances for each type of cookie and in total for Debbie's Delight Inc. in August 2000.

The sales-volume variances can also be computed as:

$$\begin{array}{c}\text{Sales-volume} \\ \text{variance of} \\ \text{contribution margin}\end{array} = \left(\begin{array}{c}\text{Actual sales} \\ \text{quantity in pounds}\end{array} - \begin{array}{c}\text{Budgeted sales} \\ \text{quantity in pounds}\end{array}\right) \times \begin{array}{c}\text{Budgeted contribution} \\ \text{margin per pound}\end{array}$$

The sales-volume variances are:

Chocolate chip	=	$(57,600 - 45,000) \times \$2.00$	=	$25,200 F
Oatmeal raisin	=	$(18,000 - 25,000) \times \$2.30$	=	16,100 U
Coconut	=	$(9,600 - 10,000) \times \$2.60$	=	1,040 U
White chocolate	=	$(13,200 - 5,000) \times \$3.00$	=	24,600 F
Macadamia nut	=	$(21,600 - 15,000) \times \$3.10$	=	20,460 F
All cookies				$53,120 F

The sales-quantity variance can also be computed as :

$$\begin{array}{c}\text{Sales-quantity} \\ \text{variance of} \\ \text{contribution margin}\end{array} = \left(\begin{array}{c}\text{Actual pounds} \\ \text{of all cookies} \\ \text{sold}\end{array} - \begin{array}{c}\text{Budgeted pounds} \\ \text{of all cookies} \\ \text{sold}\end{array}\right) \times \begin{array}{c}\text{Budgeted} \\ \text{sales-mix} \\ \text{percentage}\end{array} \times \begin{array}{c}\text{Budgeted} \\ \text{contribution} \\ \text{margin per pound}\end{array}$$

The sales-quantity variances are:

Chocolate chip	=	$(120,000 - 100,000) \times 0.45 \times \$2.00$ =	$18,000 F
Oatmeal raisin	=	$(120,000 - 100,000) \times 0.25 \times \$2.30$ =	11,500 F
Coconut	=	$(120,000 - 100,000) \times 0.10 \times \$2.60$ =	5,200 F
White chocolate	=	$(120,000 - 100,000) \times 0.05 \times \$3.00$ =	3,000 F
Macadamia nut	=	$(120,000 - 100,000) \times 0.15 \times \$3.10$ =	9,300 F
All cookies			$47,000 F

The sales-mix variance can also be computed as:

$$\begin{array}{c}\text{Sales-mix} \\ \text{variance of} \\ \text{contribution margin}\end{array} = \left(\begin{array}{c}\text{Actual sales-} \\ \text{mix percentage}\end{array} - \begin{array}{c}\text{Budgeted sales-} \\ \text{mix percentage}\end{array}\right) \times \begin{array}{c}\text{Actual pounds} \\ \text{of all cookies} \\ \text{sold}\end{array} \times \begin{array}{c}\text{Budgeted} \\ \text{contribution} \\ \text{margin per pound}\end{array}$$

16-30 (Cont'd.)

The sales-mix variances are:

Chocolate chip	=	$(0.48 - 0.45) \times 120,000 \times \$2.00$	=	\$ 7,200 F
Oatmeal raisin	=	$(0.15 - 0.25) \times 120,000 \times \$2.30$	=	27,600 U
Coconut	=	$(0.08 - 0.10) \times 120,000 \times \$2.60$	=	6,240 U
White chocolate	=	$(0.11 - 0.05) \times 120,000 \times \$3.00$	=	21,600 F
Macadamia nut	=	$(0.18 - 0.15) \times 120,000 \times \$3.10$	=	11,160 F
All cookies				\$ 6,120 F

A summary of the variances is:

Sales-Volume Variance of C.M.

Chocolate chip	$25,200 F
Oatmeal raisin	16,100 U
Coconut	1,040 U
White chocolate	24,600 F
Macadamia nut	20,460 F
All cookies	$53,120 F

Sales-Mix Variance of C.M.		**Sales-Quantity Variance of C.M.**	
Chocolate chip	$ 7,200 F	Chocolate chip	$18,000 F
Oatmeal raisin	27,600 U	Oatmeal raisin	11,500 F
Coconut	6,240 U	Coconut	5,200 F
White chocolate	21,600 F	White chocolate	3,000 F
Macadamia nut	11,160 F	Macadamia nut	9,300 F
All cookies	$ 6,120 F	All cookies	$47,000 F

4. Debbie's Delight shows a favorable sales-quantity variance because it sold more cookies in total than was budgeted. Together with the higher quantities, Debbie's also sold more of the high-contribution margin white chocolate and macadamia nut cookies relative to the budgeted mix—hence, Debbie's also showed a favorable total sales-mix variance.

SOLUTION EXHIBIT 16-30
Columnar Presentation of Sales-Volume, Sales-Quantity and Sales-Mix Variances
for Debbie's Delight Inc.

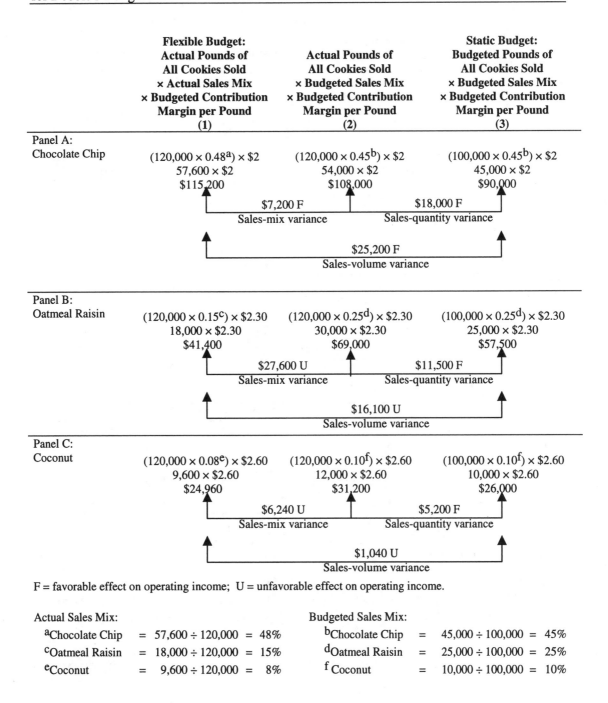

F = favorable effect on operating income; U = unfavorable effect on operating income.

Actual Sales Mix:

a Chocolate Chip = 57,600 ÷ 120,000 = 48%

c Oatmeal Raisin = 18,000 ÷ 120,000 = 15%

e Coconut = 9,600 ÷ 120,000 = 8%

Budgeted Sales Mix:

b Chocolate Chip = 45,000 ÷ 100,000 = 45%

d Oatmeal Raisin = 25,000 ÷ 100,000 = 25%

f Coconut = 10,000 ÷ 100,000 = 10%

SOLUTION EXHIBIT 16-30 (Cont'd.)
Columnar Presentation of Sales-Volume, Sales-Quantity and Sales-Mix Variances
for Debbie's Delight Inc.

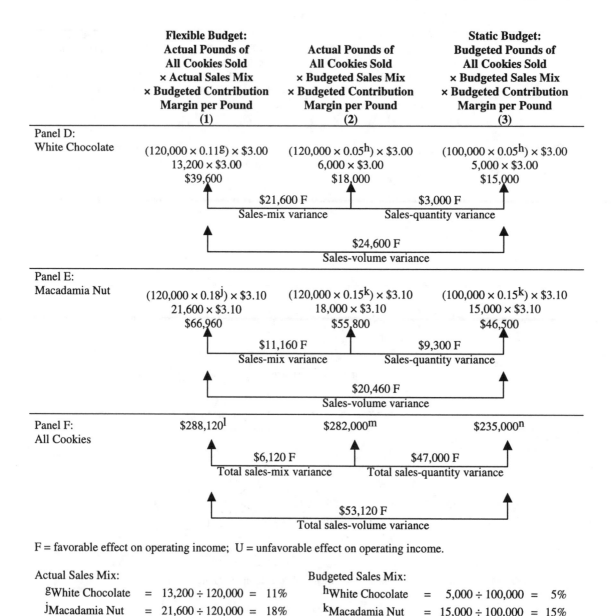

	Flexible Budget: Actual Pounds of All Cookies Sold × Actual Sales Mix × Budgeted Contribution Margin per Pound (1)	Actual Pounds of All Cookies Sold × Budgeted Sales Mix × Budgeted Contribution Margin per Pound (2)	Static Budget: Budgeted Pounds of All Cookies Sold × Budgeted Sales Mix × Budgeted Contribution Margin per Pound (3)
Panel D: White Chocolate	$(120{,}000 \times 0.11^g) \times \$3.00$ $13{,}200 \times \$3.00$ $\$39{,}600$	$(120{,}000 \times 0.05^h) \times \$3.00$ $6{,}000 \times \$3.00$ $\$18{,}000$	$(100{,}000 \times 0.05^h) \times \$3.00$ $5{,}000 \times \$3.00$ $\$15{,}000$

$\$21{,}600$ F $\$3{,}000$ F
Sales-mix variance   Sales-quantity variance

$\$24{,}600$ F
Sales-volume variance

Panel E: Macadamia Nut	$(120{,}000 \times 0.18^j) \times \$3.10$ $21{,}600 \times \$3.10$ $\$66{,}960$	$(120{,}000 \times 0.15^k) \times \$3.10$ $18{,}000 \times \$3.10$ $\$55{,}800$	$(100{,}000 \times 0.15^k) \times \$3.10$ $15{,}000 \times \$3.10$ $\$46{,}500$

$\$11{,}160$ F $\$9{,}300$ F
Sales-mix variance   Sales-quantity variance

$\$20{,}460$ F
Sales-volume variance

Panel F: All Cookies	$\$288{,}120^l$	$\$282{,}000^m$	$\$235{,}000^n$

$\$6{,}120$ F $\$47{,}000$ F
Total sales-mix variance   Total sales-quantity variance

$\$53{,}120$ F
Total sales-volume variance

F = favorable effect on operating income; U = unfavorable effect on operating income.

Actual Sales Mix:
 ^{g}White Chocolate = $13{,}200 \div 120{,}000$ = 11%
 ^{j}Macadamia Nut = $21{,}600 \div 120{,}000$ = 18%

Budgeted Sales Mix:
 ^{h}White Chocolate = $5{,}000 \div 100{,}000$ = 5%
 ^{k}Macadamia Nut = $15{,}000 \div 100{,}000$ = 15%

$^l\$115{,}200 + \$41{,}400 + \$24{,}960$
        $+ \$39{,}600 + \$66{,}960 = \$288{,}120$

$^m\$108{,}000 + \$69{,}000 + \$31{,}200$
        $+ \$18{,}000 + \$55{,}800 = \$282{,}000$

$^n\$90{,}000 + \$57{,}500 + \$26{,}000$
        $+ \$15{,}000 + \$46{,}500 = \$235{,}000$

16-32 (60 min.) **Customer-profitability analysis**

1. Solution Exhibit 16-32 shows the customer-profitability analysis. Alternative rankings are:
   a. Customer-level operating income
      1. Madison $507,440
      2. April   459,390
      3. Suitors   123,140

   b. Gross margin/Net revenues
      1. Suitors, $304,800 ÷ $863,600   35.29%
      2. Madison, $572,000 ÷ $1,830,400   31.25
      3. April, $501,600 ÷ $2,340,800   21.43

   c. Customer-level operating income/Net revenues
      1. Madison, $507, 440 ÷ $1,830,400   27.72%
      2. April, $459,390 ÷ $2,340,800   19.63
      3. Suitors, $123,140 ÷ $863,600   14.26

A breakdown of the revenues at list prices is:

	April	Madison	Suitors
Revenues at list prices	100.00%	100.00%	100.00%
Discount	30.00	20.00	15.00
Sales returns	3.50	6.20	17.11
Cost of goods sold	52.25	50.74	43.93
Gross margin	14.25	23.06	23.96
Customer-level costs	1.20	2.60	14.28
Customer-level operating Income	13.05%	20.46%	9.68%

The following conclusions relate to these percentages:

April – has high price discounting as its major differential to Madison
Madison – has lower price discounting than April and lower sales returns than Suitors
Suitors – has highest sales returns and highest customer-level costs

2. Key challenges facing Sims are:
   a. Reduce level of price discounting, especially by April,
   b. Reduce level of sales returns, especially by Suitors, and
   c. Reduce level of customer-level costs, especially by Suitors.

The ABC cost system highlights areas where the Suitors account is troublesome – it has a high number of orders, a high number of customer visits, a high number of rushed deliveries, and a high number of sales returns. Sims needs to consider whether this high level of activity can be reduced without reducing customer revenues.

SOLUTION EXHIBIT 16-32

Customer-Profitability Analysis for Zoot's Suits

	April	Madison	Suitors
Revenues at list prices			
$44 \times 400 \times \$200$; $62 \times 200 \times \$200$; $212 \times 30 \times \$200$	$3,520,000	$2,480,000	$1,272,000
Discount			
$44 \times 400 \times \$60^a$; $62 \times 200 \times \$40^b$; $212 \times 30 \times \$30^c$	1,056,000	496,000	190,800
Net revenues before returns	2,464,000	1,984,000	1,081,200
Sales returns			
$880 \times \$140$; $960 \times \$160$; $1,280 \times \$170$	123,200	153,600	217,600
Net revenues	2,340,800	1,830,400	863,600
Cost of goods sold			
$16,720^d \times 110$; $11,440^e \times 110$; $5,080^f \times 110$	1,839,200	1,258,400	558,800
Gross margin	501,600	572,000	304,800
Customer-level costs			
Order processing			
$44, 62, 212 \times \$245$	10,780	15,190	51,940
Customer visits			
$8, 12, 22 \times \$1,430$	11,440	17,160	31,460
Delivery – regular			
$41, 48, 166 \times \$300$	12,300	14,400	49,800
Delivery - rushed			
$3, 14, 46 \times \$850$	2,550	11,900	39,100
Returns processing			
$4, 6, 16 \times \$185$	740	1,110	2,960
Return stocking fee			
$880, 960, 1,280 \times \$5$	4,400	4,800	6,400
Total customer-level costs	42,210	64,560	181,660
Customer-level operating income	$ 459,390	$ 507,440	$ 123,140

[a] $\$200 - \$140 = \$60$
[b] $\$200 - \$160 = \$40$
[c] $\$200 - \$170 = \$30$
[d] $(44 \times 400) - 880 = 16,720$
[e] $(62 \times 200) - 960 = 11,440$
[f] $(212 \times 30) - 1,280 = 5,080$

16-34 (40 min.)   **Customer loyalty clubs and profitability analysis.**

1.

Gold Program

Revenues	
2,430 × 20 × ($200 × 0.90)	$ 8,748,000
2,430 × 30 × ($200 × 0.80)	11,664,000
2,430 × 10 × ($200 × 0.70)	3,402,000
Total revenues	23,814,000
Variable Costs	
Hotel variable costs, 2,430 × 60 × $65	9,477,000
Wine Costs	
2,430 × 50 × $5	607,500
2,430 × 10 × $20	486,000
Restaurant costs	
2,430 × 20 × $10	486,000
2,430 × 30 × $15	1,093,500
2,430 × 10 × $20	486,000
Total variable costs	12,636,000
Contribution margin	$11,178,000

Silver Program

Revenues	
8,340 × 20 × ($200 × 0.90)	$30,024,000
8,340 × 15 × ($200 × 0.80)	20,016,000
Total revenues	50,040,000
Variable Costs	
Hotel variable costs, 8,340 × 35 × $65	18,973,500
Wine costs, 8,340 × 35 × $5	1,459,500
Restaurant Costs	
8,340 × 20 × $10	1,668,000
8,340 × 15 × $15	1,876,500
Total variable costs	23,977,500
Contribution margin	$26,062,500

Bronze Program

Revenues, 80,300 × 10 × ($200 × 0.90)	$144,540,000
Variable costs	
Hotel variable costs, 80,300 × 10 × $65	52,195,000
Wine costs 80,300 × 10 × $5	4,015,000
Restaurant costs 80,300 × 10 × $10	8,030,000
Total variable costs	64,240,000
Contribution margin	$ 80,300,000

16-34 (Cont'd.)

No Program

Revenues, 219,000 × 1 × $200	$43,800,000
Variable costs, 219,000 × 1 × $65	14,235,000
Contribution margin	$29,565,000

Loyalty Program	Total Revenues	Variable Costs	Contribution Margin	Contrib. Margin Total Revenues
Gold	$ 23,814,000	$ 12,636,000	$ 11,178,000	46.94%
Silver	50,040,000	23,977,500	26,062,500	52.08
Bronze	144,540,000	64,240,000	80,300,000	55.56
No program	43,800,000	14,235,000	29,565,000	67.50
Total	$262,194,000	$115,088,500	$147,105,500	

The no-program group of customers has the highest contribution margin per revenue dollar. However, it comprises only 16.71% ($43,800,000 ÷ $262,194,000) of total revenues. The gold program has the lowest contribution margin per revenue dollar. However, it is misleading to evaluate each program in isolation. A key aim of loyalty programs is to promote a high frequency of return business. The contribution margin to total revenue ratio of each program in isolation does not address this issue.

2.

Revenues	$262,194,000
Variable costs	115,088,500
Contribution margin	147,105,500
Fixed costs	140,580,000
Operating income	$ 6,525,500

3. Number of room nights

Gold, 2,430 × 60	145,800
Silver, 8,340 × 35	291,900
Bronze, 80,300 × 10	803,000
No program, 219,000 × 1	219,000
	1,459,700

Average room rate per night: $\dfrac{\$262,194,000}{1,459,700} = \$179.62$

Average variable cost per night: $\dfrac{\$115,088,500}{1,459,700} = \$78.84$

16-34 (Cont'd.)

4. Sherriton Hotels has fixed costs of $140,580,000. A key challenge is to attract a high number of repeat business customers. Loyalty programs aim to have customers return to Sherriton multiple times. Their aim is increasing the revenues beyond what they would be without the program. It is to be expected that the higher the level of nights stayed, the greater the inducements necessary to keep attracting the customer to return. However, given the low level of variable costs to room rates, there is considerable cushion available for Sherriton to offer high inducements for frequent stayers.

Sherriton could adopt a net present value analysis of customers who are in the different loyalty clubs. It would be informative for Sherriton to have information on how much of each customer's total lodging industry expenditures it captures. It may well want to give higher levels of inducements to frequent stayers if the current program attracts only, say, 30% of each of its frequent customer's total business in cities where it has lodging properties available.

16-36 (15–20 min.) Customer profitability, responsibility for environmental clean-up, ethics.

1.   Customer-profitability analysis examines how individual customers differ in their profitability. The revenues and costs of each customer can be estimated with varying degrees of accuracy. Revenues of IF typically would be known at the time of sale. Many costs also would be known, e.g., the cost of materials used to manufacture the fluids sold to each customer. A major area of uncertainty is future costs associated with obligations arising from the sale. There are several issues here:

a.   Uncertainty as to the existence and extent of legal liability. Each customer has primary responsibility to dispose of its own toxic waste. However, under some U.S. laws (such as the "Superfund" laws), suppliers to a company may be partially liable for disposal of toxic material. Papandopolis needs to determine the extent of IF's liability. It would be necessary to seek legal guidance on this issue.

b.   Uncertainty as to when the liability will occur. The further in the future, the lower the amount of the liability (assuming discounting for the time-value of money occurs.)

c.   Uncertainty as to the amount of the liability, given that the liability exists and the date of the liability can be identified. Papandopolis faces major difficulties here—see the answer to requirement 2.

Many companies argue that uncertainties related to (a), (b), and (c) make the inclusion of "hard-dollar estimates meaningless." However, at a minimum, a contingent liability should be recognized and included in the internal customer-profitability reports.

2.   Papandopolis' controller may believe that if estimates of future possible legal exposure are sufficiently uncertain, then they should not be recorded. His concern about "smoking guns" may have a very genuine basis—that is, if litigation arises, third parties may misrepresent Papandopolis' concerns to the detriment of IF. Any written comments that she makes may surface 5 or 10 years later and be interpreted as "widespread knowledge" within IF that they have responsibility for large amounts of environmental clean-up.

Given this background, Papandopolis still has the responsibility to prepare a report in an objective and competent way. Moreover, she has visited 10 customer sites and has details as to their toxic-waste handling procedures. If Acme goes bankrupt and has no liability insurance, one of the "deep pockets" available to meet toxic waste handling costs is likely to be IF. At a minimum, she should report the likely bankruptcy and the existence of IF's contingent liability for toxic-waste clean-up in her report. Whether she quantifies this contingent liability is a more difficult question. Papandopolis has limited information available to make a meaningful quantification. She is not an employee of Acme Metal and has no information about Acme's liability insurance. Moreover, she does not know what other parties (such as other suppliers) are also jointly liable to pay Acme's clean-up costs.

The appropriate course appears to highlight the contingent liability but to not attempt to quantify it.

CHAPTER 17
PROCESS-COSTING

17-2   Process costing systems separate costs into cost categories according to the timing of when costs are introduced into the process. Often, only two cost classifications, direct materials and conversion costs, are necessary. Direct materials are frequently added at one point in time, often the start or the end of the process, and all conversion costs are added at about the same time, but in a pattern different from direct materials costs.

17-4   The accuracy of the estimates of completion depend on the care and skill of the estimator and the nature of the process. Aircraft blades may differ substantially in the finishing necessary to obtain a final product. The amount of work may not always be easy to ascertain in advance.

17-6   Three inventory methods associated with process costing are:
- Weighted average.
- First-in, first-out.
- Standard costing.

17-8   FIFO computations are distinctive because they assign the cost of the earliest equivalent units available (starting with equivalent units in beginning work-in-process inventory) to units completed and transferred out, and the cost of the most recent equivalent units worked on during the period to ending work-in-process inventory. In contrast, the weighted average method costs units completed and transferred out and in ending work in process at the same average cost.

17-10   A major advantage of FIFO is that managers can judge the performance in the current period independently from the performance in the preceding period.

17-12   Standard-cost procedures are particularly appropriate to process-costing systems where there are various combinations of materials and operations. Standard-cost procedures avoid the intricacies involved in detailed tracking with weighted-average or FIFO methods when there are frequent price variations over time.

17-14   No. Transferred-in costs or previous department costs are costs incurred in a previous department that have been charged to a subsequent department. These costs may be costs incurred in that previous department during this accounting period or a preceding accounting period.

17-16 (25 min.) **Equivalent units, zero beginning inventory.**

1.
Direct materials cost per unit ($720,000 ÷ 10,000)	$ 72
Conversion cost per unit ($760,000 ÷ 10,000)	76
Assembly Department cost per unit	$148

2a. Solution Exhibit 17-16A calculates the equivalent units of direct materials and conversion costs in the Assembly Department of International Electronics in February 2001.

   Solution Exhibit 17-16B computes equivalent units costs.

2b.
Direct materials cost per unit	$ 72
Conversion cost per unit	80
Assembly Department cost per unit	$152

3. The difference in the Assembly Department cost per unit calculated in requirements 1 and 2 arises because the costs incurred in January and February are the same but fewer equivalent units of work are done in February relative to January. In January, all 10,000 units introduced are fully completed resulting in 10,000 equivalent units of work done with respect to direct materials and conversion costs. In February, of the 10,000 units introduced, 10,000 equivalent units of work is done with respect to direct materials but only 9,500 equivalent units of work is done with respect to conversion costs. The Assembly Department cost per unit is, therefore, higher.

SOLUTION EXHIBIT 17-16A
Steps 1 and 2: Summarize Output in Physical Units and Compute Equivalent Units
Assembly Department of International Electronics for February 2001

		(Step 2)	
	(Step 1)	Equivalent Units	
Flow of Production	Physical Units	Direct Materials	Conversion Costs
Work in process, beginning	0		
Started during current period	10,000		
To account for	10,000		
Completed and transferred out during current period	9,000	9,000	9,000
Work in process, ending*	1,000		
1,000 × 100%; 1,000 × 50%		1,000	500
Accounted for	10,000		
Work done in current period only		10,000	9,500

*Degree of completion in this department: direct materials, 100%; conversion costs, 50%.

17-16 (Cont'd.)

SOLUTION EXHIBIT 17-16B
Compute Equivalent Unit Costs,
Assembly Department of International Electronics for February 2001

	Total Production Costs	Direct Materials	Conversion Costs
(Step 3) Costs added during February	$1,480,000	$720,000	$760,000
Divide by equivalent units of work done in current period (Solution Exhibit 17-16A)		÷ 10,000	÷ 9,500
Cost per equivalent unit		$ 72	$ 80

17-18 (25 min.) Zero beginning inventory, materials introduced in middle of process.

1. Solution Exhibit 17-18A shows equivalent units of work done in the current period of Chemical P, 50,000; Chemical Q, 35,000; Conversion costs, 45,000.

2. Solution Exhibit 17-18B calculates cost per equivalent unit of work done in the current period for Chemical P, Chemical Q, and Conversion costs, summarizes the total Mixing Department costs for July 2001, and assigns these costs to units completed (and transferred out) and to units in ending work in process.

SOLUTION EXHIBIT 17-18A
Steps 1 and 2: Summarize Output in Physical Units and Compute Equivalent Units
Mixing Department of Vaasa Chemicals for July 2001

	(Step 1) Physical Units	(Step 2) Equivalent Units		
Flow of Production		**Chemical P**	**Chemical Q**	**Conversion Costs**
Work in process, beginning	0			
Started during current period	50,000			
To account for	50,000			
Completed and transferred out during current period	35,000	35,000	35,000	35,000
Work in process, ending*	15,000			
15,000 × 100%; 15,000 × 0%; 15,000 × 66 2/3%		15,000	0	10,000
Accounted for	50,000			
Work done in current period only		50,000	35,000	45,000

*Degree of completion in this department: Chemical P, 100%; Chemical Q, 0%; conversion costs, 66 2/3%.

17-18 (Cont'd.)

SOLUTION EXHIBIT 17-18B
Steps 3, 4, and 5: Compute Equivalent Unit Costs, Summarize Total Costs to Account For, and Assign Costs to Units Completed and to Units in Ending Work in Process, Mixing Department of Vaasa Chemicals for July 2001

	Total Production Costs	Chemical P	Chemical Q	Conversion Costs
(Step 3) Costs added during February	$455,000	$250,000	$70,000	$135,000
Divide by equivalent units of work done in current period (Solution Exhibit 17-18A)		÷ 50,000	÷35,000	÷ 45,000
Cost per equivalent unit		$ 5	$ 2	$ 3
(Step 4) Total costs to account for	$455,000			
(Step 5) Assignment of costs:				
Completed and transferred out (35,000 units)	$350,000	(35,000*× $5)	+ (35,000*×$2)	+ (35,000*×$3)
Work in process ending (15,000 units)				
Chemical P	75,000	15,000† × $5		
Chemical Q	0		0† × $2	
Conversion costs	30,000			10,000†×$3
Total work in process	105,000			
Total costs accounted for	$455,000			

*Equivalent units completed and transferred out from Solution Exhibit 17-18A, Step 2.
†Equivalent units in work in process, ending from Solution Exhibit 17-18A, Step 2.

17-20 (20 min.) **Weighted-average method, assigning costs.** (Continuation of 17-19)

Solution Exhibit 17-20 calculates cost per equivalent unit of work done to date in the Assembly Department of Aerospatiale, summarizes total costs to account for, and assigns costs to units completed and to units in ending work-in-process inventory.

SOLUTION EXHIBIT 17-20
Steps 3, 4, and 5: Compute Equivalent Unit Costs, Summarize Total Costs to Account For, and Assign Costs to Units Completed and to Units in Ending Work in Process
Weighted-Average Method of Process Costing, Satellite Assembly Department of Aerospatiale for May 2001

		Total Production Costs	Direct Materials	Conversion Costs
(Step 3)	Work in process, beginning (given)	$ 5,844,000	$ 4,933,600	$ 910,400
	Costs added in current period (given)	46,120,000	32,200,000	13,920,000
	Costs incurred to date		$37,133,600	$14,830,400
	Divide by equivalent units of work done to date (Solution Exhibit 17-19)		÷ 53.2	÷ 49.6
	Cost per equivalent unit of work done to date		$ 698,000	$ 299,000
(Step 4)	Total costs to account for	51,964,000		
(Step 5)	Assignment of costs:			
	Completed and transferred out (46 units)	45,862,000	(46*× $698,000) + (46* × $299,000)	
	Work in process, ending (12 units)			
	Direct materials	5,025,600	7.2†× $698,000	
	Conversion costs	1,076,400		3.6† × $299,000
	Total work in process	6,102,000		
	Total costs accounted for	$51,964,000		

*Equivalent units completed and transferred out from Solution Exhibit 17-19, Step 2.
†Equivalent units in work in process, ending from Solution Exhibit 17-19, Step 2.

17-22 (20 min.)   **FIFO method, assigning costs.** (Continuation of 17-21)

Solution Exhibit 17-22 calculates cost per equivalent unit of work done in May 2001 in the Assembly Department of Aerospatiale, summarizes total costs to account for, and assigns costs to units completed and to units in ending work-in-process inventory.

SOLUTION EXHIBIT 17-22
Steps 3, 4, and 5: Compute Equivalent Unit Costs, Summarize Total Costs to Account For, and Assign Costs to Units Completed and to Units in Ending Work in Process
FIFO Method of Process Costing, Satellite Assembly Division of Aerospatiale for May 2001

	Total Production Costs	Direct Materials	Conversion Costs
Work in process, beginning ($4,933,600 + $910,400)	$ 5,844,000	(costs of work done before current period)	
(Step 3) Costs added in current period (given)	46,120,000	$32,200,000	$ 13,920,000
Divide by equivalent units of work done in current period (Solution Exhibit 17-21)		÷ 46	÷ 46.4
Cost per equivalent unit of work done in current period		$ 700,000	$ 300,000
(Step 4) Total costs to account for	$51,964,000		
(Step 5) Assignment of costs:			
Completed and transferred out (46 units):			
Work in process, beginning (8 units)	$ 5,844,000		
Direct materials added in current period	560,000	0.8* × $700,000	
Conversion costs added in current period	1,440,000		4.8* × $300,000
Total from beginning inventory	7,844,000		
Started and completed (38 units)	38,000,000	(38[†] × $700,000) +	(38[†] × $300,000)
Total costs of units completed & transf. out	45,844,000		
Work in process, ending (12 units)			
Direct materials	5,040,000	7.2[#] × $700,000	
Conversion costs	1,080,000		3.6[#] × $300,000
Total work in process, ending	6,120,000		
Total costs accounted for	$51,964,000		

*Equivalent units used to complete beginning work in process from Solution Exhibit 17-21, Step 2.
[†]Equivalent units started and completed from Solution Exhibit 17-21, Step 2.
[#]Equivalent units in work in process, ending from Solution Exhibit 17-21, Step 2.

17-24 (25 min.) Weighted-average method, assigning costs.

1. & 2. Solution Exhibit 17-24 calculates the cost per equivalent unit of work done to date for direct materials and conversion costs, summarizes total costs to account for, and assigns these costs to units completed and transferred out and to units in ending work-in-process inventory.

SOLUTION EXHIBIT 17-24

Steps 3, 4, and 5: Compute Equivalent Unit Costs, Summarize Total Costs to Account For, and Assign Costs to Units Completed and to Units in Ending Work in Process

Weighted-Average Method of Process Costing, Chatham Company for July 2001

		Total Production Costs	Direct Materials	Conversion Costs
(Step 3)	Work in process, beginning (given)	$130,000	$ 60,000	$ 70,000
	Costs added in current period (given)	651,000	280,000	371,000
	Costs incurred to date		$340,000	$441,000
	Divide by equivalent units of work done to date (given)		÷ 50,000	÷ 42,000
	Cost per equivalent unit of work done to date		$ 6.80	$ 10.50
(Step 4)	Total costs to account for	$781,000		
(Step 5)	Assignment of costs:			
	Completed and transferred out (34,000 units)	588,200	(34,000* × $6.80) + (34,000* × $10.50)	
	Work in process, ending (16,000 units)			
	Direct materials	108,800	16,000† × $6.80	
	Conversion costs	84,000		8,000† × $10.50
	Total work in process	192,800		
	Total costs accounted for	$781,000		

*Equivalent units completed and transferred out (given).
†Equivalent units in work in process, ending (given).

17-26 (30 min.) **Standard-costing method, assigning costs.**

1. The calculations of equivalent units for direct materials and conversion costs are identical to the calculations of equivalent units under the FIFO method. Solution Exhibit 17-26A shows the equivalent unit calculations for standard costing given by the equivalent units of work done in July 2001. Solution Exhibit 17-26B uses the standard costs (direct materials, $6.50; conversion costs, $10.30) to summarize total costs to account for, and to assign these costs to units completed and transferred out and to units in ending work-in-process inventory.

2. Solution Exhibit 17-26B shows the direct materials and conversion costs variances for

Direct materials	$20,000 U
Conversion costs	$10,500 U

SOLUTION EXHIBIT 17-26A

Steps 1 and 2: Summarize Output in Physical Units and Compute Equivalent Units
FIFO Method of Process Costing, Chatham Company for July 2001

	(Step 1)	(Step 2) Equivalent Units	
Flow of Production	**Physical Units**	**Direct Materials**	**Conversion Costs**
Work in process, beginning (given)	10,000	(work done before current period)	
Started during current period (given)	40,000		
To account for	50,000		
Completed and transferred out during current period:			
From beginning work in process[§]	10,000		
10,000 × (100% − 100%); 10,000 × (100% − 70%)		0	3,000
Started and completed	24,000[†]		
24,000 × 100%, 24,000 × 100%		24,000	24,000
Work in process, ending* (given)	16,000		
16,000 × 100%; 16,000 × 50%		16,000	8,000
Accounted for	50,000		
Work done in current period only		40,000	35,000

[§]Degree of completion in this department: direct materials, 100%; conversion costs, 70%.
[†]34,000 physical units completed and transferred out minus 10,000 physical units completed and transferred out from beginning work-in-process inventory.
*Degree of completion in this department: direct materials, 100%; conversion costs, 50%.

SOLUTION EXHIBIT 17-26B

Steps 3, 4, and 5: Compute Equivalent Unit Costs, Summarize Total Costs to Account For, and Assign Costs to Units Completed and to Units in Ending Work in Process
Use of Standard Costs in Process Costing, Chatham Company for July 2001.

	Total Production Costs	Direct Materials	Conversion Costs
(Step 3) Standard cost per equivalent unit (given)		$ 6.50	$ 10.30
Work in process, beginning (given)			
Direct materials, 10,000 × $6.50; Conversion costs, 7,000 × $10.30	$137,100		
Costs added in current period at standard costs			
Direct materials, 40,000 × $6.50;			
Conversion costs, 35,000 × $10.30	620,500	260,000	360,500
(Step 4) Costs to account for	$757,600		
(Step 5) Assignment of costs at standard costs:			
Completed and transferred out (34,000 units):			
Work in process, beginning (10,000 units)	$137,100		
Direct materials added in current period	0	0* × $6.50	
Conversion costs added in current period	30,900		3,000* × $10.30
Total from beginning inventory	168,000		
Started and completed (24,000 units)	403,200	(24,000† × $6.50) +	(24,000† × $10.30)
Total costs of units transferred out	571,200		
Work in process, ending (16,000 units)			
Direct materials	104,000	16,000# × $6.50	
Conversion costs	82,400		8,000# × $10.30
Total work in process, ending	186,400		
Total costs accounted for	$757,600		
Summary of variances for current performance:			
Costs added in current period at standard prices (see above)		$260,000	$360,500
Actual costs incurred (given)		280,000	371,000
Variance		$ 20,000 U	$ 10,500 U

*Equivalent units to complete beginning work in process from Solution Exhibit 17-26A, Step 2.
†Equivalent units started and completed from Solution Exhibit 17-26A, Step 2.
#Equivalent units in work in process, ending from Solution Exhibit 17-26A, Step 2.

17-28   (35–40 min.)   **Transferred-in costs, FIFO method.**

1. & 2.   Solution Exhibit 17-28A calculates the equivalent units of work done in the current period (for transferred-in costs, direct-materials, and conversion costs) to complete beginning work-in-process inventory, to start and complete new units, and to produce ending work in process. Solution Exhibit 17-28B calculates the cost per equivalent unit of work done in the current period for transferred-in costs, direct materials, and conversion costs, summarizes total costs to account for, and assigns these costs to units completed and transferred out and to units in ending work-in-process inventory.

SOLUTION EXHIBIT 17-28A

Steps 1 and 2: Summarize Output in Physical Units and Compute Equivalent Units
FIFO Method of Process Costing
Cooking Department of Hideo Chemicals for June 2001

| | (Step 1) | (Step 2) Equivalent Units | | |
| | Physical Units | Transferred-in Costs | Direct Materials | Conversion Costs |
Flow of Production				
Work in process, beginning (given)	40	(work done before current period)		
Transferred-in during current period (given)	80			
To account for	120			
Completed and transferred out during current period:				
From beginning work in process[§]	40			
$40 \times (100\% - 100\%)$; $40 \times (100\% - 0\%)$;				
$40 \times (100\% - 75\%)$		0	40	10
Started and completed	50[†]			
$50 \times 100\%$; $50 \times 100\%$; $50 \times 100\%$		50	50	50
Work in process, ending* (given)	30			
$30 \times 100\%$; $30 \times 0\%$; $30 \times 50\%$		30	0	15
Accounted for	120			
Work done in current period only		80	90	75

[§]Degree of completion in this department: Transferred-in costs, 100%; direct materials, 0%; conversion costs, 75%.
[†]90 physical units completed and transferred out minus 40 physical units completed and transferred out from beginning work-in-process inventory.
*Degree of completion in this department: transferred-in costs, 100%; direct materials, 0%; conversion costs, 50%.

17-28 (Cont'd.)

SOLUTION EXHIBIT 17-28B
Steps 3, 4, and 5: Compute Equivalent Unit Costs, Summarize Total Costs to Account For,
and Assign Costs to Units Completed and to Units in Ending Work in Process
FIFO Method of Process Costing
Cooking Department of Hideo Chemicals for June 2001

	Total Production Costs	Transferred -in Costs	Direct Materials	Conversion Costs
Work in process, beginning ($39,200 + $0 + $18,000)	$ 57,200	(Costs of work done before current period)		
(Step 3) Costs added in current period (given)	171,325	$85,600	$36,000	$49,725
Divide by equivalent units of work done in current period (Solution Exhibit 17-28A)		÷ 80	÷ 90	÷ 75
Cost per equiv. unit of work done in current period		$ 1,070	$ 400	$ 663
(Step 4) Total costs to account for	$228,525			
(Step 5) Assignment of costs:				
Completed and transferred out (90 units):				
Work in process, beginning (40 units)	$ 57,200			
Transferred-in costs added in current period	0	0*×$1,070		
Direct materials added in current period	16,000		40*×$400	
Conversion costs added in current period	6,630			10*×$663
Total from beginning inventory	79,830			
Started and completed (50 units)	106,650	(50†×$1,070) + (50†× $400)+ (50†×$663)		
Total costs of units completed & tfd. out	186,480			
Work in process, ending (30 units)				
Transferred-in costs	32,100	30#×$1,070		
Direct materials	0		0#×$30	
Conversion costs	9,945			15#×$663
Total work in process, ending	42,045			
Total costs accounted for	$228,525			

*Equivalent units used to complete beginning work in process from Solution Exhibit 17-28A, Step 2.
†Equivalent units started and completed from Solution Exhibit 17-28A, Step 2.
#Equivalent units in work in process, ending from Solution Exhibit 17-28A, Step 2.

17-30 (25 min.) Weighted-average method.

1.   Solution Exhibit 17-30A shows equivalent units of work done to date
      Direct materials   100 equivalent units
      Conversion costs   97 equivalent units

2. & 3. Solution Exhibit 17-30B calculates cost per equivalent unit of work done to date,
summarizes the total Assembly Department costs for October 2001, and assigns these costs to
units completed (and transferred out) and to units in ending work in process using the weighted-
average method.

17-30 (Cont'd.)

SOLUTION EXHIBIT 17-30A

Steps 1 and 2: Summarize Output in Physical Units and Compute Equivalent Units
Weighted-Average Method of Process Costing, Assembly Department of Global Defense Inc. for October 2001

Flow of Production	(Step 1) Physical Units (given)	(Step 2) Equivalent Units	
		Direct Materials	Conversion Costs
Work in process beginning	20		
Started during current period	80		
To account for	100		
Completed and transferred out during current period	90	90	90
Work in process, ending*	10		
10 × 100%; 10 × 70%		10	7
Accounted for	100		
Work done to date		100	97

*Degree of completion in this department: direct materials, 100%; conversion costs, 70%.

SOLUTION EXHIBIT 17-30B

Steps 3, 4, and 5: Compute Equivalent Unit Costs, Summarize Total Costs to Account For, and Assign Costs to Units Completed and to Units in Ending Work in Process
Weighted-Average Method of Process Costing, Assembly Department of Global Defense Inc. for October 2001

		Total Production Costs	Direct Materials	Conversion Costs
(Step 3)	Work in process, beginning (given)	$ 580,000	$ 460,000	$ 120,000
	Costs added in current period (given)	2,935,000	2,000,000	935,000
	Costs incurred to date		$2,460,000	$1,055,000
	Divide by equivalent units of work done to date (Solution Exhibit 17-30A)		÷ 100	÷ 97
	Cost per equivalent unit of work done to date		$ 24,600	$10,876.29
(Step 4)	Total costs to account for	$3,515,000		
(Step 5)	Assignment of costs:			
	Completed and transferred out (90 units)	$3,192,866	(90* × $24,600) + (90* × $10,876.29)	
	Work in process, ending (10 units)			
	Direct materials	246,000	10† × $24,600	
	Conversion costs	76,134		7† × $10,876.29
	Total work in process	322,134		
	Total costs accounted for	$3,515,000		

*Equivalent units completed and transferred out from Solution Exhibit 17-30A, Step 2.
†Equivalent units in work in process, ending from Solution Exhibit 17-30A, Step 2.

17-32 (20 min.) FIFO method.

1. The equivalent units of work done in the current period in the Assembly Department in October 2001 for direct materials and conversion costs are shown in Solution Exhibit 17-32A.

2. The cost per equivalent unit of work done in the current period in the Assembly Department in October 2001 for direct materials and conversion costs is calculated in Solution Exhibit 17-32B.

3. Solution Exhibit 17-32B summarizes the total Assembly Department costs for October 2001, and assigns these costs to units completed (and transferred out) and units in ending work in process under the FIFO method.

The cost per equivalent unit of beginning inventory and of work done in the current period differ:

	Beginning Inventory	Work Done in Current Period
Direct materials	$23,000 ($460,000 ÷ 20 equiv. units)	$25,000
Conversion costs	$10,000 ($120,000 ÷ 12 equiv. units)	$11,000

The following table summarizes the costs assigned to units completed and those still in process under the weighted-average and FIFO process-costing methods for our example.

	Weighted Average (Solution Exhibit 17-30B)	FIFO (Solution Exhibit 17-32B)	Difference
Cost of units completed and transferred out	$3,192,866	$3,188,000	–$4,866
Work in process, ending	322,134	327,000	+$4,866
Total costs accounted for	$3,515,000	$3,515,000	

The FIFO ending inventory is higher than the weighted-average ending inventory by $4,866. This is because FIFO assumes that all the lower-cost prior-period units in work in process are the first to be completed and transferred out while ending work in process consists of only the higher-cost current-period units. The weighted-average method, however, smoothes out cost per equivalent unit by assuming that more of the higher-cost units are completed and transferred out, while some of the lower-cost units in beginning work in process are placed in ending work in process. Hence, in this case, the weighted-average method results in a higher cost of units completed and transferred out and a lower ending work-in-process inventory relative to FIFO.

17-32 (Cont'd.)

SOLUTION EXHIBIT 17-32A
Steps 1 and 2: Summarize Output in Physical Units and Compute Equivalent Units
FIFO Method of Process Costing, Assembly Department of Global Defense Inc. for October 2001

		(Step 2) Equivalent Units	
	(Step 1)		
Flow of Production	Physical Units	Direct Materials	Conversion Costs
Work in process, beginning (given)	20	(work done before current period)	
Started during current period (given)	80		
To account for	100		
Completed and transferred out during current period:			
From beginning work in process[§]	20		
20 × (100% − 100%); 20 × (100% − 60%)		0	8
Started and completed	70[†]		
70 ×100%, 70 × 100%		70	70
Work in process, ending* (given)	10		
10 × 100%; 10 × 70%		10	7
Accounted for	100		
Work done in current period only		80	85

[§]Degree of completion in this department: direct materials, 100%; conversion costs, 60%.
[†]90 physical units completed and transferred out minus 20 physical units completed and transferred out from beginning work-in-process inventory.
*Degree of completion in this department: direct materials, 100%; conversion costs, 70%.

17-32 (Cont'd.)

SOLUTION EXHIBIT 17-32B
Steps 3, 4, and 5: Compute Equivalent Unit Costs, Summarize Total Costs to Account For, and Assign Costs to Units Completed and to Units in Ending Work in Process
FIFO Method of Process Costing, Assembly Department of Global Defense Inc. for October 2001

	Total Production Costs	Direct Materials	Conversion Costs
Work in process, beginning ($460,000 + $120,000)	$ 580,000	(costs of work done before current period)	
(**Step 3**) Costs added in current period (given)	2,935,000	$2,000,000	$935,000
Divide by equivalent units of work done in current period (Solution Exhibit 17-32A)		÷ 80	÷ 85
Cost per equivalent unit of work done in current period		$ 25,000	$ 11,000
(**Step 4**) Total costs to account for	$3,515,000		
(**Step 5**) Assignment of costs:			
Completed and transferred out (90 units):			
Work in process, beginning (20 units)	$ 580,000		
Direct materials added in current period	0	0* × $25,000	
Conversion costs added in current period	88,000		8* × $11,000
Total from beginning inventory	668,000		
Started and completed (70 units)	2,520,000	(70† × $25,000) + (70† × $11,000)	
Total costs of units completed & transf. out	3,188,000		
Work in process, ending (10 units)			
Direct materials	250,000	10# × $25,000	
Conversion costs	77,000		7# × $11,000
Total work in process, ending	327,000		
Total costs accounted for	$3,515,000		

*Equivalent units used to complete beginning work in process from Solution Exhibit 17-32A, Step 2.
†Equivelant units started and completed from Solution Exhibit 17-32A, Step 2.
#Equivalent units in work in process, ending from Solution Exhibit 17-32A, Step 2.

17-34 (30 min.) **Transferred-in costs, FIFO method.** (Continuation of 17-33)

1.   As explained in Problem 17-33, requirement 1, transferred-in costs are 100% complete and direct materials are 0% complete in both beginning and ending work-in-process inventory.

2.   The equivalent units of work done in October 2001 in the Testing Department for transferred-in costs, direct materials, and conversion costs are calculated in Solution Exhibit 17-34A.

3.   Solution Exhibit 17-34B calculates the cost per equivalent unit of work done in October 2001 in the Testing Department for transferred-in costs, direct materials, and conversion costs, summarizes total Testing Department costs for October 2001, and assigns these costs to units completed and transferred out and to units in ending work in process using the FIFO method.

17-34 (Cont'd.)

4. Journal entries:

   a.   Work in Process—Testing Department   3,188,000
          Work in Process—Assembly Department   3,188,000
       Cost of goods completed and transferred out
          during October from the Assembly Dept. to
          the Testing Dept.

   b.   Finished Goods   9,281,527
          Work in Process—Testing Department   9,281,527
       Cost of goods completed and transferred out
          during October from the Testing Department
          to Finished Goods inventory.

SOLUTION EXHIBIT 17-34A

Steps 1 and 2: Summarize Output in Physical Units and Compute Equivalent Units
FIFO Method of Process Costing
Testing Department of Global Defense Inc. for October 2001

| | (Step 1) | (Step 2) Equivalent Units | | |
Flow of Production	Physical Units	Transferred-in Costs	Direct Materials	Conversion Costs
Work in process, beginning (given)	30	(work done before current period)		
Transferred-in during current period (given)	90			
To account for	120			
Completed and transferred out during current period:				
From beginning work in process§	30			
30 × (100% − 100%); 30 × (100% − 0%);				
30 × (100% − 70%)		0	30	9
Started and completed	75†			
75 × 100%; 75 × 100%; 75 × 100%		75	75	75
Work in process, ending* (given)	15			
15 × 100%; 15 × 0%; 15 × 60%		15	0	9
Accounted for	120			
Work done in current period only		90	105	93

§ Degree of completion in this department: Transferred-in costs, 100%; direct materials, 0%; conversion costs, 70%.
† 105 physical units completed and transferred out minus 30 physical units completed and transferred out from beginning work-in-process inventory.
*Degree of completion in this department: transferred-in costs, 100%; direct materials, 0%; conversion costs, 60%.

17-34 (Cont'd.)

SOLUTION EXHIBIT 17-34B
Steps 3, 4, and 5: Compute Equivalent Unit Costs, Summarize Total Costs to Account For, and Assign Costs to Units Completed and to Units in Ending Work in Process
FIFO Method of Process Costing
Testing Department of Global Defense Inc. for October 2001

		Total Production Costs	Transferred-in Costs	Direct Materials	Conversion Costs
	Work in process, beginning ($331,800 + $0 + $980,060))	$1,311,860	(Costs of work done before current period)		
(Step 3)	Costs added in current period (given)	8,654,000	$3,188,000	$3,885,000	$1,581,000
	Divide by equivalent units of work done in current period (Solution Exhibit 17-34A)		$\div$ 90	$\div$ 105	$\div$ 93
	Cost per equiv. unit of work done in current period		$ 35,422.22	$ 37,000	$ 17,000
(Step 4)	Total costs to account for	$9,965,860			
(Step 5)	Assignment of costs:				
	Completed and transferred out (105 units):				
	Work in process, beginning (30 units)	$1,311,860			
	Tfd-in costs added in current period	0	0*$\times$ $35,422.22		
	Dir materials added in current period	1,110,000		30*$\times$$37,000	
	Conversion costs added in current period	153,000			9*$\times$$17,000
	Total from beginning inventory	2,574,860			
	Started and completed (75 units)	6,706,667	(75[†]$\times$$35,422.22)+(75[†]$\times$$37,000)+(75[†]$\times$$17,000)		
	Total costs of units completed & tfd. out	9,281,527			
	Work in process, ending (15 units)				
	Transferred-in costs	531,333	15[#] $\times$ $35,422.22		
	Direct materials	0		0[#]$\times$$37,000	
	Conversion costs	153,000			9[#]$\times$$17,000
	Total work in process, ending	684,333			
	Total costs accounted for	$9,965,860			

*Equivalent units used to complete beginning work in process from Solution Exhibit 17-34A, Step 2.
[†]Equivalent units started and completed from Solution Exhibit 17-34A, Step 2.
[#]Equivalent units in work in process, ending from Solution Exhibit 17-34A, Step 2.

17-36 (5–10 min.) **Journal entries.** (Continuation of 17-35)

1. Work in Process—Forming Department   70,000
       Accounts Payable   70,000
     To record direct materials purchased and
        used in production during April

2. Work in Process—Forming Department   42,500
       Various Accounts   42,500
     To record Forming Department conversion
        costs for April

3. Work in Process—Finishing Department   104,000
       Work in Process—Forming Department   104,000
     To record cost of goods completed and transferred
        out in April from the Forming Department
        to the Finishing Department

Work in Process—Forming Department			
Beginning inventory, April 1	9,625	3. Transferred out to	
1. Direct materials	70,000	Work in Process—Finishing	104,000
2. Conversion costs	42,500		
Ending inventory, April 30	18,125		

17-38 (30 min.) **Transferred-in costs, weighted average.**

(Related to 17-35 through 17-37)

1. Solution Exhibit 17-38A computes the equivalent units of work done to date in the Finishing Department for transferred-in costs, direct materials, and conversion costs.

Solution Exhibit 17-38B calculates the cost per equivalent unit of work done to date in the Finishing Department for transferred-in costs, direct materials, and conversion costs, summarizes total Finishing Department costs for April 2001, and assigns these costs to units completed and transferred out and to units in ending work in process using the weighted-average method.

2. Journal entries:
    a.   Work in Process—Finishing Department   104,000
         Work in Process—Forming Department   104,000
       Cost of goods completed and transferred out
         during April from the Forming Department
         to the Finishing Department

    b.   Finished Goods   168,552
         Work in Process—Finishing Department   168,552
       Cost of goods completed and transferred out
         during April from the Finishing Department
         to Finished Goods inventory

17-38 (Cont'd.)

SOLUTION EXHIBIT 17-38A
Steps 1 and 2: Summarize Output in Physical Units and Compute Equivalent Units
Weighted-Average Method of Process Costing
Finishing Department of Star Toys for April 2001

| | (Step 1) Physical Units (given) | (Step 2) Equivalent Units | | |
| | | Transferred-in Costs | Direct Materials | Conversion Costs |
Flow of Production				
Work in process beginning	500			
Transferred in during current period	2,000			
To account for	2,500			
Completed and transferred out during current period	2,100	2,100	2,100	2,100
Work in process, ending*	400			
400 × 100%; 400 × 0%; 400 × 30%		400	0	120
Accounted for	2,500			
Work done to date		2,500	2,100	2,220

*Degree of completion in this department: transferred-in costs, 100%; direct materials, 0%; conversion costs, 30%.

SOLUTION EXHIBIT 17-38B
Steps 3, 4, and 5: Compute Equivalent Unit Costs, Summarize Total Costs to Account For, and Assign Costs to Units Completed and to Units in Ending Work in Process
Weighted-Average Method of Process Costing
Finishing Department of Star Toys for April 2001

	Total Production Costs	Transferred-in Costs	Direct Materials	Conversion Costs
(Step 3) Work in process, beginning (given)	$ 25,000	$ 17,750	$ 0	$ 7,250
Costs added in current period (given)	165,500	104,000	23,100	38,400
Costs incurred to date		$121,750	$23,100	$45,650
Divide by equivalent units of work done to date (Solution Exhibit 17-38A)		÷ 2,500	÷ 2,100	÷ 2,220
Equivalent unit costs of work done to date		$ 48.70	$ 11	$20.563
(Step 4) Total costs to account for	$190,500			
(Step 5) Assignment of costs:				
Completed and transferred out (2,100 units)	$168,552	(2,100*×$48.70)+(2,100* × $11)+(2,100*× $20.563)		
Work in process, ending (400 units)				
Transferred-in costs	19,480	400†×$48.70		
Direct materials	0		0† × $11	
Conversion costs	2,468			120† × $20.563
Total work in process	21,948			
Total costs accounted for	$190,500			

*Equivalent units completed and transferred out from Solution Exhibit 17-38A, Step 2.
†Equivalent units in work in process, ending from Solution Exhibit 17-38A, Step 2.

17-40 (45 min.) Transferred-in costs, weighted-average and FIFO.

1. Solution Exhibit 17-40A computes the equivalent units of work done to date in the Drying and Packaging Department for transferred-in costs, direct materials, and conversion costs. Solution Exhibit 17-40B calculates the cost per equivalent unit of work done to date in the Drying and Packaging Department for transferred-in costs, direct materials, and conversion costs, summarizes total Drying and Packaging Department costs for week 37, and assigns these costs to units completed and transferred out and to units in ending work in process using the weighted-average method.

2. Solution Exhibit 17-40C computes the equivalent units of work done in week 37 in the Drying and Packaging Department for transferred-in costs, direct materials, and conversion costs. Solution Exhibit 17-40D calculates the cost per equivalent unit of work done in week 37 in the Drying and Packaging Department for transferred-in costs, direct materials, and conversion costs, summarizes total Drying and Packaging Department costs for week 37, and assigns these costs to units completed and transferred out and to units in ending work in process using the FIFO method.

SOLUTION EXHIBIT 17-40A
Steps 1 and 2: Summarize Output in Physical Units and Compute Equivalent Units
Weighted-Average Method of Process Costing
Drying and Packaging Department of Frito-Lay Inc. for Week 37

Flow of Production	(Step 1) Physical Units (given)	(Step 2) Equivalent Units		
		Transferred-in Costs	Direct Materials	Conversion Costs
Work in process beginning	1,250			
Transferred in during current period	5,000			
To account for	6,250			
Completed and transferred out during current period	5,250	5,250	5,250	5,250
Work in process, ending*	1,000			
1,000 × 100%; 1,000 × 0%; 1,000 × 40%		1,000	0	400
Accounted for	6,250			
Work done to date		6,250	5,250	5,650

*Degree of completion in this department: transferred-in costs, 100%; direct materials, 0%; conversion costs, 40%.

17-40 (Cont'd.)

SOLUTION EXHIBIT 17-40B

Steps 3, 4, and 5: Compute Equivalent Unit Costs, Summarize Total Costs to Account For, and Assign Costs to Units Completed and to Units in Ending Work in Process
Weighted-Average Method of Process Costing
Drying and Packaging Department of Frito-Lay Inc. for Week 37

	Total Production Costs	Transferred-in Costs	Direct Materials	Conversion Costs
(Step 3) Work in process, beginning (given)	$ 38,060	$ 29,000	$ 0	$ 9,060
Costs added in current period (given)	159,600	96,000	25,200	38,400
Costs incurred to date		$125,000	$25,200	$47,460
Divide by equivalent units of work done to date (Solution Exhibit 17-40A)		÷ 6,250	÷ 5,250	÷ 5,650
Equivalent unit costs of work done to date		$ 20	$ 4.80	$ 8.40
(Step 4) Total costs to account for	$197,660			
(Step 5) Assignment of costs:				
Completed and transferred out (5,250 units)	$174,300	5,250*× $20 + 5,250*× $4.80 + 5,250*× $8.40		
Work in process, ending (1,000 units)				
Transferred-in costs	20,000	1,000†× $20		
Direct materials	0		0† × $480	
Conversion costs	3,360			400† × $8.40
Total work in process	23,360			
Total costs accounted for	$197,660			

*Equivalent units completed and transferred out from Solution Exhibit 17-40A, Step 2.
†Equivalent units in work in process, ending from Solution Exhibit 17-40A, Step 2.

17-40 (Cont'd.)

SOLUTION EXHIBIT 40C
Steps 1 and 2: Summarize Output in Physical Units and Compute Equivalent Units
FIFO Method of Process Costing
Drying and Packaging Department of Frito-Lay Inc. for Week 37

Flow of Production	(Step 1) Physical Units	(Step 2) Equivalent Units		
		Transferred-in Costs	Direct Materials	Conversion Costs
Work in process, beginning (given)	1,250	(work done before current period)		
Transferred-in during current period (given)	5,000			
To account for	6,250			
Completed and transferred out during current period:				
From beginning work in process[§]	1,250			
1,250 × (100% − 100%); 1,250 × (100% − 0%);				
1,250 × (100% − 80%)		0	1,250	250
Started and completed	4,000[†]			
4,000 × 100%; 4,000 × 100%; 4,000 × 100%		4,000	4,000	4,000
Work in process, ending* (given)	1,000			
1,000 × 100%; 1,000 × 0%; 1,000 × 40%		1,000	0	400
Accounted for	6,250			
Work done in current period only		5,000	5,250	4,650

[§]Degree of completion in this department: Transferred-in costs, 100%; direct materials, 0%; conversion costs, 80%.
[†]5,250 physical units completed and transferred out minus 1,250 physical units completed and transferred out from beginning work-in-process inventory.
*Degree of completion in this department: transferred-in costs, 100%; direct materials, 0%; conversion costs, 40%.

17-40 (Cont'd.)

SOLUTION EXHIBIT 17-40D
Steps 3, 4, and 5: Compute Equivalent Unit Costs, Summarize Total Costs to Account For, and Assign Costs to Units Completed and to Units in Ending Work in Process
FIFO Method of Process Costing
Drying and Packaging Department of Frito-Lay Inc. for Week 37

		Total Production Costs	Transferred-in Costs	Direct Materials	Conversion Costs
	Work in process, beginning ($9,060 + $0 + $28,920)	$ 37,980	(Costs of work done before current period)		
(Step 3)	Costs added in current period (given)	157,600	$94,000	$25,200	$38,400
	Divide by equivalent units of work done in current period (Solution Exhibit 17-40C)		÷ 5,000	÷ 5,250	÷ 4,650
	Cost per equiv. unit of work done in current period		$ 18.80	$ 4.80	$ 8.258
(Step 4)	Total costs to account for	$195,580			
(Step 5)	Assignment of costs:				
	Completed and transferred out (5,250 units):				
	Work in process, beginning (1,250 units)	$ 37,980			
	Transferred-in costs added in current period	0	0* × $18.80		
	Direct materials added in current period	6,000		1,250* × $4.80	
	Conversion costs added in current period	2,065			250* × $8.258
	Total from beginning inventory	46,045			
	Started and completed (4,000 units)	127,432	(4,000† × $18.80)+(4,000† × $4.80) +(4,000† ×$8.258)		
	Total costs of units completed & tfd. out	173,477			
	Work in process, ending (1,000 units)				
	Transferred-in costs	18,800	1,000# ×$18.80		
	Direct materials	0		0# ×$4.80	
	Conversion costs	3,303			400# ×$8.258
	Total work in process, ending	22,103			
	Total costs accounted for	$195,580			

*Equivalent units used to complete beginning work in process from Solution Exhibit 17-40C, Step 2.
†Equivalent units started and completed from Solution Exhibit 17-40C, Step 2.
#Equivalent units in work in process, ending from Solution Exhibit 17-40C, Step 2.

17-42 (15–30 min.) **Operation costing, equivalent units.**

1. Materials and conversion costs of each operation, the total units produced, and the material and conversion cost per unit for the month of May are as follows:

	Extrusion	Form	Trim	Finish
Units produced	16,000	11,000	5,000	2,000
Materials costs	$192,000	$ 44,000	$15,000	$12,000
Materials cost per unit	12.00	4.00	3.00	6.00
Conversion costs*	392,000	132,000	69,000	42,000
Conversion cost per unit	24.50	12.00	13.80	21.00

*Direct manufacturing labor and manufacturing overhead

The unit cost and total costs in May for each product are as follows:

Cost Elements	Plastic Sheets	Standard Model	Deluxe Model	Executive Model
Extrusion materials (EM)	$ 12.00	$ 12.00	$ 12.00	$ 12.00
Form materials (FM)	–	4.00	4.00	4.00
Trim materials (TM)	–	–	3.00	3.00
Finish materials	–	–	–	6.00
Extrusion conversion (EC)	24.50	24.50	24.50	24.50
Form conversion (FC)	–	12.00	12.00	12.00
Trim conversion (TC)	–	–	13.80	13.80
Finish conversion	–	–	–	21.00
Total unit cost	$ 36.50	$ 52.50	$ 69.30	$ 96.30
Multiply by units produced	× 5,000	× 6,000	× 3,000	× 2,000
Total product costs	$182,500	$315,000	$207,900	$192,600

2.

	Equivalent Units			
	Materials		Conversion Costs	
	Percent Complete	Quantity	Percent Complete	Quantity
Entering trim operation:				
2,000 Deluxe units	100	2,000	100	2,000
1,000 Deluxe units	100	1,000	60	600
2,000 Executive units	100	2,000	100	2,000
Total equivalent units		5,000		4,600

Conversion cost per equivalent unit in trim operation:
   ($30,000 + $39,000) ÷ 4,600 units = $15 per unit

Materials cost per equivalent unit in trim operation (as before)
   $15,000 ÷ 5,000 units = $3 per unit

	Unit Cost	Equivalent Units	Total Costs
Deluxe model work-in-process costs at the trim operation			
Extrusion material (100% complete when transferred in)	$12.00	1,000	$12,000
Extrusion conversion (100% complete when transferred in)	24.50	1,000	24,500
Form material (100% complete when transferred in)	4.00	1,000	4,000
Form conversion (100% complete when transferred in)	12.00	1,000	12,000
Trim material (100% complete)	3.00	1,000	3,000
Trim conversion (60% complete)	15.00	600	9,000
Work-in-process costs	$70.50		$64,500

17-44 (45 min.) Transferred-in costs, equivalent unit costs, working backwards.

1. The equivalent units of work done in the current period for each cost category are computed in Solution Exhibit 17-44B using data on costs added in current period and cost per equivalent unit of work done in current period.

	Transferred-In Costs	Direct Materials	Conversion Costs
Costs added in current period	$58,500	$57,000	$57,200
Divided by equivalent units of work done in current period	÷ $6.50	÷ $3	÷ $5.20
Equivalent units of work done in current period	9,000	19,000	11,000

2.
$$\text{Physical units completed and transferred out} = \text{Physical units in beginning work in process} + \text{Physical units added} - \text{Physical units in ending work in process}$$

$$= 15,000 + 9,000 - 5,000 = 19,000$$

Solution Exhibit 17-44A shows the equivalent units of work done in June to complete beginning work in process and the equivalent units of work done in June to start and complete 4,000 units. Note that direct materials in beginning work in process is 0% complete because it is added only when the process is 80% complete and the beginning WIP is only 60% complete. We had calculated the total equivalent units of work done in the current period in requirement 1: transferred-in costs, 9,000; direct materials, 19,000; and conversion costs, 11,000. The missing number is the equivalent units of each cost category in ending work in process (see Solution Exhibit 17-44A).

Transferred-in costs	5,000
Direct materials	0
Conversion costs	1,000

17-44 (Cont'd.)

3. Percentage of completion for each cost category in ending work in process can be calculated by dividing equivalent units in ending work in process for each cost category by physical units of work in process (5,000 units).

Transferred-in costs	$5{,}000 \div 5{,}000 =$	100%
Direct materials	$0 \div 5{,}000 =$	0%
Conversion costs	$1{,}000 \div 5{,}000 =$	20%

4. Solution Exhibit 17-44B summarizes the total costs to account for, and assigns these costs to units completed and transferred out and to units in ending work in process.

SOLUTION EXHIBIT 17-44A
Steps 1 and 2: Summarize Output in Physical Units and Compute Equivalent Units
FIFO Method of Process Costing
Thermo-assembly Department of Lennox Plastics for September 2001

	(Step 1)	(Step 2) Equivalent Units		
Flow of Production	**Physical Units**	**Transferred-in Costs**	**Direct Materials**	**Conversion Costs**
Work in process, beginning (given)	15,000	(work done before current period)		
Transferred-in during current period (given)	9,000			
To account for	24,000			
Completed and transferred out during current period:				
From beginning work in process[§]	15,000			
15,000 × (100% − 100%); 15,000 × (100% − 0%);				
15,000 × (100% − 60%)		0	15,000	6,000
Started and completed	4,000[†]			
4,000 × 100%; 4,000 × 100%; 4,000 × 100%		4,000	4,000	4,000
Work in process, ending* (given)	5,000			
5,000 × 100%; 5,000 × 0%; 5,000 × 20%		5,000	0	1,000
Accounted for	24,000			
Work done in current period only (from Solution Exhibit 17-44B)		9,000	19,000	11,000

[§]Degree of completion in this department: Transferred-in costs, 100%; direct materials, 0%; conversion costs, 60%.

[†]19,000 physical units completed and transferred out minus 15,000 physical units completed and transferred out from beginning work-in-process inventory.

*Degree of completion in this department: transferred-in costs, 100%; direct materials, 0%; conversion costs, 80%.

17-44 (Cont'd.)

SOLUTION EXHIBIT 17-44B

Steps 3, 4, and 5: Compute Equivalent Unit Costs, Summarize Total Costs to Account For, and Assign Costs to Units Completed and to Units in Ending Work in Process
FIFO Method of Process Costing
Thermo-assembly Department of Lennox Plastics for September 2001

		Total Production Costs	Transferred-in Costs	Direct Materials	Conversion Costs
	Work in process, beginning ($90,000 + $0 + $45,000)	$135,000	(Costs of work done before current period)		
(Step 3)	Costs added in current period (given)	172,700	$58,500	$57,000	$57,200
	Divide by equivalent units of work done in current period		÷ 9,000	÷19,000	÷11,000
	Cost per equiv. unit of work done in current period		$ 6.50	$ 3	$ 5.20
(Step 4)	Total costs to account for	$307,700			
(Step 5)	Assignment of costs:				
	Completed and transferred out (19,000 units):				
	Work in process, beginning (15,000 units)	$135,000			
	Transferred-in costs added in current period	0	0* × $6.50		
	Direct materials added in current period	45,000		15,000* × $3	
	Conversion costs added in current period	31,200			6,000* × $5.20
	Total from beginning inventory	211,200			
	Started and completed (4,000 units)	58,800	(4,000† × $6.50) + (4,000† × $3) + (4,000† × $5.20)		
	Total costs of units completed & tfd. out	270,000			
	Work in process, ending (5,000 units)				
	Transferred-in costs	32,500	5,000# ×$6.50		
	Direct materials	0		0# × $3	
	Conversion costs	5,200			1,000# ×$5.20
	Total work in process, ending	37,700			
	Total costs accounted for	$307,700			

*Equivalent units used to complete beginning work in process from Solution Exhibit 17-44A, Step 2.
†Equivalent units started and completed from Solution Exhibit 17-44A, Step 2.
#Equivalent units in work in process, ending from Solution Exhibit 17-44A, Step 2.

CHAPTER 18
SPOILAGE, REWORK, AND SCRAP

18-2 Spoilage—unacceptable units of production that are discarded or sold for net disposal proceeds.

Rework—unacceptable units of production that are subsequently repaired and sold as acceptable finished goods.

Scrap—material left over when making a product(s). It has low sales value compared with the sales value of the product(s).

18-4 Abnormal spoilage is spoilage that is not expected to arise under efficient operating conditions. Costs of abnormal spoilage are "lost costs," measures of inefficiency that should be written off directly as losses for the accounting period.

18-6 Normal spoilage typically is expressed as a percentage of good units passing the inspection point. Given actual spoiled units, we infer abnormal spoilage as follows:

Abnormal spoilage = Actual spoilage – Normal spoilage

18-8 Yes. Normal spoilage rates should be computed from the good output or from the *normal* input, not the *total* input. Normal spoilage is a given percentage of a certain output base. This base should never include abnormal spoilage, which is included in total input. Abnormal spoilage does not vary in direct proportion to units produced, and to include it would cause the normal spoilage count to fluctuate irregularly but not vary in direct proportion to the output base.

18-10 No. If abnormal spoilage is detected at a different point in the production cycle than normal spoilage, then unit costs would differ. If, however normal and abnormal spoilage are detected at the same point in the production cycle, their unit costs would be the same.

18-12 No. Unless there are special reasons for charging rework to jobs that contained the bad units, the costs of extra materials, labor, and so on are usually charged to manufacturing overhead and allocated to all jobs.

18-14 A company is justified in inventorying scrap when its estimated net realizable value is significant and the time between storing it and selling or reusing it is quite long.

18-16 (5-10 min.) **Normal and abnormal spoilage in units.**

1. Total spoiled units   12,000
    Normal spoilage in units, 5% × 132,000   6,600
    Abnormal spoilage in units   5,400

2. Abnormal spoilage, 5,400 × $10 $ 54,000
    Normal spoilage, 6,600 × $10   66,000
    Potential savings, 12,000 × $10 $120,000

Regardless of the targeted normal spoilage, abnormal spoilage is non-recurring and avoidable. The targeted normal spoilage rate is subject to change. Many companies have reduced their spoilage to almost zero, which would realize all potential savings. Of course, zero spoilage usually means higher-quality products, more customer satisfaction, more employee satisfaction, and various effects on nonmanufacturing (for example, purchasing) costs of direct materials.

18-18 (20–25 min.) **Weighted-average method, assigning costs.**
(Continuation of 18-17)

Solution Exhibit 18-18 calculates the costs per equivalent unit for direct materials and conversion costs, summarizes total costs to account for, and assigns these costs to units completed and transferred out (including normal spoilage), to abnormal spoilage, and to units in ending work in process.

SOLUTION EXHIBIT 18-18
Compute Equivalent Unit Costs, Summarize Total Costs to Account For, and Assign Costs to Units Completed, to Spoilage Units, and to Units in Ending Work in Process
Weighted-Average Method of Process Costing
Gray Manufacturing Company, November 2000

		Total Production Costs	Direct Materials	Conversion Costs
(Step 3)	Work in process, beginning (given)	$ 2,533	$ 1,423	$ 1,110
	Costs added in current period (given)	39,930	12,180	27,750
			13,603	28,860
	Divided by equivalent units of work done to date		÷11,150	÷ 9,750
	Equivalent unit costs of work done to date		$ 1.22	$ 2.96
(Step 4)	Total costs to account for	$42,463		
(Step 5)	Assignment of costs			
	Good units completed and transferred out (9,000 units)			
	Costs before adding normal spoilage	$37,620	(9,000[#] × $1.22) + (9,000[#] × $2.96)	
	Normal spoilage (100 units)	418	(100[#] × $1.22) + (100[#] × $2.96)	
(A)	Total cost of good units completed & transf. out	38,038		
(B)	Abnormal spoilage (50 units)	209	(50[#] × $1.22) + (50[#] × $2.96)	
	Work in process, ending (2,000 units)			
	Direct materials	2,440	2,000[#] × $1.22	
	Conversion costs	1,776		600[#] × $2.96
(C)	Total work in process, ending	4,216		
(A)+(B)+(C)	Total costs accounted for	$42,463		

[#]Equivalent units of direct materials and conversion costs calculated in Step 2 in Solution Exhibit 18-17.

18-20 (20–25 min.) **FIFO method, assigning costs.** (Continuation of 18-19)

Solution Exhibit 18-20 calculates the costs per equivalent unit for direct materials and conversion costs, summarizes total costs to account for, and assigns these costs to units completed and transferred out (including normal spoilage), to abnormal spoilage, and to units in ending work in process

SOLUTION EXHIBIT 18-20
Compute Equivalent Unit Costs, Summarize Total Costs to Account For, and Assign Costs to Units Completed, to Spoilage Units, and to Units in Ending Work in Process
FIFO Method of Process Costing
Gray Manufacturing Company, November 2000

		Total Production Costs	Direct Materials	Conversion Costs
(Step 3)	Work in process, beginning (given: $1,423 + $1,110)	$ 2,533		
	Costs added in current period (given)	39,930	$12,180	$27,750
	Divided by equivalent units of work done in current period		÷10,150	÷ 9,250
	Equivalent unit costs of work done in current period		$ 1.20	$ 3
(Step 4)	Total costs to account for	$42,463		
(Step 5)	Assignment of costs:			
	Good units completed and transferred out (9,000 units)			
	Work in process, beginning (1,000 units)	$ 2,533		
	Direct materials added in current period	0	$0^{\S} \times \$1.20$	
	Conversion costs added in current period	1,500		$500^{\S} \times \$3$
	Total from beginning inventory before normal spoilage	4,033		
	Started and completed before normal spoilage (8,000 units)	33,600	$(8,000^{\S} \times \$1.20) +$	$(8,000^{\S} \times \$3)$
	Normal spoilage (100 units)	420	$(100^{\S} \times \$1.20) +$	$(100^{\S} \times \$3)$
(A)	Total cost of good units transferred out	38,053		
(B)	Abnormal spoilage (50 units)	210	$(50^{\S} \times \$1.20) +$	$(50 \times \$3)$
	Work in process, ending (2,000 units)			
	Direct materials	2,400	$2,000^{\S} \times \$1.20$	
	Conversion costs	1,800		$600^{\S} \times \$3$
(C)	Total work in process, ending	4,200		
(A)+(B)+(C)	Total costs accounted for	$42,463		

§Equivalent units of direct materials and conversion costs calculated in Step 2 in Solution Exhibit 18-19.

18-22 (25 min.) **FIFO method, spoilage.**

1. & 2. Solution Exhibit 18-22 calculates the cost per equivalent unit of work done in the current period for direct materials and conversion costs, summarizes total costs to account for, and assigns these costs to units completed and transferred out (including normal spoilage), to abnormal spoilage, and to units in ending work in process using the FIFO method.

18-22 (Cont'd.)

3. From Solution Exhibit 18-22, under the FIFO method,

$$\text{Costs of a good unit completed (and transferred out)} = \frac{\text{Total production costs of good units transferred out}}{\text{Number of good units completed}}$$

$$= \frac{\$428,400}{20,000} = \$21.42$$

Note that this cost is higher than the cost per equivalent unit of $19.20 (direct materials, $8.40 and conversion costs, $10.80). Why? Because the costs of good units completed and transferred out also include the cost of normal spoilage of 15%.

SOLUTION EXHIBIT 18-22
First-in, First-out (FIFO) Method of Process Costing with Spoilage
Anderson Plastics, April 2001

PANEL A: Steps 1 and 2—Summarize Output in Physical Units and Compute Equivalent Units

	(Step 1)	(Step 2) Equivalent Units	
Flow of Production	**Physical Units**	**Direct Materials**	**Conversion Costs**
Work in process, beginning (given)	15,000		
Started during current period (given)	25,000		
To account for	40,000		
Good units completed and transferred out during current period:			
From beginning work in process[ll]	15,000		
15,000 × (100% −100%); 15,000 × (100% − 60%)		0	6,000
Started and completed	5,000[#]		
5,000 × 100%; 5,000 × 100%		5,000	5,000
Normal spoilage*	3,000		
3,000 × 100%; 3,000 × 100%		3,000	3,000
Abnormal spoilage[†]	1,000		
1,000 × 100%; 1,000 × 100%		1,000	1,000
Work in process, ending[‡]	16,000		
16,000 × 100%; 2,000 × 75%		16,000	12,000
Accounted for	40,000		
Work done in current period only		25,000	27,000

[ll]Degree of completion in this department: direct materials, 100%; conversion costs, 60%.

[#]20,000 physical units completed and transferred out minus 15,000 physical units completed and transferred out from beginning work-in-process inventory.

*Normal spoilage is 15% of good units transferred out: 15% × 20,000 = 3,000 units. Degree of completion of normal spoilage in this department: direct materials, 100%; conversion costs, 100%.

[†]Abnormal spoilage = Actual spoilage − Normal spoilage = 4,000 − 3,000 = 1,000 units. Degree of completion of abnormal spoilage in this department: direct materials, 100%; conversion costs, 100%.

[‡] Degree of completion in this department: direct materials, 100%; conversion costs, 75%.

18-22 (Cont'd.)

PANEL B: Steps 3, 4, and 5—Compute Equivalent Unit Costs, Summarize Total Costs to Account For, and Assign Costs to Units Completed, to Spoilage Units, and to Units in Ending Work in Process

		Total Production Costs	Direct Materials	Conversion Costs
(Step 3)	Work in process, beginning (given: $120,000 + $90,000)	$210,000		
	Costs added in current period (given)	501,600	$210,000	$291,600
	Divided by equivalent units of work done in current period		÷ 25,000	÷ 27,000
			$ 8.40	$ 10.80
	Equivalent unit costs of work done in current period	$711,600		
(Step 4)	Total costs to account for			
(Step 5)	Assignment of costs:			
	Good units completed and transferred out (20,000 units)			
	Work in process, beginning (15,000 units)	$210,000		
	Direct materials added in current period	0	$0^\S \times \$8.40$	
	Conversion costs added in current period	64,800		$6,000^\S \times \$10.80$
	Total from beginning inventory before normal spoilage	274,800		
	Started and completed before normal spoilage (5,000 units)	96,000	$(5,000^\S \times \$8.40) + (5,000^\S \times \$10.80)$	
	Normal spoilage (3,000 units)	57,600	$(3,000^\S \times \$8.40) + (3,000^\S \times \$10.80)$	
(A)	Total cost of good units transferred out	428,400		
(B)	Abnormal spoilage (1,000 units)	19,200	$(1,000^\S \times \$8.40) + (1,000 \times \$10.80)$	
	Work in process, ending (16,000 units)			
	Direct materials	134,400	$16,000^\S \times \$8.40$	
	Conversion costs	129,600		$12,000^\S \times \$10.80$
(C)	Total work in process, ending	264,000		
(A)+(B)+(C)	Total costs accounted for	$711,600		

§Equivalent units of direct materials and conversion costs calculated in Step 2 in Panel A.

18-24 (25 min.) **Weighted-average method, spoilage.**

1.   Solution Exhibit 18-24, Panel A, calculates the equivalent units of work done to date for each cost category in September 2000.

2. & 3. Solution Exhibit 18-24, Panel B, calculates the costs per equivalent unit for each cost category, summarizes total costs to account for, and assigns these costs to units completed (including normal spoilage), to abnormal spoilage, and to units in ending work in process using the weighted-average method.

SOLUTION EXHIBIT 18-24
Weighted-Average Method of Process Costing with Spoilage
Superchip, September 2000

PANEL A: Steps 1 and 2—Summarize Output in Physical Units and Compute Equivalent Units

Flow of Production	(Step 1) Physical Units (given)	(Step 2) Equivalent Units Direct Materials	Conversion Costs
Work in process, beginning	400		
Started during current period	1,700		
To account for	2,100		
Good units completed and transferred out during current period:	1,400	1,400	1,400
Normal spoilage*	210		
210 × 100%; 210 × 100%		210	210
Abnormal spoilage[†]	190		
190 × 100%; 190 ×100%		190	190
Work in process, ending[‡]	300		
300 × 100%; 300 × 40%		300	120
Accounted for	2,100		
Work done to date		2,100	1,920

*Normal spoilage is 15% of good units transferred out: 15% × 1,400 = 210 units. Degree of completion of normal spoilage in this department: direct materials, 100%; conversion costs, 100%.
[†]Abnormal spoilage = Actual spoilage − Normal spoilage = 400 − 210 = 190 units. Degree of completion of abnormal spoilage in this department: direct materials, 100%; conversion costs, 100%.
[‡]Degree of completion in this department: direct materials, 100%; conversion costs, 40%.

18-24 (Cont'd.)

Panel B: Steps 3, 4, and 5—Compute Equivalent Unit Costs, Summarize Total Costs to Account For, and Assign Costs to Units Completed, to Spoilage Units, and to Units in Ending Work in Process

		Total Production Costs	Direct Materials	Conversion Costs
(Step 3)	Work in process, beginning (given)	$ 74,200	$ 64,000	$ 10,200
	Costs added in current period (given)	531,600	378,000	153,600
			442,000	163,800
	Divided by equivalent units of work done to date		÷ 2,100	÷ 1,920
	Equivalent unit costs of work done to date		$210.476	$85.3125
(Step 4)	Total costs to account for	$605,800		
(Step 5)	Assignment of costs			
	Good units completed and transferred out (1,400 units)			
	Costs before adding normal spoilage	$414,104	$(1,400^\# \times \$210.476) + (1,400^\# \times \$85.3125)$	
	Normal spoilage (210 units)	62,116	$(210^\# \times \$210.476) + (210^\# \times \$85.3125)$	
(A)	Total cost of good units completed & transf. out	476,220		
(B)	Abnormal spoilage (190 units)	56,199	$(190^\# \times \$210.476) + (190^\# \times \$85.3125)$	
	Work in process, ending (300 units)			
	Direct materials	63,143	$300^\# \times \$210.476$	
	Conversion costs	10,238		$120^\# \times \$85.3125$
(C)	Total work in process, ending	73,381		
(A)+(B)+(C)	Total costs accounted for	$605,800		

$^\#$ Equivalent units of direct materials and conversion costs calculated in Step 2 in Panel A.

18-26   (30 min.) **Standard costing method, spoilage.**

1.   Solution Exhibit 18-26, Panel A, shows the computation of the equivalent units of work done in September 2000 for direct materials (1,700 units) and conversion costs (1,800 units).

2.   The direct materials cost per equivalent unit of beginning work in process and of work done in September 2000 is the standard cost of $205 given in the problem.
       The conversion cost per equivalent unit of beginning work in process and of work done in September 2000 is the standard cost of $80 given in the problem.

3.   Solution Exhibit 18-26, Panel B summarizes the total costs to account for, and assigns these costs to units completed (including normal spoilage), to abnormal spoilage, and to units in ending work in process using the standard costing method.

SOLUTION EXHIBIT 18-26
Standard-Costing Method of Process Costing with Spoilage
Superchip, September 2000

PANEL A: Steps 1 and 2—Summarize Output in Physical Units and Compute Equivalent Units

Flow of Production	(Step 1) Physical Units	(Step 2) Equivalent Units Direct Materials	Conversion Costs
Work in process, beginning (given)	400		
Started during current period (given)	1,700		
To account for	2,100		
Good units completed and transferred out during current period:			
From beginning work in process[‖]	400		
400 × (100% −100%); 400 × (100% − 30%)		0	280
Started and completed	1,000[#]		
1,000 × 100%; 1,000 × 100%		1,000	1,000
Normal spoilage*	210		
210 × 100%; 210 × 100%		210	210
Abnormal spoilage[†]	190		
190 × 100%; 190 × 100%		190	190
Work in process, ending[‡]	300		
2,000 × 100%; 2,000 × 40%		300	120
Accounted for	2,100		
Work done in current period only		1,700	1,800

[‖]Degree of completion in this department: direct materials, 100%; conversion costs, 30%.

[#]1,400 physical units completed and transferred out minus 400 physical units completed and transferred out from beginning work in process inventory.

*Normal spoilage is 15% of good units transferred out: 15% × 1,400 = 210 units. Degree of completion of normal spoilage in this department: direct materials, 100%; conversion costs, 100%.

[†]Abnormal spoilage = Actual spoilage − Normal spoilage = 400 − 210 = 190 units. Degree of completion of abnormal spoilage in this department: direct materials, 100%; conversion costs, 100%.

[‡]Degree of completion in this department: direct materials, 100%; conversion costs, 40%.

18-26 (Cont'd.)

PANEL B: Steps 3, 4, and 5—Compute Equivalent Unit Costs, Summarize Total Costs to Account For, and Assign Costs to Units Completed, to Spoilage Units, and to Units in Ending Work in Process

		Total Production Costs	Direct Materials	Conversion Costs
(Step 3)	Standard costs per equivalent unit (given)	$ 285	$ 205	$ 80
	Work in process, beginning*	91,600		
	Costs added in current period at standard prices			
	Direct materials, 1,700 × $205; conversion costs, 1,800 × $80	492,500	348,500	$144,000
(Step 4)	Costs to account for	$584,100		
(Step 5)	Assignment of costs at standard costs:			
	Good units completed and transferred out (1,400 units)			
	Work in process, beginning (400 units)	$ 91,600		
	Direct materials added in current period	0	$0^§ × $205	
	Conversion costs added in current period	22,400		280^§ × $80
	Total from beginning inventory before normal spoilage	114,000		
	Started and completed before normal spoilage (1,000 units)	285,000	(1,000^§ × $205) + (1,000^§ × $80)	
	Normal spoilage (210 units)	59,850	(210^§ × $205) + (210^§ × $80)	
(A)	Total cost of good units transferred out	458,850		
(B)	Abnormal spoilage (190 units)	54,150	(190^§ × $205) + (190^§ × $80)	
	Work in process, ending (300 units)			
	Direct materials	61,500	300^§ × $205	
	Conversion costs	9,600		120^§ × $80
(C)	Total work in process, ending	71,100		
(A)+(B)+(C)	Total costs accounted for	$584,100		

*Work in process, beginning has 400 equivalent units (400 physical units × 100%) of direct materials and 120 equivalent units (400 physical units × 30%) of conversion costs. Hence work in process, beginning inventory at standard costs equals ($205 × 400) + ($80 × 120) = $82,000 + $9,600 = $91,600.

§Equivalent units of direct materials and conversion costs calculated in Step 2 in Solution Exhibit 18-25, Panel A.

18-28 (15 min.) **Reworked units, costs of rework.**

1. The two alternative approaches to accounting for the materials costs of reworked units are:
   a. To charge the costs of rework to the current period as a separate expense item. This approach would highlight to White Goods the costs of the supplier problem.
   b. To charge the costs of the rework to manufacturing overhead.

2. The $50 tumbler cost is the cost of the actual tumblers included in the washing machines. The $44 tumbler units from the new supplier units were never used in any washing machine and that supplier is now bankrupt.

3. The total costs of rework due to the defective tumbler units include:
   a. The labor and other conversion costs spent on substituting the new tumbler units.
   b. The costs of any extra negotiations to obtain the replacement tumbler units.
   c. Any higher price the existing supplier may have charged to do a rush order for the replacement tumbler units.

18-30 (30 min.) Weighted-average method, spoilage.

Solution Exhibit 18-30 calculates the equivalent units of work done to date for each cost category, presents computations of the costs per equivalent unit for each cost category, summarizes total costs to account for, and assigns these costs to units completed (including normal spoilage), to abnormal spoilage, and to units in ending work in process using the weighted-average method.

SOLUTION EXHIBIT 18-30
Weighted-Average Method of Process Costing with Spoilage
Cleaning Department of the Alston Company for May

PANEL A: Steps 1 and 2—Summarize Output in Physical Units and Compute Equivalent Units

	(Step 1) Physical Units (given)	(Step 2) Equivalent Units	
Flow of Production		Direct Materials	Conversion Costs
Work in process, beginning	1,000		
Started during current period	9,000		
To account for	10,000		
Good units completed and transferred out during current period:	7,400	7,400	7,400
Normal spoilage*	740		
740 × 100%; 740 × 100%		740	740
Abnormal spoilage†	260		
260 × 100%; 260 ×100%		260	260
Work in process, ending‡	1,600		
1,600 × 100%; 1,600 × 25%		1,600	400
Accounted for	10,000		
Work done to date		10,000	8,800

*Normal spoilage is 10% of good units transferred out: 10% × 7,400 = 740 units. Degree of completion of normal spoilage in this department: direct materials, 100%; conversion costs, 100%.

†Abnormal spoilage = 260 units. Degree of completion of abnormal spoilage in this department: direct materials, 100%; conversion costs, 100%.

‡Degree of completion in this department: direct materials, 100%; conversion costs, 25%.

18-30 (Cont'd.)

Panel B: Steps 3, 4, and 5—Compute Equivalent Unit Costs, Summarize Total Costs to Account For, and Assign Costs to Units Completed, to Spoilage Units, and to Units in Ending Work in Process

		Total Production Costs	Direct Materials	Conversion Costs
(Step 3)	Work in process, beginning (given)	$ 1,800	$ 1,000	$ 800
	Costs added in current period (given)	17,000	9,000	8,000
			10,000	8,800
	Divided by equivalent units of work done to date		÷10,000	÷ 8,800
	Equivalent unit costs of work done to date		$ 1	$ 1
(Step 4)	Total costs to account for	$18,800		
(Step 5)	Assignment of costs			
	Good units completed and transferred out (7,400 units)			
	Costs before adding normal spoilage	$14,800	7,400# × $1 +	7,400# × $1
	Normal spoilage (740 units)	1,480	740# × $1 +	740# × $1
(A)	Total cost of good units completed & transferred out	16,280		
(B)	Abnormal spoilage (260 units)	520	260# × $1 +	260# × $1
	Work in process, ending (1,600 units)			
	Direct materials	1,600	1,600# × $1	
	Conversion costs	400		400# × $1
(C)	Total work in process, ending	2,000		
(A)+(B)+(C)	Total costs accounted for	$18,800		

#Equivalent units of direct materials and conversion costs calculated in Step 2 in Panel A above.

18-32 (35 min.) Weighted-average method, Milling Department.
(Continuation of 18-30)

For the Milling Department, Solution Exhibit 18-32 calculates the equivalent units of work done to date for each cost category, presents computations of the costs per equivalent unit for each cost category, summarizes total costs to account for, and assigns these costs to units completed (including normal spoilage), to abnormal spoilage, and to units in ending work in process using the weighted-average method.

SOLUTION EXHIBIT 18-32
Weighted-Average Method of Process Costing with Spoilage
Milling Department of the Alston Company for May

PANEL A: Steps 1 and 2—Summarize Output in Physical Units and Compute Equivalent Units

	(Step 1) Physical Units (given)	(Step 2) Equivalent Units		
Flow of Production		Transferred-in Costs	Direct Materials	Conversion Costs
Work in process, beginning	3,000			
Started during current period	7,400			
To account for	10,400			
Good units completed and transferred out during current period:	6,000	6,000	6,000	6,000
Normal spoilage*	300			
300 × 100%; 300 × 100%; 300 × 100%		300	300	300
Abnormal spoilage†	100			
100 × 100%; 100 ×100%, 100 × 100%		100	100	100
Work in process, ending‡	4,000			
4,000 × 100%; 4,000 × 0%; 4,000 × 25%		4,000	0	1,000
Accounted for	10,400			
Work done to date		10,400	6,400	7,400

*Normal spoilage is 5% of good units transferred out: 5% × 6,000 = 300 units. Degree of completion of normal spoilage in this department: transferred-in costs, 100%; direct materials, 100%; conversion costs, 100%.
†Abnormal spoilage = 100 units. Degree of completion of abnormal spoilage in this department: transferred-in costs, 100%; direct materials, 100%; conversion costs, 100%.
‡Degree of completion in this department: transferred-in costs, 100%; direct materials, 0%; conversion costs, 25%.

18-32 (Cont'd.)

Panel B: Steps 3, 4, and 5—Compute Equivalent Unit Costs, Summarize Total Costs to Account For, and Assign Costs to Units Completed, to Spoilage Units, and to Units in Ending Work in Process

		Total Production Costs	Transferred-in costs	Direct Materials	Conversion Costs
(Step 3)	Work in process, beginning (given)	$ 8,900	$ 6,450	$ 0	$2,450
	Costs added in current period (given)	21,870	16,280	640	4,950
			22,730	640	7,400
	Divided by equivalent units of work done to date		÷10,400	÷ 6,400	÷7,400
	Equivalent unit costs of work done to date		$2.1856	$ 0.10	$ 1
(Step 4)	Total costs to account for	$30,770			
(Step 5)	Assignment of costs				
	Good units completed and transferred out (6,000 units)				
	Costs before adding normal spoilage	$19,713	6,000# × ($2.1856 + $0.10 + $1)		
	Normal spoilage (300 units)	986	300# × ($2.1856 + $0.10 + $1)		
(A)	Total cost of good units completed & transferred out	20,699			
(B)	Abnormal spoilage (100 units)	329	100# × ($2.1856 + $0.10 + $1)		
	Work in process, ending (4,000 units)				
	Transferred-in costs	8,742	4,000# × $2.1856		
	Direct materials	0		0# × $0.10	
	Conversion costs	1,000			1,000# × $1
(C)	Total work in process, ending	9,742			
(A)+(B)+(C)	Total costs accounted for	$30,770			

#Equivalent units of direct materials and conversion costs calculated in Step 2 in Panel A.

18-34 (20–25 min.) **Job-costing spoilage and scrap.**

1. a. Materials Control   600
        Manufacturing Department Overhead Control   800
            Work-in-Process Control   1,400
            (650 + 500 + 250 = 1,400)

    b. Accounts Receivable   1,250
            Work-in-Process Control   1,250

2. a. The clause does not specify whether the 1% calculation is to be based on the input cost ($26,951 + $15,076 + $7,538) or the cost of the good output before the "1% normal spoilage" is added.

    b. *If the inputs are used to determine the 1%:*

$$\$26,951 + \$15,076 + \$7,538 = \$49,565$$

1% of $49,565 = $495.65 or $496, rounded. Then, the entry to leave the $496 "normal spoilage" cost on the job, remove the salvageable material, and charge manufacturing overhead would be:

Materials Control   600
Manufacturing Department Overhead Control   304
    Work-in-Process Control   904
($800 spoilage minus $496 = $304 spoilage
cost that is taken out of the job;
$600 salvage value plus $304 = $904; or
$1,400 minus $496 = $904)

If the outputs are used to determine the 1%:

$$\$26,951 - \$650 = \$26,301$$
$$15,076 - 500 = 14,576$$
$$\underline{7,538 - 250 = \underline{7,288}}$$
$$\underline{\$49,565} \qquad \underline{\$48,165}$$

Then, $48,165 × 1% = $481.65 or $482, rounded. The journal entry would be:

Materials Control   600
Manufacturing Department Overhead Control   318
    Work-in-Process Control   918

18-36 (30 min.) Job costing, scrap.

1. Materials Control 7,000

        Materials–Related Manufacturing Overhead Control 7,000

    (To record scrap common to all jobs at the time it is
    returned to the storeroom)

2. Cash or Accounts Receivable 7,000

        Materials Control 7,000

    (To record sale of scrap from the storeroom)

3. A summary of the manufacturing costs for HM3 and JB4 before considering the value of scrap are as follows:

	HM3		JB4		Total Costs
	Cost per Unit (1)	Total Costs (2) = (1) × 20,000	Cost per Unit (3)	Total Costs (4) = (3) × 10,000	(5) = (2)+(4)
Direct materials	$10	$200,000	$15	$150,000	$350,000
Direct manufacturing labor	3	60,000	4	40,000	100,000
Materials-related manufacturing overhead (20% of direct materials)	2	40,000	3	30,000	70,000
Other manufacturing overhead (200% of direct manufacturing labor)	6	120,000	8	80,000	200,000
Total	$21	$420,000	$30	$300,000	$720,000

The value of scrap of $7,000 generated during March will reduce materials-related manufacturing overhead costs by $7,000 from $70,000 to $63,000. Materials-related manufacturing overhead will then be allocated at 18% of direct materials costs ($63,000 ÷ 350,000 = 0.18)

The revised manufacturing cost per unit would then be:

	HM3		JB4		Total Costs
	Cost per Unit (1)	Total Costs (2) = (1) × 20,000	Cost per Unit (3)	Total Costs (4) = (3) × 10,000	(5) = (2)+(4)
Direct materials	$10.00	$200,000	$15.00	$150,000	$350,000
Direct manufacturing labor	3.00	60,000	4.00	40,000	100,000
Materials-related manufacturing overhead (18% of direct materials)	1.80	36,000	2.70	27,000	63,000
Other manufacturing overhead 200% of direct manufacturing labor)	6.00	120,000	8.00	80,000	200,000
Total	$20.80	$416,000	$29.70	$297,000	$713,000

18-38 (25–35 min.) **Weighted-average, inspection at 80% completion.**

The computation and allocation of spoilage is the most difficult part of this problem. The units in the ending inventory have passed inspection. Therefore, of the 80,000 units to account for (10,000 beginning + 70,000 started), 10,000 must have been spoiled in June [80,000 – (50,000 completed + 20,000 ending inventory)]. Normal spoilage is 7,000 [0.10 × (50,000 + 20,000)]. The 3,000 remainder is abnormal spoilage (10,000 – 7,000).

Solution Exhibit 18-38, Panel A, calculates the equivalent units of work done for each cost category. We comment on several points in this calculation:

- Ending work in process includes an element of normal spoilage since all the ending WIP have passed the point of inspection—inspection occurs when production is 80% complete, while the units in ending WIP are 95% complete.
- Spoilage includes no direct materials units because spoiled units are detected and removed from the finishing activity when inspection occurs at the time production is 80% complete. Direct materials are added only later when production is 90% complete.
- Direct materials units are included for ending work in process, which is 95% complete, but not for beginning work in process, which is 25% complete. The reason is that direct materials are added when production is 90% complete. The ending work in process, therefore, contains direct materials units; the beginning work in process does not.

Solution Exhibit 18-38, Panel B, computes the costs per equivalent unit for each cost category, summarizes total costs to account for, and assigns these costs to units completed (including normal spoilage), to abnormal spoilage, and to units in ending work in process using the weighted-average method. The cost of ending work in process includes the assignment of normal spoilage costs since these units have passed the point of inspection. The costs assigned to each cost category are as follows:

Cost of good units completed and transferred out (including normal spoilage costs on good units)	$1,877,350
Abnormal spoilage	67,710
Cost of ending work in process (including normal spoilage costs on ending work in process)	734,140
Total costs assigned and accounted for	$2,679,200

18-38 (Cont'd.)

SOLUTION EXHIBIT 18-38
Weighted-Average Method of Process Costing with Spoilage
Finishing Department of the Ottawa Manufacturing Company for June

PANEL A: Steps 1 and 2—Summarize Output in Physical Units and Compute Equivalent Units

	(Step 1) Physical Units (given)	(Step 2) Equivalent Units		
Flow of Production		Transferred-in Costs	Direct Materials	Conversion Costs
Work in process, beginning	10,000			
Started during current period	70,000			
To account for	80,000			
Good units completed and transferred out during current period:	50,000	50,000	50,000	50,000
Normal spoilage on good units*	5,000			
5,000 × 100%; 5,000 × 0%; 5,000 × 80%		5,000	0	4,000
Work in process, ending‡	20,000			
20,000 × 100%; 20,000 × 100%; 20,000 × 95%		20,000	20,000	19,000
Normal spoilage on ending WIP**	2,000			
2,000 × 100%; 2,000 × 0%; 2,000 × 80%		2,000	0	1,600
Abnormal spoilage†	3,000			
3,000 × 100%; 3,000 × 0%; 3,000 × 80%		3,000	0	2,400
Accounted for	80,000			
Work done to date		80,000	70,000	77,000

*Normal spoilage is 10% of good units that pass inspection: 10% × 50,000 = 5,000 units. Degree of completion of normal spoilage in this department: transferred-in costs, 100%; direct materials, 0%; conversion costs, 80%.

‡Degree of completion in this department: transferred-in costs, 100%; direct materials, 100%; conversion costs, 95%.

**Normal spoilage is 10% of the good units in ending WIP that have passed the inspection point, 10% × 20,000 = 2,000 units. Degree of completion of normal spoilage in this department: transferred-in costs, 100%; direct materials, 0%; conversion costs, 80%.

†Abnormal spoilage = Actual spoilage – Normal spoilage = 10,000 – 7,000 = 3,000 units. Degree of completion of abnormal spoilage in this department: transferred-in costs, 100%; direct materials, 0%; conversion costs, 80%.

18-38 (Cont'd.)

Panel B: Steps 3, 4, and 5—Compute Equivalent Unit Costs, Summarize Total Costs to Account For, and Assign Costs to Units Completed, to Spoilage Units, and to Units in Ending Work in Process

		Total Production Costs	Transferred-in Costs	Direct Materials	Conversion Costs
(Step 3)	Work in process, beginning (given)	$ 124,900	$ 82,900	$ –	$ 42,000
	Costs added in current period (given)	2,554,300	647,500	655,200	1,251,600
			730,400	655,200	1,293,600
	Divided by equivalent units of work done to date		÷ 80,000	÷ 70,000	÷ 77,000
	Equivalent unit costs of work done to date		$ 9.13	$ 9.36	$ 16.80
(Step 4)	Total costs to account for	$2,679,200			
(Step 5)	Assignment of costs				
	Good units completed and transferred out (50,000 units)				
	Costs before adding normal spoilage	$1,764,500	50,000# × ($9.13 + $9.36 + $16.80)		
	Normal spoilage (5,000 units)	112,850	(5,000# × $9.13) +	(0# × $9.36) + (4,000# × $16.80)	
(A)	Total cost of good units completed & transferred out	1,877,350			
(B)	Abnormal spoilage (3,000 units)	67,710	(3,000# × $9.13) +	(0# × $9.36) + (2,400# × $16.80)	
	Work in process, ending (20,000 units)				
	WIP ending, before normal spoilage	689,000	(20,000# × $9.13) + (20,000# × $9.36)+(19,000# × $16.80)		
	Normal spoilage on ending WIP	45,140	(2,000# × $9.13) +	(0# × $9.36) + (1,600# × $16.80)	
(C)	Total costs of ending WIP	734,140			
(A)+(B)+(C)	Total costs accounted for	$2,679,200			

#Equivalent units of transferred-in costs, direct materials, and conversion costs calculated in Step 2 in Panel A.

18-40 (35 min.) FIFO method, spoilage, working backwards.

1. Equivalent units of work done in the current period can be calculated using Step 2 as follows:

	Direct Materials	Conversion Costs
Costs added in January	$1,480,000	$942,000
Divided by costs per equivalent unit of work done in January	÷ $20	÷ $12
Equivalent units of work done in January	74,000	78,500

2. Solution Exhibit 18-40, Panel A, shows the equivalent units of work done (a) to complete beginning work-in-process inventory, (b) to start and complete new units, (c) for normal spoilage, and (d) for abnormal spoilage. The sum of these equivalent units is then subtracted from the total equivalent units of work done in January (direct materials, 74,000, and conversion costs, 78,500) to determine the equivalent units in ending work in process (direct materials, 15,000, and conversion costs, 12,000).

18-40 (Cont'd.)

3.   The physical units of ending work in process can be calculated by taking total physical units to account for, 84,000 (beginning work in process, 10,000 plus units started 74,000) and subtracting good units completed and transferred out, 61,000; normal spoilage, 6,710; and abnormal spoilage, 1,290, to obtain 15,000 physical units in ending work in process.

   The percentage of completion of ending work in process for each cost category can then be calculated as follows:

	Direct Materials	Conversion Costs
Equivalent units of ending work in process (requirement 2)	15,000	12,000
Divided by physical units of ending work in process	÷15,000	÷15,000
Percentage of completion of ending work in process	100%	80%

4.   Solution Exhibit 18-40, Panel B summarizes total costs to account for, and assigns these costs to units completed and transferred out (including normal spoilage), to abnormal spoilage, and to units in ending work in process.

SOLUTION EXHIBIT 18-40
First-in, First-out (FIFO) Method of Process Costing with Spoilage
Cooking Department of Spicer Inc. for January

PANEL A: Steps 1 and 2—Summarize Output in Physical Units and Compute Equivalent Units

		(Step 2) Equivalent Units	
	(Step 1)		
	Physical	Direct	Conversion
Flow of Production	Units	Materials	Costs
Work in process, beginning (given)	10,000		
Started during current period (given)	74,000		
To account for	84,000		
Good units completed and transferred out during current period:			
From beginning work in process[||]	10,000		
$10,000 \times (100\% - 100\%); 10,000 \times (100\% - 25\%)$		0	7,500
Started and completed	51,000[#]		
$51,000 \times 100\%; 51,000 \times 100\%$		51,000	51,000
Normal spoilage*	6,710		
$6,710 \times 100\%; 6,710\% \times 100\%$		6,710	6,710
Abnormal spoilage[†]	1,290		
$1,290 \times 100\%; 1,290 \times 100\%$		1,290	1,290
Work in process, ending[‡]	15,000		
$15,000 \times 100\%; 15,000 \times 80\%$		15,000	12,000
Accounted for	84,000		
Work done in current period only		74,000	78,500

[||]Degree of completion in this department: direct materials, 100%; conversion costs, 25%.

[#]61,000 physical units completed and transferred out minus 10,000 physical units completed and transferred out from beginning work-in-process inventory.

*Normal spoilage is 11% of good units transferred out: 11% × 61,000 = 6,710 units. Degree of completion of normal spoilage in this department: direct materials, 100%; conversion costs, 100%.

[†]Abnormal spoilage = Actual spoilage – Normal spoilage = 8,000 – 6,710 = 1,290 units. Degree of completion of abnormal spoilage in this department: direct materials, 100%; conversion costs, 100%.

[‡]Degree of completion in this department: direct materials, 100%; conversion costs, 80%.

18-40 (Cont'd.)

PANEL B: Steps 3, 4, and 5—Compute Equivalent Unit Costs, Summarize Total Costs to Account For, and Assign Costs to Units Completed, to Spoilage Units, and to Units in Ending Work in Process

		Total Production Costs	Direct Materials	Conversion Costs
(Step 3)	Work in process, beginning (given: $220,000 + $30,000)	$ 250,000		
	Costs added in current period (given)	2,422,000	$1,480,000	$942,000
	Divided by equivalent units of work done in current period		÷ 74,000	÷ 78,500
	Equivalent unit costs of work done in current period		$ 20	$ 12
(Step 4)	Total costs to account for	$2,672,000		
(Step 5)	Assignment of costs:			
	Good units completed and transferred out (61,000 units)			
	Work in process, beginning (10,000 units)	$ 250,000		
	Direct materials added in current period	0	0[§] × $20	
	Conversion costs added in current period	90,000		7,500[§] × $12
	Total from beginning inventory before normal spoilage	340,000		
	Started and completed before normal spoilage (51,000 units)	1,632,000	51,000[§] × $20 +	51,000[§] × $12
	Normal spoilage (6,710 units)	214,720	6,710[§] × $20 +	6,710[§] × $12
(A)	Total cost of good units transferred out	2,186,720		
(B)	Abnormal spoilage (1,290 units)	41,280	1,290[§] × $20 +	1,290 × $12
	Work in process, ending (15,000 units)			
	Direct materials	300,000	15,000[§] × $20	
	Conversion costs	144,000		12,000[§] × $12
(C)	Total work in process, ending	444,000		
(A)+(B)+(C)	Total costs accounted for	$2,672,000		

[§]Equivalent units of direct materials and conversion costs calculated in Step 2 in Panel A.

CHAPTER 19
QUALITY, TIME, AND THE THEORY OF CONSTRAINTS

19-2   Quality of design refers to how closely the characteristics of a product or service meet the needs and wants of customers. Conformance quality refers to the performance of a product or service relative to its design and product specifications.

19-4   An internal failure cost differs from an external failure cost on the basis of when the nonconforming product is detected. An internal failure is detected *before* a product is shipped to a customer, whereas an external failure is detected *after* a product is shipped to a customer.

19-6   No, companies should emphasize financial as well as nonfinancial measures of quality, such as yield and defect rates. Nonfinancial measures are not directly linked to bottom-line performance but they indicate and direct attention to the specific areas that need improvement. Tracking nonfinancial measures over time directly reveals whether these areas have, in fact, improved over time. Nonfinancial measures are easy to quantify and easy to understand.

19-8   Examples of nonfinancial measures of internal performance are:
1.   The number of defects for each product line.
2.   Process yield (rates of good output to total output at a particular process).
3.   Manufacturing lead time (the amount of time from when an order is received by production to when it becomes a finished good).
4.   Employee turnover (ratio of the number of employees who left the company in a year, say, to the total number of employees who worked for the company in that year).

19-10   No. There is a trade-off between customer-response time and on-time performance. Simply scheduling longer customer-response time makes achieving on-time performance easier. Companies should, however, attempt to reduce uncertainty of arrival of orders, manage bottlenecks, reduce setup and processing time, and run smaller batches. This would have the effect of reducing both customer-response time and improving on-time performance.

19-12   No. Adding a product when capacity is constrained and the timing of customer orders is uncertain causes delays in delivering all existing products. If the revenue losses from delays in delivering existing products and the increase in carrying costs of the existing products exceed the positive contribution earned by the product that was added, then it is not worthwhile to make and sell the new product, despite its positive contribution margin. The chapter describes the negative effects (negative externalities) that one product can have on others when products share common manufacturing facilities.

19-14   The four key steps in managing bottleneck resources are:
Step 1:   Recognize that the bottleneck operation determines throughput contribution.
Step 2:   Search for, and find the bottleneck.
Step 3:   Keep the bottleneck busy, and subordinate all nonbottleneck operations to the bottleneck operation.
Step 4:   Increase bottleneck efficiency and capacity.

19-16 (30 min.) Costs of quality.

1. The ratio of each COQ category to revenues for each period is as follows:

Semi-annual Costs of Quality Report Bergen, Inc.
(in thousands)

	6/30/2000 (1)	% of Rev. (2) = (1) ÷ 4,120	12/31/2000 (3)	% of Rev. (4) = (3) ÷ 4,540	6/30/2001 (5)	% of Rev. (6) = (5) ÷ 4,650	12/31/2001 (7)	% of Rev. (8) = (7) ÷ 4,510
Prevention costs								
Machine maintenance	$ 215		$ 215		$ 190		$ 160	
Training suppliers	5		45		20		15	
Design reviews	20		102		100		95	
	240	5.8%	362	8.0%	310	6.7%	270	6.0%
Appraisal costs								
Incoming inspection	45		53		36		22	
Final testing	160		160		140		94	
	205	5.0%	213	4.7%	176	3.8%	116	2.6%
Internal failure costs								
Rework	120		106		88		62	
Scrap	68		64		42		40	
	188	4.6%	170	3.7%	130	2.8%	102	2.2%
External failure costs								
Warranty repairs	69		31		25		23	
Customer returns	262		251		116		80	
	331	8.0%	282	6.2%	141	3.0%	103	2.3%
Total quality costs	$ 964	23.4%	$1,027	22.6%	$ 757	16.3%	$ 591	13.1%
Total production and revenues	$4,120		$4,540		$4,650		$4,510	

From an analysis of the Cost of Quality Report, it would appear that Bergen Inc.'s program has been successful since

- Total quality costs as a percentage of total revenues have declined from 23.4% to 13.1%.
- External failure costs, those costs signaling customer dissatisfaction have declined from 8% of total revenues to 2.3%. These declines in warranty repairs and customer returns should translate into increased revenues in the future.
- Internal failure costs have been reduced from 4.6% to 2.2% of revenues
- Appraisal costs have decreased from 5.0% to 2.6%. Preventing defects from occurring in the first place is reducing the demand for final testing.
- Quality costs have shifted to the area of prevention where problems are solved before production starts. Maintenance, training, and design reviews have increased from 5.8% of total revenues to 6% and from 25% of total quality costs (240 ÷ 964) to 45.7% (270 ÷ 591). The $30,000 increase in these costs is more than offset by decreases in other quality costs.

Because of improved designs, quality training, and additional pre-production inspections, scrap and rework costs have declined. Production does not have to spend an inordinate amount of time with customer service since they are now making the product right the first time and warranty repairs and customer returns have decreased.

19-16 (Cont'd.)

2. To measure the opportunity cost of not implementing the quality program, Bergen Inc. could assume that

- Sales and market share would continue to decline if the quality program had not been implemented and then calculate the loss in revenue and contribution margin.
- The company would have to compete on price rather than quality and calculate the impact of having to lower product prices.

Opportunity costs are not recorded in accounting systems because they represent the results of what might have happened if Bergen had not improved quality. Nevertheless, opportunity costs of poor quality can be significant. It is important for Bergen to take these costs into account when making decisions about quality.

19-18 (30–40 min.) **Costs of quality analysis, nonfinancial quality measures.**

1. & 2.
**Revenues, Costs of Quality and Costs of Quality
as a Percentage of Revenues for Olivia**

Revenues = $2,000 × 10,000 units = $20,000,000

Costs of Quality	Cost (1)	Percentage of Revenues (2) = (1) ÷ $20,000,000
Prevention costs		
Design engineering ($75 × 6,000 hours)	$ 450,000	2.25%
Appraisal costs		
Testing and inspection ($40 × 1 hour × 10,000 units)	400,000	2.00%
Internal failure costs		
Rework ($500 × 5% × 10,000 units)	250,000	1.25%
External failure costs		
Repair ($600 × 4% × 10,000 units)	240,000	1.20%
Total costs of quality	$1,340,000	6.70%

19-18 (Cont'd.)

Revenues, Costs of Quality and Costs of Quality
as a Percentage of Revenues for Solta

Revenues: $1,500 × 5,000 units = $7,500,000

Costs of Quality	Costs (1)	Percentage of Revenues (2)=(1)÷$7,500,000
Prevention costs		
Design engineering ($75 × 1,000 hours)	$ 75,000	1.00%
Appraisal costs		
Testing and inspection ($40 × 0.5 × 5,000 units)	100,000	1.33%
Internal failure costs		
Rework ($400 × 10% × 5,000 units)	200,000	2.67%
External failure costs		
Repair ($450 × 8% × 5,000 units)	180,000	2.40%
Estimated forgone contribution margin on lost sales [($1,500 – $800) × 300]	210,000	2.80%
Total external failure costs	390,000	5.20%
Total costs of quality	$765,000	10.20%

Costs of quality as a percentage of sales are significantly different for Solta (10.20%) compared with Olivia (6.70%). Ontario spends very little on prevention and appraisal activities for Solta, and incurs high costs of internal and external failures. Ontario follows a different strategy with respect to Olivia, spending a greater percentage of sales on prevention and appraisal activities. The result: fewer internal and external failure costs and lower overall costs of quality as a percentage of sales compared with Solta.

3.   Examples of nonfinancial quality measures that Ontario Industries could monitor as part of a total quality-control effort are:
   a.   Outgoing quality yield for each product
   b.   Returned refrigerator percentage for each product
   c.   On-time delivery
   d.   Employee turnover

19-20 (25 min.) **Quality improvement, relevant costs, and relevant revenues.**

Relevant costs over the next year of choosing the new lens = $50 × 20,000 copiers = $1,000,000

	Relevant Benefits over the Next Year of Choosing the New Lens
Costs of quality items	
Savings on rework costs	
$40 × 12,000 rework hours	$ 480,000
Savings in customer-support costs	
$20 × 800 customer-support-hours	16,000
Savings in transportation costs for parts	
$180 × 200 fewer loads	36,000
Savings in warranty repair costs	
$45 × 8,000 repair-hours	360,000
Opportunity costs	
Contribution margin from increased sales	600,000
Cost savings and additional contribution margin	$1,492,000

Because the expected relevant benefits of $1,492,000 exceed the expected relevant costs of the new lens of $1,000,000, Photon should introduce the new lens. Note that the opportunity cost benefits in the form of higher contribution margin from increased sales is an important component for justifying the investment in the new lens. The incremental cost of the new lens of $1,000,000 is greater than the incremental savings in rework and repair costs of $892,000. Investing in the new lens is beneficial, provided it generates additional contribution margin of at least $108,000 ($1,000,000 − $892,000), that is, additional sales of at least $108,000 ÷ $6,000 = 18 copiers.

19-22 (20 min.) **Waiting time, banks.**

1.   If the branch expects to receive 40 customers each day and it takes 5 minutes to serve a customer, the average time that a customer will wait in line before being served is:

$$= \frac{\left(\begin{array}{c}\text{Average number}\\\text{of customers}\end{array}\right) \times \left(\begin{array}{c}\text{Time taken to}\\\text{serve a customer}\end{array}\right)^2}{2 \times \left[\begin{array}{c}\text{Available time}\\\text{counter is open}\end{array} - \left[\left(\begin{array}{c}\text{Average number}\\\text{of customers}\end{array}\right) \times \left(\begin{array}{c}\text{Time taken to}\\\text{serve a customer}\end{array}\right)\right]\right]}$$

$$= \frac{[40 \times (5)^2]}{2 \times [300 - (40 \times 5)]} = \frac{(40 \times 25)}{2 \times (300 - 200)} = \frac{1,000}{2 \times 100} = \frac{1,000}{200} = 5 \text{ minutes}$$

19-22 (Cont'd.)

2.   If the branch expects to receive 50 customers each day and the time taken to serve a customer is 5 minutes, the average time that a customer will wait in line before being served is:

$$= \frac{[50 \times (5)^2]}{2 \times [300 - (50 \times 5)]} = \frac{(50 \times 25)}{2 \times (300 - 250)} = \frac{50 \times 25}{2 \times 50} = \frac{1,250}{100} = 12.5 \text{ minutes}$$

3.   If the branch expects to receive 50 customers each day and the time taken to serve a customer is 4 minutes, the average time that a customer will wait in line before being served is:

$$= \frac{[50 \times (4)^2]}{2 \times [300 - (50 \times 4)]} = \frac{(50 \times 16)}{2 \times (300 - 200)} = \frac{50 \times 16}{2 \times 100} = \frac{800}{200} = 4 \text{ minutes}$$

19-24 (15 min.) Theory of constraints, throughput contribution, relevant costs.

1.   Finishing is a bottleneck operation. Hence, producing 1,000 more units will generate additional throughput contribution and operating income.

Increase in throughput contribution ($72 – $32) × 1,000	$40,000
Incremental costs of the jigs and tools	30,000
Net benefit of investing in jigs and tools	$10,000

Mayfield should invest in the modern jigs and tools because the benefit of higher throughput contribution of $40,000 exceeds the cost of $30,000.

2.   The Machining Department has excess capacity and is not a bottleneck operation. Increasing its capacity further will not increase throughput contribution. There is, therefore, no benefit from spending $5,000 to increase the Machining Department's capacity by 10,000 units. Mayfield should not implement the change to do setups faster.

19-26 (15 min.) Theory of constraints, throughput contribution, quality.

1.   Cost of defective unit at machining operation which is not a bottleneck operation is the loss in direct materials (variable costs) of $32 per unit. Producing 2,000 units of defectives does not result in loss of throughput contribution. Despite the defective production, machining can produce and transfer 80,000 units to finishing. Therefore, cost of 2,000 defective units at the machining operation is $32 × 2,000 = $64,000.

2.   A defective unit produced at the bottleneck finishing operation costs Mayfield materials costs plus the opportunity cost of lost throughput contribution. Bottleneck capacity not wasted in producing defective units could be used to generate additional sales and throughput contribution. Cost of 2,000 defective units at the finishing operation is:

Loss of direct materials $32 × 2,000	$ 64,000
Forgone throughput contribution ($72 – $32) × 2,000	80,000
Total cost of 2,000 defective units	$144,000

19-26 (Cont'd.)

Alternatively, the cost of 2,000 defective units at the finishing operation can be calculated as the lost revenue of $72 × 2,000 = $144,000. This line of reasoning takes the position that direct materials costs of $32 × 2,000 = $64,000 and all fixed operating costs in the machining and finishing operations would be incurred anyway whether a defective or good unit is produced. The cost of producing a defective unit is the revenue lost of $144,000.

19-28 (30 min.) Quality improvement, relevant costs, and relevant revenues.

1.   By implementing the new method, Tan would incur additional direct materials costs on all the 200,000 units started at the molding operation.

Additional direct materials costs = $4 per lamp × 200,000 lamps	$800,000

The relevant benefits of adding the new material are:
Increased revenue from selling 30,000 more lamps
$40 per lamp × 30,000 lamps $1,200,000

Note that Tan Corporation continues to incur the same total variable costs of direct materials, direct manufacturing labor, setup labor and materials handling labor, and the same fixed costs of equipment, rent, and allocated overhead that it is currently incurring, even when it improves quality. Since these costs do not differ among the alternatives of adding the new material or not adding the new material, they are excluded from the analysis. The relevant benefit of adding the new material is the extra revenue that Tan would get from producing 30,000 good lamps.

An alternative approach to analyzing the problem is to focus on scrap costs and the benefits of reducing scrap.

The relevant benefits of adding the new material are:
a.   Cost savings from eliminating scrap:
Variable costs per lamp, $19[a] × 30,000 lamps $ 570,000
b.   Additional contribution margin from selling
another 30,000 lamps because 30,000 lamps
will no longer be scrapped:
Unit contribution margin $21[b] × 30,000 lamps   630,000
Total benefits to Tan of adding new material to improve
quality $1,200,000

[a]Note that only the variable scrap costs of $19 per lamp (direct materials, $16 per lamp; direct manufacturing labor, setup labor, and materials handling labor, $3 per lamp) are relevant because improving quality will save these costs. Fixed scrap costs of equipment, rent, and other allocated overhead are irrelevant because these costs will be incurred whether Tan Corporation adds or does not add the new material.

[b]*Unit contribution margin*

Selling price		$40.00
Variable costs:		
Direct materials costs per lamp	$16.00	
Molding department variable manufacturing costs		
per lamp (direct manufacturing labor, setup labor, and		
materials handling labor)	3.00	
Variable costs		19.00
Unit contribution margin		$21.00

On the basis of quantitative considerations alone, Tan should use the new material. Relevant benefits of $1,200,000 exceed the relevant costs of $800,000 by $400,000.

2.   Other nonfinancial and qualitative factors that Tan should consider in making a decision include the effects of quality improvement on:
   a.   Gaining manufacturing expertise that could lead to further cost reductions in the future.
   b.   Enhanced reputation and increased customer goodwill which could lead to higher future revenues through greater unit sales and higher sales prices.
   c.   More worker empowerment and higher employee morale.

19-30   (30–40 min.)   **Compensation linked with profitability, on-time delivery, and external quality performance measures.**

1.

	Jan.-March	April-June	July-Sept.	Oct.-Dec.
Detroit				
Add: Profitability				
2% of operating income	$16,000	$17,000	$14,000	$18,000
Add: On-time delivery				
$10,000 if above 98%	10,000	10,000	0	0
Deduct: Quality				
50% of cost of sales returns	(9,000)	(13,000)	(5,000)	(12,500)
Total: Bonus paid	$17,000	$14,000	$ 9,000	$ 5,500
Los Angeles				
Add: Profitability				
2% of operating income	$32,000	$30,000	$36,000	$38,000
Add: On-time delivery				
$10,000 if above 98%	0	0	0	10,000
Deduct: Quality				
50% of cost of sales returns	(17,500)	(17,000)	(14,000)	(11,000)
Total: Bonus paid	$14,500	$13,000	$22,000	$37,000

19-30 (Cont'd.)

2. *Operating income as a measure of profitability*

Operating income does capture revenue and cost-related factors. However, there is no recognition of investment differences between the two plants. Los Angeles sales are approximately double that of Detroit. This difference gives the Los Angeles plant manager the opportunity to earn a larger bonus due to investment size alone. An alternative approach would be to use return on investment (perhaps relative to the budgeted ROI).

98% on-time benchmark as a measure of on-time delivery performance

This measure does reflect the ability of Pacific-Dunlop to meet a benchmark for on-time delivery. Several concerns arise with this specific measure:

    a.   It is a yes-or-no cut-off. A 10% on-time performance earns no bonus, but neither does a 97.9% on-time performance. Moreover, no extra bonus is paid for performance above 98.0%. An alternative is to have the bonus be a percentage of the on-time delivery percentage.

    b.   It can be manipulated by management. The Pacific-Dunlop plant manager may quote conservative delivery dates to sales people in an effort to "guarantee" that the 98% target is achieved.

    c.   It reflects performance relative only to scheduled delivery date. It does not consider how quickly Pacific-Dunlop can respond to customer orders.

50% of cost of sales returns as a measure of quality

This measure does incorporate one cost that arises with defective goods. However, there are several concerns with its use:

    a.   Not all sales returns are due to defective work by the plant manager. Some returns are due to tampering by the customer. Other returns arise from breakage during delivery and installation.

    b.   It does not systematically incorporate customer opinion about quality. Not all customers return defective goods.

    c.   It ignores important categories of the cost of defective goods. For example, dissatisfied customers may decline to make any subsequent purchases.

3.   Most companies use both financial and nonfinancial measures to evaluate performance, sometimes presented in a single report called a *balanced scorecard*. Using multiple measures of performance enables top management to evaluate whether lower-level managers have improved one area at the expense of others. For example, did the on-time delivery performance of the Detroit plant manager decrease in the October–December period relative to the April–June period because the manager emphasized shipment of high-margin products to increase operating income?

4.   If on-time delivery is dropped as a performance evaluation measure, managers will concentrate on increasing operating income and decreasing sales returns but will give less attention to on-time delivery. Consider the following situation. Suppose a manager must choose between (a) delivering a high margin order that will add to operating income while delaying a number of

19-30 (Cont'd.)

other orders and adversely affecting on-time performance, or (b) delaying the high margin order and sacrificing some operating income, to achieve better on-time performance. What action will the manager take? If on-time performance is excluded as a performance evaluation measure, the manager will almost certainly choose (a). Only if on-time performance is included in the manager's performance evaluation will the manager consider choosing option (b).

19-32 (20–30 min.) **Waiting times, relevant revenues, and relevant costs.**
(Continuation of 19-31)

1.   The direct approach is to look at incremental revenues and incremental costs.

Average selling price per order for Y28, which has average operating throughput time of 350 hours	$ 8,000
Variable costs per order	5,000
Additional contribution per order from Y28	3,000
Multiply by expected number of orders	× 25
Increase in expected contribution from Y28	$75,000

Expected loss in revenues and increase in costs from introducing Y28

Product (1)	Expected Loss in Revenues from Increasing Average Manufacturing Lead Times for All Products (2)	Expected Increase in Carrying Costs from Increasing Average Manufacturing Lead Times for All Products (3)	Expected Loss in Revenues Plus Expected Increases in Costs of Introducing Y28 (4) = (2) + (3)
Z39	$25,000.00[a]	$6,375.00[b]	$31,375.00
Y28	–	2,187.50[c]	2,187.50
Total	$25,000.00	$8,562.50	$33,562.50

[a]50 orders × ($27,000 - $26,500)
[b](410 hours – 240 hours) × $0.75 × 50 orders
[c](350 hours – 0) × $0.25 × 25

Increase in expected contribution from Y28 of $75,000 is greater than increase in expected costs of $33,562.50 by $41,437.50. Therefore, SRG should introduce Y28.

19-32 (Cont'd.)

Alternative calculations of incremental revenues and incremental costs of introducing Y28.

	Alternative 1: Introduce Y28 (1)	Alternative 2: Do Not Introduce Y28 (2)	Relevant Revenues and Relevant Costs (3) = (1) – (2)
Expected revenues	$1,525,000.00[a]	$1,350,000.00[b]	$175,000.00
Expected variable costs	875,000.00[c]	750,000.00[d]	125,000.00
Expected carrying costs	17,562.50[e]	9,000.00[f]	8,562.50
Expected total variable and carrying costs	892,562.50	759,000.00	133,562.50
Expected revenues minus expected costs	$ 632,437.50	$ 591,000.00	$ 41,437.50

[a]$(50 \times \$26,500) + (25 \times \$8,000)$ [b]$50 \times \$27,000$
[c]$(50 \times \$15,000) + (25 \times \$5,000)$ [d]$50 \times \$15,000$
[e]$(50 \times \$0.75 \times 410) + (25 \times \$0.25 \times 350)$ [f]$50 \times \$0.75 \times 240$

2. Introducing Y28 results in an incremental cost of $33,562.50 from the loss in revenues of Z39, the higher carrying costs for Z39, and the carrying costs of Y28 (see table on page 19-22). To break even, SRG needs to earn a total contribution of $33,562.50 over the 25 orders, or a contribution per order of $33,562.50 ÷ 25 = $1,342.50.

Variable costs per order of Y28	$5,000.00
Required contribution to break even	1,342.50
Selling price per dollar of Y28 to break even	$6,342.50

If Y28 sells above $6,342.50 per order, SRG should manufacture and sell Y28. If Y28 sells below $6,342.50 per order, SRG should not manufacture and sell Y28.

19-34 (20 min.) **Theory of constraints, throughput contribution, relevant costs.**

1. It will cost Colorado $50 per unit to reduce manufacturing time. But manufacturing is not a bottleneck operation; installation is. Therefore, manufacturing more equipment will not increase sales and throughput contribution. Colorado Industries should not implement the new manufacturing method.

2. Additional relevant costs of new direct materials, $2,000 × 320 units, $640,000
    Increase in throughput contribution, $25,000 × 20 units, $500,000

    The additional incremental costs exceed the benefits from higher throughput contribution by $140,000, so Colorado Industries should not implement the new design.

        Alternatively, compare throughput contribution under each alternative.
    Current throughput contribution is $25,000 × 300 $7,500,000
    With the modification, throughput contribution is $23,000 × 320 $7,360,000

    The current throughput contribution is greater than the throughput contribution resulting from the proposed change in direct materials. Hence, Colorado Industries should not implement the new design.

3. Increase in throughput contribution, $25,000 × 10 units $250,000
    Increase in relevant costs $ 50,000

    The additional throughput contribution exceeds incremental costs by $200,000, so Colorado Industries should implement the new installation technique.

4. Motivating installation workers to increase productivity is worthwhile because installation is a bottleneck operation, and any increase in productivity at the bottleneck will increase throughput contribution. On the other hand, motivating workers in the manufacturing department to increase productivity is not worthwhile. Manufacturing is not a bottleneck operation, so any increase in output will result only in extra inventory of equipment. Colorado Industries should encourage manufacturing to produce only as much equipment as the installation department needs, not to produce as much as it can. Under these circumstances, it would not be a good idea to evaluate and compensate manufacturing workers on the basis of their productivity.

19-36 (25 min.) Quality improvement, Pareto charts, fishbone diagrams.

1. Examples of failures in accounts receivable management are:
    a. Uncollectible amounts or bad debts
    b. Delays in receiving payments

2. Prevention activities that could reduce failures in accounts receivable management include:
    a. Credit checks on customers
    b. Shipping the correct copier to the customer
    c. Supporting installation of the copier and answering customer questions
    d. Sending the correct invoice, in the correct amount, and to the correct address, promptly
    e. Following up to see if the machine is functioning smoothly

19-36 (Cont'd.)

3.   A Pareto diagram for the problem of delays in receiving customer payments follows:

SOLUTION EXHIBIT 19-36A
Pareto Diagram for Failures in Accounts Receivables at Murray Corporation

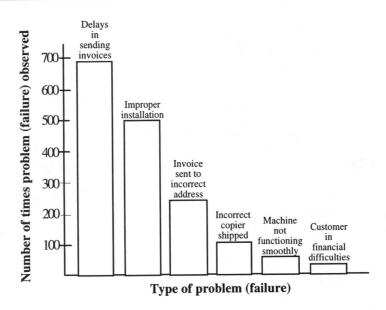

A cause-and-effect or fishbone diagram for the problem of delays in sending invoices may appear as follows:

SOLUTION EXHIBIT 19-36B
Cause-and-Effect Diagram
For Problem of Delays in Sending Invoices at Murray Corporation

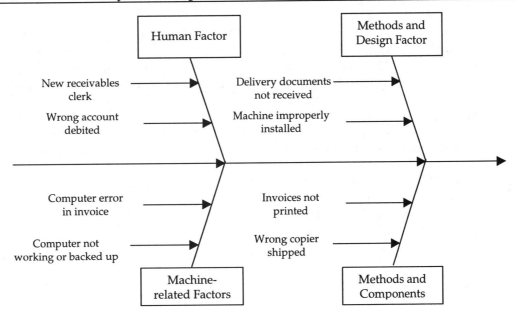

19-38 (45–50 min.)   **Quality improvement, theory of constraints.**

1.   Consider the incremental revenues and incremental costs to Wellesley Corporation of purchasing additional grey cloth from outside suppliers.

Incremental revenues, $1,250 × (5,000 rolls × 0.90)		$5,625,000
Incremental costs:		
Cost of gray cloth, $900 × 5,000 rolls	$4,500,000	
Direct materials variable costs at printing		
operation, $100 × 5,000 rolls	500,000	
Incremental costs		5,000,000
Excess of incremental revenues over incremental costs		$ 625,000

Note that, because the printing department has surplus capacity equal to 5,500 (15,000 – 9,500) rolls per month, purchasing grey cloth from outside entails zero opportunity costs. Yes, the Printing Department should buy the grey cloth from the outside supplier.

2.   By producing a defective roll in the Weaving Department, Wellesley Corporation is worse off by the entire amount of revenue forgone of $1,250 per roll. Note that, since the weaving operation is a constraint, any rolls received by the Printing Department that are scrapped result in lost revenue to the firm.

An alternative approach to analyzing the problem is to focus on scrap costs and the benefits of reducing scrap.

The relevant costs of Printing Department scrap are:	
a. Direct materials variable costs in the Weaving Department	$ 500
b. Direct materials variable costs in the Printing Department	100
c. Contribution margin forgone from not selling one roll	
$1,250 – $500 – $100	650
Amount by which Wellesley Corporation is worse off as a	
result of Printing Department scrap	$1,250

Note that only the variable scrap costs of $600 per roll (direct materials in the Weaving Department, $500 per roll; direct materials in the Printing Department, $100 per roll) are relevant because improving quality will save these costs. Fixed scrap costs attributable to other operating costs are irrelevant because these costs will be incurred whether Wellesley Corporation reduces scrap in the Printing Department or not.

Wellesley Corporation should make the proposed modifications in the Printing Department because the incremental benefits exceed the incremental costs by $125,000 per month:

Incremental benefits of reducing scrap in the Printing Department	
by 4% (from 10% to 6%)	
4% × 9,500 rolls × $1,250 per roll (computed above)	$475,000
Incremental costs of the modification	350,000
Excess of incremental benefits over incremental costs	$125,000

19-38 (Cont'd.)

3.   To determine how much Wellesley Corporation is worse off by producing a defective roll in the Weaving Department, consider the payoff to Wellesley from not having a defective roll produced in the Weaving Department. The good roll produced in the Weaving Department will be sent for further processing in the Printing Department. The relevant costs and benefits of printing and selling this roll follow:

Additional direct materials variable costs incurred in the Printing Department	$ (100)
Expected revenue from selling the finished product, 0.9 × $1,250 (since 10% of the Printing Department output will be scrapped and earn zero revenue)	1,125
Net expected benefit of producing a good roll in the Weaving Department	$1,025

By producing a defective roll in the Weaving Department, Wellesley Corporation is worse off by $1,025 per roll. Note that, since the weaving operation is a constraint, any rolls that are scrapped result in lost revenue to the firm.

An alternative approach to analyzing the problem is to focus on scrap costs and the benefits of reducing scrap.

The relevant costs of Weaving Department scrap are:	
(a) Direct materials variable costs in the Weaving Department	$ 500
(b) Expected unit contribution margin forgone from not selling one roll, ($1,250 × 0.9) – $500 – $100	525
Amount by which Wesley Corporation is worse off as a result of Weaving Department scrap	$1,025

Note that only the variable scrap costs of $500 per roll (direct materials in the Weaving Department) are relevant because improving quality will save these costs. All fixed scrap costs attributable to other operating costs are irrelevant because these costs will be incurred whether Wellesley Corporation reduces scrap in the Weaving Department or not.

Wellesley Corporation should make the proposed improvements in the Printing Department because the incremental benefits exceed the incremental costs by $30,000 per month:

Incremental benefits of reducing scrap in the Weaving Department by 2% (from 5% to 3%)	
2% × 10,000 rolls × $1,025 per roll (computed above)	$205,000
Incremental costs of the improvements	175,000
Excess of incremental benefits over incremental costs	$ 30,000

CHAPTER 20
INVENTORY MANAGEMENT, JUST-IN-TIME, AND BACKFLUSH COSTING

20-2 Five cost categories important in managing goods for sale in a retail organization are:
1. Purchasing costs
2. Ordering costs
3. Carrying costs
4. Stockout costs
5. Quality costs

20-4 Costs included in the carrying costs of inventory are *incremental costs* for such items as insurance, rent, obsolescence, spoilage, and breakage plus the *opportunity cost* of capital (or required return on investment).

20-6 The steps in computing the costs of a prediction error when using the EOQ decision model are:
Step 1: Compute the monetary outcome from the best action that could have been taken, given the actual amount of the cost input.
Step 2: Compute the monetary outcome from the best action based on the incorrect amount of the predicted cost input.
Step 3: Compute the difference between the monetary outcomes from Steps 1 and 2.

20-8 Just-in-time (JIT) purchasing is the purchase of goods or materials such that a delivery immediately precedes demand or use. Benefits include lower inventory holdings (reduced warehouse space required and less money tied up in inventory) and less risk of inventory obsolescence and spoilage.

20-10 The sequence of activities involved in placing a purchase order can be facilitated by use of the internet. The Concepts in Action box in Chapter 20 discusses how Cisco is streamlining the procurement process for its customers—e.g., having online a complete price list, information about expected shipment dates, and a service order capability that is available 24 hours a day with email or fax confirmation.

20-12 Obstacles to companies adopting a supply-chain approach include:
- Communication obstacles—the unwillingness of some parties to share information.
- Trust obstacles—includes the concern that all parties will not meet their agreed-upon commitments.
- Information system obstacles—includes problems due to the information systems of different parties not being technically compatible.
- Limited resources—includes problems due to the people and financial resources given to support a supply chain initiative not being adequate.

20-14 Traditional normal and standard costing systems use sequential tracking, which is any product-costing method where recording of the journal entries occurs in the same order as actual purchases and progress in production.

Backflush costing omits the recording of some or all of the journal entries relating to the cycle from purchase of direct materials to sale of finished goods. Where journal entries for one or more stages in the cycle are omitted, the journal entries for a subsequent stage use normal or standard costs to work backward to flush out the costs in the cycle for which journal entries were not made.

20-16 (20 min.) Economic order quantity for retailer.

1. D = 10,000, P = $225, C = $10

$$EOQ = \sqrt{\frac{2\,DP}{C}} = \sqrt{\frac{2(10,000)\$225}{10}}$$

$$= 670.82$$

$$\cong 671 \text{ jerseys}$$

2. Number of orders per year $= \dfrac{D}{EOQ} = \dfrac{10,000}{671}$

$$= 14.90$$

$$\cong \quad 15 \text{ orders}$$

3. $\dfrac{\text{Demand each}}{\text{working day}} \quad = \dfrac{D}{\text{Number of working days}}$

$$= \frac{10,000}{365}$$

$$= 27.40 \text{ jerseys per day}$$

Purchase lead time = 7 days

Reorder point   = 27.40 x 7

$$= 191.80 \cong 192 \text{ jerseys}$$

20-18 (15 min.)   **EOQ for a retailer.**

1. $D = 20,000$, $P = \$160$, $C = 20\% \times \$8 = \$1.60$

$$EOQ = \sqrt{\frac{2DP}{C}} = \sqrt{\frac{2(20,000)\$160}{\$1.60}} = 2,000 \text{ yards}$$

2.   Number of orders per year: $\dfrac{D}{EOQ} = \dfrac{20,000}{2,000} = 10 \text{ orders}$

3.   Demand each working day $= \dfrac{D}{\text{Number of working days}}$

$$= \frac{20,000}{250}$$

= 80 yards per day

= 400 yards per week

Purchasing lead time = 2 weeks
Reorder point = 400 x 2 = 800 yards

20-20 (20 min.) **Economic order quantity for retailer, ordering and carrying costs.**

1. $D = 20,000$, $P = \$120$, $C = \$10$

$EOQ \quad = \quad \sqrt{\dfrac{2(20,000)(\$120)}{\$10}}$

$= \quad 692.8 \times 693 \text{ modems}$

2. $RTC \quad = \quad \dfrac{DP}{Q} + \dfrac{QC}{2}$

$= \quad \dfrac{20,000 \times \$120}{692.8} + \dfrac{692.8 \times 10}{2}$

$= \quad \$3,464 + 3,464$

$= \quad \$6,928$

3.   Reorder point $= \begin{matrix} \text{Number of units} \\ \text{sold per} \\ \text{unit of time} \end{matrix} \times \begin{matrix} \text{Purchase - order} \\ \text{lead time} \end{matrix}$

$= \quad \dfrac{20,000}{360} \times 5$

$= \quad 277.78 \quad \cong \quad 278 \text{ modems}$

20-22 (20 min.)   JIT production, relevant benefits, relevant costs.

1.   Solution Exhibit 20-22 presents the annual net benefit of $154,000 to Evans Corporation of implementing a JIT production system.

2.   Other nonfinancial and qualitative factors that Evans should consider in deciding whether it should implement a JIT system include:
   a.   The possibility of developing and implementing a detailed system for integrating the sequential operations of the manufacturing process. Direct materials must arrive when needed for each subassembly so that the production process functions smoothly.
   b.   The ability to design products that use standardized parts and reduce manufacturing time.
   c.   The ease of obtaining reliable vendors who can deliver quality direct materials on time with minimum lead time.
   d.   Willingness of suppliers to deliver smaller and more frequent orders.
   e.   The confidence of being able to deliver quality products on time. Failure to do so would result in customer dissatisfaction.
   f.   The skill levels of workers to perform multiple tasks such as minor repairs, maintenance, quality testing and inspection.

SOLUTION EXHIBIT 20-22
Annual Relevant Costs of Current Production System and JIT Production System for Evans Corporation

Relevant Items	Incremental Costs under Current Production System	Incremental Costs under JIT Production System
Annual tooling costs	–	$150,000
Required return on investment		
12% per year × $900,000 of average inventory per year	$108,000	
12% per year × $200,000 of average inventory per year		24,000
Insurance, space, materials handling, and setup costs	200,000	140,000[a]
Rework costs	350,000	280,000[b]
Incremental revenues from higher selling prices	–	(90,000)[c]
Total net incremental costs	$658,000	$504,000
Annual difference in favor of JIT production	▲ $154,000 ↑	

[a]$200,000 (1 − 0.30) = $140,000

[b]$350,000 (1 − 0.20) = $280,000

[c] $3 × 30,000 units = $90,000

20-4

20-24 (20 min.) **Backflush costing, two trigger points, materials purchase and sale (continuation of 20-23).**

1.

(a) Purchases of raw materials	Inventory Control	2,754,000	
	Accounts Payable Control		2,754,000
(b) Incur conversion costs	Conversion Costs Control	723,600	
	Various Accounts		723,600
(c) Completion of finished goods	No entry		
(d) Sale of finished goods	Cost of Goods Sold	3,432,000	
	Inventory Control		2,692,800
	Conversion Costs Allocated		739,200
(e) Underallocated or overallocated conversion costs	Conversion Costs Allocated	739,200	
	Costs of Goods Sold		15,600
	Conversion Costs Control		723,600

2.

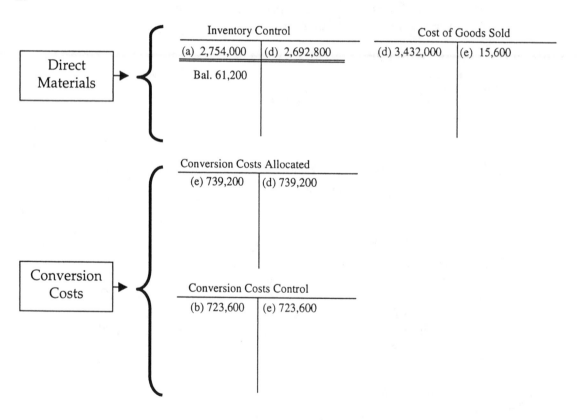

Inventory Control		Cost of Goods Sold	
(a) 2,754,000	(d) 2,692,800	(d) 3,432,000	(e) 15,600
Bal. 61,200			

Direct Materials

Conversion Costs Allocated	
(e) 739,200	(d) 739,200

Conversion Costs Control	
(b) 723,600	(e) 723,600

Conversion Costs

20-26 (30 min.) **Effect of different order quantities on ordering costs and carrying costs, EOQ.**

1. A straightforward approach to this requirement is to construct the following table for different purchase-order quantities.

D: Demand	26,000	26,000	26,000	26,000	26,000
Q: Order quantity	300	500	600	700	900
Q/2: Average inventory in units	150	250	300	350	450
D/Q: Number of purchase orders	86.67	52	43.33	37.14	28.89
(D/Q) × P: Annual ordering costs	$6,240	$3,744	$3,120	$2,674	$2,080
(Q/2) × C: Annual carrying costs	1,560	2,600	3,120	3,640	4,680
Total relevant costs of ordering and carrying inventory	$7,800	$6,344	$6,240	$6,314	$6,760

$$\qquad\qquad\qquad\qquad\qquad\qquad\qquad\qquad\qquad\qquad\uparrow$$
$$\text{Minimum}$$
$$\text{Cost}$$

D = 26,000 units
Q = order quantity
P = $72
C = $10.40

$$\text{EOQ} = \sqrt{\frac{2DP}{C}} = \sqrt{\frac{2 \times 26,000 \times \$72}{\$10.40}} = \sqrt{360,000} = 600 \text{ packages}$$

The shape of the total relevant cost function for Koala Blue is relatively flat from order quantities 500 to 700.

2. When the ordering cost per purchase order is reduced to $40:

$$\text{EOQ} = \sqrt{\frac{2 \times 26,000 \times \$40}{\$10.40}} = \sqrt{200,000} = 447.2 \text{ packages} \times 447 \text{ packages}$$

The EOQ drops from 600 packages to 447 packages when Koala Blue's ordering cost per purchase order drops from $72 to $40.

20-28 (20–30 min.) **EOQ, cost of prediction error.**

1.   EOQ $= \sqrt{\dfrac{2DP}{C}}$

D = 2,000; P = \$40; C = \$4 + (10\% \times \$50) = \$9

EOQ $= \sqrt{\dfrac{2(2000)\$40}{\$9}}$ = 133.333 tires $\simeq$ 133 tires

TRC $= \dfrac{DP}{Q} + \dfrac{QC}{2}$ where Q can be any quantity, including the EOQ

$= \dfrac{2,000 \times \$40}{133.3} + \dfrac{133.3 \times \$9}{2}$ = \$600 + \$600 = \$1,200

If students used an EOQ of 133 tires (order quantities rounded to the nearest whole number),

TRC $= \dfrac{2,000 \times \$40}{133} + \dfrac{133 \times \$9}{2}$ = \$601.5 + \$598.5 = \$1,200.

Sum of annual relevant ordering and carrying costs equals \$1,200.

2.   The prediction error affects C, which is now:

C   = \$4 + (10\% \times \$30) = \$7

D   = 2,000, P = \$40, C = \$7

EOQ $= \sqrt{\dfrac{2(2,000)\$40}{\$7}}$ = 151.186 tires = 151 tires (rounded)

20-28 (Cont'd.)

The cost of the prediction error can be calculated using a three-step procedure:

Step 1: Compute the monetary outcome from the best action that could have been taken, given the actual amount of the cost input.

$$\text{TRC} = \frac{DP}{Q} + \frac{QC}{2}$$

$$= \frac{2,000 \times \$40}{151.186} + \frac{151,186 \times \$7}{2}$$

$$= \$529.15 + \$529.15 = \$1,058.30$$

Step 2: Compute the monetary outcome from the best action based on the incorrect amount of the predicted cost input.

$$\text{TRC} = \frac{DP}{Q} + \frac{QC}{2}$$

$$= \frac{2,000 \times \$40}{133.333} + \frac{133.333 \times \$7}{2}$$

$$= \$600 + \$466.67 = \$1,066.67$$

Step 3: Compute the difference between the monetary outcomes from Step 1 and Step 2:

	Monetary Outcome
Step 1	$1,058.30
Step 2	1,066.67
Difference	$ (8.37)

The cost of the prediction error is $8.37.

Note: The $20 prediction error for the purchase price of the heavy-duty tires is irrelevant in computing purchase costs under the two alternatives because the same purchase costs will be incurred whatever the order size.

Some students may prefer to round off the EOQs to 133 tires and 151 tires, respectively. The calculations under each step in this case follow:

Step 1: $\text{TRC} = \dfrac{2,000 \times \$40}{151} + \dfrac{151 \times \$7}{2} = \$529.80 + \$528.50 = \$1058.30$

Step 2: $\text{TRC} = \dfrac{2,000 \times \$40}{133} + \dfrac{133 \times \$7}{2} = \$601.50 + \$465.50 = \$1067.00$

Step 3: Difference $= \$1,058.30 - \$1,067.00 = \$8.70$

20-30 (20 min.)   **Supply-chain analysis, company viewpoints.**

1. The major benefits to adopting a supply-chain approach include:

   a. Overall reduction in inventory levels across the supply chain:
      - "receiving better information has allowed us to forecast and reduce inventory levels...
      - "The inventory levels are lower...by not overstocking the warehouses"

   b. Fewer stockouts at the retail level.

   c. Reduced manufacturing of items not subsequently demanded by retailers:
      - "You produce only what you need"
      - "We have less waste by not overstocking the warehouses"

   d. Lower manufacturing costs due to better production scheduling and fewer expedited orders:
      - "We can fine tune our production scheduling"

These benefits can both increase revenues (fewer stockouts) and decrease costs (lower manufacturing costs, lower holding costs, and lower distribution costs).

2. Key obstacles to a manufacturer adopting a supply chain approach are:

   a. Communication obstacles—includes the unwillingness of some parties to share information.

   b. Trust obstacles—includes the concern that all parties will not meet their agreed-upon commitments.

   c. Information system obstacles—includes problems due to the information systems of different parties not being technically compatible.

   d. Limited resources—includes problems due to the people and financial resources given to support a supply chain initiative not being adequate.

20-32   (20 min.)   **Backflush, two trigger points, materials purchase and sale (continuation of 20-32).**

1.

(a) Purchases of raw materials	Inventory Control Accounts Payable Control	550,000	550,000

(b) Incur conversion costs	Conversion Costs Control
	  Various Accounts
	  (such as Accounts Payable)
	  Payable Control and Wages
		440,000	440,000

(c) Completion of finished goods	No entry		

(d) Sale of finished goods	Cost of Goods Sold
	  Inventory Control
	  Conversion Costs Allocated
		900,000	500,000
			400,000

(e) Underallocated
      or overallocated
      conversion costs
	Conversion Costs Allocated
	Cost of Goods Sold
	  Conversion Costs Control
		400,000
		40,000
			440,000

2.

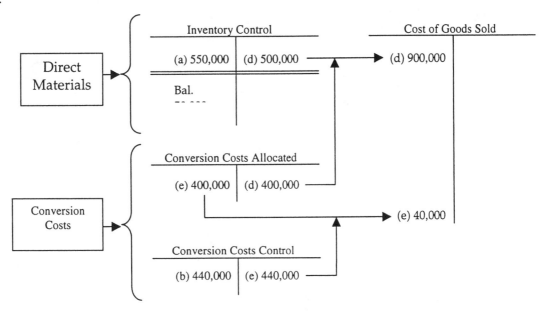

20-34 (20–25 min.)   **Backflush costing and JIT production.**

1.

(a) Purchases of raw material	Inventory: Raw and In-Process Control Accounts Payable Control	5,300,000	5,300,000
(b) Incur conversion costs	Conversion Costs Control Various Accounts	3,080,000	3,080,000

(c) Completion of finished goods	Finished Goods Control
	    Inventory: Raw and In-Process Control
	    Conversion Costs allocated
		8,200,000	5,200,000
			3,000,000

(d) Sale of finished goods	Cost of Goods Sold Finished Goods Control	7,872,000	7,872,000

2.

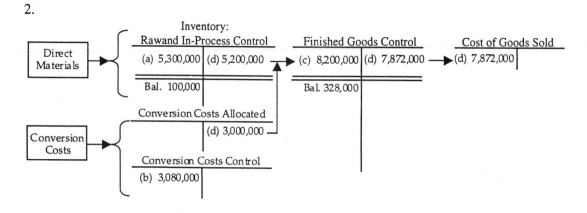

20-36 (20–25 min.) **Backflush, two trigger points, completion of production and sale (continuation of 20-34 and 20-35).**

1.

(a) Purchases of raw materials	No entry		
(b) Incur conversion	Conversion Costs Control	3,080,000	
	Various Accounts		3,080,000
(c) Completion of finished goods	Finished Goods Control	8,200,000	
	Accounts Payable Control		5,200,000
	Conversion Costs Allocated		3,000,000
(d) Sale of finished goods	Cost of Goods Sold	7,872,000	
	Finished Goods Control		7,872,000
(e) Underallocated or overallocated conversion costs	Conversion Costs Allocated	3,000,000	
	Cost of Goods Sold	80,000	
	Conversion Costs Control		3,080,000

20-36 (Cont'd.)

2.

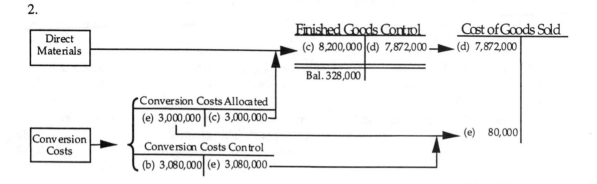

The $328,000 ending balance of Finished Goods Control consists of the 8,000 units of finished goods units in inventory at the standard cost of $41 per unit. Since the first trigger point is at the completion of production, the $100,000 of direct materials on hand (as shown in solution to Problem 20-34) are not recorded as inventory. In this version, if backflush costing, direct materials purchases are recorded only when finished goods are produced.

3.   The key difference between the accounting in Problem 20-34 and the accounting here is the absence of the Inventory: Raw and In-Process Control Account. As a result, at the end of June, $100,000 of direct materials purchased but not yet manufactured into finished units have not been entered into the Inventory Control account. (Direct materials purchased is $5,300,000.) This variation of backflush costing is suitable for a production system that has virtually no direct materials inventory and minimum work-in-process inventories. It is less feasible otherwise.

20-38 (35–40 min.)   **Backflushing.**

1.   Glendale has successfully implemented JIT in its production operations and, hence, minimized work-in-process inventory. It still has a fair amount of raw material and finished goods inventory. Glendale should, therefore, adopt a backflush costing system with two trigger points, as follows:
   a.   Direct materials purchases charged to Inventory: Raw and In-Process Control
   b.   Finished goods recorded as Finished Goods Control
The backflush approach described closely approximates the costs computed using sequential tracking. There is no work in process so there is no need for a Work in Process inventory account.

     Further, by maintaining a Raw and In-Process Inventory Control and Finished Goods Control account, Glendale can keep track of and control the inventories of direct materials and finished goods in its plant.

2a.   I would recommend that Glendale adopt a backflush costing system with trigger points at completion of finished goods and at the sale of finished goods. This would approximate the sequential tracking approach since the question assumes Glendale has no raw materials or work-in-process inventories. There is, therefore, no need for these inventory accounts.

   b.   A backflush costing system with two trigger points—when purchases of raw materials are made (debited to Inventory Control), and when Finished Goods are sold—would approximate sequential tracking, since the question assumes Glendale has no work-in-process or finished goods inventories.
   c.   A backflush costing system with a single trigger point when finished goods are sold would approximate sequential tracking, since the question assumes Glendale has no raw material, work-in-process or finished goods inventories. This is a further simplification of the three examples in the text (p.728).
     The principle here is that backflushing of costs should be triggered at the finished goods inventory stage if Glendale plans to hold finished goods inventory. If Glendale plans to hold no finished goods inventory, backflushing can be postponed till the finished goods are sold. In other words, the trigger points for backflushing relate to the points where inventory is being accumulated. As a result, backflushing matches the sequential tracking approach and also maintains a record for the monitoring and control of the inventory.

20-38 (Cont'd.)

3.   Some comments on the quotation follow:
a. The backflush system is a standard costing system, not an actual costing system.
b. If standard costing is used, an up-to-date realistic set of standard costs is always desirable—as long as the set meets the cost-benefit test as related to the task of updating.
c. The operating environments of "the present JIT era" have induced many companies toward more simplicity (backflush) and abandoning the typical standard costing system (sequential tracking).
d. Backflush is probably closer to being a periodic system than a perpetual system. However, a periodic system may be cost-effective, particularly where physical inventories are relatively low or stable.
e. The textbook points out that, to be attractive, backflush costing should generate the same financial measurements as sequential tracking—and at a lower accounting cost.
f. The choice of a product costing system is highly contextual. Its characteristics should be heavily affected by its costs, the preferences of operating managers, and the underlying operating processes. Sweeping generalizations about any cost accounting system or technique are unjustified.

CHAPTER 21
CAPITAL BUDGETING AND COST ANALYSIS

21-2 The six stages in capital budgeting are:
1. An *identification stage* to distinguish which types of capital expenditure projects are necessary to accomplish organization objectives.
2. A *search stage* that explores alternative capital investments that will achieve organization objectives.
3. An *information-acquisition stage* to consider the expected costs and expected benefits of alternative capital investments.
4. A *selection stage* to choose projects for implementation.
5. A *financing stage* to obtain project financing.
6. An *implementation and control* stage to get projects underway and monitor their performance.

21-4 No. Only quantitative outcomes are formally analyzed in capital budgeting decisions. Many effects of capital budgeting decisions, however, are difficult to quantify in financial terms. These nonfinancial or qualitative factors (for example, the number of accidents in a manufacturing plant or employee morale) are important to consider in making capital budgeting decisions.

21-6 The payback method measures the time it will take to recoup, in the form of net cash inflows, the total dollars invested in a project. The payback method is simple and easy to understand. It is a handy method when precision in estimates of profitability is not crucial and when predicted cash flows in later years are highly uncertain. The main weakness of the payback method is its neglect of profitability and the time value of money.

21-8 No. The discounted cash-flow techniques implicitly consider depreciation in rate of return computations; the compound interest tables automatically allow for recovery of investment. The net initial investment of an asset is usually regarded as a lump-sum outflow at time zero. Where taxes are included in the DCF analysis, depreciation costs are included in the computation of the taxable income number that is used to compute the tax payment cash flow.

21-10 All overhead costs are not relevant in NPV analysis. Overhead costs are relevant only if the capital investment results in a change in total overhead cash flows. Overhead costs are not relevant if total overhead cash flows remain the same but the overhead allocated to the particular capital investment changes.

21-12 The categories of cash flow that should be considered are:
1a. Initial machine investment,
  b. Initial working capital investment,
  c. After-tax cash flow from current disposal of old machine,
2a. Annual after-tax cash flow from operations (excluding depreciation effects),
  b. Income tax cash savings from annual depreciation deductions,
3a. After-tax cash flow from terminal disposal of machine, and
  b. After-tax cash flow from recovery of working capital.

21-14 A cellular telephone company manager responsible for retaining customers needs to consider the expected future revenues and the expected future costs of "different investments" to retain customers. One such investment could be a special price discount. An alternative investment is offering loyalty club benefits to long-time customers.

21-16 Exercises in compound interest, no income taxes.

The answers to these exercises are printed after the last problem, at the end of the chapter

21-18 (30 min.)   Capital budgeting methods, no income taxes.

The table for the present value of annuities (Appendix C, Table 4) shows: 10 periods at 14% = 5.216

1a.   Net present value

$$= \$28,000(5.216) - \$110,000$$
$$= \$146,048 - \$110,000 = \$36,048$$

b.   Payback period

$$= \frac{\$110,000}{\$28,000} = 3.93 \text{ years}$$

c.   Internal rate of return:

$\$110,000$ =   Present value of annuity of $28,000 at R% for 10 years, or what factor (F) in the table of present values of an annuity (Appendix C, Table 4) will satisfy the following equation.

$$\$110,000 = \$28,000F$$
$$F = \frac{\$110,000}{\$28,000} = 3.929$$

On the 10-year line in the table for the present value of annuities (Appendix C, Table 4), find the column closest to 3.929; 3.929 is between a rate of return of 20% and 22%.

Interpolation can be used to determine the exact rate:

	Present Value Factors	
20%	4.192	4.192
IRR rate	—	3.929
22%	3.923	—
Difference	0.269	0.263

Internal rate of return $= 20\% + \left[\dfrac{0.263}{0.269}\right](2\%)$

$$= 20\% + (0.978)(2\%) = 21.96\%$$

21-18 (Cont'd.)

d. Accrual accounting rate of return based on net initial investment:
Net initial investment = $110,000
Estimated useful life = 10 years
Annual straight-line depreciation = $110,000 ÷ 10 = $11,000

$$\text{Accrual accounting rate of return} = \frac{\$28,000 - \$11,000}{\$110,000}$$

$$= \frac{\$17,000}{\$110,000} = 15.46\%$$

2. Factors City Hospital should consider include:
   a. Quantitative financial aspects.
   b. Qualitative factors, such as the benefits to its customers of a better eye-testing machine and the employee-morale advantages of having up-to-date equipment.
   c. Financing factors, such as the availability of cash to purchase the new equipment.

21-20 (30 min.) Capital budgeting with uneven cash flows, no income taxes.

1. Present value of savings in cash operating costs:

$10,000 × 0.862	$ 8,620
8,000 × 0.743	5,944
6,000 × 0.641	3,846
5,000 × 0.552	2,760
4,000 × 0.476	1,904
3,000 × 0.410	1,230
3,000 × 0.354	1,062
Present value of savings in cash operating costs	25,366
Net initial investment	(28,000)
Net present value	$ (2,634)

2. Payback period:

Year	Cash Savings	Cumulative Cash Savings	Initial Investment Yet to Be Recovered at End of Year
0	–	–	$28,000
1	$10,000	$10,000	18,000
2	8,000	18,000	10,000
3	6,000	24,000	4,000
4	5,000	29,000	–

$$\text{Payback period} = 3 \text{ years} + \frac{\$4,000}{\$5,000} = 3.8 \text{ years}$$

3. From requirement 1, the net present value is negative with a 16% required rate of return. Hence, the internal rate of return must be less than 16%.

Year (1)	Cash Savings (2)	P.V. Factor at 14% (3)	P.V. at 14% (4) = (2) × (3)	P.V. Factor at 12% (5)	P.V. at 12% (6) = (2) × (5)	P.V. Factor at 10% (7)	P.V. at 10% (8) = (2) × (7)
1	$10,000	0.877	$ 8,770	0.893	$ 8,930	0.909	$ 9,090
2	8,000	0.769	6,152	0.797	6,376	0.826	6,608
3	6,000	0.675	4,050	0.712	4,272	0.751	4,506
4	5,000	0.592	2,960	0.636	3,180	0.683	3,415
5	4,000	0.519	2,076	0.567	2,268	0.621	2,484
6	3,000	0.456	1,368	0.507	1,521	0.564	1,692
7	3,000	0.400	1,200	0.452	1,356	0.513	1,539
			$26,576		$27,903		$29,334

Net present value at 14% = $26,576 – $28,000 = $(1,424)
Net present value at 12% = $27,903 – $28,000 = $ (97)
Net present value at 10% = $29,334 – $28,000 = $ 1,334
By interpolation:

$$\text{Internal rate of return} = 10\% + \left(\frac{1,334}{1,334 + 97}\right)(2\%)$$

$$= 10\% + (0.932)(2\%) = 11.86\%$$

4. Accrual accounting rate of return based on net initial investment:

$$\text{Average annual savings in cash operating costs} = \frac{\$39,000}{7 \text{ years}} = \$5,571$$

$$\text{Annual straight-line depreciation} = \frac{\$28,000}{7 \text{ years}} = \$4,000$$

$$\text{Accrual accounting rate of return} = \frac{\$5,571 - \$4,000}{\$28,000}$$

$$= \frac{\$1,571}{\$28,000} = 5.61\%$$

21-22 (30 min.) Payback and NPV methods, no income taxes.

1. a. Payback measures the time taken to recoup, in the form of expected future cash flows, the net investment in a project. Payback emphasizes the early recovery of cash as a key aspect of project ranking. Some managers argue that this emphasis on early recovery of cash is appropriate if there is a high level of uncertainty about future cash flows. Projects with shorter paybacks give the organization more flexibility because funds for other projects become available sooner.

Strengths

- Easy to understand
- One way to capture uncertainty about expected cash flows in later years of a project (although sensitivity analysis is a more systematic way)

Weaknesses

- Fails to incorporate the time value of money
- Does not consider a project's cash flows after the payback period

b.
Project A

Outflow, $200,000
Inflow, $50,000^1 + $50,000^2 + $50,000^3 + $50,000^4

Payback = 4 years

Project B

Outflow, $190,000

Inflow, $40,000^1 + $50,000^2 + $70,000^3 + $\dfrac{\$30,000^4}{\$75,000}$

Payback $= 3 + \dfrac{\$30,000}{\$75,000} = 3.4$ years

Project C

Outflow, $250,000

Inflow, $75,000^1 + $75,000^2 + $60,000^3 + $\dfrac{\$40,000^4}{\$80,000}$

Payback $= 3 + \dfrac{\$40,000}{\$80,000} = 3.5$ years

21-22 (Cont'd.)

Project D

Outflow, $210,000
Inflow, $75,000(Year 1) + $75,000(Year 2) + $60,000(Year 3)

Payback = 3 years

2. Solution Exhibit 21-22 shows the following ranking:

	NPV
1. Project C	$27,050
2. Project B	$25,635
3. Project D	$(3,750)
4. Project A	$(19,750)

3. Using NPV, Project C is the preferred project despite its having the longest payback. Project C has sizable cash inflows after the payback period. Nonfinancial qualitative factors should also be considered. For example, are there differential worker safety issues across the projects? Are there differences in the extent of learning that can benefit other projects? Are there differences in the customer relationships established with different projects that can benefit Cording Manufacturing in future projects?

SOLUTION EXHIBIT 21-22

Sketch of Relevant Cash Flows

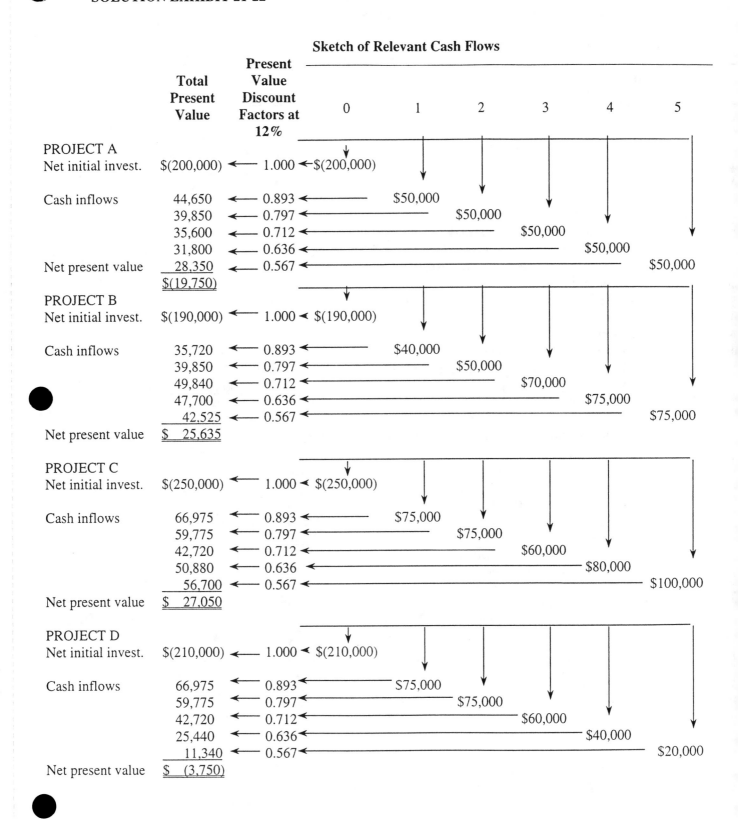

	Total Present Value	Present Value Discount Factors at 12%	0	1	2	3	4	5
PROJECT A Net initial invest.	$(200,000)	1.000	$(200,000)					
Cash inflows	44,650	0.893		$50,000				
	39,850	0.797			$50,000			
	35,600	0.712				$50,000		
	31,800	0.636					$50,000	
Net present value	28,350	0.567						$50,000
	$(19,750)							
PROJECT B Net initial invest.	$(190,000)	1.000	$(190,000)					
Cash inflows	35,720	0.893		$40,000				
	39,850	0.797			$50,000			
	49,840	0.712				$70,000		
	47,700	0.636					$75,000	
	42,525	0.567						$75,000
Net present value	$ 25,635							
PROJECT C Net initial invest.	$(250,000)	1.000	$(250,000)					
Cash inflows	66,975	0.893		$75,000				
	59,775	0.797			$75,000			
	42,720	0.712				$60,000		
	50,880	0.636					$80,000	
	56,700	0.567						$100,000
Net present value	$ 27,050							
PROJECT D Net initial invest.	$(210,000)	1.000	$(210,000)					
Cash inflows	66,975	0.893		$75,000				
	59,775	0.797			$75,000			
	42,720	0.712				$60,000		
	25,440	0.636					$40,000	
	11,340	0.567						$20,000
Net present value	$ (3,750)							

21-24 (22–30 min.) **DCF, accrual accounting rate of return, working capital, evaluation of performance, no income taxes.**

1. A summary of cash inflows and outflows (in thousands) are:

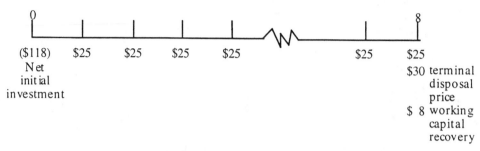

Present value of annuity of savings in cash operating costs ($25,000 per year for 8 years at 14%): $25,000 x 4.639		$115,975
Present value of $30,000 terminal disposal price of machine at end of year 8: $30,000 × 0.351		10,530
Present value of $8,000 recovery of working capital at end of year 8: $8,000 × 0.351		2,808
Gross present value		129,313
Deduct net initial investment:		
Special-purpose machine, initial investment	$110,000	
Additional working capital investment	8,000	118,000
Net present value		$ 11,313

2. Use a trial-and-error approach. First, try a 16% discount rate:

$25,000 × 4.344	$108,600
($30,000 + $8,000) x.305	11,590
Gross present value	120,190
Deduct net initial investment	(118,000)
Net present value	$ 2,190

Second, try an 18% discount rate:

$25,000 × 4.078	$101,950
($30,000 + $8,000) × .266	10,108
Gross present value	112,058
Deduct net initial investment	(118,000)
Net present value	$ (5,942)

21-24 (Cont'd.)

By interpolation:

$$\text{Internal rate of return} = 16\% + \left(\frac{2{,}190}{2{,}190 + 5{,}942} \right) \times 2\%$$

$$= 16\% + (.2693 \times 2\%)$$

$$= 16.54\%$$

3. Accrual accounting rate of return based on net initial investment:

Net initial investment = $110,000 + $8,000
= $118,000

Annual depreciation
($110,000 – $30,000) ÷ 8 years   = $10,000

$$\text{Accrual accounting rate of return} = \frac{\$25{,}000 - \$10{,}000}{\$118{,}000} = 12.71\%$$

4. If your decision is based on the DCF model, the purchase would be made because the net present value is positive, and the 16.54% internal rate of return exceeds the 14% required rate of return. However, you may believe that your performance may actually be measured using accrual accounting. This approach would show a 12.71% return on the initial investment, which is below the required rate. Your reluctance to make a "buy" decision would be quite natural unless you are assured of reasonable consistency between the decision model and the performance evaluation method.

21-26 (60 min.)   Selling a plant, income taxes.

1. *Option 1*

Current disposal price	$9,000,000
Deduct current book value	0
Gain on disposal	9,000,000
Deduct 40% taxes	3,600,000
Net present value	$5,400,000

Option 2

Waterford receives three sources of cash inflows:
  a.   Rent. Four annual payments of $2,400,000. The after-tax cash inflow is:
$$\$2{,}400{,}000 \times (1 - 0.40) = \$1{,}440{,}000 \text{ per year}$$

  b.   Discount on material purchases, payable at year-end 2000:
$$10\% \times \$2 \times 2{,}370{,}000 = \$474{,}000$$
The after-tax cash inflow is:
$$\$474{,}000 \times (1 - 0.40) = \$284{,}400$$

  c.   Sale of plant at year-end 2003. The after-tax cash inflow is:
$$\$2{,}000{,}000 \times (1 - 0.40) = \$1{,}200{,}000$$

21-9

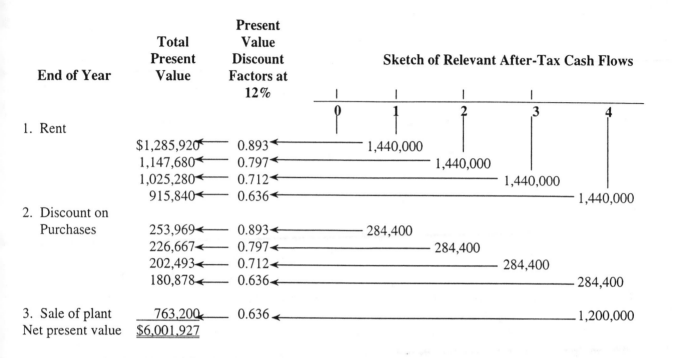

End of Year	Total Present Value	Present Value Discount Factors at 12%	Sketch of Relevant After-Tax Cash Flows			
			0	1	2	3	4
1. Rent							
	$1,285,920	0.893		1,440,000			
	1,147,680	0.797			1,440,000		
	1,025,280	0.712				1,440,000	
	915,840	0.636					1,440,000
2. Discount on Purchases							
	253,969	0.893		284,400			
	226,667	0.797			284,400		
	202,493	0.712				284,400	
	180,878	0.636					284,400
3. Sale of plant	763,200	0.636					1,200,000
Net present value	$6,001,927						

Option 3

Contribution margin per jacket:

Selling price		$42.00
Variable costs		
Direct materials	$20.80	
Direct manuf., marketing and distribution labor	6.40	
Variable manuf., marketing and distribution overhead	5.80	33.00
Contribution margin		$ 9.00

	2000	2001	2002	2003
Contribution margin $9.00 x 200,000; 300,000; 400,000; 100,000	$1,800,000	$2,700,000	$3,600,000	$900,000
Fixed overhead (cash) costs	200,000	200,000	200,000	200,000
Operating income before depreciation	1,600,000	2,500,000	3,400,000	700,000
Income taxes (40%)	640,000	1,000,000	1,360,000	280,000
Net cash inflow	$ 960,000	$1,500,000	$2,040,000	$420,000

21-26 (Cont'd.)

Depreciation:

$$\$1,500,000 \div 4 = \$375,000 \text{ per year}$$

Income tax cash savings from depreciation deduction:
$$\$375,000 \times 0.40 = \$150,000$$

Sale of plant at end of 2003:
$$\$3,000,000 \times (1 - 0.40) = \$1,800,000$$

Solution Exhibit 21-26 presents the NPV calculations.

2. Option 2 has the highest NPV:

	NPV
Option 1	$5,400,000
Option 2	$6,001,927
Option 3	$3,872,880

Option 1 gives Waterford immediate liquidity which it can use for other projects.

Option 2 has the advantage of Waterford having a closer relationship with the supplier. However, it limits Waterford's flexibility if Auburn Mill's quality is not comparable to competitors.

Option 3 has Waterford entering a new line of business. If this line of business is successful, it could be expanded to cover souvenir jackets for other major events. The risks of selling the predicted number of jackets should also be considered. For example, bribery scandals at the Olympic movement could increase the uncertainty that the predicted sales will occur.

21-26 (Cont'd.)

SOLUTION EXHIBIT 21-26

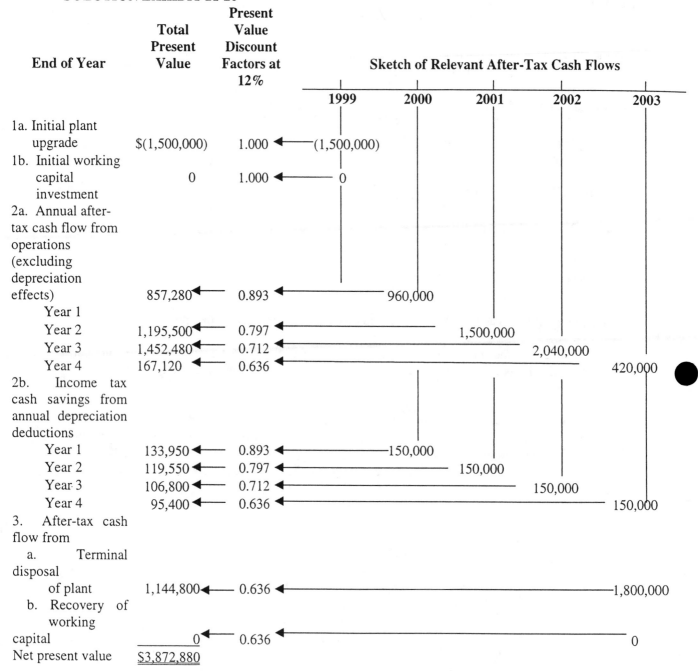

End of Year	Total Present Value	Present Value Discount Factors at 12%	Sketch of Relevant After-Tax Cash Flows				
			1999	**2000**	**2001**	**2002**	**2003**
1a. Initial plant upgrade	$(1,500,000)	1.000	(1,500,000)				
1b. Initial working capital investment	0	1.000	0				
2a. Annual after-tax cash flow from operations (excluding depreciation effects)	857,280	0.893		960,000			
Year 1							
Year 2	1,195,500	0.797			1,500,000		
Year 3	1,452,480	0.712				2,040,000	
Year 4	167,120	0.636					420,000
2b. Income tax cash savings from annual depreciation deductions							
Year 1	133,950	0.893		150,000			
Year 2	119,550	0.797			150,000		
Year 3	106,800	0.712				150,000	
Year 4	95,400	0.636					150,000
3. After-tax cash flow from							
a. Terminal disposal of plant	1,144,800	0.636					1,800,000
b. Recovery of working capital	0	0.636					0
Net present value	$3,872,880						

21-28 (40 min.)   **Equipment replacement, income taxes (continuation of 21-27).**

1. Income tax rate = 30%

Modernize Alternative

Annual depreciation:
$28,000,000 ÷ 7 years = $4,000,000 a year.

Income tax cash savings from annual depreciation deductions:
$4,000,000 × 0.30 = $1,200,000 a year.

Terminal disposal of equipment = $5,000,000.

After-tax cash flow from terminal disposal:
$5,000,000 × 0.70 = $3,500,000.

The NPV components are:

		NPV
1. Initial investment:		
$(28,000,000) × 1.000		$(28,000,000)

2a. Annual after-tax cash flow from operations
    (excluding depreciation):

Dec. 31, 2001	8,280,000 × 0.70 × 0.893	5,175,828
2002	9,180,000 × 0.70 × 0.797	5,121,522
2003	10,080,000 × 0.70 × 0.712	5,023,872
2004	10,980,000 × 0.70 × 0.636	4,888,296
2005	11,880,000 × 0.70 × 0.567	4,715,172
2006	12,780,000 × 0.70 × 0.507	4,535,622
2007	13,680,000 × 0.70 × 0.452	4,328,352

2b. Income tax cash savings from annual depreciation
    deductions (annuity of $1,200,000 for 7 years):

$1,200,000 × 4.564		5,476,800

3. After-tax cash flow from terminal sale of
equipment:

$3,500,000 × 0.452		1,582,000

Net present value	$ 12,847,464	

21-28 (Cont'd.)

Replace alternative

Initial machine replacement = $49,000,000

Sale in Jan. 1, 2001 of equipment = $3,000,000

After-tax cash flow from sale:
   $3,000,000 × 0.70 = $2,100,000

Net after-tax initial investment
   $49,000,000 − $2,100,000 = $46,900,000

Annual depreciation
   $49,000,000 ÷ 7 years = $7,000,000 a year

Income-tax cash savings from annual depreciation deductions
   $7,000,000 × 0.30 = $2,100,000

Terminal disposal of equipment = $12,000,000

After-tax cash flow from terminal disposal
   $12,000,000 × 0.70 = $8,400,000

The NPV components are:
1. Net after-tax initial investment
   $(46,900,000) × 1.000 $(46,900,000)

2a. Annual after-tax cash flow from operations (excluding depreciation)

Dec. 31,			
	2001	$11,040,000 × 0.70 × 0.893	6,901,104
	2002	12,240,000 × 0.70 × 0.797	6,828,696
	2003	13,440,000 × 0.70 × 0.712	6,698,496
	2004	14,640,000 × 0.70 × 0.636	6,517,728
	2005	15,840,000 × 0.70 × 0.567	6,286,896
	2006	17,040,000 × 0.70 × 0.507	6,047,496
	2007	18,240,000 × 0.70 × 0.452	5,771,136

2b. Income tax cash savings from annual depreciation deductions (annuity of $2,100,000 for 7 years)
   $2,100,000 × 4.564   9,584,400

3. After-tax cash flow from terminal sale of equipment
   $8,400,000 × 0.452   3,796,800

Net present value $11,532,752

21-28 (Cont'd.)

2. Superfast would prefer to:
   a. have lower tax rates,
   b. have revenue exempt from taxation,
   c. recognize taxable revenues in later years rather than earlier years,
   d. recognize taxable cost deductions greater than actual outlay costs, and
   e. recognize cost deductions in earlier years rather than later years (including accelerated amounts in earlier years).

21-30 (40 min.) **NPV and customer profitability, no income taxes.**

Homebuilders	2000	2001	2002	2003	2004	2005
Revenues (5%)*	$45,000	$47,250	$49,612	$52,093	$54,698	$57,433
COGS (4%)*	22,000	22,880	23,795	24,747	25,737	26,766
Op. Costs (4%)*	10,000	10,400	10,816	11,249	11,699	12,167
Total costs	32,000	33,280	34,611	35,996	37,436	38,933
Cash flow from operations	$13,000	$13,970	$15,001	$16,097	$17,262	$18,500
Kitchen						
Revenues (15%)*	$325,000	$373,750	$429,812	$494,284	$568,427	$653,691
COGS (4%)*	180,000	187,200	194,688	202,476	210,575	218,998
Op. Costs (4%)*	75,000	78,000	81,120	84,365	87,740	91,250
Total costs	255,000	265,200	275,808	286,841	298,315	310,248
Cash flow from operations	$ 70,000	$108,550	$154,004	$207,443	$270,112	$343,443
Subdivision						
Revenues (8%)*	$860,000	$928,800	$1,003,104	$1,083,352	$1,170,020	$1,263,622
COGS (4%)*	550,000	572,000	594,880	618,675	643,422	669,159
Op. Costs (4%)*	235,000	244,400	254,176	264,343	274,917	285,914
Total costs	785,000	816,400	849,056	883,018	918,339	955,073
Cash flow from operations	$75,000	$112,400	$154,048	$200,334	$251,681	$308,549

* Annual increases given in question.

21-30 (Cont'd.)

2.

Year	P.V. Factor for 10%	Homebuilders Cash Flow from Operations	Present Value	Kitchen Cash Flow from Operations	Present Value	Subdivision Cash Flow from Operations	Present Value
2001	0.909	$13,970	$12,699	$108,550	$98,672	$112,400	$102,172
2002	0.826	15,001	12,391	154,004	127,207	154,048	127,244
2003	0.751	16,097	12,089	207,443	155,790	200,334	150,451
2004	0.683	17,262	11,790	270,112	184,486	251,681	171,898
2005	0.621	18,500	11,488	343,443	213,278	308,549	191,609
			$60,457		$779,433		$743,374

Customer NPVs

Homebuilders	$ 60,457
Kitchen Constructors	779,433
Subdivision Erectors	743,374

3. Assume the 20% discount is given in 2001

	2000	2001	2002	2003	2004	2005
Revenues (5%)	$325,000	$260,000[a]	$273,000[b]	$286,650[b]	$300,982[b]	$316,031[b]
Total costs (4%)	255,000	265,200	275,808	286,841	298,315	310,248
Cash flow from operations	$ 70,000	$ (5,200)	$ (2,808)	$ (191)	$ 2,667	$ 5,783

[a] 20% price discount
[b] 5% annual increase

Net present value:

Year	P.V. Factor at 10%	Cash Flow from Operations	Present Value
2001	0.909	$(5,200)	$(4,727)
2002	0.826	(2,808)	(2,319)
2003	0.751	(191)	(143)
2004	0.683	2,667	1,822
2005	0.621	5,783	3,591
			$(1,776)

The 20% discount and reduced subsequent annual revenue reduces the NPV from $779,433 to ($1,776). This is a drop of $781,209 in NPV.

21-30 (Cont'd.)

Christen should consider whether the price discount demanded by Kitchen need be met in full to keep the account. The implication of meeting the full demand is that the account is minimally profitable at best. An equally serious concern is whether Christen's other two customers will demand comparable price discounts if Kitchen's full demands are met. The consequence would be very large reductions in the NPVs of all its customers.

Christen should also consider the reliability of the growth estimates used in computing the NPVs. Are the predicted differences in revenue growth rates based on reliable information? Many revenue growth estimates by salespeople turn out to be overestimates or occur over a longer time period than initially predicted.

21-32 (40 min.) **Replacement of a machine, income taxes, sensitivity.**

1. WRL Company should retain the old equipment because the net present value of the incremental cash flows is negative. The computations are presented below. In this format the present value factors appear at the bottom. All cash flows, year by year, are then converted into present values.

	After-Tax Cash Flows				
	1999a	**2000**	**2001**	**2002**	**2003**
Initial machine investment	$(120,000)				
Current disposal price of old machine	40,000				
Tax savings from loss on disposal of old machineb	4,000				
Recurring after-tax cash-operating savings:					
Variable ($0.06 × 300,000 × 0.6)c		$10,800	$10,800	$10,800	$10,800
Fixed ($1,000 × 0.6)d		600	600	600	600
Difference in income tax cash savings from depreciation deductionse		6,000	6,000	6,000	6,000
Additional after-tax cash flow from terminal disposal of new machine over old machine ($20,000 – $8,200)f					11,800
Net after-tax cash flows	$ (76,000)	$17,400	$17,400	$17,400	$29,200
Present value discount factors	1.000	0.862	0.743	0.641	0.552
Present value	$ (76,000)	$14,999	$12,928	$11,153	$16,118
Net present value	$ (20,802)				

a. Actually January 1, 2000

b.
Original cost of old machine:	$80,000
Depreciation taken during the first 3 years {[(80,000 – 10,000) ÷ 7] × 3}	30,000
Book value	50,000
Current disposal price:	40,000
Loss on disposal	$10,000
Tax rate	x 0.40
Tax savings from loss on disposal of old machine	$ 4,000

21-32 (Cont'd.)

c. Difference in recurring after-tax variable cash-operating savings, with 40% tax rate:
   $(\$0.20 - \$0.14) \times (300,000) \times (1 - 0.40) = \$10,800$

d. Difference in after-tax fixed cost savings, with 40% tax rate:
   $(\$15,000 - \$14,000) \times (1 - 0.40) = \$600$

e.

	Old Machine	New Machine
Initial machine investment	$80,000	$120,000
Terminal disposal price at end of useful life	10,000	20,000
Depreciable base	$70,000	$100,000
Annual depreciation using straight-line (7-year life)	$10,000	
Annual depreciation using straight-line (4-year life):		$ 25,000

Year (1)	Depreciation on Old Machine (2)	Depreciation on New Machine (3)	Additional Depreciation Deductions on New Machine (4) = (3) – (2)	Income Tax Cash Savings from Difference in Depreciation Deductions at 40% (4) × 40%
2000	$10,000	$25,000	$15,000	$6,000
2001	10,000	25,000	15,000	6,000
2002	10,000	25,000	15,000	6,000
2003	10,000	25,000	15,000	6,000

f.

	Old Machine	New Machine
Original cost	$80,000	$120,000
Total depreciation	70,000	100,000
Book value of machines on Dec. 31, 2003	10,000	20,000
Terminal disposal price of machines on Dec. 31, 2003	7,000	20,000
Loss on disposal of machines	3,000	0
Add tax savings on loss (40% of $3,000; 40% of $0)	1,200	0
After-tax cash flow from terminal disposal of machines ($7,000 + $1,200; $20,000 – $0)	$ 8,200	$ 20,000

Additional after-tax cash flow from terminal disposal of machines: $20,000 – $8,200 = $11,800.

21-32 (Cont'd.)

2.   Let the *additional* recurring after-tax variable cash operating savings required to make NPV = $0 be $X each year.

        The present value of an annuity of $1 per year for 4 years discounted at 16% = 2.798 (Appendix C, Table 4)

        To make NPV = 0, we need to generate cash savings with NPV of $20,802.

        That is $X (2.798)   = $20,802

                  X   =   20,802 ÷ 2.798 = $7,435

WRL must generate additional annual after-tax variable cash operating savings of $7,435.

3.   The nonquantitative factors that are important to WRL Company's decision include the following:

    a.   The lower operating costs (variable and fixed) of the new machine would enable WRL to meet future competitive or inflationary pressures to a greater degree than it could using the old machine.

    b.   If the increased efficiency of the new machine provides a labor or energy cost savings, then additional increases in these costs in the future would make the new machine more attractive.

    c.   Maintenance and servicing of both machines should be reviewed in terms of reliability of the manufacturer and the costs.

    d.   Potential technological advances in machinery over the next four years should be evaluated.

    f.   Space requirements for the new machine should be reviewed and compared with the space requirements of the present equipment to determine if more or less space is required.

21-34 (40 min.)   **Ethics, capital budgeting.**

1a. Refer to the specific standards of competence, confidentiality, integrity, and objectivity in "Standards of Ethical Conduct for Management Accountants," (Chapter 1 p.15) George Watson's conduct in giving Helen Dodge specific instructions on preparing the second revision of the proposal is unethical because his conduct violates the following specific standards.

Competence
Watson has the responsibility to perform his professional duties in accordance with relevant technical standards, such as using conservatism and realistic estimates in the net present value analysis. Management accountants should prepare complete and clear reports and recommendations after appropriate analyses of relevant and reliable information.

Confidentiality
Watson should refrain from using or appearing to use confidential information acquired in the course of his work for unethical advantage or personal gain (saving on commuting time and costs).

Integrity
Watson has the responsibility to advise all parties of any potential conflict of interest. Watson should communicate unfavorable as well as favorable information and professional judgments and opinions.

Objectivity
Watson has the responsibility to disclose fully all relevant information that can influence an intended user's understanding of the analysis.

1b. Helen Dodge's revised proposal for the warehouse conversion is unethical because her actions violate the following standards.

Competence
Although the estimates used in the analysis are based on management's judgment, Dodge's action in changing reasonable estimates to remote assumptions is unethical. Management accountants have the responsibility to prepare complete and clear reports and recommendations after appropriate analysis of relevant and reliable information.

Integrity
Dodge has the responsibility to avoid conflicts of interest, refrain from subverting the attainment of the organization's legitimate and ethical objectives (profitability), and refrain from engaging in or supporting any activity that would discredit the profession.

Objectivity
Dodge has the responsibility to communicate information fairly and objectively and to disclose fully, all relevant information that can influence an intended user's understanding.

2. Steps that Helen Dodge should follow in attempting to resolve this situation are as follows:

    - Dodge should first investigate and see if Evans Company has an established policy for resolving conflict, and she should follow this policy if it does exist.
    - Since it appears that George Watson, Dodge's superior, is involved, there is no need to confront Watson or discuss this issue with him any further. Dodge should present the situation to the next higher level, the vice president of finance, for resolution.
    - If the issue is not resolved to Dodge's satisfaction, she should continue to successive higher levels, including the Audit Committee and the Board of Directors.
    - Dodge should clarify the concepts of the issue at hand in a confidential discussion with an objective advisor, i.e., a peer.
    - If the situation is still unresolved after exhausting all levels of internal review, Dodge will have no recourse but to resign and submit an informative memorandum to an appropriate representative of the organization.
    - Unless legally bound (which does not appear to be the case in this situation), it is inappropriate to have communication about this situation with authorities and individuals not employed or engaged by the organization.

CHAPTER 22
MANAGEMENT CONTROL SYSTEMS, TRANSFER PRICING, AND MULTINATIONAL CONSIDERATIONS

22-2   To be effective, management control systems should be (a) closely aligned to an organization's strategies and goals, (b) designed to fit the organization's structure and the decision-making responsibility of individual managers, and (c) able to motivate managers and employees to put in effort to attain selected goals desired by top management.

22-4   The chapter cites five benefits of decentralization:
1.   Creates greater responsiveness to local needs
2.   Leads to quicker decision making
3.   Increases motivation
4.   Aids management development and learning
5.   Sharpens the focus of managers

The chapter cites four costs of decentralization:
1.   Leads to suboptimal decision making
2.   Results in duplication of activities
3.   Decreases loyalty toward the organization as a whole
4.   Increases costs of gathering information

22-6   No. A transfer price is the price one subunit of an organization charges for a product or service supplied to another subunit of the same organization. The two segments can be cost centers, profit centers, or investment centers. For example, the allocation of service department costs to production departments that are set up as either cost centers or investment centers is an example of transfer pricing.

22-8   Transfer prices should have the following properties. They should
1.   promote goal congruence,
2.   be useful for evaluating subunit performance,
3.   sustain a high level of management effort, and
4.   preserve a high level of subunit autonomy in decision making.

22-10   Transferring products or services at market prices generally leads to optimal decisions when (a) the intermediate market is perfectly competitive, (b) interdependencies of subunits are minimal, and (c) there are no additional costs or benefits to the corporation as a whole in using the market instead of transacting internally.

22-12   Reasons why a dual-pricing approach to transfer pricing is not widely used in practice include:
1.   The manager of the division using a cost-based method does not have sufficient incentives to control costs.
2.   This approach does not provide clear signals to division managers about the level of decentralization top management wants.
3.   This approach tends to insulate managers from the frictions of the market place.

22-14 Yes. The general transfer-pricing guideline specifies that the minimum transfer price equals the additional *outlay costs* per unit incurred up to the point of transfer *plus* the *opportunity costs* per unit to the supplying division. When the supplying division has idle capacity, its opportunity costs are zero; when the supplying division has no idle capacity, its opportunity costs are positive. Hence, the minimum transfer price will vary depending on whether the supplying division has idle capacity or not.

22-16 (25 min.) **Decentralization, responsibility centers**.

1. The manufacturing plants in the Manufacturing Division are cost centers. Senior management determines the manufacturing schedule based on the quantity of each type of lighting product specified by the sales and marketing division and detailed studies of the time and cost to manufacture each type of product. Manufacturing managers are accountable only for costs. They are evaluated based on achieving target output within budgeted costs.

2a. If manufacturing and marketing managers were to directly negotiate the prices for manufacturing various products, Quinn should evaluate manufacturing plant managers as profit centers—revenues received from marketing minus the costs incurred to produce and sell output.

2b. Quinn Corporation would be better off decentralizing its marketing and manufacturing decisions and evaluating each division as a profit center. Decentralization would encourage plant managers to increase total output to achieve the greatest profitability, and motivate plant managers to cut their costs to increase margins. Manufacturing managers would be motivated to design their operations according to the criteria that meet the marketing managers' approval, thereby improving cooperation between manufacturing and marketing.

Under Quinn's existing system, manufacturing managers had every incentive not to improve. Manufacturing managers' incentives were to get as high a cost target as possible so that they could produce output within budgeted costs. Any significant improvements could result in the target costs being lowered for the next year, increasing the possibility of not achieving budgeted costs. By the same line of reasoning, manufacturing managers would also try to limit their production so that production quotas would not be increased in the future. Decentralizing manufacturing and marketing decisions overcomes these problems.

22-18 (35 min.) **Multinational transfer pricing, effect of alternative transfer-pricing methods, global income tax minimization.**

1.   This is a three-country, three-division transfer-pricing problem with three alternative transfer-pricing methods. Summary data in U.S. dollars are:

China Plant

Variable costs:	1,000 Yuan ÷ 8 Yuan per $ = $125 per subunit
Fixed costs:	1,800 Yuan ÷ 8 Yuan per $ = $225 per subunit

South Korea Plant

Variable costs:	360,000 Won ÷ 1,200 Won per $ = $300 per unit
Fixed costs:	480,000 Won ÷ 1,200 Won per $ = $400 per unit

U.S. Plant

Variable costs:	= $100 per unit
Fixed costs:	= $200 per unit

Market prices for private-label sale alternatives:

China Plant:	3,600 Yuan ÷ 8 Yuan per $	= $450 per subunit
South Korea Plant:	1,560,000 Won ÷ 1,200 Won per $	= $1,300 per unit

The transfer prices under each method are:

a.   Market price
   • China to South Korea = $450 per subunit
   • South Korea to U.S. Plant = $1,300 per unit

b.   200% of full costs
   • China to South Korea
       2.0 ($125 + $225) = $700 per subunit
   • South Korea to U.S. Plant
       2.0 ($700 + $300 + $400) = $2,800 per unit

c.   300% of variable costs
   • China to South Korea
       3.0 ($125) = $375 per subunit
   • South Korea to U.S. Plant
       3.0 ($375 + $300) = $2,025 per unit

	Method A Internal Transfers at Market Price	Method B Internal Transfers at 200% of Full Costs	Method C Internal Transfers at 300% of Variable Costs
1. *China Division*			
Division revenues per unit	$ 450	$ 700	$ 375
Deduct:			
Division variable costs per unit	125	125	125
Division fixed costs per unit	225	225	225
Division operating income per unit	100	350	25
Income tax at 40%	40	140	10
Division net income per unit	$ 60	$ 210	$ 15
2. *South Korea Division*			
Division revenues per unit	$1,300	$2,800	$2,025
Deduct:			
Transferred-in costs per unit	450	700	375
Division variable costs per unit	300	300	300
Division fixed costs per unit	400	400	400
Division operating income per unit	150	1,400	950
Income tax at 20%	30	280	190
Division net income per unit	$ 120	$1,120	$ 760
3. *United States Division*			
Division revenues per unit	$3,200	$3,200	$3,200
Deduct:			
Transferred-in costs per unit	1,300	2,800	2,025
Division variable costs per unit	100	100	100
Division fixed costs per unit	200	200	200
Division operating income per unit	1,600	100	875
Income tax at 30%	480	30	262.5
Division net income per unit	$1,120	$ 70	$ 612.5

2. Division net income:

	Market Price	200% of Full Costs	300% of Variable Cost
China Division	$ 60	$ 210	$ 15.00
South Korea Division	120	1,120	760.00
U.S. Division	1,120	70	612.50
User Friendly Computer Inc.	$1,300	$1,400	$1,387.50

User Friendly will maximize its net income by using the 200% of full costs, transfer-pricing method. This is because the 200% of full cost method sources most income in the countries with the lower income tax rates.

22-20 (30 min.) **Effect of alternative transfer-pricing methods on division operating income.**

	Internal Transfers at Market Prices Method A	Internal Transfers at 110% of Full Costs Method B
1. *Mining Division*		
Revenues:		
$90, $66[1] × 400,000 units	$36,000,000	$26,400,000
Deduct:		
Division variable costs:		
$52[2] × 400,000 units	20,800,000	20,800,000
Division fixed costs:		
$8[3] × 400,000 units	3,200,000	3,200,000
Division operating income	$12,000,000	$ 2,400,000
Metals Division		
Revenues:		
$150 × 400,000 units	$60,000,000	$60,000,000
Deduct:		
Transferred-in costs:		
$90, $66 × 400,000 units	36,000,000	26,400,000
Division variable costs:		
$36[4] × 400,000 units	14,400,000	14,400,000
Division fixed costs:		
$15[5] × 400,000 units	6,000,000	6,000,000
Division operating income	$ 3,600,000	$13,200,000

[1] $66 = $60 × 110%

[2] Variable cost per unit in Mining Division = Direct materials + Direct manufacturing labor + 75% of Manufacturing overhead = $12 + $16 + 75% × $32 = $52

[3] Fixed cost per unit = 25% of Manufacturing overhead = 25% × $32 = $8

[4] Variable cost per unit in Metals Division = Direct materials + Direct manufacturing labor + 40% of Manufacturing overhead = $6 + $20 + 40% × $25 = $36

[5] Fixed cost per unit in Metals Division = 60% of Manufacturing overhead = 60% × $25 = $15

22-20 (Cont'd.)

2.   Bonus paid to division managers at 1% of division operating income will be as follows:

	Method A Internal Transfers at Market Prices	Method B Internal Transfers at 110% of Full Costs
Mining Division manager's bonus		
(1% × $12,000,000; 1% × $2,400,000)	$120,000	$ 24,000
Metals Division manager's bonus		
(1% × $3,600,000; 1% × $13,200,000)	36,000	132,000

The Mining Division manager will prefer Method A (transfer at market prices) because this method gives $120,000 of bonus rather than $24,000 under Method B (transfers at 110% of full costs). The Metals Division manager will prefer Method B because this method gives $132,000 of bonus rather than $36,000 under Method A.

3.   Brian Jones, the manager of the Mining Division, will appeal to the existence of a competitive market to price transfers at market prices. Using market prices for transfers in these conditions leads to goal congruence. Division managers acting in their own best interests make decisions that are also in the best interests of the company as a whole.

Jones will further argue that setting transfer prices based on cost will cause Jones to pay no attention to controlling costs since all costs incurred will be recovered from the Metals Division at 110% of full costs.

22-22 (25 min.) General guideline, transfer price range.

1.   If the Screen Division sells screens in the outside market, it will receive, for each screen, the market price of the screen minus variable marketing and distribution costs per screen = $110 − $4 = $106. The incremental cost of manufacturing each screen is $70. The Screen Division is operating at capacity. Hence, the opportunity cost per screen of selling the screen to the Assembly Division rather than in the outside market is the contribution margin the Screen Division would forgo if it transferred screens internally rather than sold them in the outside market.

Contribution margin per screen = $106 − $70 = $36.

Using the general guideline,

$$\text{Minimum transfer price per screen} = \text{Incremental costs per screen up to the point of transfer} + \text{Opportunity costs per screen to the selling division}$$

That is,   Minimum transfer price per screen = $70 + $36 = $106

22-22 (Cont'd.)

2. If the two division managers were to negotiate a transfer price, the range of possible transfer prices is between $106 and $112 per screen. As calculated in requirement 1, the Screen Division will be willing to supply screens to the Assembly Division only if the transfer price equals or exceeds $106 per screen.

If the Assembly Division were to purchase the screens in the outside market, it will incur a cost of $112, the cost of the screen equal to $110 plus variable purchasing costs of $2 per screen. Hence, the Assembly Division will be willing to buy screens from the Screen Division only if the price does not exceed $112 per screen. Within the price range of $106 and $112 per screen, each division will be willing to transact with the other. The exact transfer price between $106 and $112 will depend on the bargaining strengths of the two divisions.

22-24   (30 min.)   Multinational transfer pricing, goal congruence.
(Continuation of 22-23)

1. After-tax operating income if Mornay Company sold all 1,000 units of Product 4A36 in the United States is

Revenues, $600 × 1,000 units	$600,000
Full manufacturing costs, $500 × 1,000 units	500,000
Operating income	100,000
Income taxes at 40%	40,000
After-tax operating income	$ 60,000

From Exercise 22-23, requirement 1, Mornay Company's after-tax operating income if it transfers 1,000 units of Product 4A36 to Austria at full manufacturing cost and sells the units in Austria is $112,000. Therefore, Mornay should sell the 1,000 units in Austria.

2. Transferring Product 4A36 at the full manufacturing cost of the U.S. Division minimizes import duties and taxes (Exercise 22-23, requirement 2), but creates zero operating income for the U.S Division. Acting autonomously, the U.S. Division manager would maximize division operating income by selling Product 4A36 in the U.S. market, which results in $60,000 in after-tax division operating income as calculated in requirement 1, rather than by transferring Product 4A36 to the Austrian division at full manufacturing cost. Hence, the transfer price calculated in requirement 2 of Exercise 22-23 will not result in actions that are optimal for Mornay Company as a whole.

3. The minimum transfer price at which the U.S. division manager acting autonomously will agree to transfer Product 4A36 to the Austrian division is $600 per unit. Any transfer price less than $600 will leave the U.S. Division's performance worse than selling directly in the U.S. market. Because the U.S. Division can sell as many units of Product 4A36 in the U.S. market, there is an opportunity cost of transferring the product internally equal to $250 (selling price $600 − variable manufacturing costs, $350).

22-24 (Cont'd.)

$$
\begin{aligned}
\text{Minimum transfer} \atop \text{price per unit} \quad = \quad &\text{Incremental costs per} \atop \text{unit up to the point of} \atop \text{transfer} \quad + \quad \text{Opportunity costs per} \atop \text{unit to the selling} \atop \text{(U.S.) division}
\end{aligned}
$$

$$= \quad \$350 + \$250 = \$600$$

This transfer price will result in Mornay Company as a whole paying more import duties and taxes than the answer to Exercise 22-23, requirement 2, as calculated below:

U.S. Division

Revenues, $600 × 1,000 units	$600,000
Full manufacturing costs	500,000
Division operating income	100,000
Division income taxes at 40%	40,000
Division after-tax operating income	$ 60,000

Austrian Division

Revenues, $750 × 1,000 units`	$750,000
Transferred in costs, $600 × 1,000 units	600,000
Import duties at 10% of transferred-in price, $60 × 1,000 units	60,000
Division operating income	90,000
Division income taxes at 44%	39,600
Division after-tax operating income	$ 50,400

Total import duties and income taxes at transfer prices of $500 and $600 per unit for 1,000 units of Product 4A36 follow:

		Transfer Price of $500 per Unit (Exercise 22-23, Requirement 2)	Transfer Price of $600 per Unit
(a)	U.S. income taxes	$ 0	$ 40,000
(b)	Austrian import duties	50,000	60,000
(c)	Austrian income taxes	88,000	39,600
		$138,000	$139,600

The minimum transfer price that the U.S. division manager acting autonomously would agree to results in Mornay Company paying $1,600 in additional import duties and income taxes.

A student who has done the calculations shown in Exercise 22-23, requirement 2, can calculate the additional taxes from a $600 transfer price more directly, as follows:

22-24 (Cont'd.)

Every $1 increase in the transfer price per unit over $500 results in additional import duty and taxes of $0.016 per unit

So, a $100 increase ($600 – $500) per unit will result in additional import duty and taxes of $0.016 × 100 = $1.60

For 1,000 units transferred, this equals $1.60 × 1,000 = $1,600

22-26 (5 min) **Transfer-pricing problem.** (Continuation of 22-25)

The company as a whole would benefit in this situation if C purchased from outside suppliers. The $15,000 disadvantage to the company as a whole by purchasing from the outside supplier would be more than offset by the $30,000 contribution margin of A's sale of 1,000 units to other customers.

Purchase costs from outside supplier, 1,000 units × $135		$135,000
Deduct variable cost savings, 1,000 units × $120		120,000
Net cost to company as a whole by buying from outside		$ 15,000
A's sales to other customers, 1,000 units × $155		$155,000
Deduct:		
Variable manufacturing costs, $120 × 1,000 units	$120,000	
Variable marketing costs, $5 × 1,000 units	5,000	
Variable costs		125,000
Contribution margin from selling A to other customers		$ 30,000

22-28 (30–40 min.) **Pricing in imperfect markets.** (Continuation of 22-27)

An alternative presentation, which contains the same numerical answers, can be found at the end of this solution.

1.   Potential contribution from external intermediate sale is

1,000 × ($195 – $120)	$75,000
Contribution through keeping price at $200 is	
800 × $80.	64,000
Forgone contribution by transferring 200 units	$11,000

Opportunity cost per unit to the supplying division by transferring internally:

$$\frac{\$11,000}{200} = \$55$$

Transfer price = $120 + $55 = $175

22-9

22-28 (Cont'd.)

An alternative approach to obtaining the same answer is to recognize that the incremental or outlay cost is the same for all 1,000 units in question. Therefore, the total revenue desired by A would be the same for selling outside or inside.

Let X equal the transfer price at which Division A is indifferent between selling all units outside versus transferring 200 units inside.
$$1{,}000\ (\$195) = 800\ (\$200) + 200X$$
$$X = \$175$$

The $175 price will lead to the correct decision. Division B will not buy from Division A because its total costs of $175 + $150 will exceed its prospective selling price of $300. Division A will then sell 1,000 units at $195 to the outside; Division A and the company will have a contribution margin of $75,000. Otherwise, if 800 units were sold at $200 and 200 units were transferred to Division B, the company would have a contribution of $64,000 plus $6,000 (200 units of final product × $30), or $70,000.

A comparison might be drawn regarding the computation of the appropriate transfer prices between the preceding problem and this problem:

$$\begin{matrix}\text{Minimum} \\ \text{transfer price}\end{matrix} = \begin{pmatrix}\text{Additional } incremental\ costs \\ \text{per unit incurred up} \\ \text{to the point of transfer}\end{pmatrix} + \begin{pmatrix}Opportunity\ costs \\ \text{per unit to} \\ \text{Division A}\end{pmatrix}$$

Perfect markets: = $120 + (Selling price – Outlay costs per unit)
= $120 + ($200 – $120) = $200

Imperfect markets: $= \$120 + \dfrac{\text{Marginal revenues} - \text{Outlay costs}}{\text{Number of units transferred}}$

$$= \$120 + \frac{\$35{,}000^a - \$24{,}000^b}{200} = \$175$$

[a]Marginal revenues of Division A from selling 200 units outside rather than transferring to Division B
= ($195 × 1,000) – ($200 × 800) = $195,000 – $160,000 = $35,000.
[b]Incremental (outlay) costs incurred by Division A to produce 200 units
= $120 × 200 = $24,000.

Therefore, selling price ($195) and marginal revenues per unit ($175 = $35,000 ÷ 200) are not the same.

The following discussion is optional. These points should be explored only if there is sufficient class time:

Some students will erroneously say that the "new" market price of $195 is the appropriate transfer price. They will claim that the general guideline says that the transfer price should be $120 + ($195 – $120) = $195, the market price. This conclusion assumes a perfect market.

22-28 (Cont'd.)

But, here, there are imperfections in the intermediate market. That is, the market price is *not* a good approximation of alternative revenue. If a division's sales are heavy enough to reduce market prices, marginal revenue will be less than market price.

It is true that *either* $195 or $175 will lead to the correct decision by B in this case. But suppose that B's variable costs were $120 instead of $150. Then B would buy at a transfer price of $175 (but not at a price of $195, because then B would earn a negative contribution of $15 per unit [$300 − ($195 + $120)]. Note that if B's variable costs were $120, transfers would be desirable:

Division A contribution is:
  $800 \times (\$200 - \$120) + 200\ (\$175 - \$120)$ = $75,000
Division B contribution is:
  $200 \times [\$300 - (\$175 + \$120)]$ = <u>1,000</u>
  Total contribution   <u>$76,000</u>

Or the same facts can be analyzed for the company as a whole:

Sales of intermediate product,
  $800 \times (\$200 - \$120)$ = $64,000
Sales of final products,
  $200 \times [300 - (\$120 + \$120)]$ = <u>12,000</u>
  Total contribution   <u>$76,000</u>

If the transfer price were $195, B would not accept the transfer and would not earn any contribution. As shown above, Division A and the company as a whole will earn a total contribution of $75,000 instead of $76,000.

2. a. Division A can sell 900 units at $195 to the outside market and 100 units to Division B, or 800 at $200 to the outside market and 200 units to Division B. Note that, under both alternatives, 100 units can be transferred to Division B at no opportunity cost to A.

Using the general guideline, the minimum transfer price of *the first 100 units* [901–1000] is:

$$TP_1 = \$120 + 0 = \$120$$

If Division B needs 100 additional units, the opportunity cost to A is not zero, because Division A will then have to sell only 800 units to the outside market for a contribution of $800 \times (\$200 - \$120) = \$64,000$ instead of 900 units for a contribution of $900\ (\$195 - \$120) = \$67,500$. Each unit sold to B in addition to the first 100 units has an opportunity cost to A of $(\$67,500 - \$64,000) \div 100 = \$35$.

Using the general guideline, the minimum transfer price of *the next 100 units* [801–900] is:

$$TP_2 = \$120 + \$35 = \$155$$

22-28 (Cont'd.)

Alternatively, the computation could be:

Increase in contribution from 100 more units, 100 × $75	$7,500
Loss in contribution on 800 units, 800 × ($80 − $75)	<u>4,000</u>
Net "marginal revenue"	<u>$3,500</u> ÷ 100 units = $35

(Minimum) transfer price applicable to first 100 units offered by A is $120 + $0	=	$120 per unit
(Minimum) transfer price applicable to next 100 units offered by A is $120 + ($3,500 ÷ 100)	=	$155 per unit
(Minimum) transfer price applicable to next 800 units	=	$195 per unit

b.   The manager of Division B will not want to purchase more than 100 units because the units at $155 would decrease his contribution ($155 + $150 > $300). Because the manager of B does not buy more than 100 units, the manager of A will have 900 units available for sale to the outside market. The manager of A will strive to maximize the contribution by selling them all at $195.

This solution maximizes the company's contribution:

900 × ($195 − $120)	=	$67,500
100 × ($300 − $270)	=	<u>3,000</u>
		<u>$70,500</u>

which compares favorably to:

800 × ($200 − $120)	=	$64,000
200 × ($300 − $270)	=	<u>6,000</u>
		<u>$70,000</u>

ALTERNATIVE PRESENTATION (by James Patell)

1.   Company Viewpoint

a: *Sell 1,000 outside at $195*			b: *Sell 800 outside at $200, transfer 200*		
Price	$195		Transfer price	$200	
Variable costs	<u>120</u>		Variable costs	<u>120</u>	
Contribution	<u>$ 75</u> × 1,000 = $75,000		Contribution	<u>$ 80</u> × 800 = $64,000

Total contribution given up if transfer occurs[*]
   = $75,000 − $64,000 = $11,000

22-28 (Cont'd.)

On a per-unit basis, the relevant costs are:

$$\underset{\text{point of transfer}}{\text{Incremental costs to}} + \underset{\text{Division A of transfer}}{\text{Opportunity costs to}} = \text{Transfer price}$$

$$\$120 + \frac{\$11,000}{200} = \$175$$

By formula, costs are:

$$\begin{bmatrix} \text{Incremental costs} \\ \text{to point} \\ \text{of transfer} \end{bmatrix} + \begin{bmatrix} \text{Lost opportunity to} \\ \text{sell 200 at \$195, for} \\ \text{contribution of \$75} \end{bmatrix} - \begin{bmatrix} \text{Gain when 1st 800} \\ \text{sell at \$200} \\ \text{instead of \$195} \end{bmatrix}$$

$$= \qquad \$120 + \frac{200 \times \$75}{200} - \frac{[(\$200 - \$195) \times 800]}{200}$$

$$= \qquad \$120 + \$75 - \$20 = \$175$$

*Contribution of $30 per unit by B is not given up if transfer occurs, so it is not relevant here.

2. a.   At most, Division A can sell only 900 units and can produce 1,000. Therefore, at least 100 units should be transferred, at a transfer price no less than $120. The question is whether or not a second 100 units should be transferred.

Company Viewpoint

a: *Sell 900 outside at $195*		b: *Sell 800 outside at $200, transfer 100*	
Transfer price	$195	Transfer price	$200
Variable cost	120	Variable cost	120
Contribution	$ 75 × 900 = $67,500	Contribution	$ 80 × 800 = $64,000

Total contribution forgone if transfer of 100 units occurs
= $67,500 − $64,000 = $3,500 (or $35 per unit)

$$\underset{\text{point of transfer}}{\text{Incremental costs to}} + \underset{\text{Division A of transfer}}{\text{Opportunity costs to}} = \text{Transfer price}$$

$$\$120 \quad + \qquad \$35 \qquad = \qquad \$155$$

22-28 (Cont'd.)

b. By formula:

$$\left[\begin{array}{c}\text{Incremental costs}\\ \text{to point}\\ \text{of transfer}\end{array}\right] + \left[\begin{array}{c}\text{Lost opportunity to}\\ \text{sell 100 at \$195, for}\\ \text{contribution of \$75}\end{array}\right] - \left[\begin{array}{c}\text{Gain when 1st 800}\\ \text{sell at \$200}\\ \text{instead of \$195}\end{array}\right]$$

$$= \ \$120 + \frac{100 \times \$75}{100} - \frac{[(\$200 - \$195) \times 800]}{100}$$

$$= \ \$120 + \$75 - \$40 = \$155$$

Transfer Price Schedule (minimum acceptable transfer price)

Units	Transfer Price
0–100	$120
101–200	$155
201–1,000	$195

22-30 (30 min.) Goal congruence problems with cost-plus transfer-pricing methods, dual-pricing system. (Continuation of 22-29)

1. Two examples of goal congruence problems are:
   a. Division managers using an outside supplier when Oceanic Product's operating income is maximized by buying from an internal division.
   b. Division managers selling to an outside purchaser when it is better for Oceanic Products to further process internally.

2. *Transfers to buying divisions at market price*
   Harvesting Division to Processing Division = $1.00 per pound of raw tuna
   Processing Division to Marketing Division = $5.00 per pound of processed tuna

   Transfers out to selling divisions at 150% of full costs
   Harvesting Division to Processing Division
   $$= 1.5 \ (\$0.20 + \$0.40) = \$0.90 \text{ per pound of raw tuna}$$
   Processing Division to Marketing Division
   $$= 1.5 \ [(\$1.00 \times 2)^* + \$0.80 + \$0.60] = \$5.10 \text{ per pound of processed tuna}$$

   *The transferred-in cost is $1.00 per pound of raw tuna. It takes two pounds of raw tuna to produce one pound of tuna fillets.

22-30 (Cont'd.)

Tuna Harvesting Division

Division revenues, $0.90 × 1,000	$ 900
Division variable costs, $0.20 × 1,000	200
Division fixed costs, $0.40 × 1,000	400
Division total costs	600
Division operating income	$ 300

Tuna Processing Division

Division revenues, $5.10 × 500	$2,550
Transferred-in costs, $1.00 × 1,000	1,000
Division variable costs, $0.80 × 500	400
Division fixed costs, $0.60 × 500	300
Division total costs	1,700
Division operating income	$ 850

Tuna Marketing Division

Division revenues, $12 × 300	$3,600
Transferred-in costs, $5 × 500	2,500
Division variable costs, $0.30 × 300	90
Division fixed costs, $0.70 × 300	210
Division total costs	2,800
Division operating income	$ 800

3.

	Division Operating Income
Tuna Harvesting Division	$ 300
Tuna Processing Division	850
Tuna Marketing Division	800
Oceanic Products	$1,950

The overall company operating income from harvesting 1,000 pounds of raw tuna and its further processing and marketing is $2,000 (see Problem 22-29, requirement 1).

A dual transfer-pricing method entails using different transfer prices for transfers into the buying division and transfers out of the supplying division. There is no reason why the sum of division operating incomes should equal the total company operating income.

4. Problems which may arise if Oceanic Products uses the dual transfer-pricing system include:

    a.   It may reduce the incentives of the supplying division to control costs since every $1 of cost of the supplying division is transferred out to the buying division at $1.50. It may also reduce the incentives of the supplying divisions to keep abreast of market conditions.

    b.   A dual transfer-pricing system does not provide clear signals to the individual divisions about the level of decentralization top management seeks.

22-32 (30–40 min.)   **Multinational transfer pricing and taxation.**

1.   Anita Corporation and its subsidiaries' operating income if it manufactures the machine and sells it in Brazil or in Switzerland follows:

	If Sold in Brazil	If Sold in Switzerland
Revenue	$1,000,000	$950,000
Costs		
Manufacturing costs	500,000	500,000
Transportation and modification costs	200,000	250,000
Total costs	700,000	750,000
Operating income	$ 300,000	$200,000

Anita Corporation maximizes operating income by manufacturing the machine and selling it in Brazil.

2.   *Anita Corporation will not sell if the transfer price is less than $500,000*—its outlay costs of manufacturing the machine.

The Brazilian subsidiary will not agree to a transfer price of more than $800,000. At a price of $800,000, the Brazilian subsidiary's incremental operating income from purchasing and selling the milling machine will be $0 ($1,000,000 – $200,000 – $800,000).

The Swiss subsidiary will not agree to a transfer price of more than $700,000. At a price of $700,000, the Swiss subsidiary's incremental operating income from purchasing and selling the milling machine will be $0 ($950,000 – $250,000 – $700,000).

Any transfer price between $700,000 and $800,000 will achieve the optimal actions determined in requirement 1. For prices in this range, Anita Corporation will be willing to sell, the Brazilian Corporation willing to buy, and the Swiss subsidiary not interested in acquiring the machine.

Where within the range of $700,000 to $800,000 that the transfer price will be set depends on the bargaining powers of the Anita Corporation and the Brazilian subsidiary managers. Anita Corporation's main source of bargaining power comes from the threat of selling the machine to the Swiss subsidiary. If the transfer price is set at $700,000, then

Anita's operating income, $700,000 – $500,000	$200,000
Brazilian subsidiary's operating income, $1,000,000 – $700,000 – $200,000	100,000
Overall operating income of Anita and subsidiaries	$300,000

Note that the general guideline could be used to derive the minimum transfer price.

$$\begin{matrix} \text{Minimum} \\ \text{transfer price} \end{matrix} = \begin{pmatrix} \text{Additional } \textit{incremental} \text{ costs} \\ \text{per unit incurred up} \\ \text{to the point of transfer} \end{pmatrix} + \begin{pmatrix} \textit{Opportunity} \text{ costs} \\ \text{per unit to the} \\ \text{supplying division} \end{pmatrix}$$

$$= \quad \$500,000 + \$200,000 = \$700,000$$

22-16

22-32 (Cont'd.)

Anita's opportunity cost of supplying the machine to the Brazilian subsidiary is the $200,000 in operating income it forgoes by not supplying the machine to the Swiss subsidiary. Note that competition between the Brazilian and Swiss subsidiaries means that the transfer price will be at least $700,000.

3.   Consider the optimal transfer prices that can be set to minimize taxes (for Anita and its subsidiaries) (a) for transfers from Anita to the Brazilian subsidiary and (b) for transfers from Anita to the Swiss subsidiary.

a.   Transfers from Anita to the Brazilian subsidiary should "allocate" as much of the operating income to Anita as possible, since the tax rate in the United States is lower than in Brazil for this transaction. Therefore, these transfers should be priced at the highest allowable transfer price of $700,000 to minimize overall company taxes.

Taxes paid:

Anita, 0.40 × ($700,000 – $500,000)	$ 80,000
Brazilian subsidiary, 0.60 × ($1,000,000 – $700,000 – $200,000)	60,000
Total taxes paid by Anita Corporation and its subsidiaries on transfers to Brazil	$140,000

After-tax operating income:

Anita, ($700,000 – $500,000) – $80,000	$120,000
Brazilian subsidiary ($1,000,000 – $700,000 – $200,000) – $60,000	40,000
Total after-tax operating income for Anita Corporation and its subsidiaries on transfers to Brazil	$160,000

b.   Transfers from Anita to the Swiss subsidiary should "allocate" as little of the operating income to Anita as possible, since the tax rate in the United States is higher than in Switzerland for this transaction. Therefore, these transfers should be priced at the lowest allowable transfer price of $500,000 to minimize overall company taxes.

Taxes paid:

Anita, 0.40 × ($500,000 – $500,000)	$ 0
Swiss subsidiary, 0.15 × ($950,000 – $500,000 – $250,000)	30,000
Total taxes paid by Anita Corporation and its subsidiaries on transfers to Switzerland	$30,000

After-tax operating income

Anita, ($500,000 – $500,000) – $0	$ 0
Swiss subsidiary ($950,000 – $500,000 – $250,000) – $30,000	170,000
Total net income for Anita Corporation and its subsidiaries on transfers to Switzerland	$170,000

From the viewpoint of Anita Corporation and its subsidiaries together, overall after-tax operating income is maximized if the machine is transferred to the Swiss subsidiary (after-tax operating income of $170,000 versus after-tax operating income of $160,000 if the machine is transferred to the Brazilian subsidiary). Note that the corporation and its subsidiaries trade off the lower overall before-tax operating income achieved by transferring to the Swiss subsidiary

22-32 (Cont'd.)

with the lower taxes that result from such a transfer. Hence, (a) the equipment should be manufactured by Anita, and (b) it should be transferred to the Swiss subsidiary at a price of $500,000.

4.   As in requirement 2, the Brazilian subsidiary would be willing to bid up the price to $800,000, while the Swiss subsidiary would be willing to pay only up to $700,000. Anita Corporation, acting autonomously, would like to maximize its own after-tax operating income by transferring the machine at as high a transfer price as possible. As in requirement 2, the price would end up being at least $700,000. Since the taxing authorities will not allow prices above $700,000, the transfer price will be $700,000. At this transfer price, the Swiss subsidiary makes zero operating income and will not be interested in the machine. Hence, Anita Corporation will sell the machine to the Brazilian subsidiary at a price of $700,000.

The answer is not the same as in requirement 3, because, acting autonomously, the objective of each manager is to maximize after-tax operating income of his or her own company rather than after-tax operating income of Anita Corporation and its subsidiaries as a whole. Goal congruence is not achieved in this setting.

Can the company induce the managers to take the right actions without infringing on their autonomy? This outcome is probably not going to be easy.

One possibility might be to implement a dual-pricing scheme in which the machine is transferred at cost ($500,000), but under which Anita Corporation is credited with after-tax operating income earned on the machine by the subsidiary it ships the machine to (in this example, $170,000 of net income earned by the Swiss subsidiary). A negative feature of this arrangement is that the $170,000 of after-tax operating income will be "double counted" and recognized on the books of both Anita Corporation and the Swiss subsidiary.

Another possibility might be to evaluate the managers on the basis of overall after-tax operating income of Anita Corporation and its subsidiaries. This approach will induce a more global perspective, but at the cost of inducing a larger noncontrollable element in each manager's performance measure.

22-34 (40–50 min.)   Transfer pricing, utilization of capacity.

1.

	Super-chip	Okay-chip
Selling price	$60	$12
Direct materials	2	1
Direct manufacturing labor	28	7
Contribution margin per unit	$30	$ 4
Contribution margin per hour		
($30 ÷ 2; $4 ÷ 0.5)	$15	$ 8

Because the contribution margin per hour is higher for Super-chip than for Okay-chip, CIC should produce and sell as many Super-chips as it can and use the remaining available capacity to produce Okay-chip.

The total demand for Super-chips is 15,000 units, which would take 30,000 hours (15,000 × 2 hours per unit). CIC should use its remaining capacity of 20,000 hours (50,000 – 30,000) to produce 40,000 Okay-chips (20,000 ÷ 0.5).

22-34 (Cont'd.)

2. Options for manufacturing process-control unit

	Using Circuit Board	Using Super-chip
Selling price	$132	$132
Direct materials	60	2
Direct manufacturing labor (Super-chip)	0	28
Direct manufacturing labor (Process-control unit)	50	60
Contribution margin per unit	$ 22	$ 42

Overall Company Viewpoint

Alternative 1: No Transfer of Super-chips

Sell 15,000 Super-chips at contribution margin per unit of $30	$450,000
Transfer 0 Super-chips	0
Sell 40,000 Okay-chips at contribution margin per unit of $4	160,000
Sell 5,000 Control units at contribution margin per unit of $22	110,000
Total contribution margin	$720,000

Alternative 2: Transfer 5,000 Super-chips to Process-Control Division. These Super-chips would require 10,000 hours to manufacture, leaving only 10,000 hours for the manufacture of 20,000 Okay-chips (10,000 ÷ 0.5)

Sell 15,000 Super-chips at contribution margin per unit of $30	$450,000
Transfer 5,000 Super-chips to Process-Control Division	0
Sell 20,000 Okay-chips at contribution margin per unit of $4	80,000
Sell 5,000 Control units at contribution margin per unit of $42	210,000
Total contribution margin	$740,000

CIC is better off transferring 5,000 Super-chips to the Process-Control Division.

3.   For each Super-chip that is transferred, two hours of time (labor capacity) are given up in the Semiconductor Division, and, in those two hours, four Okay-chips could be produced, each contributing $4.

$$\begin{array}{rcl} \text{Minimum transfer price per Super-chip} & = & \text{Incremental cost per unit to the point of transfer} + \text{Opportunity cost per unit for the Semiconductor Division} \\ & = & \$30 \quad + \quad \$16 \\ & = & \$46 \text{ per unit} \end{array}$$

If the selling price for the process-control unit were firm at $132, the Process-Control Division would accept any transfer price up to $50 ($60 price of circuit board − $10 incremental labor cost if Super-chip used).

22-34 (Cont'd.)

However, consider what happens if the transfer price of Super-chip is set at, say, $49, and the price of the control unit drops to $108. From CIC's viewpoint:

	Using Circuit Board	Using Super-chip
Selling price	$108	$108
Direct materials	60	49
Direct manufacturing labor	50	60
Contribution margin per hour	$ –2	$ –1

Process-Control Division will not produce any control units. From the company's viewpoint, the contribution margin on the control unit if the Super-chip is used is:

Selling price	$108
Direct materials	2
Direct manufacturing labor (Super-chip)	28
Direct manufacturing labor (process-control unit)	60
Contribution margin per unit	$ 18

The contribution margin per unit from producing Super-chips for the process-control unit exceeds the contribution margin of $16 from producing 4 Okay-chips, each yielding a contribution margin of $4 per unit. Hence the Semiconductor Division should transfer 5,000 Super-chips as the following calculations show:

Alternative 1—No transfer (and, therefore, no sales of process-control units)

Sell 15,000 Super-chips at contribution margin per unit of $30	$450,000
Sell 40,000 Okay-chips at contribution margin per unit of $4	160,000
	$610,000

Alternative 2—Transfer 5,000 Super-chips.

Sell 15,000 Super-chips at contribution margin per unit of $30	$450,000
Sell 20,000 Okay-chips at contribution margin per unit of $4	80,000
Sell 5,000 control units at contribution margin per unit of $18	90,000
	$620,000

Therefore, if the price for the control unit is uncertain, the transfer price must be set at the minimum acceptable transfer price of $46.

4.   For a transfer of any amount between 0 and 10,000 Super-chips (which require 2 hours each to produce), the opportunity cost is the production of Okay-chips (which require ½ hour each). In this range, the relevant costs are equal to the transfer price of $46 established in part 3.

If more than 10,000 Super-chips are transferred, the opportunity cost becomes the sale of Super-chips on the outside market. Now the minimum transfer price per Super-chip becomes

22-34 (Cont'd.)

$$\begin{array}{l} \text{Incremental} \\ \text{cost per Super -} \\ \text{chip up to the} \\ \text{point of} \\ \text{transfer} \end{array} + \begin{array}{l} \text{Opportunity} \\ \text{cost per Super -} \\ \text{chip to the} \\ \text{Semiconductor} \\ \text{Division} \end{array} = \$30 + (\$60 - \$30) = \$60, \text{ the market price.}$$

At this transfer price, it is cheaper for the Process-Control Division to buy the circuit board for $60, since $10 of additional direct manufacturing labor cost is saved.

The Semiconductor Division should at most transfer 10,000 Super-chips.

Internal Demand	Transfer
0–10,000	$46
10,000–25,000	60

22-36 (40–50 min.) Goal congruence, income taxes, different market conditions.

1.

	New Engine	Existing Engine Used by Assembly
Selling price	$375	
Savings in purchase costs by making engines in-house		$400
Manufacturing costs:		
Direct materials	$100	$125
Direct manufacturing labor	40	50
Variable manufacturing overhead	25	25
Total costs of manufacturing	165	200
Contribution margin from New Engine	$210	
Net savings in costs by making existing engine in-house		$200

If order for the new engine is accepted, San Ramon earns a contribution margin of $210 × 2,000 units. $420,000

In this case, Engine Division will be in a position to supply only 2,000 units to Assembly, and Assembly will have to purchase 1,200 engines from outside. The incremental cost of buying engines from outside is $200 × 1,200   240,000

Net benefit from accepting order $180,000

An alternative approach is to compare relevant costs of the accept order and reject order alternatives.

	Accept Order	Reject Order
1. Contribution margin from selling 2,000 units of new engine, $210 × 2,000	$(420,000)	
2. Incremental cost of making and transferring 2,000 units or 3,200 units of old engines, $200 × 2,000; $200 × 3,200	400,000	$640,000
3. Incremental costs of purchasing 1,200 units from outside, $400 × 1,200	480,000	
	$460,000	$640,000

San Ramon Corporation should
    a.   make 2,000 units of the new engine in the Engine Division
    b.   make 2,000 units of the existing engine for the Assembly Division
    c.   have the Assembly Division purchase 1,200 existing engines from the outside market

2.   The options facing the Engine Division manager are (a) to sell 2,000 units of the special order engine and make 2,000 units for the Assembly Division, or (b) to make 3,200 units for the Assembly Division. The contribution margin per unit from accepting the special order is $210 per unit. Let the transfer price be $X. Then, we want to find X such that

$$\$210 \times 2,000 + (\$X - \$200)\,2,000 = (\$X - \$200)\,3,200$$
$$(\$X - \$200)(3,200 - 2,000) = \$420,000$$
$$\$X - \$200 = \frac{\$420,000}{1,200} = \$350$$
$$X = \$550$$

For transfer prices below $550, the Engine Division gets more by selling 2,000 units outside and transferring 2,000 units to Assembly Division. It will not transfer more than 2,000 units to Assembly even though the transfer price is greater than the variable costs of manufacturing the existing engine, $200 plus the contribution margin per unit from accepting the special order of $210 equal to $410 ($500, say). Why? Because by transferring an additional 1,200 units (say), it will have to give up $420,000 ($210 × 2,000) of contribution margin by not accepting the special order. The Engine Division manager would be willing to transfer 2,000 units for which it has capacity (after fulfilling the outside order) to the Assembly Division provided the transfer price covers the Engine Division's variable costs. So, the range of transfer price that will induce the Engine Division manager to implement the optimal solution in requirement 1 is:

TP ≥ $200 for the first 2,000 units

TP ≥ $550 for the next 1,200 units

The Assembly Division manager would be willing to buy from the Engine Division so long as the transfer price is less than or equal to the price at which the Assembly Division can buy the engines on the outside market.

TP ≤ $400

22-36 (Cont'd.)

It will not buy the engines from the Engine Division if TP > $400. The range of TP that will result in both managers favoring the optimal actions in requirement 1 are TPs that satisfy the respective constraints described above.

$$\$200 \leq TP \leq \$400 \text{ for the first 2,000 units}$$

$$TP = \$550 \text{ for the next 1,200 units}$$

This transfer-pricing scheme will induce both managers to transfer 2,000 units between the Engine and Assembly Divisions, but no more. Because the Assembly Division manager is willing to pay no more than $400 and the Engine Division manager is unwilling to transfer unless the transfer price is above $550, no transfers will occur beyond the first 2,000 units.

3a. The full manufacturing costs of the engines transferred to the Assembly Division are:

Direct materials	$125
Direct manufacturing labor	50
Variable manufacturing overheads	25
Fixed manufacturing overheads	

$$\left(\frac{\$520,000}{2} = \$260,000 \div 2,000 \text{ engines} \right)$$

since the engines transferred to the Assembly Division use up half the Engine Division's capacity	130
Total manufacturing cost	$330

b. A transfer price of $330 is in the optimal range identified in requirement 2 and, so, will achieve the optimal actions of selling 2,000 engines under the outside offer and transferring 2,000 engines to the Assembly Division as identified in requirement 1. At the transfer price of $550 for the next 1,200 units, the Assembly Division will prefer to purchase engines at $400 from the outside market.

c. One advantage of full cost transfer pricing is that it is useful for the firm's long-run pricing decisions.

One disadvantage of full cost transfer pricing is that costs that are fixed for the corporation as a whole look like variable costs from the viewpoint of the Assembly Division manager. This is because, by choosing not to have a unit transferred from the Engine Division, the Assembly Division manager would appear to save both the variable and fixed costs of the engine. This could lead to suboptimal decisions.

4a. To minimize taxes, San Ramon should transfer the engines at the highest price it can, the market price of $400. The Engine Division would pay no taxes on any income that it would report. By setting the transfer price as high as possible, the Assembly Division would minimize the income it would report and, hence, the taxes it would pay.

22-23

b. Yes, as in part 3b, the transfer price of $400 is also within the range identified in requirement 2 and so will achieve the outcome desired in requirement 1 (sell 2,000 engines under the outside offer and transfer 2,000 engines to the Assembly Division).

5.   San Ramon should use a transfer price of $400 for the first 2,000 units and $550 for the next 1,200 units when transferring engines from the Engine Division to the Assembly Division. This transfer price minimizes tax payments for the San Ramon Corporation as a whole and also achieves goal congruence. That is, at the transfer prices indicated, both Divisions will be content with the following arrangement

a.   The Engine Division will make 2,000 engines for outside customers and 2,000 engines for the Assembly Division

b.   The Assembly Division will take 2,000 engines from the Engine Division and 1,200 engines from the outside market

Of course, the Assembly Division manager would like to negotiate a price lower than $400 (but greater than $200) for the first 2,000 engines from the Engine Division, but this would increase San Ramon's tax payments.

At a transfer price of $400, San Ramon can still evaluate each division's performance on the basis of division operating income because the transfer price of $400 approximates the market prices for the engines transferred from the Engine Division to the Assembly Division. Market-based transfer prices give top management a reasonably good picture of the contributions of the individual divisions to overall companywide profitability.

CHAPTER 23
PERFORMANCE MEASUREMENT, COMPENSATION, AND MULTINATIONAL CONSIDERATIONS

23-2 The six steps in designing an accounting-based performance measure are:
1. Choose performance measures that align with top management's financial goal(s)
2. Choose the time horizon of each performance measure in Step 1
3. Choose a definition of the components in each performance measure in Step 1
4. Choose a measurement alternative for each performance measure in Step 1
5. Choose a target level of performance
6. Choose the timing of feedback

23-4 Yes. Residual income (RI) is not identical to return on investment (ROI). ROI is a percentage with investment as the denominator of the computation. RI is an absolute amount in which investment is used to calculate an imputed interest charge.

23-6 Definitions of investment used in practice when computing ROI are:
1. Total assets available
2. Total assets employed
3. Working capital (current assets minus current liabilities) plus other assets
4. Stockholders' equity

23-8 Special problems arise when evaluating the performance of divisions in multinational companies because
 a. The economic, legal, political, social, and cultural environments differ significantly across countries.
 b. Governments in some countries may impose controls and limit selling prices of products.
 c. Availability of materials and skilled labor, as well as costs of materials, labor, and infrastructure may differ significantly across countries.
 d. Divisions operating in different countries keep score of their performance in different currencies.

23-10 Moral hazard describes contexts in which an employee is tempted to put in less effort (or report distorted information) because the employee's interests differ from the owner's and because the employee's effort cannot be accurately monitored and enforced.

23-12 Measures of performance that are superior (measures that change significantly with the manager's performance and not very much with changes in factors that are beyond the manager's control) are the key to designing strong incentive systems in organizations. When selecting performance measures, the management accountant must choose those performance measures that change with changes in the actions taken by managers. For example, if a manager has no authority for making investments, then using an investment-based measure to evaluate the manager imposes risk on the manager and provides little information about the manager's performance. The management accountant might suggest evaluating the manager on the basis of costs, or costs and revenues, rather than ROI.

23-14 When employees have to perform multiple tasks as part of their jobs, incentive problems can arise when one task is easy to monitor and measure while the other task is more difficult to evaluate. Employers want employees to intelligently allocate time and effort among various tasks. If, however, employees are rewarded on the basis of the task that is more easily measured, they will tend to focus their efforts on that task and ignore the others.

23-16 (30 min.) **ROI, comparisons of three companies.**

1. The separate components highlight several features of return on investment not revealed by a single calculation:
   a. The importance of investment turnover as a key to income is stressed.
   b. The importance of revenues is explicitly recognized.
   c. The important components are expressed as ratios or percentages instead of dollar figures. This form of expression often enhances comparability of different divisions, businesses, and time periods.
   d. The breakdown stresses the possibility of trading off investment turnover for income as a percentage of revenues so as to increase the average ROI at a given level of output.

2. (Filled-in blanks are in bold face.)

	Companies in Same Industry		
	A	B	C
Revenue	$1,000,000	$ 500,000	$10,000,000
Income	$ 100,000	$ 50,000	$ 50,000
Investment	$ 500,000	$5,000,000	$ 5,000,000
Income as a % of revenue	10%	10%	0.5%
Investment turnover	2.0	0.1	2.0
Return on investment	20%	1%	1%

Income and investment alone shed little light on comparative performances because of disparities in size between Company A and the other two companies. Thus, it is impossible to say whether B's low return on investment in comparison with A's is attributable to its larger investment or to its lower income. Furthermore, the fact that Companies B and C have identical income and investment may suggest that the same conditions underlie the low ROI, but this conclusion is erroneous. B has higher margins but a lower investment turnover. C has very small margins (1/20th of B) but turns over investment 20 times faster.

I.M.A. Report No. 35 (page 35) states:

"Introducing revenues to measure level of operations helps to disclose specific areas for more intensive investigation. Company B does as well as Company A in terms of income margin, for both companies earn 10% on revenues. But Company B has a much lower turnover of investment than does Company A. Whereas a dollar of investment in Company A supports two dollars in revenues each period, a dollar investment in Company B supports only ten cents in revenues each period. This suggests that the analyst should look carefully at Company B's investment. Is the company keeping an inventory larger than necessary for its revenue level? Are receivables being

23-16 (Cont'd.)

collected promptly? Or did Company A acquire its fixed assets at a price level that was much lower than that at which Company B purchased its plant?"

"On the other hand, C's investment turnover is as high as A's, but C's income as a percentage of revenue is much lower. Why? Are its operations inefficient, are its material costs too high, or does its location entail high transportation costs?"

"Analysis of ROI raises questions such as the foregoing. When answers are obtained, basic reasons for differences between rates of return may be discovered. For example, in Company B's case, it is apparent that the emphasis will have to be on increasing turnover by reducing investment or increasing revenues. Clearly, B cannot appreciably increase its ROI simply by increasing its income as a percent of revenue. In contrast, Company C's management should concentrate on increasing the percent of income on revenue."

23-18 (10–15 min.) **ROI and RI.**

$$\text{ROI} \quad = \quad \frac{\text{Operating income}}{\text{Investment}}$$

$$\text{Operating income} \quad = \quad \text{ROI} \times \text{Investment}$$

[No. of menhirs sold (Selling price – Var. cost per unit)] – Fixed costs = ROI × Investment

Let X = minimum selling price per unit to achieve a 20% ROI

1. $10,000 (X - \$300) - \$1,000,000$ = 20% ($1,600,000)
    $10,000X$ = $320,000 + $3,000,000 + $1,000,000 = $4,320,000
    X = $432

2. $10,000 (X - \$300) - \$1,000,000$ = 15% ($1,600,000)
    $10,000X$ = $240,000 + $3,000,000 + $1,000,000 = $4,240,000
    X = $424

23-20 (25 min.) **Financial and nonfinancial performance measures, goal congruence.**

1. Operating income is a good summary measure of short-term financial performance. By itself, however, it does not indicate whether operating income in the short run was earned by taking actions that would lead to long-run competitive advantage. For example, Summit's divisions might be able to increase short-run operating income by producing more product while ignoring quality or rework. Harrington, however, would like to see division managers increase operating income without sacrificing quality. The new performance measures take a balanced scorecard approach by evaluating and rewarding managers on the basis of direct measures (such as rework costs, on-time delivery performance, and sales returns). This motivates managers to take actions that Harrington believes will increase operating income now and in the future. The nonoperating income measures serve as surrogate measures of future profitability.

2. The semiannual installments and total bonus for the Charter Division are calculated as follows:

Charter Division Bonus Calculation
For Year Ended December 31, 2000

January 1, 2000 to June 30, 2000

Profitability	(0.02 × $462,000)	$ 9,240
Rework	(0.02 × $462,000) – $11,500	(2,260)
On-time delivery	No bonus—under 96%	0
Sales returns	[(0.015 × $4,200,000) – $84,000] × 50%	(10,500)
Semiannual installment		$ (3,520)
Semiannual bonus awarded		$ 0

July 1, 2000 to December 31, 2000

Profitability	(0.02 × $440,000)	$ 8,800
Rework	(0.02 × $440,000) – $11,000	(2,200)
On-time delivery	96% to 98%	2,000
Sales returns	[(0.015 × $4,400,000) – $70,000] × 50%	(2,000)
Semiannual installment		$ 6,600
Semiannual bonus awarded		$ 6,600
Total bonus awarded for the year		$ 6,600

23-20 (Cont'd.)

The semiannual installments and total bonus for the Mesa Division are calculated as follows:

Mesa Division Bonus Calculation
For Year Ended December 31, 2000

January 1, 2000 to June 30, 2000

Profitability	(0.02 × $342,000)	$ 6,840
Rework	(0.02 × $342,000) – $6,000	0
On-time delivery	Over 98%	5,000
Sales returns	[(0.015 × $2,850,000) – $44,750] × 50%	(1,000)
Semiannual bonus installment		$10,840
Semiannual bonus awarded		$10,840

July 1, 2000 to December 31, 2000

Profitability	(0.02 × $406,000)	$ 8,120
Rework	(0.02 × $406,000) – $8,000	0
On-time delivery	No bonus—under 96%	0
Sales returns	[(0.015 × $2,900,000) – $42,500] which is greater than zero, yielding a bonus of	3,000
Semiannual bonus installment		$11,120
Semiannual bonus awarded		$11,120
Total bonus awarded for the year		$21,960

3.   The manager of the Charter Division is likely to be frustrated by the new plan, as the division bonus is more than $20,000 less than the previous year. However, the new performance measures have begun to have the desired effect—both on-time deliveries and sales returns improved in the second half of the year, while rework costs were relatively even. If the division continues to improve at the same rate, the Charter bonus could approximate or exceed what it was under the old plan.

The manager of the Mesa Division should be as satisfied with the new plan as with the old plan, as the bonus is almost equivalent. However, there is no sign of improvements in the performance measures instituted by Harrington in this division; as a matter of fact, on-time deliveries declined considerably in the second half of the year. Unless the manager institutes better controls, the bonus situation may not be as favorable in the future. This could motivate the manager to improve in the future but currently, at least, the manager has been able to maintain his bonus without showing improvements in the areas targeted by Harrington.

23-20 (Cont'd.)

Ben Harrington's revised bonus plan for the Charter Division fostered the following improvements in the second half of the year despite an increase in sales:
- increase of 1.9% in on-time deliveries.
- $500 reduction in rework costs.
- $14,000 reduction in sales returns.

However, operating income as a percent of sales has decreased (11 to 10%).

The Mesa Division's bonus has remained at the status quo as a result of the following effects
- increase of 2.0 % in operating income as a percent of sales (12% to 14%).
- decrease of 3.6% in on-time deliveries.
- $2,000 increase in rework costs.
- $2,250 decrease in sales returns.

This would suggest that there needs to be some revisions to the bonus plan. Possible changes include:

- increasing the weights put on on-time deliveries, rework costs, and sales returns in the performance measures while decreasing the weight put on operating income.
- a reward structure for rework costs that are below 2% of operating income that would encourage managers to drive costs lower.
- reviewing the whole year in total. The bonus plan should carry forward the negative amounts for one six-month period into the next six-month period incorporating the entire year when calculating a bonus.
- developing benchmarks, and then giving rewards for improvements over prior periods and encouraging continuous improvement.

23-22   (25 min.)   RI, EVA®.

1.

	Truck Rental Division	Transportation Division
Total assets	$650,000	$950,000
Current liabilities	120,000	200,000
Investment		
(Total assets – current liabilities)	530,000	750,000
Required return		
(12% × Investment)	63,600	90,000
Operating income before tax	75,000	160,000
Residual income		
(Optg. inc. before tax – reqd. return)	11,400	70,000

2.   After-tax cost of debt financing $= (1- 0.4) \times 10\% = 6\%$
After-tax cost of equity financing $= 15\%$

$$\text{Weighted average cost of capital} = \frac{\$900,000 \times 6\% + 600,000 \times 15\%}{\$900,000 + 600,000} = 9.6\%$$

23-22 (Cont'd.)

Required return for EVA 9.6% × Investment (9.6% × $530,000; 9.6% × $750,000)	$50,880	$72,000
Operating income after tax 0.6 × operating income before tax	45,000	96,000
EVA (Optg. inc. after tax – reqd. return)	(5,880)	24,000

3.   Both the residual income and the EVA calculations indicate that the Transportation Division is performing better than the Truck Rental Division. The Transportation Division has a higher residual income ($70,000 versus $11,400) and a higher EVA [$24,000 versus $(5,880)]. The negative EVA for the Truck Rental Division indicates that, on an after-tax basis, the division is destroying value—the after-tax economic return from the Truck Rental Division's assets is less than the required return. If EVA continues to be negative, Burlingame may have to consider shutting down the Truck Rental Division.

23-24   (20 min.)   Multinational performance measurement, ROI, RI.

1a.   U.S. Division's ROI in 2000 $= \dfrac{\text{Operating income}}{\text{Total assets}} = \dfrac{\text{Operating income}}{\$8,000,000} = 15\%$

Hence operating income = 15% × $8,000,000 = $1,200,000.

1b.   Swedish Division's ROI in 2000 in kronas $= \dfrac{9{,}180{,}000 \text{ kronas}}{60{,}000{,}000 \text{ kronas}} = 15.3\%$

2.   Convert total assets into dollars at December 31, 1999 exchange rate, the rate prevailing when assets were acquired (8 kronas = $1)

24,000,000 kronas $= \dfrac{60{,}000{,}000 \text{ kronas}}{8 \text{ kronas per dollar}} = \$7{,}500{,}000$

Convert operating income into dollars at the average exchange rate prevailing during 2000 when operating income was earned equal to

$\dfrac{9{,}180{,}000 \text{ kronas}}{8.5 \text{ kronas per dollar}} = \$1{,}080{,}000$

Comparable ROI for Swedish Division $= \dfrac{\$1{,}080{,}000}{\$7{,}500{,}000} = 14.4\%$

23-24 Cont'd.)

The Swedish Division's ROI calculated in kronas is helped by the inflation that occurs in Sweden in 2000. Inflation boosts the division's operating income. Since the assets are acquired at the start of the year on 1-1-2000, the asset values are not increased by the inflation that occurs during the year. The net effect of inflation on ROI calculated in kronas is to use an inflated value for the numerator relative to the denominator. Adjusting for inflationary and currency differences negates the effects of any differences in inflation rates between the two countries on the calculation of ROI. After these adjustments, the U.S. Division shows a higher ROI than the Swedish Division.

3. U.S. Division's RI in 2000 = $1,200,000 – 12% × $8,000,000
                                = $1,200,000 – $960,000 = $240,000

Swedish Division's RI in 2000 (in U.S. dollars) is

$1,080,000 – 12% × $7,500,000 = $1,080,000 – $900,000 = $180,000.

The U.S. Division's RI also exceeds the Swedish Division's RI in 2000 by $60,000 ($240,000 – $180,000).

23-26 (20–30 min.) Risk sharing, incentives, benchmarking, multiple tasks.

1. An evaluation of the three proposals to compensate Marks, the general manager of the Dexter Division follows:

(i) Paying Marks a flat salary will not subject Marks to any risk, but will provide no incentives for Marks to undertake extra physical and mental effort.

(ii) Rewarding Marks only on the basis of Dexter Division's ROI would motivate Marks to put in extra effort to increase ROI because Marks's rewards would increase with increases in ROI. But compensating Marks solely on the basis of ROI subjects Marks to excessive risk because the division's ROI depends not only on Marks's effort but also on other random factors over which Marks has no control. For example, Marks may put in a great deal of effort, but, despite this effort, the division's ROI may be low because of adverse factors (such as high interest rates or a recession) which Marks cannot control.

To compensate Marks for taking on uncontrollable risk, AMCO must pay him additional amounts within the structure of the ROI-based arrangement. Thus, compensating Marks only on the basis of performance-based incentives will cost AMCO more money, on average, than paying Marks a flat salary. The key question is whether the benefits of motivating additional effort justify the higher costs of performance-based rewards.

Furthermore, the objective of maximizing ROI may induce Marks to reject projects that, from the viewpoint of the organization as a whole, should be accepted. This would occur for projects that would reduce Marks's overall ROI but which would earn a return greater than the required rate of return for that project.

23-26 (Cont'd.)

(iii) The motivation for having some salary and some performance-based bonus in compensation arrangements is to balance the benefits of incentives against the extra costs of imposing uncontrollable risk on the manager.

2.   Marks's complaint does not appear to be valid. The senior management of AMCO is proposing to benchmark Marks's performance using a relative performance evaluation (RPE) system. RPE controls for common uncontrollable factors that similarly affect the performance of managers operating in the same environments (for example, the same industry). If business conditions for car battery manufacturers are good, all businesses manufacturing car batteries will probably perform well. A superior indicator of Marks's performance is how well Marks performed relative to his peers. The goal is to filter out the common noise to get a better understanding of Marks's performance. Marks's complaint will be valid only if there are significant differences in investments, assets, and the business environment in which AMCO and Tiara operate. Given the information in the problem, this does not appear to be the case.

3.   Superior performance measures change significantly with the manager's performance and not very much with changes in factors that are beyond the manager's control. If Marks has no authority for making capital investment decisions, then ROI is not a good measure of Marks's performance—it varies with the actions taken by others rather than the actions taken by Marks. AMCO may wish to evaluate Marks on the basis of operating income rather than ROI.

ROI, however, may be a good measure to evaluate Dexter's economic viability. Senior management at AMCO could use ROI to evaluate if the Dexter Division's income provides a reasonable return on investment, regardless of who has authority for making capital investment decisions. That is, ROI may be an inappropriate measure of Marks's performance but a reasonable measure of the economic viability of the Dexter Division. If, for whatever reasons—bad capital investments, weak economic conditions, etc.—the Division shows poor economic performance, as computed by ROI, AMCO management may decide to shut down the division even though they may simultaneously conclude that Marks performed well.

4.   There are two main concerns with Marks's plans. First, creating very strong sales incentives imposes excessive risk on the sales force, because a salesperson's performance is affected not only by his or her own effort, but also by random factors (such as a recession in the industry) that are beyond the salesperson's control. If salespersons are risk averse, the firm will have to compensate them for bearing this extra uncontrollable risk. Second, compensating salespersons only on the basis of sales creates strong incentives to sell, but may result in lower levels of customer service and sales support (this was the story at Sears auto repair shops where a change in the contractual terms of mechanics to "produce" more repairs caused unobservable quality to be negatively affected). Where employees perform multiple tasks, it may be important to "blunt" incentives on those aspects of the job that can be measured well (for example, sales) to try and achieve a better balance of the two tasks (for example, sales and customer service and support). In addition, the division should try to better monitor customer service and customer satisfaction through surveys, or through quantifying the amount of repeat business.

23-28 (25 min.)   **Historical-cost and current-cost ROI measures.**

1.

	City Plaza	South Station	Central Park
$\dfrac{\text{Operating income}}{\text{Investment at historical cost}}$	$\dfrac{\$90,000}{\$300,000} = 30.0\%$	$\dfrac{\$120,000}{\$500,000} = 24.0\%$	$\dfrac{\$60,000}{\$240,000} = 25.0\%$
$\dfrac{\text{Operating income}}{\text{Investment at current cost}}$	$\dfrac{\$90,000}{\$600,000} = 15.0\%$	$\dfrac{\$120,000}{\$700,000} = 17.1\%$	$\dfrac{\$60,000}{\$450,000} = 13.3\%$

2.   Using investments at historical cost as the denominator, City Plaza has the highest ROI and South Station the lowest. Using investment at current cost as the denominator, South Station has the highest ROI and Central Park the lowest.

The choice of an appropriate measure depends on how Nobillo Corporation judges the performance of its convenience stores.

If Nobillo uses a single benchmark (say, 16%) in judging the performance of each store, the current cost measure will promote comparability among stores that were bought at different times or in areas with different real estate markets. Historical cost will give rise to differences in ROI among convenience stores that are unrelated to differences in operating efficiency. For example, in times of rising prices, the oldest store (City Plaza) will have a lower historical cost investment level than the newest store (South Station) for comparable amounts of square feet of store space in comparable locations. The current cost differences of the investment in the City Plaza and South Station stores, for example, are much smaller than the differences in historical costs, due largely to the different time periods in which the two stores were build. A drawback of current cost is that current cost estimates are difficult to obtain.

If Nobillo tailors the performance benchmark for each convenience store in its budgeting process, then the choice of a specific investment measure is less contentious. For example, if historical cost is used, the budgeted ROI benchmark for the South Station store could be, say, 25% whereas the budgeted ROI benchmark for the City Plaza store could be, say, 30%. Another benefit of tailoring the budget to each manager is that more incentives are provided to managers who are put in charge of poorly performing stations or stations in highly competitive markets.

23-30 (40–50 min.) **Evaluating managers, ROI, value-chain analysis of cost structure.**

1.

	$\dfrac{\text{Revenues}}{\text{Total Assets}}$	×	$\dfrac{\text{Operating Income}}{\text{Revenues}}$	=	$\dfrac{\text{Operating Income}}{\text{Total Assets}}$
Computer Power					
1999	1.111		0.250		0.278
2000	0.941		0.125		0.118
Peach Computer					
1999	1.250		0.100		0.125
2000	1.458		0.171		0.250

Computer Power's ROI has declined sizably from 1999 to 2000, largely because of a decline in operating income to revenues. Peach Computer's ROI has doubled from 1999 to 2000, in large part due to an increase in operating income to revenues.

2.

Business Function	Computer Power		Peach Computer	
	1999	2000	1999	2000
Research and development	12.0%	6.0%	10.0%	15.0%
Design	5.0	3.0	2.0	4.0
Production	34.0	40.0	46.0	34.0
Marketing	25.0	33.0	20.0	23.0
Distribution	9.0	8.0	10.0	8.0
Customer Service	15.0	10.0	12.0	16.0
Total costs	100.0%	100.0%	100.0%	100.0%

23-30 (Cont'd.)

Business functions with increases/decreases in the percentage of total costs from 1999 to 2000 are:

	Computer Power	**Peach Computer**
Increases	Production Marketing	Research and development Design Marketing Customer service
Decreases	Research and development Design Distribution Customer service	Production Distribution

Computer Power has decreased expenditures in several key business functions that are critical to its long-term survival—notably research and development and design. These costs are (using the Chapter 8 appendix terminology) discretionary and can be reduced in the short run without any short-run effect on customers, but such action is likely to create serious problems in the long run.

3.   Based on the information provided, Provan is the better candidate for president of User Friendly Computer. Both Computer Power and Peach Computer are in the same industry. Provan has headed Peach Computer at a time when it has considerably outperformed Computer Power:

a.   The ROI of Peach Computer has increased from 1999 to 2000, while that of Computer Power has decreased.
b.   The computer magazine has increased the ranking of Peach Computer's main product, while it has decreased the ranking of Computer Power's main product.
c.   Peach Computer has received high marks for new products (the lifeblood of a computer company), while Computer Power new-product introductions have been described as "mediocre."

23-32 (20–30 min.)   **Division manager's compensation, risk sharing, incentives.**
(Continuation of 23-31)

1.   Consider each of the three proposals that the management of Mason Industries is considering:

a.   *Compensate Grieco on the basis of a fixed salary without any bonus.*
Paying Grieco a flat salary will not subject Grieco to any risk, but will provide no incentives for Grieco to undertake extra physical and mental effort.

b.   *Compensate Grieco on the basis of division residual income (RI).*
The benefit of this arrangement is that Grieco would be motivated to put in extra effort to increase RI because Grieco's rewards would increase with increases in RI.   But compensating Grieco largely on the basis of RI subjects Grieco to excessive risk, because the division's RI depends not only on Grieco's effort but also on random factors over which Grieco has no control. Grieco may put in a great deal of effort, but the division's RI may be low because of adverse factors (high interest rates, recession) that the manager cannot control.   For example, general market conditions will influence Grieco's revenues and costs.

To compensate Grieco for taking on uncontrollable risk, Mason Industries must pay her additional amounts within the structure of the RI-based arrangement.   Thus, only using performance-based incentives costs Mason more money, on average, than paying a flat salary. The key question is whether the benefits of motivating additional effort justify the higher costs of performance-based rewards.

c.   *Compensate Grieco using other companies that also manufacture go-carts and recreational vehicles as a benchmark.*

The benefit of benchmarking or relative performance evaluation is to cancel out the effects of common noncontrollable factors that affect a performance measure.   Taking out the effects of these factors provides better information about management performance.   However, benchmarking and relative performance evaluation are effective only when similar noncontrollable factors affect each of the companies in the benchmark group.   If this is the case, as it appears to be here, benchmarking is a good idea.   If, however, the companies in the benchmark group are not exactly comparable because, for example, they have other areas of business that cannot be separated from their go-cart and recreational vehicle business, or they operate under different market conditions, benchmarking may not be a good idea.   If the noncontrollable factors are not the same, then comparing the RI of Grieco's division to the RI of the other companies will not provide useful relative performance evaluation information.

2.   Mason should use a compensation arrangement that includes both a salary component and a bonus component based on residual income.   The motivation for having some salary and some performance-based bonus in Grieco's compensation is to balance the benefits of incentives against the extra costs of imposing uncontrollable risk on the manager.   If similar noncontrollable factors affect the performance of the benchmark companies that also manufacture and sell go-carts and recreational vehicles, I would recommend that the bonus be based on the JSD's residual income relative to the residual income earned by the benchmark companies.

23-34 (20–30 min.) **Division manager's compensation.** (Continuation of 23-33)

Consider each of the three proposals that Rupert Prince is considering:

1. *Compensate managers on the basis of division ROI.*

    The benefit of this arrangement is that managers would be motivated to put in extra effort to increase ROI because managers' rewards would increase with increases in ROI. But compensating managers largely on the basis of ROI subjects the managers to excessive risk, because each division's ROI depends not only on the manager's effort but also on random factors over which the manager has no control. A manager may put in a great deal of effort, but the division's ROI may be low because of adverse factors (high interest, recession) that the manager cannot control.

    To compensate managers for taking on uncontrollable risk, Prince must pay them additional amounts within the structure of the ROI-based arrangement. Thus, using mainly performance-based incentives will cost Prince more money, on average, than paying a flat salary. The key question is whether the benefits of motivating additional effort justify the higher costs of performance-based rewards. The motivation for having some salary and some performance-based bonus in compensation arrangements is to balance the benefits of incentives against the extra costs of imposing uncontrollable risk on the manager.

    Finally, rewarding a manager only on the basis of division ROI will induce managers to maximize the division's ROI even if taking such actions are not in the best interests of the company as a whole.

2. *Compensate managers on the basis of companywide ROI.*

    Rewarding managers on the basis of companywide ROI will motivate managers to take actions that are in the best interests of the company rather than actions that maximize a division's ROI.

    A negative feature of this arrangement is that each division manager's compensation will now depend not only on the performance of that division manager but also on the performance of the other division managers. For example, the compensation of Ken Kearney, the manager of the Newspaper Division, will depend on how well the managers of the Television and Film studios perform, even though Kearney himself may have little influence over the performance of these divisions. Hence, compensating managers on the basis of companywide ROI will impose extra risk on each division manager.

3. *Compensate managers using the other divisions' average ROI as a benchmark.*

    The benefit of benchmarking or relative performance evaluation is to cancel out the effects of common noncontrollable factors that affect a performance measure. Taking out the effects of these factors provides better information about a manager's performance. What is critical, however, for benchmarking and relative performance evaluation to be effective is that similar noncontrollable factors affect each division. It is not clear that the same noncontrollable factors that affect the performance of the Newspaper Division (cost of newsprint paper, for example) also affect the performance of the Television and Film studios divisions. If the noncontrollable factors are not the same, then comparing the ROI of one division to the average ROI of the other two divisions will not provide useful information for relative performance evaluation.

    A second factor for Prince to consider is the impact that benchmarking and relative performance evaluation will have on the incentives for the division managers of the Newspaper, Television, and Film studios Divisions to cooperate with one another. Benchmarking one division against another means that a division manager will look good by improving his or her own performance, or by making the performance of the other division managers look bad.

23-36 (30 min.)   **ROI, RI.**

1.   ROS $= \dfrac{\text{Operating Income}}{\text{Sales}} = \dfrac{1,800,000}{15,000,000} = 12\%$

   ROI $= \dfrac{\text{Operating Income}}{\text{Total Assets}} = \dfrac{1,800,000}{10,000,000} = 18\%$

2a.   ROI $= 20\% = \dfrac{\text{Operating income}}{\text{Total Assets}} = \dfrac{X}{10,000,000}$

   Hence operating income = 20% × 10,000,000 = $2,000,000
   Operating income = Revenue – Costs
   Therefore, Costs = $15,000,000 – $2,000,000 = $13,000,000
   Currently,
   Costs = Revenues – Operating income = $15,000,000 – $1,800,000 = $13,200,000

   Costs need to be reduced by $200,000 ($13,200,000 – $13,000,000)

b.   ROI $= 20\% = \dfrac{\text{Operating income}}{\text{Total assets}} = \dfrac{\$1,800,000}{X}$

   Hence X = 1,800,000 ÷ 20% = $9,000,000
   PD would need to decrease total assets in 2001 by $1,000,000 ($10,000,000 – $9,000,000)

3.   RI   =   Income – (Required rate of return × Investment)
      = $1,800,000 – (0.15 × 10,000,000)
      = $300,000

4.   PD wants RI to increase by 50% × $300,000 = $150,000
   That is PD wants RI in 2001 to be $300,000 + $150,000 = $450,000
   If PD cuts costs by $45,000 its operating income will increase to
         $1,800,000 + $45,000 = $1,845,000
            RI_{2001} = $450,000 = $1,845,000 – (0.15 × Assets)
         $1,395,000   =   0.15 × Assets
            Assets   = $1,395,000 ÷ 0.15 = $9,300,000
   PD would need to decrease total assets by $700,000 ($10,000,000 – $9,300,000).

5.   Barrington could use ROS to some degree. That way there is less focus on cutting costs and reduction in assets and more emphasis on actual revenues and how they translate into operating income.

   Barrington may also want to consider nonfinancial measures such as customer satisfaction and market share, quality, yield and on-time performance as well as monitor employee satisfaction and the development of employee skills.